Building Contr

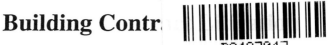

D0497047

Fourth E

Erratum

Please note the following changes.

On page 43, with regard to *Team Services PLC v Tier Management and Design Limited* [1992] CILL 786:

> The decision was appealed by both sides. On 7 April 1993 the Court of Appeal disallowed the plaintiff's cross-appeal from the order of His Honour Judge Bowsher QC that the defendant may make an interim payment late and thereby lose the discount on the payment, but recover that lost discount by making a subsequent payment on time, and allowed the defendant's appeal from his Honour's order that their entitlement to deduct cash discounts from interim payments was dependent upon payment of those interim payments within the time for payment required by the sub-contract. Leave to appeal to the House of Lords was refused by the Court of Appeal and subsequently by the House of Lords itself.
>
> The effect of the Court of Appeal's decision is that where there is a provision for cash discount, there is no implied term that the cash discount is only allowable if payment is made timeously. Most standard terms, however, include express wording to that effect.

On page 83, the reference to *Pratt v Swanmore Builders Limited* (1980) 15 BLR 37, should, in fact, be *George G Hill Associates (A Firm)* (1987) 38 BLR 29.

On page 224, in the case of *Fairweather v Wandsworth* (1988) 12 BLR 40, the citation should read (1988) 39 BLR 106.

The publishers apologise for any inconvenience.

Building Contract Litigation

Building Contract Litigation

Fourth Edition

Robert Fenwick Elliott

Solicitor

LONGMAN

© Longman Group UK Ltd Ltd 1993

ISBN 0 85121 973 X

First edition	1981
Reprinted	1983
Second edition	1985
Third edition	1988
Fourth edition	1993

Published by

Longman Law, Tax and Finance
Longman Group UK Limited
21–27 Lamb's Conduit Street, London WC1N 3NJ

Associated Offices
Australia, Hong Kong, Malaysia, Singapore, USA

A CIP catalogue record for this book is available from the British
Library

Typeset by Servis Filmsetting Ltd, Manchester, England
Printed and bound by Biddles

Contents

Preface

Most general practitioners in the law become involved from time to time in building contract disputes. Sometimes these disputes are resolved by correspondence or in straightforward litigation in the county court. Sometimes, however, they are more complex, and the general practitioner can be at a disadvantage when an opponent is a specialist in this field. The purpose of this book is to provide a practical guide to building contract litigation and arbitration for the general practitioner solicitor.

When this book was first written it was intended only for the use of solicitors who were not wholly familiar with the construction world. In subsequent editions, however, its ambit has been somewhat expanded in order hopefully, to be of use also to lay-people who are concerned in the field.

This edition of the book takes account of the continuing number of changes in substantive and procedural law, and also includes a new chapter on the subject of Retrospective Delay Analysis. This material is designed to reflect what is currently the most important development in construction law, namely the reaction of the courts against substantial but often casually thought out loss and expense claims.

This edition also contains new material on the subject of ADR (Alternative Dispute Resolution) which has been achieving an increasing importance in resolving building contract disputes. It remains to be seen what place ADR eventually takes within the system, but at present it is an area which is rapidly gaining importance.

The preparation of this edition would have been entirely impossible without the considerable assistance of my partner Tony Francis, and I am deeply indebted to him and to my colleague Miss Jean Doull.

I should also express my gratitude to Longman, the publishers of this book, for their patience in waiting for the manuscript of this edition in competition with the demands of clients.

As for the previous editions of this book, all reference to court rules are to the Rules of the Supreme Court. Likewise, references to practice and procedure relate to practice and procedure in the central office of

the High Court, and I leave it to the reader to rely upon their experience
of the practice of their own District Registry or county court.

Robert Fenwick Elliott
Fenwick Elliott
353 Strand
London, WC2R 0HS.

September 1993.

Abbreviations

ADR
Alternative Dispute Resolution

BLR
Building Law Reports, Humphrey Lloyd and Colin Reese (Eds)
(George Godwin)

CILL
Construction Industry Law Letter, Phillip Capper and John Dobson
(Eds) (Legal Studies and Services Limited)

Const LJ
Construction Law Journal, (Sweet and Maxwell)

CLR
Construction Law Reports, Michael Furmston and Vincent Powell-
Smith (Eds) (The Architectural Press)

Fay
Official Referees' Business, His Honour Edgar Fay QC (Sweet and
Maxwell)

FIDIC
Fédération Internationale des Ingenieurs-Conseils

Hudson
Hudson's Building and Engineering Contracts, 10th edn (Sweet and
Maxwell)

ICC
International Chamber of Commerce

ICE Contract
Standard Form of Civil Engineering Contract, 6th edn 1991

JCT Contract
The JCT Standard Form of Building Contract, 1980 edn. Local Authorities Edition with quantities.

Keating
Building Contracts, Donald Keating (fourth edn with first and second supplements) (Sweet and Maxwell)

ORSA
Official Referees Solicitors Association

RIBA
Royal Institute of British Architects

RICS
Royal Institute of Chartered Surveyors

White Book
The Supreme Court Practice, 1988 (Sweet and Maxwell)

Table of Cases

Table of Statutes

Table of Statutory Instruments

Chapter 1

Forms of contract

There are a variety of contractual or quasi-contractual bases upon which contractors carry out building work. These bases can be fundamentally different as to the principal obligations of the parties (ie the obligation on the contractor to do the work properly and the obligation on the employer to pay). Many of the day-to-day matters concerning the contract proceed more or less regardless of the form of contract, but it is impossible to obtain any clear view as to the legal position concerning a building contract without first understanding the basis of the contractual relationship in question. So beguiling can the use of familiar expressions be that it is by no means unknown for substantial building contract litigation to reach, or nearly reach, trial pleaded upon an entirely inappropriate basis. An error of that sort can change building contract litigation from mildly tedious into a positive nightmare.

It would be impossible, and in any event beyond the scope of this book, to set out a comprehensive classification of building contracts. There are, however, certain major features which are fundamental both to the method of payment (where the main contrast is between lump sum contracts and cost contracts) and to the obligations of the builder (where much depends upon the extent to which the contractor undertakes any design obligation).

There follows a brief classification of the sorts of contract most commonly in use and a survey of some of the standard forms commonly used. Neither is exhaustive.

1 The classification of contracts

(a) Lump sum contracts

A lump sum contract is a contract whereby the contractor agrees for a pre-agreed price to execute certain defined building works (the building work undertaken by the contractual obligation is usually called the 'Works'). In principle, the contract is very simple but in practice there are many complicating factors.

The general rule in ordinary lump sum contracts is that the contractor is entitled to be paid the pre-agreed lump sum as and when he

1

substantially completes the Works (*Hoenig v Isaacs* [1952] 2 All ER 176). Substantial completion does not necessarily entail the perfect execution of every detail of the Works, and if the contractor is guilty of only comparatively minor defects and/or omissions then he is entitled to be paid the lump sum less a set-off in respect of his failings. In exceptional cases the parties may by clear and unambiguous words enter into an entire contract, which is 'one where the entire fulfilment of the promise by either party is a condition precedent to the right to call for the fulfilment of any part of the promise by the other' (*Hudson's Building and Engineering Contracts*, 10th edn; p 243). In these very exceptional circumstances the contractor is not entitled to be paid anything unless he completes the Works without any defects or omissions at all.

Where there has been a failure by the contractor to achieve substantial completion (or, in the exceptional case, entire completion) then it may be possible for the employer to deny that the contractor is entitled to any payment at all. This is, however, 'swimming against the tide' and the courts are most reluctant to see a contractor receive no payment at all for work that the contractor has done. As Lord Denning said in *Hoenig v Isaacs* at p 180; 'When a contract provides for a specific sum to be paid on completion of specified work, the courts lean against a construction of the contract which would deprive the contractor of any payment at all simply because there are some defects or omissions'.

The parties might arrive at the lump sum in one of a number of ways. Very often the contractor places a price against each item in a bill of quantities or specification describing the work to be done on an item by item basis. The total is often subject to additions for overheads and profit, and to negotiation one way or the other. All this is irrelevant to the basic entitlement of the contractor, ie to the lump sum.

Although the lump sum is always the starting point, it is comparatively rare for the price the contractor is entitled to receive at the end of the day to be exactly the same as the lump sum. The lump sum is usually subject to adjustment for extra work, fluctuations, sub-contractors, and so on; a description of the more common adjustments appears in Chapter 4, section 1. The lump sum is, however, the starting point for calculating the final entitlement.

Note that in the absence of any contractual provision to the contrary the contractor is not obliged to accept variations, although it is rare for a contractor to avail himself of this right. Even where there is a contractual provision entitling the employer or his architect or engineer to order variations there is some limit to the extent of variations which the employer may order. For example, in *Blue Circle Industries plc v Holland Dredging Co* (1987) 37 BLR 40 the Court of Appeal found that a dredging contractor was not obliged by Clause 41 of the ICE conditions (Fifth Edition) to construct an artificial island as a variation to a dredging contract.

(b) Cost contracts

Cost contracts may have various titles, such as, cost plus contracts, prime cost contracts, or fee contracts, but irrespective of their title they are all a species of measurement and value contracts. Some cost contracts are also described as management contracts (see page 6 below).

The basis of payment for the works under a cost contract is not any pre-agreed lump sum but the actual cost (or prime cost) of the Works as performed. There is a term (implied if not expressed) in cost contracts that the contractor will perform the Works efficiently and not wastefully, but subject to that the contractor is entitled to be paid whatever the work actually costs him. In addition, the contractor is almost always entitled to an additional payment, sometimes described as a fee, to cover his overheads and profit.

Particular care should be exercised with regard to estimates in cost contracts. These estimates are sometimes reproduced in the formal contract document and can have a contractual significance. They should, however, be rigidly distinguished from lump sums. Confusion particularly arises in the case of small informal building contracts where the contractor gives an estimate for the Works. Whether he can be held to that estimate, or whether he can say that the job cost more than he anticipated, depends upon whether the contract is a lump sum contract or a cost contract. Thus, in *Croshaw v Pritchard* (1899) 16 TLR, the defendant's estimate was construed as being an offer capable of acceptance.

Many small informal contracts are cost contracts. In the case of more substantial work, however, cost contracting has always been less common than contracting on a lump sum basis and remains a steady minority preference.

(c) Lump sum contracts and cost contracts compared

The fundamental difference as to payment between lump sum contracts and cost contracts leads to a number of differences between the detailed clauses.

It is fundamental to lump sum contracts that the contract price is agreed at the time of the formation of the contract, which is usually at about the time of the commencement of work. The price in the case of cost contracts, on the other hand, cannot be ascertained until the Works are complete and the cost calculated and so of course the price cannot appear in the contract documents.

In the case of lump sum contracts, the precise extent of the work needs to be defined with some care, otherwise it would not be possible to know how much work the contractor has to do for the pre-agreed price. In the case of cost contracts, on the other hand, precise definition of the contract work is of less importance because the price is dependent upon the amount of work that the contractor actually does. Lump sum contracts usually contain a provision (and sometimes a complex formula) to fix the price of any extra work that may be ordered by the employer after the contract is formed. There is no need for this in a cost contract, where the contractor is paid in the same way for both original contract work and extras.

In lump sum contracts the contractor stands to gain or lose substantial sums of money according to the accuracy of his estimating. If the Works are unexpectedly difficult, or if there is an unexpected rise in the cost of labour or materials, or if the charges of sub-contractors are unexpectedly high, then a lump sum contractor must bear the cost and, unless there is express provision in the contract, is entitled only to the pre-agreed lump sum. In order to pass some of the burden of these risks from the contractor's shoulders to the employer's, sophisticated lump sum contracts such as the standard JCT (Joint Contracts Tribunal) contract contain complex clauses designed to adjust the lump sum in certain circumstances. In particular, there are often fluctuations clauses, extremely complex clauses as to the payment for the work of nominated sub-contractors, and far-reaching clauses as to the payment of loss and expense to the contractor in certain circumstances. All these clauses are unnecessary in a cost contract since (subject to his obligation to perform the Works efficiently and not wastefully) the contractor is indemnified against whatever the cost of the work turns out to be.

Cost contracts usually contain a precise definition of what type of cost is recoverable by the contractor directly (these costs are called either prime cost or actual cost) and what type of cost the contractor is expected to recover within the fee or percentage addition. Typically, definitions of prime cost include the cost of labour, materials and sub-contractors as well as other costs incurred on the site but exclude head office and administrative costs. Such a definition of prime cost is unnecessary in a lump sum contract, although it can form part of the formula for the valuation of extras, as in Clause 13.5.4 of the JCT contract.

There are other features of formal building contracts that are common both to typical lump sum contracts and to typical cost contracts. In particular, both forms of contract usually contain provisions:
 (1) as to when the contractor must complete the Works;
 (2) for extension of time in certain circumstances;
 (3) for liquidated damages in the event of delay;
 (4) for certification of interim and final payments due;
 (5) as to determination of the contract by either party; and
 (6) as to retention of sums due and as to insurance.

(d) Re-measurement contracts

Re-measurement contracts are a sort of hybrid between lump sum contracts and cost contracts. In re-measurement contracts the parties do not pre-agree any price for the work as a whole, but they do pre-agree the rates of remuneration to which the contractor is to be entitled. These rates can either be by reference to the amount of work that is done (eg so much per brick laid) or by reference to the amount of labour and materials expended (eg so much per hour for labourers).

Re-measurement contracts are sometimes easily recognisable, particularly where they are described as day-works contracts or are in the JCT form of contract with approximate quantities. They are sometimes less easy to recognise where, for example, the parties change what would otherwise be a lump sum contract into a re-measurement contract by the use of the words 'all works are subject to re-measurement on completion'.

(e) Design-and-build contracts

Traditionally, substantial building works are undertaken by an employer who commissions a design by professionals and then enters into a contract with a contractor to execute that design. Increasingly, however, contractors enter into contracts not only to build the Works but also to design them.

The obligations of the contractor where he designs the Works as well as builds them are obviously different from his obligations where the works are designed by a professional agent of the employer. In particular, the design-and-build contractor is usually absolutely liable on his promise that the Works will be fit for their intended purpose; this is capable of arising by implication if not expressly (*Independent Broadcasting Authority v EMI Electronics Limited* (1981) 14 BLR 1). This contrasts with the position under the traditional system where the professional designers promise only to use reasonable care in the design.

Design-and-build contracts may be either lump sum contracts or cost contracts. The cost arrangement is, however, often preferable both from the contractor's point of view (because he is unable to estimate exactly the cost of executing a design that is usually incomplete at the time the contract is made) and from the employer's point of view (because he would otherwise be especially vulnerable to the danger of the contractor cutting corners). Design-and-build contracts are often also regarded as particularly suitable for target arrangements, and there are a variety of sophisticated provisions as to payment.

Equally, very minor work where no professional designer is involved is frequently carried out under informal design-and-build contracts, although they are not usually described as such by the parties at the time of the formation of an informal contract.

As an alternative to the out and out design-and-build arrangement, some employers are now trying hybrid arrangements. These arrangements come in a variety of forms and have no widely accepted label; 'primary design procurement' probably describes it as well as anything. A typical scheme is as follows:

(1) The employer gets his architect to prepare generalised plans,

showing the overall dimensions of the work, where the walls are, and the general appearance of the building.

(2) The employer's architect also prepares a performance specification, describing such things as the insulation properties required of the roof, the power and controllability of the heating system and so forth.

(3) Lump sum tenders are then obtained from contractors.

(4) The successful contractor then completes the design work— — within the parameters of the architect's primary design and such as will comply with the performance specification — and then carries out the work.

There are numerous variations among these schemes as to how the employer maintains quality control, whether the original architect may work for the contractor at the detailed design stage and as to the contractor's responsibility for the primary design. There is little or no authority as to how the courts approach such arrangements.

The 'primary design' concept is very common in the area of sub-contracts. In a traditional no-design lump sum main contract, such as JCT80, it is not normal for the architect or engineer to design everything; details such as the mechanisms of the lifts and the Mechanical and Electrical Engineering Services are left to the specialist sub-contractors. Sometimes these specialists will sign warranties with the employer as to their design work; in the absence of warranties the courts have to try to reconcile two well established, but often complicating principles:

(1) liability should flow up the contractual chain; and

(2) under JCT80, responsibility for producing the design rests with the architect as employer's agent, not with the contractor.

(f) Management contracts

It may be that the trend during the 1980s towards the use of management contracts was caused by a feeling that architects are not the best qualified people to manage a major building contract, and that by appointing a building contractor to manage the contract on his behalf the employer is setting a thief to catch a thief. Be that as it may, there has since the early 1980s been a marked increase in the use of management contracts and also in the number of management contracts that have run into legal difficulties.

There are two distinct forms of 'management contracts'. Often terminology can be confusing in that a distinction is now made between 'construction management agreements' and 'management contract agreements'. In the case of construction management, an employer engages a construction manager to act as his agent in much the same way as he would engage an architect or a quantity surveyor to manage the works. The work will be divided up into many 'packages'. The construction manager will be responsible for engaging, on behalf of the employer, trade contractors to carry out each package. The important feature of this type of arrangement is that the contracts are entered into directly between the employer and the various trade contractors. In management contracts generally, the trade contractors enter into contracts with the management contractor. Accordingly, the form of contractual arrangement can have very important implications for the trade contractor, particularly in relation to payment. In the case of a construction manager and a management contractor in sub-letting work, the employer is looking for the benefit of their experience in getting the best possible deal from the trade contractors. In the case of a construction manager, his role is that of agent, not principal, and his authority to deal with the trade contractor may well be limited by requirements that he should obtain approval from the employer's quantity surveyor or architects on various matters. The scope of a construction manager's ostensible authority is often greater than the scope of his actual authority. For management contractor's the role is that of principal and there is usually some sort of restriction on him which requires him to consult or obtain the approval of the employer's architect or quantity surveyor before accepting any tenders. A management contractor is, of course, liable to pay the sub-contractors and usually includes a 'pay when paid' clause in the sub-contract terms to protect his own position. Such 'pay when paid' clauses have in the past caused, and continue to cause, a number of problems. In this situation, where the employer becomes insolvent and is unable to pay the management contractor, the result is that the sub-contractor is not paid for works that have been properly carried out. To date, there is limited authority as to the efficacy of 'pay when paid' clauses, but so far the approach of the courts in this country is to uphold such clauses. The management contractor recovers the cost of the works from the employer pursuant to a widely drawn prime cost recovery clause which entitles the management contractor to recover from the employer virtually everything spent or to be spent by the management contractor on the works.

There are some features common to both forms of arrangement:

(1) The fee is usually low. Calculated on a percentage basis, fees of 3 or 5 per cent are not unusual, far below the returns that may be earned by contractors on a successful lump sum project. Some care is needed, however, to see whether the management contractor's fee is not augmented by the management contractor being permitted to keep the benefit of the traditional main contractor's discount of $2\frac{1}{2}$ per cent.

(2) The risk is correspondingly low. It is typical to see clauses which limit the management contractor's liability to the employer for delay or defects; sometimes the clause limits the liability of the management contractor to the amounts (if any) that the management contractor is able to recover from the trade contractors in respect of such matters.

(3) The form of contract used is often unique, frequently originating

from the offices of the contractor and much amended on behalf of the employer. Regrettably, the standard of drafting is not universally high. The Joint Contracts Tribunal (JCT) has now produced a standard form of management contract, but it will be many years before the courts have finished dealing with the one-off forms.

2 The standard forms

There are a number of forms of building contract in standard use. In the centre of the range of the standard forms is the JCT contract in its six current versions, each of which runs to some 40,000 words and is designed for use with the standard form of sub-contract (which runs to some 30,000 words).

(a) The Joint Contracts Tribunal

The JCT is a body whose constituents are:

the Royal Institute of British Architects,
the Building Employers Confederation,
the Royal Institution of Chartered Surveyors,
the Association of County Councils,
the Association of Metropolitan Authorities,
the Association of District Councils,
the Confederation of Associations of Specialist Engineering Contractors,
the Federation of Associations of Specialists and Sub-contractors,
the Association of Consulting Engineers,
the British Property Federation and the Scottish Building Contract Committee.

The JCT publishes not only the Standard Form of Building Contract (in six versions) but also a series of documents designed for use with the main contract, an Agreement for Minor Building Works, an Intermediate Form and a Fixed Fee Form of Prime Cost Contract.

The JCT contracts are published by RIBA Publications Ltd and can be obtained from the RIBA bookshop, 66 Portland Place, London, W1N 4AD, or by mail order from RIBA Publications Limited, Finsbury Mission, Moreland Street, London, EC1V 8VB (071-251 0791).

(b) The JCT Standard Form of Building Contract 1980 Edition

This contract is the latest in a long line that stretches back into the nineteenth century. For many years the Royal Institute of British Architects published the contract, and it was popularly known as the RIBA Contract. Now the RIBA is only one of the constituent bodies of the JCT. The contract comes in six versions: Private With Quantities; Private Without Quantities; Private With Approximate Quantities; Local Authorities With Quantities; Local Authorities Without Quantities and Local Authorities With Approximate Quantities.

The versions 'With Quantities' and 'Without Quantities' are lump sum contracts. The lump sum is stated in the Articles at the beginning of the contract, but it is subject to adjustment for many things. The editions 'With Approximate Quantities' are not lump sum contracts at all, but are re-measurement contracts. They achieve this end by deleting all references to the contract sum and extending the application of the valuation of variations clause in the lump sum contract to the whole of the work done.

The 1980 edition of the contract re-numbered the clauses from the previous 1963 edition and has made a number of changes. Some of the major features of the JCT form are set out below. This description is intended as an overview of the contract as a whole. Many of the clauses in the contract have been the subject of judicial interpretation or comment, either in their present form or in the form of JCT63. The reader is referred to Appendix B for the text of the more important of these provisions and notes on them. The comments apply to the edition 'With Quantities'.

Article 2 — This sets out the lump sum, which is referred to in the contract as 'the Contract Sum'.

Article 3 — This names the architect, who not only has power to issue instructions as to various matters which the contractor is obliged to follow but also has the power and indeed the duty to issue certificates which are binding upon the parties unless and until they are reviewed upon arbitration. The more important certificates determine the amount due to the contractor as the Works proceed (Clause 30.1.1), the amount due at the conclusion of the contract (Clause 30.8) and as to what extension of time if any the contractor is entitled (Clause 25).

Article 4 — This names the quantity surveyor whose essential function is to advise the architect as to the value of work done by the contractor.

Article 5 — This is a wide-reaching arbitration clause.

Clause 1 — This is the interpretation and definition clause.

Clause 2 — This shows that the contractor's obligation is to carry out and complete the Works shown on the contract drawings and other contract documents; there is no obligation on the contractor as to the efficacy of the design.

Clause 13.2 — This empowers the architect to issue instructions requiring a variation to the work. Despite the width of the words used it is suggested in Keating, *Building Contracts* that:

there must be some limit to the nature and extent of the variations which can be achieved. Clause 4 states that the contractor shall forthwith comply with all instructions save where such instruction is one requiring a variation to the contract and need not comply to the extent that he makes reasonable objections. Therefore, the architect has no authority to issue unreasonable instructions; what would be unreasonable under one contract may not be so under another. Moresoever, it is likely that an architect would not have authority to vary the whole nature of the works, for example to change works designed as a single dwelling house into a block of flats.

Clause 13.5 — This sub-clause sets out the rules for the payment for variations and extra work. In broad terms, the rules provide for extrapolation from the bills of quantities if possible; if this is not possible variations are valued at cost. The importance of the valuation rules can be overestimated, since if they do not reimburse the contractor the direct loss and/or expense incurred by the contractor by reason of the variation, then the contractor can apply under Clause 26.1 for ascertainment (and hence payment; Clause 26.5) of such loss and expense. In other words Clause 26 'tops up' the valuation rules in Clause 13.5.

Clause 17.1 — This provides that the architect is to certify the date of Practical Completion. Unless and until that certificate is overturned in arbitration or litigation, it is conclusive.

Clause 17.3 — After Practical Completion there is a Defects Liability Period (usually but not necessarily six months) and the architect may require the contractor to make good any defects appearing within that time. The contractor does not get paid for this.

Clause 19.2 — The contractor needs the written consent of the architect (not to be unreasonably withheld) before sub-contracting any part of the works. This requirement is frequently ignored and does not necessarily affect the contractor's right to payment.

Clause 24.2.1 — This is the liquidated damages clause, whereby the employer may recover liquidated damages at whatever rate is set out in the appendix to the contract if the architect certifies that the contractor has failed to complete the works by the Completion Date.

Clause 25 — The 'Completion Date' as defined in the 1980 edition can be varied; the architect must revise the Completion Date if the contractor is delayed by a 'Relevant Event'. Relevant Events include such matters as bad weather, strikes, extra work being ordered, delays by the architect in providing necessary instructions and delay on the part of nominated sub-contractors.

Clause 26 — Delay usually costs both the employer and the contractor money. The point about the Relevant Events is that they *all* allow the contractor more time to complete the work; the contractor is relieved from paying the employer's liquidated damages. Clause 26 goes further in respect of *some* of the Relevant Events, in particular delay by the architect in providing necessary instructions (Clause 26.2.1) and extra work (Clause 26.2.7); it entitles the contractor to be reimbursed for his own loss and expense. The contractor may be entitled to loss and expense under Clause 26 not only if the Works as a whole are delayed (prolongation) but also if the regular progress of any part of the Works is materially affected (disruption). See page 51 as to the quantification of loss and expense.

Clauses 27 and 28 — These clauses are the determination clauses, and although they are expressly without prejudice to any other rights or remedies of the parties, for practical purposes they codify within the contract the effect of what would otherwise be regarded as a repudiatory breach or frustrating event. In practice, it is far more common for a party to determine the contract under the express clauses than it is to rely on his common law right to accept repudiatory conduct as such, but it is frequently argued that the wrongful exercise of the determination clauses amounts itself to repudiation.

Clause 30.1 — This clause provides for the architect to issue interim certificates, usually monthly, for payments on account to the contractor.

Clause 30.4 — The employer retains 5 per cent of whatever would otherwise be payable on interim certificates. Of this, $2\frac{1}{2}$ per cent is released to the contractor on Practical Completion, and the other $2\frac{1}{2}$ per cent is released when the architect certifies that the contractor has made good the defects appearing within the defects liability period.

Clause 30.6.2 — This is the clause which sets out how much the contractor gets paid at the end of the day. The basic entitlement is to the contract sum but this is adjusted in a number of respects.

Clause 30.8 — The Final Certificate is usually due about a year after Practical Completion. It sets out the final state of the account and operates by way of conclusive evidence that where the work has to be to the satisfaction of the architect it is to such satisfaction. It is unlike all the other certificates in that it is not subject to review in arbitration or litigation unless and to the extent that such arbitration or litigation is commenced within fourteen days after the certificate is issued. Note, however, that the Final Certificate does not generally inhibit a claim in respect of defective workmanship or inadequate materials because the contractual requirements in these instances are usually defined by the contract drawings and specification, rather than left to the satisfaction of the architect.

Clause 35 — This is the nominated sub-contractors' clause. It is extremely complex, but the basic scheme is that in respect of certain parts of the work the architect reserves to himself (usually by the use of a prime cost sum in the bills of quantities) the right of nomination. The contractor must (subject to certain limited rights of objection) then enter into a nominated sub-contract with whichever sub-contractor is chosen by the architect. Each interim certificate directs the contractor precisely how much to pay to each nominated sub-contractor, and the employer then pays the contractor that amount in respect of that work. The standard form of nominated sub-contract (NSC/4) is specifically designed to fit in with the nomination clause in the main contract, and under it the sub-contractors' entitlement to payment is fixed by the architect under the main contract. Contractors who are not nominated (domestic sub-contractors) are not subject to the nominated subcontractor provisions.

Clauses 38, 39 and 40 — These are the fluctuations clauses and are alternatives for the parties to choose. Each of them in its different way is designed to share between the employer and the contractor the effects of inflation. Clause 38 (which is the least generous to the contractor) allows the contractor to recover increases in taxes, etc. Clause 39 (which contains better protection for a contractor) also allows the contractor to recover increases in the cost of labour and materials by a complex set of rules related to increases in the wage rates agreed with the relevant unions and market prices of the relevant materials, goods, electricity and fuels. Clause 40 applies the formula rules issued by the JCT, which work on an index basis.

(c) JCT Nominated Sub-Contract NSC/4

The range of standard forms for nominated sub-contractors is as follows:

NSC/1 Nominated Sub-Contract Tender and Agreement

NSC/2 Employer/Nominated Sub-Contractor Agreement for use where Sub-Contractor tendered on NSC/1

NSC/2a Employer/Nominated Sub-Contractor Agreement for use where Tender NSC/1 not used

NSC/3 Standard Form of Nomination of a Sub-Contractor where Tender NSC/1 has been used

NSC/4 Sub-Contract for sub-contractors who have tendered on Tender NSC/1 and executed Agreement NSC/2 and have been nominated by Nomination NSC/3

NSC/4a Sub-Contract NSC/4 adapted for use where Tender NSC/1, Agreement NSC/2 and Nomination NSC/3 have not been used.

The central document among these is NSC/4. This runs to about 30,000 words, bears a parasitic relationship to the main contract and incorporates the tender document (NSC/1) by reference. NSC/4 is either a lump sum contract or a re-measurement contract according to how the tender form NSC/1 (if there is one) has been completed. There is an alternative on the tender form between a 'sub-contract sum', which leads to a lump sum contract, and a 'tender sum', which leads to a re-measurement contract. If the parties choose the lump sum arrangement then the sub-contract sum is adjusted under Clause 21.10.2 in much the same way as under the main contract forms 'With Quantities' or 'Without Quantities'. If the re-measurement option is chosen, then the sub-contractors' final entitlement ('the Ascertained Final Sub-Contract Sum') is calculated under Clause 21.11.2 and does not necessarily bear any close relationship to the tender sum, the latter having little contractual significance.

The contractor's obligation as to payment is to pay the sub-contractors as and when the architect under the main contract so certifies. The intention is that the architect should in each interim certificate under the main contract direct the contractor as to what sum is to be payable to each of the nominated sub-contractors. The contractor then has seventeen days from the date of the issue of each interim certificate to make payment to those sub-contractors, and, provided he does so, he may retain a cash discount of $2\frac{1}{2}$ per cent (Clause 21.3.1.1). As far as final payment of nominated sub-contractors is concerned, the architect has an obligation under Clause 35.16 of the main contract to certify practical completion of nominated sub-contract work, and must within a year after that certify the amount finally due to that sub-contractor (main contract Clause 35.17).

NSC/4 contains a time for completion (which is usually earlier than the time for completion under the main contract) and like the main contract contains many detailed clauses as to architects' instructions, insurance, determination, defects liability period, valuation of variations etc. It also contains a choice of fluctuations clauses, though it should be noted that it is by no means imperative that the fluctuations clause under a sub-contract must be in the same form as a fluctuations clause under the main contract; indeed it is quite common to have a fixed-price main contract with fluctuating sub-contracts, or vice versa.

It was said by the Court of Appeal in *Tersons Limited v Stevenage Development Corporation* [1965] 1 QB 37 that the Green Form was not to be construed *contra proferentum* against either the contractor or the sub-contractor, and the same presumably goes for NSC/4.

(d) JCT Management and Associated Works Contract Conditions

The JCT87 Management Contract consists of the Standard Form Management Contract Conditions, the Works Contract to be entered into by the management contractor and the works contractor and an employer/works contractor warranty. Some of the JCT87 wording is similar to that of the JCT80; it is divided into nine sections and incorporates five schedules. Schedule 3 lists 54 services to be provided by the management contractor pursuant to article 1 of the contract which are carried out in conjunction with the employer's professionals. The overriding obligations of the management contractor is to endeavour to see that the project is carried out economically and as expeditiously as possible.

The works contract consists of an invitation to tender, tender, articles of agreement and conditions. Although it is not obligatory to use the works contract conditions with the management contract, it is usual, and the two documents have been drafted for use in conjunction with one another. In general, payment of the works contractor depends upon certification under the management contract and it is not uncommon for the works contract conditions to be amended by the management contractor to incorporate a 'pay when paid' clause. Again, the contract is divided into nine sections and in a number of respects the Works Contract is similar to NSC/4. Like NSC/4 the Works Contract is either a lump sum contract or a re-measurement contract, depending on how the articles of agreement have been completed.

(e) Intermediate Form of Contract IFC84

In addition to the full standard form itself, JCT issued an intermediate form of contract for use in the range between those for which the standard form contract and the JCT Agreement for Minor Building Works are issued. The narrative to the contract advises that the form is only suitable where the proposed building works are of simple content and only involve a recognised basic skill of the industry, without any buildings or installations of a complex nature and the works are adequately specified. This form of contract incorporates a number of features of JCT80, but in a more simplified manner.

(f) JCT Agreement for Minor Works

In addition to the full standard form itself, the JCT has for some years issued a much shorter 'Agreement for Minor Building Works' (sometimes referred to as the 'Minor Works' or 'Small Works' Agreement), which is an eight page document headed as follows:

This Form of Agreement is designed for use where minor building works are to be carried out for an agreed sum and where an Architect/Supervising Officer has been appointed on behalf of the Employer. The Form is not for use for works for which bills of quantities have been prepared or where the Employer wishes to nominate sub-contractors or suppliers, or where the duration is such that full labour and materials fluctuations are required; nor for works of a complex nature which involve complex services or require more than a short period of time for their execution.

Despite the modesty of these words, this contract is widely and successfully used, and indeed represents a very much less dangerous vehicle than the full JCT80 contract for many of those in the contracting industry.

Although the overall scheme of the contractual arrangement is the same there are a number of important differences of detail between the workings of this contract and JCT80. First, there is no express provision entitling the contractor to be paid loss and/or expense arising from late instructions or any of the other matters listed in Clause 26 of JCT80. It is thought that the contractor under the Minor Works Agreement may nevertheless achieve a similar result by making a claim for damages at common law; such a claim would not of course fall within the certification scheme.

Secondly, there is a particular importance attached in the Minor Works Agreement to the penultimate certificate under Clause 10(ii). This clause provides that ten days after practical completion the architect should certify 95 per cent of the anticipated final account figure. Although somewhat crude, the aim of this provision is that the contractor should be paid this amount promptly upon completion without the need to wait for the finalisation of the account. It recognises that small contractors often have modest cash resources to finance their work and need that prompt payment.

The certification procedure in the Minor Works Agreement was considered by the Court of Appeal in *Crestar v Carr* (1987) 37 BLR 113. The court found that a final certificate is not valid unless the architect has certified under Clause 9 (iii) that the contractor has complied with its defects liability obligations, and unless a penultimate certificate under Clause 10 (ii) has also been issued. This decision is of particular interest because it is not uncommon in practice for final certificates under Minor Works Agreements to be issued without one or both of the preceding certificates. It was also found in that case that a valid final certificate would not prevent the employer from making claims for damages for breach of contract, and further that the parties are at liberty to challenge the final certificate in arbitration either before or after the expiration of fourteen days from the issue of the certificate.

(g) ICE Conditions of Contract

A form of contract for civil engineering works is issued under the sponsorship and approval of the Institution of Civil Engineers, the Association of Consulting Engineers and the Federation of Civil Engineering Contractors. It occupies in the civil engineering world the central position occupied by the JCT contract in the building world.

The current edition, the sixth, was issued in 1991 and in the main incorporates a number of revisions made to the fifth edition between 1973 and 1986. The changes introduced by the sixth edition are not particularly wide ranging, although the engineers' powers are wider. The ICE Contract is a re-measurement contract; see Chapter 1, section 1(d). The engineer appointed under the contract has wide powers of certification and is in a somewhat more powerful position than the architect under the JCT contract. The contract contains detailed provisions as to such matters as variations, delay, sub-contractors, determination, interim certificates and many other matters. One of the unique features of this form of contract, however, is Clause 12 which enables the contractor to claim an extension of time and additional payment where, in the opinion of the engineer, the contractor has encountered unforeseen physical conditions or artificial obstructions.

The detailed wording of the ICE conditions differs from the JCT wording in practically every respect. There does not appear to be any logical reason for this and indeed the Banwell Report in 1974 recommended unification. Since that time both the ICE and the JCT have issued new editions, but neither makes any significant advance towards unification.

There is a form of sub-contract designed for use with the ICE form known as 'the Blue Form'. This document is not related to the non-nominated Blue Form of sub-contract designed for use with JCT63. Although commonly accepted by sub-contractors, the ICE Blue Form is a document containing far more comfort for a main contractor than for a sub-contractor.

(h) CPA Conditions

When contractors require cranes, earth moving equipment and other plant, they frequently hire it. The hiring is almost always in the terms or substantially in the terms of the Model Conditions for the Hiring of Plant (with effect from September 1979) which are the copyright of the Contractors' Plant Association, 28 Eccleston Street, London, SW1 9PY (071-730 7117). The Model Conditions replace the General Conditions for Hiring of Plant previously issued by the CPA.

There are two noteworthy features of the CPA conditions. The first is that they pass much of the risk of damage to the hirer, including the risk of negligence on the part of a competent operator provided by the owner. Condition 8 provides as follows:

When a driver or operator is supplied by the Owner with the plant, the Owner shall supply a person competent in operating the plant and such person shall be under the direction and control of the Hirer. Such drivers or operators shall for all purposes in connection with their employment in the working of the plant be regarded as the servants or agents of the Hirer (but without prejudice to any of the provisions of Clause 13) who alone shall be responsible for all claims in connection with the operation of the plant by the said drivers or operators. The Hirer shall not allow any other person to operate such plant without the Owner's previous consent to be confirmed in writing.

Condition 13 provides as follows:

(a) For the avoidance of doubt it is hereby declared and agreed that nothing in this Clause affects the operation of Clauses 5, 8 and 9 of this Agreement.
(b) During the continuance of the hire period the Hirer shall subject to the provisions referred to in subparagraph (a) make good to the Owner all loss of or damage to the plant from whatever cause the same may arise fair wear and tear excepted, and except as provided in Clause 9 herein, and shall also fully and completely indemnify the Owner in respect of all claims by any person whatsoever for injury to person or property caused by or in connection with or arising out of the use of the plant and in respect of all costs and charges in connection therewith whether arising under statute or common law. In the event of loss of or damage to the plant, hire charges shall be continued at idle time rates until settlement has been effected.
(c) Notwithstanding the above the Owner shall accept liability for damage, loss or injury due to or arising
    (i) prior to delivery of any plant to the site of the hirer where the plant is in transit by transport of the Owner or as otherwise arranged by the Owner
    (ii) during the erection of any plant, where such plant requires to be completely erected on site, always provided that such erection is under the exclusive control of the Owner or his Agent
    (iii) during the dismantling of any plant, where plant requires to be dismantled after use prior to removal from site, always provided that such dismantling is under the exclusive control of the Owner or his Agent
    (iv) after the plant has been removed from the site and is in transit on to the Owner by transport of the Owner or as otherwise arranged by the Owner
    (v) where plant is travelling to or from a site under its own power with a driver supplied by the Owner.

The effectiveness of the predecessors to these clauses was affirmed by the House of Lords in *Arthur White (Contractors) Ltd v Tarmac Civil Engineering Ltd* [1967] 1 WLR 1508. They are however within the scope of the Unfair Contract Terms Act 1977 and in *Phillips Products Limited v Hyland* (1984) *The Times*, 24 December, CA upheld the trial judge's finding that Condition 8 was not fair and reasonable, and was therefore ineffective as an exclusion clause.

The other noteworthy point about the CPA conditions relates to their universality. It is clear from *British Crane Hire v Ipswich Plant Hire* [1974] 1 All ER 1059 that the courts will readily infer the incorporation of the CPA conditions as between commercial entities who regularly contract under such conditions.

A commentary on the Model Conditions appeared in the magazine *Contract Journal* on 3 January 1980 (p 37) and 10 January 1980 (p 22).

(i) Other standard forms

Traditionally, the JCT contract and its forerunner the RIBA contract have been by far the most widely used of the standard forms. Since the formation of the Joint Contracts Tribunal, however, the form has consistently shown a tendency to grow in length and complexity; it has been pointed out that the contract has grown from 17 pages in 1952, to 33 pages in 1963, and is now (with quantities) 59 pages long but in smaller print. This tendency has created a reaction in the industry against the use of the form and since the introduction of the 1980 Edition contracting parties have often sought to avoid its use.

Where local authorities or regional health authorities instruct substantial building works, they usually do so under the Local Authorities Editions of the JCT Standard Form. Where central government is the employer, the form of contract is often the government's own form, GC/Works/1, which replaced their earlier form CC/Works/1. A form of sub-contract suitable for use with domestic sub-contractors is known as DOM/1. The wording and format of this contract is similar to that of other JCT forms of contract.

In the case of contracts to be carried out overseas, whether they are building contracts or civil engineering contracts, the form used is often the FIDIC form prepared by the Fédération Internationale des Ingénieurs-Conseils and the Fédération Internationale Européeanne de la Construction, and this contract shares many of the provisions of the ICE contract.

In addition to the above, there are a number of other standard contracts in current use that have been prepared by various professional bodies and by particular contractors and sub-contractors for their own use.

Chapter 2

Contractual procedure

1 Design

The traditional starting point for an employer is to engage the services of an architect or a surveyor to design the required work. This design may be in many stages and commence with a feasibility study, but eventually the design progresses into the form of detailed drawings which show precisely the required work. In due course these drawings are incorporated by reference into the contract between the employer and the contractor and represent the basic description of the work which the contractor is required to execute. The drawings are frequently amplified by one or more specifications and/or by sections of the bills of quantities.

The preparation of the design can take various forms, usually according to the magnitude of the project. In major building works for the construction or substantial alteration of buildings it is usual for the basic design to be in the hands of an architect. Detailed parts of the design are frequently delegated; for example the design of foundations and frame is put in the hands of consulting or structural engineers and the design of heating and air conditioning installations is entrusted to heating and ventilation engineers. The architect generally retains responsibility for coordinating the designs of these specialists. In medium-sized works, the whole of the design is frequently in the hands of a single architect or surveyor. In the case of small works, it is often the case that neither the employer nor any architect or surveyor employed by him does any of the design work, save to indicate the nature of the work he requires. Where, for example, an employer simply requires a road across his land he may merely indicate to the contractor that he requires a road along such a route suitable for such traffic. The design of the road is left to the contractor. This last example is a simple example of a design-and-build contract. It is unusual for a design-and-build contract to give rise to any difficult questions as to design: the responsibility for ensuring that the work is effected properly rests squarely with the contractor and if defects appear it is irrelevant whether they are defects of design or of workmanship.

18

In the normal case of traditional contracts (ie where the design is not the responsibility of the contractor but that of the employer's architect) then much importance can attach to the question of whether a defect is a design defect or a defect of workmanship. It is impossible to lay down hard and fast rules as to whether any particular defect will be one or another, for the choice between a flat roof and a pitched roof will be a matter of design, but the choice between a screw and a nail may well be a matter of workmanship. As a rule of thumb, the shape, dimensions, choice of material and other matters apparent from the drawings are generally regarded as design matters and the things left over for the good sense of the contractor are generally regarded as matters of workmanship.

Sometimes an employer or his architect nominates a sub-contractor or supplier who offers more than mere workmanship. For example, where the Works include a lift it is obvious that the manufacturer of the lift will design the lift installation. It is beyond the scope of this book to consider in detail the design liabilities of sub-contractors and suppliers, but in such an example the supplier of the lift may be liable to the employer for breach of collateral warranty if the lift had a design defect (*Shanklin Pier Co Ltd v Detel Products* [1951] 2 KB 854). Such collateral warranty may have been reduced to a formal direct warranty agreement between the employer and the nominated sub-contractor as in the JCT form NSC/2. In the past it is possible that the sub-contractor or supplier in question could also have been liable to the employer in negligence. However, throughout the latter part of the 1980s the courts have severely restricted the type of losses recoverable in negligence, culminating in the House of Lords decisions in *D & F Estates Limited v Church Commissioners* [1989] 2 All ER 992 and *Murphy v Brentwood District Council* [1990] 3 WLR 414. These cases establish that in claims for negligence other than claims for personal injuries, the damages recoverable are limited to damage caused to other property and not the cost of remedying the defective work itself, which is pure economic loss.

2 Bills of quantities

Bills of quantities are usually prepared by a quantity surveyor once the drawings have been prepared by the architect. The purpose of bills of quantities is to set out in itemized form all the work that is shown by the drawings and the opportunity is also usually taken to describe in further detail what the contractor must do. The process of preparing bills of quantities from drawings is known as 'taking off'. In an effort to simplify and unify the method of description of works, the Royal Institution of Chartered Surveyors and the National Federation of Building Trades Employers produce a book known as the *Standard Method of Measurement of Building Works* (usually abbreviated to the *Standard Method of Measurement (SMM)*) and it is normal for bills of quantities to be prepared in accordance with it. Clause 2.2.2.1 of the JCT contract expressly so provides.

Once the bills of quantities have been prepared, copies of them are given to the contractor to prepare his tender. The contractor goes through the bills of quantities item by item, placing against each item his price for that particular item of work. The contractor then totals all the items (often including an item for profit) and so arrives at the lump sum. The process of the contractor putting a price against each item is known as 'pricing' and a bill of quantities which has prices inserted (traditionally in a column on the right hand side of the page) is known as a 'priced bill of quantities'.

It is plain that in respect of original contract work the distribution of the lump sum among the items in the bills of quantities is irrelevant. The contractor's entitlement is to the lump sum, and it does not matter how he has arrived at it. There are, however, two particularly important consequences of the way in which the lump sum is distributed.

The first consequence relates to the valuation of variations under the JCT system. Under Clause 13.5.1.1 there is a rule that 'where the (extra) work is of similar character to, is executed under similar conditions as, and does not significantly change the quantity of, work set out in the bills of quantities the rates and prices for the work so set out shall determine the valuation'. In other words, the price set against each individual item not only represents a part of the total lump sum, but also sets out the prima facie entitlement of the contractor where more of the same thing is ordered. Because of this it has been known for contractors to indulge in the entertaining but dangerous exercise known as 'loading'. When considering alternative tenders, the employer is interested in the total lump sum but not usually the breakdown of this as between the individual items. Accordingly, if a contractor upon receipt of the bills of quantities thinks that the employer is likely to require more, say, painting work, then he sometimes 'loads' the painting rates and correspondingly reduces the rates for some other area of the work that he does not think will be increased. In this way, he hopes to be paid at a premium when the additional painting is ordered. If the contractor does this, however, he runs the risk that the employer might omit the painting and order more of the very sort of work that the contractor has underpriced.

The second consequence is that contractors sometimes indulge in what is known as 'front end loading'. The contractor increases his rates for the initial work at the expense of his rates for the finishing work so that he receives a greater proportion of the eventual recovery in the early interim payments rather than the late interim payments.

3 Tenders

Once the architect has prepared the design, and the quantity surveyors have prepared the bills of quantities, and the contractors on the tendering list have priced those bills of quantities, then the contractors submit their tender forms in sealed envelopes. All these tenders are then opened at the same time by the employer or his architect, and the employer enters into a contract with the successful tenderer.

Ordinarily, there is no implication that a contractor is to be paid for the costs of preparing his tender (*William Lacey (Hounslow) Ltd v Davis* [1957] 1 WLR 932), but a contractor may be entitled to payment for preparatory work, even if a contract for the main work is never placed (*Marston v Kigass* (1989) 46 BLR 109).

The normal intention is that the hopeful contractors should prepare their tenders independently. Occasionally, however, tendering contractors 'take a cover'. This might occur where a contractor, because of his current work load, is not in a position to undertake a contract for which he has been invited to tender, and yet does not wish to be seen to turn work away. He therefore contacts a friendly contractor who is also tendering and pitches his own price a little higher than that other contractor's price. The taking of covers is of course carefully concealed from the employer. It should be noted in passing that agreements between contractors as to tendering are potentially within the scope of the Restrictive Trade Practices Act 1976. Further, agreements between contractors relating to the tenders are likely to fall foul of EEC Competition Law; Article 85 of the Treaty of Rome prohibits all agreements between undertakings and concerted practices which may affect trade between member states. Also, EEC legislation may provide a remedy to a tendering party who feels that he has been discriminated against by a body in favour of a contractor from its own country (*Commission of the European Communities v Ireland* (1988) 44 BLR 1). There is, in fact, a growing body of EEC procurement legislation presently confined to government contracts, but this is likely to continue to be a developing area of law.

A party requesting tenders which are submitted in accordance with the required tender process should give these tenders due consideration (*Blackpool and Fylde Aeroclub Limited v Blackpool Borough Council* [1990] 1 WLR 1195). It is unclear as to how much consideration should actually be given to the tender and in *Fairclough Building Limited v Borough Council of Port Talbot* [1992] CILL 779 it was decided that provided a recipient of the tender gives the tender some consideration and behaves reasonably in rejecting the tender, then the tenderer can have no cause for complaint.

Tenders should be distinguished from estimates. A tender is in the nature of an offer which is capable of acceptance in the legal sense. It is usually a document which incorporates a priced bill of quantities or something similar. The term 'estimate' is used far more widely and can either represent an offer capable of acceptance so as to form a lump sum contract or it can merely be the contractor's view as to the eventual claim he will make for payment under a cost contract or in *quantum meruit*. There is certainly no rule of law that the use of the word 'estimate' on a document prevents it amounting to an offer (*Croshaw v Pritchard* (1899) 16 TLR 45), and where such a document carries standard terms and conditions then that will generally be a strong indication that the document is an offer capable of giving rise to a contract if accepted expressly or by conduct. Estimates may of course take verbal form as well as written form.

The precise terms of estimates should be carefully considered to establish whether they constitute an offer or merely a view as to the likely cost. Even if the estimate is merely a view as to the likely cost, the contractor may be liable for its accuracy in misrepresentation, for breach of collateral warranty, or in negligence (*Esso v Mardon* [1976] QB 801).

Contractors are not infrequently concerned about being taken off the tender lists of local authorities. Where there is no reason for such removal it may be reversed (*R v Enfield ex p Unwin* (1989) 46 BLR 1).

4 Letters of intent

It can take a long time for the formalities of a substantial building contract to be concluded, and where the employer wishes the contractor to get started as soon as possible he sometimes sends a letter expressing his intention to enter into a formal contract in due course. Such letters are sometimes expressed to be 'subject to contract'.

Such a letter of intent is not usually regarded as capable of giving rise to a binding contract for the execution of the works as a whole. Where a contract is entered into in due course, then that contract may have retrospective effect (see *Trollope & Colls Ltd v Atomic Power Constructions Ltd* [1963] 1 WLR 333) and the letter of intent will ultimately have little effect. However, in the case of *Wilson Smithett v Bangladesh Sugar* [1986] 1 Lloyd's Rep 370, a letter of intent amounted to an acceptance of an offer with the result that a binding contract was formed. Further, a letter of intent may result in what is known as an 'if' contract under which a party is asked to carry out certain works and in return, if these works are carried out, he will be paid the cost of carrying out the works. Where a contract is not entered into but the contractor has undertaken works, it seems that the court will lean towards a construction of a letter of intent that allows the contractor to be paid in respect of work done in reliance upon the letter of intent (*Turriff Construction Ltd v Regalia Knitting Mills Ltd* (1971) 9 BLR 20). In these circumstances, the contractor will usually be entitled to be paid upon a *quantum meruit* basis.

5 Contractual documents

Once the employer and contractor have reached agreement they usually embody that agreement in a number of contractual documents. The central document is the document usually referred to as 'the contract'. In the JCT form, it comprises the Articles of Agreement and the Conditions. The contract itself does not usually describe the extent of the Works in any detail. This description usually appears in the drawings and the bills of quantities, all of which are incorporated into the contract by reference.

6 Nomination

It frequently happens that the employer wishes to have certain parts of the works carried out not by the main contractor but by some other building company, often a specialist. The normal way for an employer to proceed in these circumstances in England and Wales is not for him to enter into parallel contracts with the builders but to engage a main contractor with a contract which provides that the main contractor must enter into sub-contracts with sub-contractors nominated by the employer. It is very common for sub-contractors to be nominated to perform heating and ventilation works, lift installation, window installation, steel frame construction and any other parts of building works which involve specialist building techniques or patented or unique building materials. Sometimes, the employer is interested in particular materials rather than particular workmanship and he may then nominate the supplier.

The term 'nomination' is used loosely to describe any instruction from an employer or his architect to a builder to enter into a contract with a nominated sub-contractor or supplier. The main contractor has the right under Clause 35 to make reasonable objection to the nomination of a particular sub-contractor. There is little authority as to what constitutes 'reasonable objection', although Keating says this could cover objections as to the sub-contractor's financial standing and also the sub-contractor's actual technical abilities. It is the employer or the architect who enters into the negotiations with the intended sub-contractor, and when those negotiations are at a stage when the employer is satisfied with the sub-contractor's tender, then the main contractor is instructed to accept it. In theory, difficult questions of law as to purported acceptance of offers by persons other than the offeree can arise, but in practice nomination is widespread and a proposed nominated sub-contractor who addresses his tender to the architect will probably anticipate that the offer will be taken up by a main contractor of whom he may never even have heard.

7 Certification and interim payment

Where a contractor is involved in substantial building works, it is usually essential to him to receive payment for the works as they proceed. Most formal building contracts (including the JCT form) provide that the architect named in the contract should issue interim certificates as to the amount to be paid to the contractor month by month. The arbitration clause in the contract usually empowers the arbitrator to open up and review such certificates. It used to be widely accepted that the courts had equivalent power to an arbitrator, but in *Northern Regional Health Authority v Crouch* [1984] 2 WLR 676 it was held by the Court of Appeal that the court does not ordinarily have power to open up and review certificates and other decisions of the architect.

In summary, the position as regards interim certificates appears to be as follows:

(1) If the contractor is content with any interim or final certificate that has been issued, then he can issue proceedings in the court for the recovery of moneys due on the certification in question. The employer cannot ask the court to review certificates but can seek a stay of the court proceedings under s 4 of the Arbitration Act 1950 if the contract does contain an arbitration clause. However, the employer can also avail himself of such rights of set off as he may have. In *Enco Civil Engineering Limited v Zeuss International Development Limited* (1992) 9 CLD 8, an application for summary judgment by a contractor on the basis of two certificates issued by the engineer under ICE Conditions of Contract failed as the court held that the defendants had raised substantial counterclaims against the plaintiffs in respect of defective work and delay.

(2) If the contractor is not satisfied with the interim certification, he *may* nevertheless be able to obtain a judgment in the courts. There is a line of cases, now fairly old, which establishes that the contractor may sue in the courts if the architect disqualifies himself from certification by reason of fraud, collusion or dishonesty (*South Eastern Railway v Warton* (1861) 2 F&F 457). Far more common than actual fraud or dishonesty is the position where the architect is found to be failing to act impartially and independently and is, instead, certifying according to the instructions of the employer. In such circumstances the architect is disqualified so that the contractor may recover payment without a certificate (*Hickman v Roberts* [1913] AC 299 HL). In the *Panamena* case (see Chapter 3, section 2 (1)) the House of Lords went further in permitting the contractor to circumvent the certification requirement on the ground of persistent error; it is not clear what impact the *NRHA v Crouch* decision (above) has upon these cases.

(3) As an alternative to an action for payment under the contract the contractor *may* be able to bring a claim for damages for breach of contract. In *Croudace Ltd v London Borough of Lambeth* (1986) 33 BLR 20 the architect named by the contract was a member of the employer's staff. When he retired the employer took no steps to replace him, and although the employer purported to appoint an independent firm to assess the plaintiff's loss and expense, it did not in fact do so. The Court of Appeal found that the employer was in breach of contract *inter alia* in not appointing a successor architect and the plaintiff was entitled to summary judgment and interim payment on account of its claim. In this connection, it might be noted that an architect cannot delegate his role of certifier, although the architect can consult others to assist him in issuing certificates.

(4) Subject to the foregoing, a contractor who is dissatisfied with interim certification generally has no option but to commence arbitration proceedings (see Chapter 16).

One major practical effect of interim certificates is that they are generally regarded as sufficient to entitle a contractor to judgment under Ord 14 unless the employer has a set-off (eg for defective work). Where the contractor has the benefit of a certificate duly given pursuant to a contractual provision, the court does not generally require any further proof that the money is due.

There was formerly a line of cases, commencing with the Court of Appeal decision in *Dawnays Ltd v FC Minter Ltd and Trollope and Colls Ltd* [1971] 1 WLR 1205, which held that cash was the life blood of the building industry and that certificates for payment were to be treated as in the nature of negotiable instruments — that is to say to be paid without any set-off except arising out of fraud. The 'no set-off' rule was overturned by the House of Lords in *Modern Engineering (Bristol) Ltd v Gilbert Ash (Northern) Ltd* [1974] AC 689, where it was held that building contracts were subject to the ordinary rule as to set-off. It remains the case, however, that the court will not be dissuaded from awarding judgment under Ord 14 where the defendant makes bare allegations as to defective work or some other cross-claim; the set-off must be properly detailed and quantified, as was the case in *Enco Civil Engineering Limited v Zeuss International Development Limited* (1992) referred to above.

Although the *Gilbert Ash* case (above) is of importance as to the principle that ordinary rules of set-off apply to claims based on certificates for payment, it is of limited application upon its particular circumstances. The claim in the case was by a sub-contractor against a main contractor under a certificate issued under the main contract. The sub-contract was not, however, in the usual form (then the Green Form). If it had been in the usual form the contractor would only have been entitled to its set-off if the architect had issued a certificate as to the delay of the nominated sub-contractor under Clause 27(d) (ii) of the then current form, which now appears in a slightly modified form as Clause 35.15.1 (see *Brightside Kilpatrick Engineering Services v Mitchell Construction (1973) Ltd* [1975] 2 Lloyd's Rep 483).

It is usual for the certifier under the contract to be the architect who has designed the work and he will remain the employer's agent for the purpose of such matters as issuing instructions. There are, however, many cases which show that, when certifying, the architect must act fairly and independently between the parties to the contract (in particular *Hickman & Co v Roberts* [1913] AC 229 HL and *Panamena Europea Navigacion v Leyland & Co Ltd* [1947] AC 428). The architect acts as the agent of the employer in all these matters, but his duty to his employer in certification is to act in a fair and professional manner (*Sutcliffe v Thackrah* [1974] AC 727 HL).

There is usually a provision in a building contract also giving the architect the function of certifying what extensions of time are due to the contractor. Under the 1963 edition of the JCT form there was some doubt about the precise extent of the architect's right to make such certificates upon an interim basis, but under the 1980 edition there is express power for the architect to certify as to time on an interim basis. The same principles as to impartiality apply to such certification as apply to certification of interim payments.

8 Practical completion and defects liability periods

Building works, like the arrow of Eleatic paradox, have a propensity to get closer and closer to completion but never quite to arrive. The building industry has accordingly evolved the concept of practical completion, which in broad terms means the stage at which the Works are reasonably ready for their intended use, notwithstanding that there may be some minor defects or omissions.

The date of practical completion is important in a number of respects. It is generally the date on which the works are deemed to be complete for the purpose of liquidated damages. It is usually the time at which the architect ceases to have power to vary the works and it ordinarily marks the commencement of the defects liability period.

The defects liability period is akin to a guarantee period and the contractor usually has the obligation, and indeed the right, to remedy defects appearing within this time. The contractor is usually required to remedy these defects free of charge but the practice is to the benefit of both parties since the contractor would otherwise be liable for the greater cost of another contractor remedying the defects.

Ordinarily, a provision for the making good of defects within a defects liability period does not deprive the employer of his damages for defects appearing outside that period (*Hancock and Others v B W Anerley Brazier Ltd* [1966] WLR 1316) nor does it operate to extend the time allowed to the contractor to finish the Works correctly (*H W Nevill (Sunblest) Ltd v Williams Press & Son Ltd* (1981) 20 BLR 78 at 89). In the JCT form, the time for issue of the final certificate (whereby the architect certifies that the Works are satisfactory) is fixed by reference to the certificate of completion of making good defects (Clause 30.8) but there is no attempt to limit the contractor's liability to the defects that appear within the defects liability period. If a contractor were to seek such a limit to his liability in the contract he might well be thwarted by the Unfair Contract Terms Act 1977.

Issue of the final certificate is of significance and under JCT 1980 unless proceedings are commenced twenty-eight days after the issue of the final certificate, then the final certificate is conclusive as to the amount of the contractor's final account and also in respect of the quality of materials and the standard of workmanship of the contractor where such matters are to be to the reasonable satisfaction of the architect. The case of *Culbert Limited v H Kumar* [1992] CILL 752 appears to have extended the effect of the final certificate to include quality of materials and workmanship where the approval of such matters was actually inherently something for the opinion of the architect.

9 The final account

The final account, as its name suggests, is the document which shows the total price eventually to be paid for the Works. A positive final account is one which shows a further sum due to the contractor; a negative final account is one which shows that the contractor has been overpaid through the interim payments. Although the expression 'final account' is not expressly used in the JCT contract, it is colloquially used to describe the computation referred to in Clause 30.6.3.

Chapter 3

Terms of the contract

1 Express terms

Sometimes there is a formal agreement entered into and signed by both parties in one of the standard forms. There may be more than one such agreement relating to successive parts of the same project; if so, it is common for them to be in the same standard form. Where there is a formal document such as a JCT form of contract, then it is a mistake to assume that it contains the whole of the contract. It will usually incorporate by reference bills of quantities, drawings and often a specification. These may well contain information pertinent to the dispute. The contract documentation in such a case can often be substantial and it requires some experience to be able quickly to locate the relevant provisions.

Where there is no document signed by both parties, then isolating the terms of the contract can be extremely difficult and may not be resolved until trial. Frequently one or both parties attempt to incorporate their own standard conditions, their own programme or a particular letter that they may have written. Sometimes the standard conditions contain a clause such as 'The purchaser's order shall be construed as an express acceptance of these conditions and insofar as any provision of the purchaser's order is inconsistent herewith, these conditions shall be deemed to prevail'. Such a condition is not conclusive (*Butler Machine Tool Co Ltd v Ex-Cell-O Corporation (England) Ltd* [1979] 1 All ER 965), and it is necessary to analyse the contract on the traditional basis of offer and acceptance.

In many cases the parties make a series of counter-offers to each other and the acceptance does not occur until one party or the other accepts the last made offer by his conduct in starting work. It is, therefore, particularly important to establish when the works were commenced.

When looking at the formation of the contract, it is helpful to bear in mind the following points.

(a) Essential terms

A contract cannot come into being until the essential terms are agreed. It is said in Keating that agreement as to parties, price, time and description of works is normally the minimum necessary, although an obligation to complete within a reasonable time will be implied if the other essential terms are agreed. In the case of contracts other than lump sum contracts the description of the work may be in extremely broad terms, and even in the case of the lump sum contracts it is often succinct.

(b) Retrospective agreement

It is apparent from *Trollope and Colls Ltd v Atomic Power Construction Ltd* [1963] 1 WLR 333 that it is perfectly possible for the parties not to form their contract until some time after the work has commenced, such that the terms of the contract operate retrospectively.

(c) Quasi-contract

If there is no agreement as to price then there is no contract, but nonetheless a builder is entitled in quasi-contract to be paid a reasonable sum if he carries out work at the request of the other party.

(d) Incorporation by reference

It is common in the industry for offers to contain such words as 'JCT 1980 Private Edition Without Quantities to apply'. It is perfectly possible for such conditions to be incorporated by reference but conditions such as the JCT conditions are to a large measure meaningless without appointment of an architect or supervising officer, deletion of alternative clauses (such as the clauses which deal with fluctuations) and completion of the appendix which contains such matters as the liquidated damages figure.

(e) Formal requirements

It should be noted that there is no requirement for a building contract to be in writing, because in normal circumstances the building contract does not dispose of any interest in land. The builder is merely given a licence to enter the land. In the case of a building lease there is a disposition of an interest in land and as a result of s 2 of the Law of Property (Miscellaneous Provisions) Act 1989 the contract must be in writing and must contain all of the terms of the contract between the parties.

(f) Agency

It is a feature of building contracts that negotiations are frequently carried out on behalf of the employer by an agent, often an architect or surveyor. In such cases the fact of the agency and the identity of the principal are usually disclosed to the contractor. Sometimes, however, the architect or surveyor appears to contract in his own name. In such a case, the contractor can sue either the agent or the principal once the principal's identity is discovered, although the doctrine of election may cause the builder to lose his right to sue one by an unequivocal election to sue the other (*Clarkson Booker v Andjel* [1964] 2 QB 775). Usually, either the employer or his agent may sue, although it may be necessary to consider the many cases upon exclusion of undisclosed principals before establishing whether the undisclosed principal may sue in his own name rather than be obliged to sue in the name of his agent.

(g) Unfair Contract Terms Act 1977

Where one or other party puts forward its standard conditions, then substantial parts of those conditions may be written standard terms of business which fail to satisfy the requirement of reasonableness under the terms of the Unfair Contract Terms Act 1977, s 3. There have been some decisions under the Act which have particular relevance to the construction field:

1983 *George Mitchell (Chesterhall) Ltd v Finney Lock Seeds Ltd* [1983] 3 WLR 163. The House of Lords found that a seed merchant's clause limiting liability to the cost of the seeds was *not reasonable*.

1984 *Rees Hough v Redland Reinforced Plastics Ltd* (1984) 27 BLR 136. Pipe suppliers' clause limiting liability to replacement of defective pipes notified within three months was *not reasonable*.

1984 *Stevenson v Nationwide Building Society* (1984) 272 EG 663. Building society disclaimer for liability on valuation report when alternative full structural survey was offered as an alternative was *reasonable*.

1984 *Phillips Products Ltd v Hyland* [1987] 1 WLR 659. Condition 8 of CPA Model Conditions *not reasonable*.

1990 *Smith v Eric S Bush* [1990] AC 831. Surveyor's disclaimer *not reasonable* because the property was at the lower end of the market, the surveyor knew that the plaintiff would rely on the report, and she was unlikely to instruct another surveyor to inspect the property.

1991 *The Chester Grosvenor Hotel Company Limited v Alfred McAlpine Management Limited and Others* [1991] CILL 740: A clause limiting a management contractor's liability to the employer for delay to the amounts that the management contractor was able to recover from trade contractors was *reasonable*.

1992 *Barnard Pipeline Technology Limited v Maston Construction Company Limited* [1992] CILL 743. A clause limiting liability in respect of defective materials supplied, or work done limited to the cost of repairing or paying for the repair or replacement of goods was reasonable.

It is submitted in Keating that the JCT form is not to be construed *contra proferentum* either the employer or the contractor. There has, however, been some speculation as to whether the JCT form might be the 'written standard terms of business' of one or both parties within the meaning of the Unfair Contract Terms Act 1977, s 3(1). It seems unlikely that the draftsman of the Act can have intended to affect the JCT form (if indeed he was even conscious of it), but if the courts were ever to bring the JCT form within the scope of the 1977 Act then it would seem likely that many of the clauses would be affected. In the meantime the courts continue to apply the nineteenth century rules of strict construction to the contract, even where to do so leads to manifest absurdity (*Jarvis v Westminster Corporation* [1970] 1 WLR 637 HL).

(h) Liquidated damages clauses

Subject to express agreement, there is normally to be implied into a building contract a term that the contractor will complete the works within a reasonable time. If, without sufficient excuse, the contractor is late in completing the works then he is liable to pay damages at common law assessed under the common law principles that derive from *Hadley v Baxendale* (1854) 9 Ex 341 and *Victoria Laundry (Windsor) Ltd v Newman Industries Ltd* [1949] 2 KB 528.

Formal building contracts usually quantify precisely both of these common law matters. Not only is the completion date agreed but the amount recoverable by an employer for delay in completion of the works is fixed by a liquidated damages clause. Such a clause appears at Clause 24 of the JCT form of contract.

Unlike the provision at Clause 26 of the JCT contract relating to loss and expense (which deals with the entitlement of the contractor who is delayed by his employer), Clause 24 does not operate to adjust the contract sum, but creates a separate debt due from the contractor to the employer and gives the employer a contractual right of set-off. In other words, the amount of any liquidated damages is not reflected in the amount of the architect's certificates for payment, but is deductible from what would otherwise be payable under those certificates.

There is a distinction in English law between a liquidated damages clause (which is perfectly valid) and a penalty clause (which is unenforceable). Unfortunately, the expression 'penalty clause' is widely used in the industry to mean a liquidated damages clause, and in some other English speaking legal systems the terms are used by lawyers interchangeably. Whether a clause is a penalty clause or a liquidated damages clause depends principally upon its amount; the following test was formulated by the House of Lords in *Dunlop Pneumatic Tyre Co Ltd v New Garage & Motor Co Ltd* [1915] AC 79.

(1) Though the parties to a contract who use the words 'penalty' or 'liquidated damages' may *prima facie* be supposed to mean what they say, yet the expression used is not conclusive. The court must find out whether the payment stipulated is in truth a penalty or liquidated damages . . .

(2) The essence of a penalty is a payment of money stipulated as *in terrorem* of the offending party; the essence of liquidated damages is a genuine pre-estimate of damage . . .

(3) The question whether a sum stipulated is a penalty or liquidated damages is a question of construction to be decided upon the terms and inherent circumstances of each particular contract

judged as at the time of the making of the contract, not as at the time of the breach . . .

(4) To assist this task of construction various tests have been suggested, which if applicable to the case under consideration, may prove helpful, or even conclusive. Such are:

    (a) It will be held to be a penalty if the sum stipulated for is extravagant and unconscionable in amount in comparison with the greatest loss which could conceivably be proved to have followed from the breach . . .

    (b) It will be held to be a penalty if the breach consists only in not paying a sum of money, and the sum stipulated is a sum greater than the sum which ought to have been paid . . .

    (c) There is presumption (but no more) that it is a penalty when 'a single lump sum is made payable by way of compensation, on the occurrence of one or more or all of several events, some of which may occasion serious and others but trifling damage' . . .

On the other hand:

    (d) It is no obstacle to the sum stipulated being a genuine pre-estimate of damage, that the consequences of the breach are such as to make precise pre-estimation almost an impossibility. On the contrary, that is just the situation when it is probable that pre-estimated damage was the true bargain between the parties . . .

If a clause is found to be a penalty clause, then the employer is entitled to receive by way of damages only that sum which would compensate him for his actual loss, and it seems that the employer may be put to an election as to whether to seek to rely on the clause or not (*Watts, Watts & Co Ltd v Mitsui & Co Ltd* [1917] AC 227 HL).

In practice it is comparatively rare to find penalty clauses (in the strict sense of these words) in substantial building contracts. The sum is frequently calculated by reference to interest rates applied to the capital value of the completed works, and it requires only a simple calculation to show that a genuine pre-estimate of the damages that flow from loss of use of a building worth a million pounds can be of the order of £3,000 per week.

It has sometimes been suggested by commentators that a liquidated damages clause might be unenforceable if the benefiting party has in fact suffered no loss whatsoever as a result of the delay. The suggestion has been that the purpose of the clause is to quantify damages, not to create them. This argument was rejected in *BFI Group of Companies Ltd v DCB Integration Systems Ltd* [1987] CILL 348.

2 Implied terms

Some of the law concerning implied terms in building contracts has now been codified by the Supply of Goods and Services Act 1982.

Building contracts fall within Part 1 of the Act ('Supply of Goods') which applies to contracts made on or after 4 January 1983. Building contracts also fall within Part 2 of the Act ('Supply of Services') which applies to contracts made on or after 4 July 1983. Section 13 states that a supplier acting in the course of a business will carry out the service with reasonable care and skill and, subject to what the parties have agreed in relation to completion within a reasonable time (s 14). The supplier is entitled to be paid a reasonable sum for the services supplied (s 15).

Part I of the Act deals with title (s 2), correspondence with description (s 3), and quality and fitness (s 4). The implied terms in s 2 regarding title are unlikely to affect the present position significantly; the terms substantially mirror s 12 of the Sale of Goods Act 1979. Section 3 of the 1982 Act is rather more difficult. It provides that where the transferor agrees to transfer the property and the goods by description (which will almost invariably be the case in a building contract) there is an implied condition (not merely a warranty) that the goods will correspond with their description (thus mirroring s 13 of the Sale of Goods Act 1979). There is nothing remarkable about the content of this term; what is remarkable is its status as a condition. Will this import a right of rejection for any breach, however trivial? There has in the past been a distinction between the stringent rules sometimes applied in sale of goods cases (see *Arcos Ltd v E A Ronaasen & Son* [1933] AC 470) and the more pragmatic approach which has ordinarily been applied in building cases (see *Wm Cory & Son Ltd v Wingate Investments (London Colney) Ltd* (1980) 17 BLR 104). The position is further complicated by the rule that materials become the property of the owner of the land upon incorporation in the works. Notwithstanding that the Act appears to draw a clear distinction between conditions and warranties, it is difficult to see how to make sense of the distinction as regards building contracts and the courts will probably have to find that the remedies for breach of this condition cannot be more extensive than if it had merely been a warranty.

Section 4 of the 1982 Act carries the same difficulty as well as other difficulties. There is an implied condition under s 4(2) that, where the transferor transfers the goods in the course of a business, the goods supplied under the contract are of merchantable quality. There is a saving at s 4(3) for defects specifically drawn to the transferee's attention before the contract is made, or for defects which an examination ought to reveal, but since a contractor has usually not even acquired the materials at the time that he makes this contract these savings are unlikely to be of widespread application. By s 4(5) there is an implied condition that the goods supplied should be reasonably fit for their intended purpose, expressly or by implication made known. There is a saving as regards s 4(5) where the circumstances show that the transferee does not rely, or that it is unreasonable for him to rely, on the skill or judgment of the transferor. In addition to the difficulty about these terms being referred to as conditions, there are other provisions that make it difficult to know what effect, if any, s 4 of this Act will have upon the ordinary common law implied terms. Section 4(7) provides that an implied condition or warranty about quality or fitness for a particular purpose may be annexed by usage to a contract for the transfer of goods, and s 11(3) provides that nothing in the preceding provisions or the Act prejudices the operation of any other enactment or rule of law whereby any condition or warranty (other than one relating to quality or fitness) is to be implied in a contract for the transfer of goods.

In the face of all these unfathomable uncertainties the courts have sometimes been more or less ignoring the Supply of Goods and Services Act, or in any event merely paying it lip service, and continuing to apply the common law principles.

There are some significant statutory incursions into common law principles, such as the Defective Premises Act 1972 (which affects new dwellings outside the NHBC Scheme) and the Building Act 1984, s 38 (which, when it comes into effect, will create a statutory cause of action for breach of building regulations). Section 38 has still not been brought into force and, therefore, there is no statutory cause of action for breach of Building Regulations. However, it is likely that any contractor who builds in breach of Building Regulations is likely to be in breach of contract with the employer, as most building contracts meet a condition of the contract that the contractor will carry out the works in accordance with Building Regulations.

Where the parties contract under a lengthy standard form, such as the JCT form, the express provisions will leave little room for substantial implication of terms. On the other hand, where the parties agree the minimum of express terms, then the common law will imply terms that have a familiar ring to those used to sale of goods contracts, such as the fitness for purpose, the quality of the workmanship and materials, and the time for performance.

The more important of the implied terms are considered further below, but it is important to note that in building contracts, especially where both parties do or ought to know what they are doing, the courts are often slow to imply terms so as to make the contract reasonable or to iron out the nonsense and inconsistencies that frequently appear. Indeed, one of the leading cases on the limits to implication of terms is a building case, *Trollope & Colls Ltd v North West Metropolitan Regional Hospital Board* [1973] 1 WLR 601. In it, the House of Lords said that its function is to interpret and apply the contract which the parties have made for themselves. The court held, in effect, that if the parties contract for a nonsense, then a nonsense they shall have. They said at p 609:

If the express terms are perfectly clear and free from ambiguity, there is no choice to be made between different possible meanings: the clear terms must be applied even if the court thinks some other terms would have been more suitable. An unexpressed term can be implied if and only if the court finds that the parties must have intended that term to form part of their contract: it is not enough for the court to find that such a term would have been adopted by the parties as reasonable men if it had been suggested to them: it must have been a term that went without saying, a term *necessary* to give business efficacy to the contract, a term which, though tacit, formed part of the contract which the parties made for themselves.

The *Trollope & Colls* case represents the House of Lords in a strict constructionist mood. The Court of Appeal has in the past adopted a more adventurous approach (as in *Greaves & Co Contractors v Baynham Meikle & Partners* [1975] 1 WLR 1095), and indeed it is clear from the judgments in *Young & Marten Ltd v McManus Childs Ltd* [1969] 1 AC 454 that even the House of Lords is prepared to look at policy considerations when considering the implication of terms. In brief, the position seems to be that the terms as to workmanship and materials, fitness for purpose, completion and other matters of principle are now well established and readily implied, whereas the courts are not generally prepared to imply terms to iron out nonsense arising out of detailed wording in particular contracts.

(a) Fitness for purpose

A warranty is usually implied on the part of the contractor that the material used in the Works and the completed Works themselves should be reasonably fit for the purpose for which they are required. There is remarkably little case law supporting this implication since the obligation as to the Works as a whole is not generally thought to apply where the contractor is bound to follow a detailed design prepared by the employer's architect. In those circumstances the contractor's obligation is to build what he has been told to build, and it is not his fault if that is ineffective. This term is, however, of particular importance in design-and-build contracts where the contractor's obligation as to the fitness of the completed Works is an absolute one, and goes beyond the obligation merely to use reasonable skill and care. (Keating in *Building Contracts* points to *Greaves v Baynham Meikle* [1975] 1 WLR 1075; Hudson in *Building and Engineering Contracts* points to the reasoning of the House of Lords in *Young & Marten v McManus Childs* [1969] 1 AC 454. Also see *Independent Broadcasting Authority v EMI Electronics Ltd* (1981) 14 BLR 1).

Ordinarily, it is for the court to determine upon expert evidence whether the Works are fit for their purpose in any particular respect. Sometimes, however, the parties pre-agree what is to be expected of the works in a performance specification. Where, for example, the parties pre-agree the required speed of a lift, the employer will not be able to complain that that speed is not fast enough.

The term for fitness for purpose may be implied in relation to part only of the contract works (*Cammell Laird v Manganese Bronze & Brass Co*

Ltd [1934] AC 402). This term was also considered, along with (*b*) and (*c*) below, in *Hancock and Others v B W Brazier (Anerley) Ltd* [1966] 1 WLR 1317 (see (*c*) below for details).

In *John Lelliott (Contracts) Limited v Byrne Brothers (Formwork) Limited* (1992) (unreported), having found that there was an oral contract to provide a temporary support system for steelwork, the court held that there was an implied term in the contract at common law that the temporary support system would be fit for the purpose for which it was required and further that a term as to fitness could be implied under s 9(4) of the Supply of Goods and Services Act 1982.

(b) Materials

A warranty is usually implied on the part of the contractor that the materials used should be of good quality. This warranty is not overridden by the selection by the employer or the architect of a particular sort of material; in such a case the materials used must be good of their expressed kind. The extent of this term was considered at length by the House of Lords in *Young & Marten v McManus Childs* [1969] 1 AC 454. Particularly difficult questions can arise where the architect nominates a particular supplier or where the materials specified are only obtainable from one manufacturer. It seems from *Young & Marten v McManus Childs* that the court will pay particular regard to whether the contractor has any recourse against his sub-contractor or supplier; if so, the court will be more ready to find the contractor liable for any shortcomings in the material, thereby preserving the chain of liability. This term was also considered, along with (*a*) and (*c*), in *Hancock v Brazier (Anerley) Ltd* [1966] 1 WLR 1317 (see (*c*) below for details).

(c) Workmanship

A warranty is usually implied on the part of the contractor that the Works will be carried out in good and workmanlike manner. This term is not affected by any requirement on the contractor to follow a particular design or to use particular materials. By definition, workmanship is that element left to the discretion of the workman.

It may be arguable as a matter of principle that the warranty is excluded where the work is to be carried out to the satisfaction of the employer's architect. In practice, contractors are always held responsible for defects arising out of the bad workmanship of themselves or their sub-contractors, whether nominated or domestic.

This term was considered along with the previous two in relation to a contract for the sale of a house in the course of erection in *Hancock v B W Brazier (Anerley) Ltd* [1966] 1 WLR 1317. In that case, the sale was made subject to the National Conditions of Sale so far as not inconsistent with the other contract conditions, and Clause 12 of the National Conditions of Sale provided that the purchaser should be deemed to buy with full notice of the actual state of the property and take it as it was.

Upon the facts of the case the Court of Appeal rejected Clause 12 of the National Conditions of Sale for repugnance, and found that there was a threefold obligation: to do the work in a good and workmanlike manner, to supply good and proper materials and to provide a house reasonably fit for human habitation. The builder's liability was absolute in the sense of being independent of fault and applied to work done before the contract was entered into as well as subsequent work.

In practice, cases upon the sale of partly completed dwellings will often contain the additional element of a NHBC house purchaser's agreement, and it will then be necessary to consider the terms of that agreement.

In the case referred to above, *John Lelliott Limited v Byrne Brothers*, it was also held that in the same circumstances there was an implied term at common law requiring that the sub-contractor uses reasonable skill and care in carrying out the work in a good and workmanlike manner and that such a term could also be implied under s 13 of the Supply of Goods and Services Act 1982.

(d) Limitation on liability

Where there is a collateral contract between an employer and a sub-contractor or supplier, the sub-contractor's or supplier's implied duties to the employer under that collateral contract are not modified by any exclusions or limitations of liability as between the sub-contractor or supplier and the main contractor, unless the employer not only knew of but also assented to such exclusion or limitation (*Rumbelow v AMK* (1980) 17 BLR 25 at 49).

(e) Design defects

It has been held by the Supreme Court of Canada in *Brunswick Construction v Nowlan* (1974) 21 BLR 27, that a contractor executing work in accordance with plans of the employer's architect is under a duty to warn the employer of obvious design defects. A contrary conclusion was reached in *University of Glasgow v Whitfield* (1988) 42 BLR 66.

(f) Indispensably necessary work

Building contracts are usually entire in the sense that the contractor undertakes to complete the Works. This imports an obligation not only to do those things particularly described in the contract but also everything else that is indispensably necessary for the completion of the work. In ordinary circumstances a contractor is not entitled to any additional payment for such indispensably necessary work (*Williams v Fitzmaurice* (1858) 3 H&N 844).

This obligation may be seen either as a matter of construction of the express terms of the contract or as a matter of implication. In practice, the same result arises upon either analysis.

(g) Progress

Formal building contracts usually include an express provision as to when the contractor must complete the Works and also an obligation that the contractor should regularly and diligently proceed with them. Such a provision appears in Clause 23.1 of the JCT form.

It is generally agreed that in the absence of such an express provision there is an implied obligation on the contractor to complete the Works as a whole in a reasonable time (see *Charnock v Liverpool Corporation* [1968] 1 WLR 1498; *Franks & Collingwood v Gates* (1983) 1 CLR 21). There is controversy as to whether, in the absence of an express term there is an implied term as to regular and diligent progress. Hudson suggests that there is such an implied term but Keating suggests that there is not.

Where a building contract contains an express completion date and the employer does something sufficient to release the contractor from the express completion obligation, then the implied obligation on the contractor to complete within a reasonable time will arise.

(h) By-laws

It is usual for formal contracts to contain an express obligation on the part of the contractor to comply with by-laws and other statutory requirements. Such a clause appears at Clause 6 of the JCT form. In the absence of such an express provision, it is suggested by Keating that such a term arises by implication.

(i) Economy in cost contracts

Where there is a cost contract under which the contractor is entitled to be paid the cost of the Works, then there is usually an express term requiring the contractor to carry out the Works efficiently and not wastefully. If there is not, then it is generally thought that the contractor is not entitled to be paid the costs incurred wastefully or extravagantly.

There is little or no reported case law upon this topic, and although there is general agreement as to the result that the courts would bring about, it is by no means clear whether they would do so as a matter of construction or as a matter of implication of a term.

(j) Possession

It is obvious that the employer must allow the contractor to come onto the site in order to execute the Works; the right of the contractor to enter upon the land is generally regarded as a licence (*Hudson* at p 681). In practice, the enforceability of the contractor's licence may be limited by the 'balance of convenience' test on interlocutory injunctions: see page 66 below.

It is suggested in *Hudson* (at p 317) that in the case of a new project the contractor will normally be entitled to exclusive possession of the entire site in the absence of express stipulation to the contrary but that a lesser degree of possession need be afforded in such cases as works of repairs or re-instatement of existing premises while still occupied or in the case of sub-contracts.

Subject to express agreement it is to be implied that the employer should give possession within a reasonable time (*Freeman & Son v Hensler* (1900) HBC (4th Ed), Vol 2, p 292).

(k) Instructions

The obligation on the part of the employer to give possession of the site arises as part of an overall implication that he agrees to do all that is necessary on his part to bring about completion of the contract (*MacKay v Dick* (1881) 6 App Cas 251). Depending upon the terms of the contract there will generally be other things which the employer must do, such as to supply within a reasonable time particulars of an incomplete design (*Roberts v Bury Improvement Commissioners* (1870) LR S CP 310) or to correct a defective design (*Holland Hannen & Cubitts (Northern) Ltd v Welsh Health Technical Services Organisation* (1981) 18 BLR 80); and, if the contract requires one, to appoint an architect (*Hunt v Bishop* (1853) 8 Ex 675); and, if a nominated sub-contractor goes into liquidation, to re-nominate another (*Bickerton & Son Ltd v North West Metropolitan Regional Hospital Board* [1969] 1 WLR 607) within a reasonable time (*Bilton v GLC* (1981)17 BLR 1).

In *London Borough of Merton v Stanley Hugh Leach Ltd* (1985) 32 BLR 51, the court considered a comprehensive list of preliminary issues arising under the JCT63 contract, and found for the following implied terms:

(1) that the employer would not hinder or prevent the contractor from carrying out its obligations in accordance with the terms of the contract and from executing the works in a regular and orderly manner;

(2) that the employer and the architect would do all things necessary to enable the contractor to carry out the work, and the employer is liable for any breach of this duty on the part of the architect;

(3) that the architect would provide the contractor with correct information concerning the works.

These terms are only remarkable insofar as they extend into areas, such as the supply of information, which are dealt with by express provisions in the contract. They appear to be equally applicable to JCT80 as to JCT63.

(l) Certification

Where the contract provides that an architect or other person has the power to certify as to such matters as interim payment, then the architect must be neutral in that he must act fairly and impartially as between the employer and the contractor. So much is common ground between the reported decisions and the textbooks. What, however, are the rights of the parties if the architect does not so act? The approach taken by the courts has varied from case to case.

(1) The position has been established by the Court of Appeal decisions in *Northern Regional Health Authority v Derek Crouch Construction Ltd and Crown Houses Engineering Ltd* [1984] 2 WLR 676 (as to which see page 88) and *Lubenham Fidelities & Investment Co v South Pembrokeshire District Council and Wigley Fox Partnership* (1986) 6 CLR 85 CA. The effect of these cases is that, subject to any arbitrator's award, the contractor's entitlement under JCT contracts is not to the agreed contract sum adjusted as provided for by the contract, but to whatever the architect has certified even if the architect is palpably wrong. The court will not assume the powers of an arbitrator to correct errors in certification. Depending on one's viewpoint, these cases represent either lack of robustness on the part of the courts, or a rigid enforcement of a 'play to the whistle' policy.

(2) There is a line of earlier cases including the House of Lords decisions in *Hickman v Roberts* [1913] AC 229 and *Panamena Europea Navigacion v Frederick Leyland & Co Ltd* [1947] AC 428 which adopts a different approach, tending to allow the contractor to recover the contract sum adjusted as required by the contract regardless of whether the sum is certified or not. The earlier cases are framed in terms of disqualification, the contractor becoming freed from the requirement to obtain a certificate if the architect disqualifies himself by reason of some fraud, or undisclosed interest or simply by reason of his following the instructions of the employer as to certification instead of exercising his own judgment. Other cases were framed in terms of prevention; if the employer prevents or impedes the issue of a certificate he cannot then rely upon the absence of a certificate in a claim by the contractor for payment. Thus in the *Panamena* case it was found that if, to the employer's knowledge, the architect persists in applying the contract rules wrongly in his capacity as certifier then the employer will be in breach of an implied term if he does not dismiss the architect and appoint another, and the contractor is entitled to payment with or without a certificate. In *Lubenham*, the *Panamena* decision was distinguished on the grounds that there was no arbitration clause in the *Panamena* contract and thus no other remedy for an aggrieved contractor.

In practice it is extremely rare for an employer to dismiss an architect in consequence of the architect's bias towards the employer; the point is usually of academic interest by the time any dispute comes to trial, but for tactical reasons contractors sometimes demand that the employer dismiss the architect for failure to issue proper certificates when due.

As between the architect and the employer there is a term implied if not express that the architect will exercise his certification functions according to the terms of the contract (*Townsend v Stone Toms & Partners (No 2)* (1984) 27 BLR 26).

(m) Interim payment

There is surprisingly little case law upon a contractor's implied right to interim payment. The most important recent decision is *Lester Williams v Roffey Nicholls (Contractors) Limited* [1989] CILL 552, where it was held in the first instance that there was an implied term for interim payments on a reasonable valuation and this was subsequently upheld by the Court of Appeal.

There was found to be an implied term for interim payment in a contract for renovation and modernisation of a derelict cottage in *F R Cosford v Rice* (Northampton County Court (1982) 8 CL 27a). In practical terms the courts are quick to find a provision for interim payment as a matter of construction, and the use of such vague expressions as 'terms monthly' will probably be sufficient for the court to find an agreement for interim payment.

There is a practical importance of whether there is an implied term, if none is expressed, for interim payment as regards repudiation. If a contractor is not being paid and has in mind to abandon the works then either the contractor or the employer will have been in breach according to whether there is a term calling for interim payment. In either case the contractor will be entitled to payment or credit for the work he has done but the result as regards the contractor's loss of profit and the employer's loss of bargain in respect of the remaining work is usually very different.

(n) Final payment

Where a contractor does work for and at the request of an employer and there is no express agreement as to price, then the law implies an obligation on the employer to pay the contractor a reasonable sum for the contractor's labour and materials supplied (*Moffatt v Laurie* (1855) 15 CB 583). It is usually immaterial in practice whether, upon a true analysis, the obligation arises in contract or in quasi-contract.

Likewise, where an employer orders extra work, then he impliedly, if not expressly, agrees to pay for it. Where such extra work is of the kind contemplated by the contract and there are contract rates for it, then the employer must pay at the contract rate. Where there are no contract rates or the work is outside the scope of the original contract, then the employer must pay a reasonable sum (*Thorn v London Corporation* (1876) 1 App Cas 120).

There are no universally applicable rules used by the courts in determining what is a reasonable sum. Sometimes the court takes the actual cost of the works to the contractor and adds a reasonable percentage for profit; sometimes it takes expert evidence upon what an employer could reasonably expect to have to pay for the sort of work in question.

In *Crown House Engineering v Amec Projects* (1989) 48 BLR the Court of Appeal suggested that in considering a claim on a quantum meruit basis the contractor's tardy performance can be taken into account.

(o) Examples of no implication

There are a number of terms which are frequently put forward as implied terms but which in law cannot be supported as such.

There is no implied term in a lump sum contract that the contractor will be paid the reasonable value of his work. The contractor is to be paid according to the contract he has entered into.

There is no implied term that the employer will pay the contractor any additional sum to cover VAT; if a price is quoted without reference to VAT, then VAT should be regarded as included within the price (*Franks & Collingwood v Gates* (1983) 1 CLR 21). But note that this case involved an employer who was not VAT registered. The position may be different as between two commercial organisations where the party receiving the supply would be expected to receive input credit in respect of any VAT charged.

There is no implied term that where the employer engages an architect the architect is to issue certificates for payment. Certificates are only appropriate where the contract expressly calls for them.

In cases where there is a certification provision, there is no implied term that the certifier will certify in accordance with what he conceives to be reasonable or fair. His obligation is to certify in accordance with the terms of the contract.

Where there is an agreed date for completion there is no implied term that that time will be extended if the employer orders additional work or otherwise prevents or impedes progress. Unless there is an extension of time provision in the contract the effect of such matters is to set time at large, thus nullifying the original completion date altogether.

There is no implied term in JCT63 contracts that nominated sub-contracts should be in standard form (*James Longley & Co Ltd v Borough of Reigate* (1982) 22 BLR 31 CA). But note the different express provisions of Clause 35 of JCT80.

There are no implied terms in JCT contracts requiring the contractor to obtain the consent of the employer before determining a nominated sub-contract, nor empowering the architect to order the dismissal of a nominated sub-contractor (*North West Metropolitan Regional Hospital Board v Bickerton* [1970] 1 WLR 607).

There is no implied term in nominated sub-contracts that the standard form should apply.

In a sub-contract which requires the sub-contractor to carry out the work at times required by the main contractor, there is no implied term requiring the main contractor to make sufficient work available to allow the sub-contractor to work economically; *Martin Grant & Co Ltd v Sir*

Lindsay Parkinson & Co Ltd (1984) 29 BLR 31 CA. In *Kelly Pipelines v British Gas PLC* [1990] CILL 555, where a tender contained details of the minimum and maximum number of teams, the contractor proposed to provide by way of resources, the minimum being 30. It was held that there was no implied term in the contract that at least enough work for 30 gangs would be provided.

There is no implication in sub-contracts that the main contractor should allow the sub-contractor $2\frac{1}{2}$ per cent or any other discount. However, in *Team Services PLC v Kier Management and Design Limited* [1992] CILL 786 it was held at first instance that a main contractor's entitlement to deduct cash discounts from interim payments to a sub-contractor was dependent upon the payment of the interim payments by the main contractor within the time for payment required by the sub-contract, notwithstanding that in that case there were no express words to that effect. The decision was appealed. On 7 April 1993 the Court of Appeal confirmed, by a majority decision, the findings of Judge Bowsher QC at first instance. At the time of writing leave to appeal to the House of Lords was refused.

In the engagement of architects, there is no implied term that standard RIBA terms apply (*Sidney Kaye, Eric Firmin & Partners v Bronesky* (1973) 4 BLR 1).

There is no implied term in an architect's retainer permitting the employer to terminate the architect's services during the project.

There is not ordinarily any absolute warranty as to the effectiveness of the work of an architect or engineer (*George Hawkins v Chrysler (UK) Ltd* (1986) 38 BLR 36 CA), although there may be in exceptional circumstances (*Greaves & Co (Contractors) Ltd v Baynham Meikle & Partners* [1975] 3 All ER 99 CA).

Chapter 4

Payment under lump sum contracts

1 Adjustments to the lump sum

Where the consideration for a building contract is a pre-agreed lump sum, then that lump sum is *prima facie* the sum which the contractor is ultimately entitled to at the end of the day. It is, however, usually the case that the lump sum will be subject to adjustment in respect of such matters as variations, fluctuations, prime cost sums, provisional sums, and loss and expense. If the contract is described as 'fixed price' this merely means that the lump sum is not to be adjusted in respect of fluctuations; it remains liable to be adjusted in respect of the other matters.

There follows a brief description of the more important of these adjustments. There are others which sometimes fall to be made; the adjustment clause in the JCT contract, Clause 30.6.2, provides 16 separate heads of adjustment.

(a) Variations

In most standard form building contracts there is a provision expressly entitling the architect to issue instructions requiring a variation from the work originally contracted for. Such a provision appears at Clause 13.2 of the JCT contract. Such a variation may be for the addition, omission or substitution of any of the original work, although in practice many variations amount to the ordering of extras. In informal contracts the employer may simply change his mind as to the work he requires. In either case, the contractor is entitled to be paid for extra work. In the JCT contract there are rules at Clause 13.5 as to the rate of payment in respect of variations.

Where there is no express agreement as to the rate of payment for extra work but the lump sum is calculated by reference to contract rates, then there may be an implication that extra work of the same kind should be paid for at the same rates. If not then the employer must pay a reasonable sum in respect of varied work (*Sir Lindsay Parkinson & Co Ltd v Commissioners of His Majesty's Works and Public Buildings* [1949] 2 KB 632).

It is traditional for the effect of variations in the works upon the lump sum to be set out in the form of a bill of variations. A bill of variations is usually set out as an account that starts with the contract sum, deducts by way of omission any item which has been varied and adds back the total price of such items as varied.

(b) Fluctuations

Inflation in the construction industry is as much a fact of modern life as elsewhere. Contractors frequently have to estimate the cost of work many months or even sometimes years before that work is to be performed. They often also work to comparatively small profit margins, and they therefore frequently protect themselves against the effect of increases of cost of both labour and materials by inserting an express provision in the contract for the lump sum to be adjusted to reflect changes in the cost of taxes, labour and materials. Where such clauses envisage only rises in costs they are often called 'increased-cost clauses'. Where they also envisage the possibility of decreases in cost, then they are generally known as 'fluctuations clauses'.

Fluctuations clauses can take many forms. The fluctuations clause in the present JCT form of contract contains complex alternatives and runs to some 7,500 words. At the other end of the scale, small builders often insert the simplest clauses in their standard conditions entitling them to pass on increased costs to the employer.

Fluctuations clauses are not generally regarded as unreasonable provisions entitling contractors to extra money upon demand. Indeed, it is commonly found that the complex provisions in the JCT form of contract allow a contractor to recover only about 60 per cent of the true cost to him of any increases in cost that occur after the date of the tender. A properly worded fluctuations clause represents an entirely reasonable agreement to share the risk of inflation.

The expression 'fixed-price contract' is used to denote a contract which does not contain a fluctuations or an increased costs clause. The expression does *not* mean that the price is fixed for all other purposes, and indeed the lump sum will frequently be subject to adjustment in respect of such matters as variations. For a brief description of the fluctuations clauses in the JCT form of contract, see page 11.

(c) Prime-cost sums

Where the employer nominates a sub-contractor, the entitlement of the contractor in respect of such sub-contracted work is usually what the contractor must pay the sub-contractor plus a $2\frac{1}{2}$ per cent main contractor's discount. The amount the contractor must pay the sub-contractor is usually not known until after completion of the sub-contract work, and it is traditional for the employer's architect or quantity surveyor to include a prime-cost sum in the bills of quantities. This is, in effect, the architect or quantity surveyor's pre-estimate of what the nominated sub-contractor's final account will eventually be, and at the conclusion of the main contract the prime-cost sums are deducted and there is substituted the amount finally payable to the nominated sub-contractor. In the JCT form of contract these adjustments appear at Clause 30.6.2.1 and 30.6.2.7.

(d) Provisional sums

It sometimes happens that at the time of the formation of the contract the employer or his architect has yet to decide upon the precise extent of a part of the work but does anticipate that some work in that area will be necessary. It is of course possible for such work to be ignored altogether in the bills of quantities and for the work to be subsequently ordered as extra work. Alternatively, the architect or quantity surveyor may include a provisional sum in the bills of quantities, and such a provisional sum is the architect's or quantity surveyor's approximate estimate of the value of the work which will in due course be ordered. The architect must then, during the course of the work, issue an instruction to the contractor as to what work is required in that area, and if he decides to have the work performed by a nominated sub-contractor he is usually entitled to do so.

Where there is a provisional sum, the contract sum is adjusted by omitting the provisional sum and adding back the actual price of the work ordered. In the JCT form of contract such work is valued in the same way as variations under Clause 13, and the adjustment to the contract sum falls to be made under Clauses 30.6.2.2 and 30.6.2.12.

(e) Loss and expense

Many contracts reserve to the employer or his architect a wide ranging right to issue instructions to the contractor. These instructions can frequently cause the contractor extra expense that is not necessarily reflected in any additional payment he receives for any variation of the work itself. Likewise, delay by the employer's architect in providing the contractor with necessary details of the design of the works is likely to cause delay to the contractor. Similarly, other acts or defaults of the employer or his architect, such as failure to give prompt possession of the site or unnecessary requirements for the opening up for the inspection of work, can cause loss to the contractor. For these reasons it is common to insert a provision in building contracts that in such circumstances the contractor is entitled to an addition to the contract sum, and this addition is usually described as 'loss and expense'.

Frequently, a provision for loss and expense merely means that the contractor is entitled to be paid in respect of some matter *under* the contract rather than by way of damages for *breach* of contract. Sophisticated arguments can arise as to whether such a matter gives rise to a claim for loss and expense by the contractor under the contract or a claim for damages for breach of contract. The argument is usually sterile since the measure of compensation for the contractor is the same in either case (*Wraight Ltd v P H & T (Holdings) Ltd* (1968) 13 BLR 26).

Loss and expense frequently arises where the works are delayed for some reason. Sub-contractors are often involved and a complex web of claims, and cross-claims can occur (see below). In the JCT form of contract the loss and expense clause appears at Clause 26 and the appropriate adjustment to the contract sum falls to be made under Clause 30.6.2.13.

2 Delay, prolongation and disruption

Things can and do go wrong in building contracts. The ordering of extra work can disrupt progress, the architect can be late in producing drawings, the contractor can be slow in getting on with the work, one of the nominated or domestic sub-contractors can delay things, or the Works might be disrupted by some entirely neutral cause (like exceptionally adverse weather conditions). All these matters can cause substantial financial losses to the parties involved, and there follows a review of the basic consequences of these matters in the case of a lump sum contract where the JCT form has been used. In preparing a claim for loss and expense associated with delay, prolongation and disruption, it is now necessary to consider a number of recent decisions of the courts, in particular the case of *Wharf Properties v Eric Cumine Associates* (1984) 45 BLR 72, that is considered in more detail in Chapter 21.

(a) Extra work

Where the employer orders extra work, then he must pay for it. Further, if the extra work disturbs or delays the contract as a whole, the contractor is entitled to loss and expense under Clause 26.2.7. Where the extra work affects the regular progress of a nominated sub-contractor (whether or not it is the sub-contractor himself who is required to execute the extra work), then the nominated sub-contractor is also entitled to loss and expense (Clause 13.1.2.7 of NSC/4).

The position of a domestic sub-contractor depends upon the terms of the contract between the main contractor and the domestic sub-contractor. If the regular progress of the domestic sub-contractor's work is disturbed by extra work executed by the contractor or by another sub-contractor, then the domestic sub-contractor may be entitled to damages at common law against the main contractor.

If the extra works cause a delay in the completion of the Works as a whole, then the contractor is entitled to an extension of time under Clause 25.4.5.1 of the main contract. Nominated sub-contractors get an extension of time under Clause 11.2.5.5.1 of NSC/4. Domestic sub-contractors usually get an extension under comparable provisions.

(b) Employer default

It is not uncommon for contracts to be delayed by reason of the architect, who is the agent of the employer, being late in providing necessary instructions, drawings, details or levels to the contractor. If such delay disrupts the regular progress of the Works, then the contractor is entitled to be paid loss and expense (Clause 26.2.1). The same result flows from a number of other matters listed in Clause 26.2, and the position is much the same as in the case of extra work. Nominated sub-contractors may be entitled to loss and expense under Clause 13.1 of NSC/4 and domestic sub-contractors may have a claim for damages against the main contractor at common law.

The main contractor gets an extension of time under Clause 25. Nominated sub-contractors get an extension of time under Clause 11 of NSC/4 and domestic sub-contractors usually get an extension of time under comparable provisions.

(c) Time at large

It is convenient at this point to consider the position where time is 'set at large' by some act of prevention on the part of the employer which is not provided for by any clause for the extension of time. The leading authority on the point is the Court of Appeal decision in *Peak Construction (Liverpool) Ltd v McKinney Foundations Ltd* (1970) 1 BLR 111, where Salmon LJ said:

A clause giving the employer liquidated damages at so much a week or month which elapses between the date fixed for completion and the actual date of completion is usually coupled, as in the present case, with an extension of time clause. The liquidated damages clause contemplates a failure to complete on time due to the fault of the contractor ... If the failure to complete on time is due to the fault of both the employer and the contractor, in my view, the clause does not bite. I cannot see how, in the ordinary course, the employer can insist on compliance with a condition if it is partly his own fault that it cannot be fulfilled: *Wells v Army & Navy Co-operative Society Ltd*; *Amalgamated Building Contractors v Waltham Urban District Council*; and *Holme v Guppy*. I consider that unless the contract expresses a contrary intention, the employer, in the circumstances postulated, is left to his ordinary remedy; that is to say, to recover such damages as he can prove to flow from the contractor's breach. No doubt if the extension of time clause provided for a postponement of the completion date on account of delay caused by some breach or fault on the part of the employer the position would be different ... In such a case the architect would extend the date for completion, and the contractor would then be liable to pay liquidated damages for delay as from the extended completion date.

One of the failings of JCT63 was that it did not make any provision for the not uncommon inability of an employer to give possession of or access to the site at the outset of the contract. Thus, for example, in *Rapid Building Group Ltd v Ealing Family Housing Association Ltd* (1984) 29 BLR 5 the employer was unable to set off any liquidated damages at all against certificates (notwithstanding that the architect had issued a certificate of delay) because of a few days' delay at the outset caused by the need to evict some squatters. Note however that the employer was able to set up a cross-claim in damages for unliquidated damages and the court expressly declined to deal with the point as to whether those unliquidated damages could exceed the liquidated damages.

(d) Contractor default

The main contractor sometimes fails to complete the Works by the completion date and has no one but himself to blame. If so, the architect must issue a certificate to that effect (Clause 24.1); and if the employer so requires, the contractor must pay or allow liquidated damages at the rate stated in the appendix to the contract (Clause 24.2.1). In other words, the contractor must compensate the employer for the employer's loss arising out of the delay, and of course the contractor has no claim against the employer for his own additional costs arising out of his own delay.

The terminology under the 1980 edition of the JCT form is confusing, and the completion date must be distinguished from the date for completion. The date for completion is the date that appears in the appendix to the contract and *prima facie* this is the date by which the contractor must finish the works. The completion date, on the other hand, can be altered and broadly means the date for completion as extended (Clause 1.3). Accordingly, the obligation on the contractor to complete the works by the completion date represents an obligation on the contractor to complete by the date for completion as extended. Any matter which entitles the contractor to an extension is called a 'relevant event' (Clause 25). If the contractor's defaults affect the regular progress of the work of the nominated sub-contractor then the sub-contractor gets an extension of time as against the main contractor (Clause 11.2.2.1 of NSC/4). That extension of time is dealt with by the written consent of the architect. The sub-contractor is further entitled to be paid loss and expense (or perhaps damages) by the main contractor but this is not dealt with through the certification process. If the amount of such loss and expense can be agreed between the contractor and the sub-contractor, then Clause 13.2 of NSC/4 applies; if agreement is not possible then either a reasonable amount is due under the sub-contract or the sub-contractor may be entitled to damages at common law.

The position of the domestic sub-contractor is much the same as the nominated sub-contractor, except that the architect is not involved in the sub-contractor's entitlement to an extension of time. A provision similar to Clause 13.2 of NSC/4 appears at Clause 10 (2) of the Blue Form.

(e) Nominated sub-contractor default

Where a nominated sub-contractor delays completion of the whole works, complex provisions come into play, the effect of which is that the sub-contractor must pay the losses of every affected party.

Under the main contract, the contractor is entitled to an extension of time from the employer (Clause 25.4.7) but is not entitled as against the employer to loss and expense. The employer, therefore, does not recover his losses from the contractor. The employer may, however, have a claim against the nominated sub-contractor directly under Clause 3.4 of NSC/2 (in which the nominated sub-contractor warrants to the employer directly that the contractor will not become entitled to any extension of time under Clause 25.4.7). It is not clear from NSC/2 whether the amount of damages payable by a nominated sub-contractor under this provision is supposed to be liquidated at the rate of liquidated damages in the main contract.

Under the nominated sub-contract NSC/4 the sub-contractor is liable to the main contractor for any loss or damage suffered or incurred by the contractor and caused by the failure of the nominated sub-contractor to complete on time (Clause 12.2 of NSC/4). There is a proviso, however, that the contractor is not entitled to claim such loss or damage unless the architect has issued an appropriate certificate under Clause 35.15 of the main contract. Certificates under Clause 35.15 of the main contract have continued to be known by the clause numbering in the 1963 edition — Clause 27 (d) (ii). Interestingly, this proviso only applies where the sub-contractor delays and not where the sub-contractor disrupts the main contractor's progress without delaying completion (Clause 13.3 of NSC/4).

The amount of the main contractor's claim against the nominated sub-contractor does not, of course, generally include the employer's losses (which are recovered by the employer directly from the nominated sub-contractor under Clause 3.4 of NSC/2) and this is an exception to the normal rule that liability flows 'up the line'.

(f) Domestic sub-contractor default

Where the works are delayed by the default of the domestic sub-contractor, the end result is much the same as in the case of default by a nominated sub-contractor but the mechanism is different.

Under the main contract, the contractor is not entitled to any extension of time, and it is as though the default of the domestic sub-contractor was the default of the main contractor himself. The main contractor must therefore pay liquidated damages to the employer in respect of such delay as is caused by the domestic sub-contractor.

Under the sub-contract, the domestic sub-contractor will usually be liable to the main contractor in damages at common law not only for the main contractor's own losses but also for what liquidated damages the main contractor must pay or allow to the employer.

Ordinarily of course there is no direct contractual nexus between an employer and a domestic sub-contractor, and hence nothing analogous to Clause 3.4 of NSC/2.

(g) Neutral causes

Sometimes the works are disrupted or delayed by matters such as exceptionally adverse weather conditions or strikes, which are beyond the control of any of the parties. In these circumstances the effect of the rule is generally that the losses lie where they fall.

The main contractor is entitled to an extension of time under Clause 25, and therefore does not have to pay the employer liquidated damages in respect of delay occasioned by neutral causes. There is no right for the contractor to be paid loss and expense following the occurrence of neutral causes, and a similar position arises in the standard sub-contract forms applicable to both nominated sub-contractors (NSC/4) and domestic sub-contractors.

3 Quantification of loss and/or expense

(a) General principles

The principles applicable to the quantification of loss and expense pursuant to the terms of a building contract are the same as the principles for the assessment of damages for breach of contract (*Wraight Ltd v P H & T (Holdings) Ltd* (1968) 13 BLR 26). The context of the calculation is, however, firmly that of the construction industry, and proper quantification of loss and expense in a complex case requires both the knowledge and experience of professional quantity surveyors and the application of legal principles by lawyers.

There are two main heads of loss and expense that usually accompany delay. Firstly, the contractor will have to maintain on site those things that are exclusively referable to the particular contract. Examples of such things are the cost of the site office, site supervision, scaffolding, plant, canteen and so on. The proper reimbursement under this head is the actual cost of these things to the contractor during the period of delay. It is a matter of arithmetic. Sometimes, contractors prepare a claim on the basis of 'extended preliminaries', where they extrapolate the rates in the preliminaries bill in the bills of quantities; that is thought among specialist practitioners to be wrong in principle. In *Wraight Ltd v P H & T (Holdings) Ltd* Megaw J said:

In my judgment, there are no grounds for giving to the words 'direct loss and/or damage caused to the contractor by the determination' any other meaning than that which they have, for example, in a case of breach of contract or other question of the relationship of a fault to damage in a legal context.

That judgment related to a determination clause, but it is thought that there is no difference in principle in the case of a loss and expense clause; loss and expense is quantified in the same way as damages at common law, and that means the actual cost to the contractor (see *Hadley v Baxendale* (1854) 9 Ex 341 and *Victoria Laundry (Windsor) Ltd v Newman Industries Coulson & Co* [1949] 2 KB 528).

(b) Overheads and profit

There is also another head, that of head office overheads (also known as off-site costs) and profit. These two are sometimes known as gross profit, and the contractor is entitled to be compensated in respect of them *(Wraight Ltd v P H & T Holdings Ltd* (1968) 13 BLR 26). The calculation of loss and expense in this area is far more difficult than for the on-site costs since head office overheads and profit cannot usually be seen as exclusively referable to any particular contract. It is necessary to adopt some sort of formula method.

The formula most commonly used is the 'Hudson Formula', which appears in *Hudson* at p 599. The Hudson Formula obtained judicial approval in *J F Finnegan Limited v Sheffield City Council* (1988) 43 BLR 124 which stated as follows:

It is generally accepted that, on principle, a contractor who is delayed in completing a contract due to the default of his employer, may properly have a claim for head office or off site overheads during the period of delay, on the basis that the workforce, but for the delay, might have had the opportunity of being employed on another contract which would have had the effect of funding the overheads during the . . . period.

Effectively by adopting a formula method a contractor is endeavouring to do its best to demonstrate to the court's satisfaction that it has indeed actually suffered the loss claimed and it could be that a court would refuse to accept the type of calculation put forward by Hudson where, in fact, better evidence could have been presented by the contractor.

The formula says that a contractor's loss and expense in terms of head office overheads and profit resulting from delay is:

$$\frac{HO/Profit\ Percentage}{100} \times \frac{Contract\ Sum}{Contract\ Period} \times Period\ of\ Delay$$

The effect of the formula is to calculate the rate at which the contractor would have earned gross profit had the contract run to time and to extrapolate that rate into the period of delay.

The Hudson Formula is of vital importance in loss and expense cases. Quantity surveyors frequently fail to understand it, and contractors who ignore it often pass up a large proportion of their total entitlement. However, it raises difficult issues as to the measure of damages at common law and all too often it is beyond the professional experience of both the general practitioner lawyer and the quantity surveyor.

In order to put some colour into these points the reader is invited to make an analogy. Compare the position of the contractor with that of a river steamer company which has hired one of its steamers to a party of revellers for a four hour trip around the lake for £400. After some time the revellers, who are enjoying themselves in the steamer's excellent bar, demand a variation to the route which adds another hour to the trip. The contract makes no express provision for the detour save to say that it should be calculated and paid for in accordance with common law damages principles.

First, there is a matter of causation to consider. The formula proceeds upon the basis that during the period of delay the contractor's head office resources are tied up when they could have been profitably engaged elsewhere. This in turn presupposes that the contractor's ability to take on work profitably is limited by the contractor's resources (rather than by the available market). If the contractor cannot show that he has turned away (or perhaps did not seek or deliberately tendered high for) other profitable work, then he cannot show that he has suffered the Hudson Formula loss by reason of the employer's delay. The contractor may yet be able to show that he has incurred some loss in terms of head office expenditure in, for example, the cost of additional telephone calls and stationery or of staff which the contractor would otherwise have fired or not hired — such losses as these, however, are notoriously difficult to quantify except in very small numbers. To revert to the analogy, the steamer operator can only recover the hourly hire charge if he can show that he would have been able to have hired his steamer out to some other party of revellers but for the original party's delay. If not, he will be limited to such matters as the additional diesel fuel that he used during the additional hour.

Secondly, the contractor must give credit for the amount of head office overhead and profit recovery, if any, that he obtains though the valuation of extra work under Clause 13.5. The reason for this credit is simply that if and to the extent that the contractor is delayed by carrying out extras for which he is recovering his overheads and profit, he is reducing the loss he would otherwise have made. Reverting to the analogy, if and to the extent that the original party of revellers is swelling the operator's bar profits by continuing to drink, it is as good as the next party of revellers who are waiting on the quayside.

Thirdly, there is a suggestion in the text of *Hudson* that the relevant percentage to be taken is the percentage within the instant contract. Applying ordinary principles of quantification of loss, however, suggests that the right percentage is the percentage within the work that has been lost. In the analogy, the right rate is not the £100 per hour that was being earned under the contract with the original revellers, but the amount per hour (if any) that the operator would have earned from the next party on the quayside.

Fourthly, there is a small mathematical error in the formula. The text talks of the percentage as something added to the cost in the calculation of the tender. The formula, however, proceeds as though the percentage were the percentage within the whole tender figure. This error will typically exaggerate the result produced by the formula by about 10 per cent.

(c) Financing charges

Building contract litigation can take a long time and there is a great difference between simple interest at the judgment rate and compound interest at a commercial rate. Take, for example, a loss of £10,000 incurred five years ago. Simple interest at the rate of 12 per cent would be £6,250. Compound interest at 18 per cent with quarterly rests would be £13,078.

It is because of this major factor that attention has recently focused upon the possibility of claiming financing charges as loss and expense rather than interest under the Law Reform (Miscellaneous Provisions) Act 1934. The principle of this was vindicated by the Court of Appeal in *F C Minter Ltd v Welsh Health Technical Services Organisation* (1980) 13 BLR 1. Stephenson LJ said:

I do not think that today we should allow medieval abhorrence to usury to make us shrink from implying a promise to pay interest in a contract if by refusing to imply it we thereby deprive a party of what the contract appears on its natural interpretation to give him . . .

In the context of this building contract and the accepted 'cash flow' procedure and practice I have no doubt that the two kinds of interest claimed here are direct loss and/or expense unless there is something in the contractual machinery for paying direct loss and/or expense which excludes this loss and expense of interest by the claimants.

In principle, therefore, financing charges are recoverable, although the period for which they are recoverable will depend upon the precise wording of the contract. In the *Minter* case, which was decided on an amended JCT63 contract, the contractor was found to be entitled to financing charges on loss and/or expense between the time that the loss and/or expense was incurred and the time of the contractor's application for it, but not for any other period. Recovery was thus dependent upon the contractor making a series of applications for financing charges. The wording of JCT80 at Clause 26.1 is somewhat more liberal in that the contractor may make his application for loss that he is likely to incur as well as for loss that he has already incurred.

Chapter 5

Preliminary considerations

There are those who consider litigation as being a last resort. If they are unable to achieve their desired results by commercial means they pass their papers to a litigation solicitor and expect that the next step (apart from some merely procedural matters) will be trial. In building contract matters, that attitude is generally a disastrous mistake. It can lead to vast unnecessary cost, delay, and lost opportunity.

The principal and distinguishing feature of building contracts litigation is the multiplicity of issues to which it gives rise. Very commonly, the failure of the parties to resolve one issue upon a commercial basis does not mean that there is no prospect of resolving other issues upon a commercial basis. There are frequently several parties involved, some of whom may be involved in the litigation and some of whom may not be. The issue of a writ or the service of an arbitration notice should not shock the parties into inaction.

What follows is not intended to be a comprehensive check list. Every case is different. It is, however, intended to indicate the sort of points which merit consideration at an early stage when the prospect of litigation first emerges.

1 Claim by employer for defects

The legal consequences of defects in work are extremely diverse. The observations that follow concern matters of general importance and are in no particular order. (As to who to sue, see Chapter 6.)

(a) Notices

When a defect in building work occurs it is almost always desirable to give notice of the fact to every party that is or may be responsible for it. There are at least three reasons for this.

First, the responsible party may be willing to do something about the defect at his own cost, particularly where the responsible party is a contractor or sub-contractor. Some contracts, such as the JCT standard form, contain express provision that the contractor should not only be obliged but is also entitled to remedy defects appearing within the defects liability period. As a matter of common law, an employer who fails to give a contractor an opportunity to make good his defects without good cause is in breach of his duty to mitigate his loss; in practice, good cause usually means performance by the contractor so abysmal that the employer could not reasonably be expected to allow the contractor back on site. Many employers are reluctant to allow contractors back to remedy works. They should, however, reflect very carefully before turning down any offer by a contractor to rectify defects without cost.

Secondly, identifying the cause of a defect is often more difficult than it seems. A defect that appears to be a defect of workmanship attributable to a contractor frequently turns out, upon listening to the contractor's account, to be wholly or partly a design matter, the responsibility of the architect. The sooner an employer can form an accurate view as to responsibility the better, and putting a party on notice of a defect implies an invitation to that party to put forward his own account of the cause of the defect.

Thirdly, on the whole, the later a claim for defects is made, the more likely it is to be regarded as a mere excuse for non-payment. For this reason, where the contractor has a claim for payment, the sooner the employer makes a complaint of the defect, the better chance the employer has of resisting an application by the contractor for summary judgment.

The list of potential claimees is a lengthy one. The employer should consider the potential liability not only of the contractor but also of any sub-contractor under a direct warranty agreement that there may be.

Where the employer suspects that there are defects in the works under a JCT contract, then he should urgently consider the position if the architect issues a final certificate, because unless proceedings are commenced within 28 days, this operates as conclusive evidence that, where the quality of materials or the standard of workmanship are to be to the satisfaction of the architect, they are to such satisfaction. The significance of the final certificate in this regard has sometimes been overstated because the wording in earlier JCT contracts rendered the final certificate much more important. There are two major cases on the conclusiveness of final certificates; *P & M Kaye v Hossier & Dickinson Ltd* [1972] 1 WLR 146 and *H W Nevill (Sunblest) Ltd v William Press & Son Ltd* (1981) 20 BLR 78. Neither of these cases is directly relevant to post 1976 JCT contracts and it is thought that *Kaye's* case would have been differently decided if it had been adequately pleaded. In *Culbert Limited v H Cumer* [1992] CILL 752 it was held that the final certificate was conclusive not only as to matters expressly reserved by the contract to the opinion of the architect, namely the approval of quality and standards of materials and workmanship respectively, but to all materials and workmanship where approval of such matters was inherently something for the opinion of the architect. It is not yet known whether the Court of Appeal would uphold this decision that appears to extend the conclusiveness of the final certificate.

(b) Leases

Sometimes the employer is either the landlord or the tenant under a lease. If so it is necessary to look at the lease to see whether it is the landlord or the tenant who is responsible *inter se* for the defects. That party is not always the same as the building employer, and the loss caused by the defects may not be that of the building employer.

In these circumstances it can be very useful for the landlord and the tenant to co-operate from the outset and arrangements are sometimes made for one to take the other's name in litigation or for the landlord and the tenant to sue as joint plaintiffs, one giving the other an indemnity as to costs.

(c) Pre-contract surveys

If there appears to be a claim against a surveyor engaged by the purchaser who carried out a pre-contract survey, it is as well to check from the outset that the purchaser did indeed receive and rely upon the report *before* exchanging contracts on the purchase. If not (which, surprisingly, is quite usual, particularly in the case of specialist damp and timber surveys) then a claim based on the written report will generally fail, although there may be another claim to be made on any verbal report that may have preceded the written report.

(d) Formal contracts

Where there is a formal contract (eg the JCT standard form), then there are special considerations that arise.

Formal contracts almost always vest powers in the architect concerning defects. Usually, the architect has powers exercisable during the execution of the work to require the contractor to remedy defective work and to open up for inspection any suspect work. If the architect fails to exercise these powers, then it is often useful for the employer to invite him to do so in writing.

Formal contracts also generally contain determination clauses that entitle either party to terminate the contract upon certain specified breaches and usually subject to service of notices. No general guidance can be given as to the desirability of operating such a clause, save that the decision is frequently difficult and that, if it is decided to determine, every care should be taken to ensure that the procedures in the clause are precisely followed. It is widely said that the wrongful purported use of a determination clause is itself a repudiatory breach of contract, which gives rise to liability in damages.

The scheme of the JCT contract is that the architect should not issue a *final* certificate until the contractor has remedied all defects. If, however, the architect is on the point of issuing a final certificate notwithstanding the possibility of defects, then the employer is well advised to consider the protection of issuing a generally endorsed writ and serving an arbitration notice. If he fails to do so, the final certificate may be fatal to his claim.

Where the contractor is in delay in achieving completion of the works, the employer may be entitled to deduct liquidated damages. The old procedure in the 1963 edition of the JCT contract has been altered in the 1980 form of contract; in each case it is necessary for the architect and the employer to have careful regard to the necessary notices required.

(e) Clerk of works

In a claim for defective supervision against an architect, it may be relevant whether the employer engaged a clerk of works. A clerk of works is ordinarily engaged as the servant of the employer, although he will in practice work largely at the direction of the architect. In *Kensington and Chelsea and Westminster Health Authority v Wettern Composites* (1984) 31 BLR 57 damages against architects were reduced by 20 per cent because of the contributory negligence of the clerk of works, which the court described as 'the negligence of the chief petty officer as compared with that of the captain of the ship'.

A clerk of works manual was published in 1984 providing guidance as to the duties of the clerk of works; this was produced following consultation with both the RIBA and the Institute of Clerk of Works.

(f) Repudiation

Even where there is no formal contract, a contractor's workmanship may be of such an appalling standard that the employer is entitled to regard the contract as repudiated and to order the contractor from the site (see *Sutcliffe v Chippendale & Edmundson* (1971) 18 BLR 157).

Repudiation is a common law right, and because of the generally cumulative nature of building defects sufficiently severe to amount to repudiation, it is important that the right be exercised clearly and decisively, without half measures.

If during the course of an informal building contract the contractor appears to be doing everything wrong during the course of the Works, then it is usually best if the employer wishes to repudiate to require the contractor first of all to remedy all the accumulated defects within, say, seven days. If the contractor fails to comply with this requirement, then the notice of repudiation should be written promptly and unequivocally, containing such words as:

These defects, and your failure to remedy them, represent a repudiatory breach of contract, which our client accepts as such. You are required to vacate the site immediately, and in due course a claim will be made against you for the losses suffered by our client.

In the now rare case of a lump sum contract in which there is no right for the contractor to be paid in instalments, a failure on the part of the contractor to achieve substantial completion disentitles the contractor to any payment at all, see page 2. This can be a factor in deciding when, if at all, to accept appalling workmanship as repudiatory breach. If the repudiation is accepted early enough then the employer may not have to pay anything to the contractor. If the repudiation is left too late it may be difficult to persuade the court that the contractor should receive nothing for his work done, and the employer would have to pay the agreed price less a proper set-off for defects and omissions.

(g) NHBC

The procedure for making a claim under the National House Builders Council rules is apparent from the House Purchasers Agreement and the claim form. It is, however, worth bearing in mind the restrictive meaning given to the word 'structure' in the House Purchasers Agreement and it seems clear from *County & District Properties v C Jenner & Son Ltd* [1976] 2 Lloyd's Rep 728 that an employer or house owner is entitled to sue the contractor for declaratory relief before or at the same time as making a claim against the NHBC, notwithstanding clause 8(b) of the House Purchasers Agreement, which reads as follows:

Nothing in this Clause shall be construed as relieving the Vendor of any of his obligations to the Purchaser howsoever they may arise provided that the Purchaser shall before pursuing any claim against the Vendor on account of any defect in the dwelling appearing after the Initial Guarantee Period in respect of which he may by virtue of this Clause have any claim against the Council first pursue his remedy against the Council and any relief obtained from the Council shall be taken into account in mitigation of damages against the Vendor.

There is usually little point in making such a claim prematurely unless there is a limitation danger. If there is a limitation danger which renders it desirable to bring protective proceedings against the contractor, the costs position will be improved if the contractor has declined a written invitation prior to the issue of proceedings to accept responsibility for the defects if and to the extent that the NHBC fails to do so.

The address of the NHBC is Chiltern Avenue, Amersham, Bucks, HP6 5AP, (0494-434477).

(h) Inspection

Employers sometimes overlook the desirability of contractors and their advisers being offered the opportunity to inspect defects. Without inspection, a contractor may not have any details of latent defects. Defects frequently appear only after the contractor has left the site, and it is entirely reasonable that not only the contractor but also his advisers and experts should be permitted to inspect the defects (and, where appropriate, take photographs, measurements and samples).

The courts have power to order such steps under Ord 16 of the Rules of the Supreme Court and a similar power is to be found in the Arbitration Act 1950 in relation to arbitration proceedings. An unreasonable refusal by an employer to offer or allow inspection is bound to influence a court or an arbitrator against the employer. Where a claim has been made against an architect or some other person not being the contractor, the need to offer inspection is of even more importance.

The courts generally recognise the importance of remedying building works, and it is rarely necessary for an employer to delay necessary remedial work merely because of inspection. Seven days' notice to inspect may be entirely sufficient, and if a contractor or his advisers cannot re-arrange their diaries so as to inspect before remedial works commence, then they have no one but themselves to blame.

Is it necessary for the lawyers to inspect the *locus in quo*? In practice, it is surprisingly rare for such an inspection to be of great value. It can, however, be very useful to enable the lawyers to understand the geography of the site, not only where the site is a large building or complex of buildings but also where it is a small semi-detached house. Without a view, expressions like 'the main area flat roof' and 'the dining room' can be difficult to relate to expressions like 'the production hall roof' or 'the front room'.

As regards defects themselves, lawyers inspecting the site must beware of drawing their own conclusions. What looks to the layman like surface cracking can be symptomatic of major structural damage and an area that looks like a bomb site may require only clearing away. In many cases, a good annotated plan is far more useful to the lawyers than a site inspection.

(i) Photographs and videos

Photographs and videos may be admissible in evidence in litigation and in arbitration. Whoever takes the film or photographs should make a contemporaneous record setting out precisely when and where each photograph is taken together with, if possible, a written description of what is being photographed.

It is sometimes worth bearing in mind that film is very cheap, and it may be worthwhile taking many photographs which may or may not subsequently merit the expense of developing.

(j) Immediate settlement

In a formal building contract there are elaborate provisions as to payment of the contractor and the remedying of defects during the execution of the works and during the defects liability period. In the case of informal contracts, however, it is sometimes tempting for an employer to seek an immediate resolution of the issue of defects by agreeing a reduction with the contractor of the contractor's account in respect of the shortcomings in the Works. Where there is a possibility that there may be further defects in the Works, then this is a dangerous course for the employer to take since he may have compromised the whole of his rights of action against the contractor (*Conquer v Boot* [1928] 2 KB 336). It seems that what is settled is not the rights in respect of the *defect* in question (eg the leaking roof) but the *breach* (eg the breach of obligation to do the work in a good and workmanlike manner). If the employer wishes a settlement at the outset, he must therefore limit the terms of that settlement to the particular defects that he has in mind.

Arbitration is sometimes seen as a species of settlement. This may be so in theory but in practice arbitrators are required to adhere as closely as possible to the procedure in the courts of law, and in the ordinary course of events arbitration is no short cut. There are, however, three devices that are sometimes used.

(1) It is sometimes possible and desirable to agree a simplified arbitration process, whereby a pre-agreed arbitrator makes a single inspection to the site and makes an immediate award without any pleadings or other representation, or discovery, or trial. This device can be useful where both parties have a genuine desire to resolve a dispute about a straightforward matter and to abide by the decision of a mutually agreed arbitrator. Where there is not that mutual desire, the procedure can be a recipe for disaster and leads only to further complication of the issues.

(2) Where there are defects about which there is a dispute as to responsibility but which require prompt remedying, there may be scope for a without prejudice funding arrangement. (See Chapter 18, section 1.)

(3) Alternatively, such a dispute may be suitable for some form of non-binding ADR. (See Chapter 16.)

(k) Limitation

Allowing a limitation period to expire without taking protective steps is often understandable but usually inexcusable and often very costly. A fuller discussion of limitation issues appears in Chapter 17.

At this point it should be noted that limitation often operates as a gradual erosion rather than as a sudden event and the date to note in a diary for the issue of a writ and service of an arbitration notice (if there is an arbitration clause), is six years from the date when the employer first discussed the works with his architect and/or contractor, and/or sub-contractors, since that is when he can begin to lose any rights in misrepresentation and collateral warranty.

(l) Remedial work

Where an employer has a claim in respect of defects where remedial work is necessary, it is almost always best if he can have had these works executed and paid for before trial. Courts tend to be conservative about estimates of building cost and the best possible evidence of the cost of remedial work is to have spent it. Accordingly, if an employer can afford remedial works it is usually best from a legal point of view for him to do so. Once the remedial work has been done, particularly if the employer has taken advice as to their extent, it will be rare for the courts to enquire about whether it was, in fact, necessary (*Hospitals for Sick Children v McLaughlin & Harvey* (1990) 19 CLR 25).

2 Claims by contractor for payment

In their simplest form, claims by contractors for payment are debts, recoverable under Ord 14. It is in the employer's interest to introduce complications to deprive the claim of its quality as a debt; it is in the contractor's interest to present his claim as simply as possible, and as like to a debt as possible. See Chapter 9, section 3.

The basic procedure on behalf of a contractor claiming payment is, therefore, to write a seven-day letter, followed by a writ in as uncomplicated a form as possible, followed by an Ord 29 and/or Ord 14 summons (see Chapter 9).

(a) Non-certification

Where there is a formal contract containing a provision for certification of sums due, the contractor is in difficulties without the necessary certificate or certificates for payment.

It is often the case that architects issue certificates where there is no formal contract empowering them to do so. In those circumstances the contractor does not need a certificate and can simply sue for the price of his work.

Where there is a contract that plainly envisages certification, then the contractor should obtain proper certification from the architect if he can. If the architect is showing bias in favour of the employer, then it is proper to write to him pointing out that he is in breach of his duty to act fairly and impartially between the parties.

If the architect is not showing bias in the employer's favour, a different tactical position arises. The architect should be persuaded into issuing the appropriate certificate and assisted in the task of explaining the position to the employer. If the architect persists in his refusal properly to certify payment, then there may be no alternative but to serve an arbitration notice or perhaps issue proceedings.

(b) Notice

Under most formal contracts it is necessary for the contractor to give notice of various matters before becoming entitled to extensions of time and loss and expense. The importance of these notices in the ICE form of contract was recognised in *Crosby v Portland UDC* (1967) 5 BLR 121 and any steps that can be taken to give notices where necessary should be taken. The JCT form does impose a condition that such notices must be given within a reasonable time. The question of what is a reasonable time was considered in *London Borough of Merton v Stanley Hugh Leach* (1985) 32 BLR 51, in which it was said:

(The contractor) must make his application within a reasonable time: It must not be made so late that, for instance, the architect can no longer form a competent opinion or satisfy himself that the contractor has suffered the loss or expense claimed. But in considering whether the contractor has acted reasonably and with reasonable expedition it must be borne in mind that the architect is not a stranger to the work and may in some cases have a very detailed knowledge of the progress of the work and the contractor's planning.

Where the architect issues a final certificate under the JCT contract, then the parties have 28 days from the issue of that certificate to commence arbitration or other proceedings (Clause 30.9.3). If proceedings are not commenced within that time the final certificate is expressed to represent conclusive evidence as to various matters connected with payment.

(c) Determination and repudiation

In the case of a formal contract there will generally be a provision entitling the contractor to determine his employment under the contract under a number of circumstances and particularly if the employer fails to pay on certificates or interferes with the certification process. The right to determine is usually subject to the contractor giving notice of his intention to determine; sometimes these notice provisions have been construed strictly and sometimes they have not. For example, in *Central Provident Fund Board v Ho Bock Kee* (1981) 17 BLR 21 the Court of Appeal in Singapore found that a notice was invalid on the grounds that it was given by the superintending officer and not the chairman of the board as required by the contract and also because the notice was delivered by hand and not by registered post as required by the contract. Conversely, in *Goodwin & Sons v Fawcett* (1965) 195 EG 27 a notice was upheld notwithstanding that it was served by recorded delivery instead of registered post. See also the cases referred to under Clauses 27 and 28 of JCT80 in Appendix B. To avoid difficulty with this point it is of course highly desirable for a party wishing to determine to follow the formal requirements in the contract with care.

Where there is no formal right of repudiation, the contractor may nevertheless have a right at common law to treat non-payment by the employer as repudiatory. This right will only exist in contracts containing an express or implied right to interim payment, and there is no very sure way of knowing how serious the underpayment position must become before the right to repudiate arises. See page 41.

In practice, the courts tend to hesitate before giving an Ord 14 judgment on a determination or repudiation claim. The court often sees such cases as 'six of one and half a dozen of the other'. It is, therefore. usually desirable from a contractor's point of view not to determine or accept a repudiation towards the end of building works but to complete them and then sue for the price in the ordinary way.

(d) Defects and set-off

An employer is ordinarily entitled to set-off against a contractor's claim for payment his own claim for defective work or losses arising as a result of the contractor's delay if liquidated damages have not already been deducted.

There was a line of cases, commencing with *Dawnays v F C Minter and Trollope and Colls* [1971] 1 WLR 1205 that held that this set-off did not exist where the contractor sought certified sums. The certificate was said to be like a cheque, such that set-off was not available against it. *Dawnays v Minter* was overruled by the House of Lords in *Gilbert-Ash (Northern) Ltd v Modern Engineering (Bristol) Ltd* [1974] AC 689. Some care is needed, however, when looking at the *Gilbert-Ash* case, since it concerns the construction of a particular set-off clause in the standard sub-contract form of the Bovis group of companies; Lords Reid and Morris of Borth-y-Gest each thought that *Dawnays v Minter* was correct upon its particular facts. The principle that emerges, however, is that there is no rule of law that certificates are to be treated like cheques, without any right of set-off.

In ordinary cases, where there is no certification, the same principle applies. The contractor must give credit for the cost of remedying defects but may recover the balance either at trial or under Ord 14.

In practice it is frequently desirable for a contractor to offer to remedy any defects that he accepts as his responsibility; the cost to the contractor of doing so is almost certainly going to be less than the price of another contractor. If the employer does not take up such offer, he may have failed to mitigate his loss. In appropriate circumstances the contractor may consider a without prejudice funding agreement (see Chapter 18, section 1).

(e) Limitation

As in the case of an employer's claim for defects, contractors' claims for payment usually erode gradually rather than suddenly become statute barred. Contractors' rights to payment generally start eroding about six years after the date of commencement of work. The limitation period is 12 years where the contractor enters into a contract with the employer that is under seal.

Where there is a limitation danger concerning a contract with an arbitration clause, the contractor should protect his position by issuing a writ *and* serving an arbitration notice. Where the architect issues an unsatisfactory final certificate, the contractor should serve an arbitration notice immediately and perhaps issue a writ.

(f) Claim documents

Contractors sometimes spend much time and/or money in the preparation of claim documents that are frequently lengthy claims for extensions of time and payment by way of loss and expense. These claims often have the relevant documents appended to them. In many cases, such documents are prepared, presented and rejected before the prospect of litigation emerges. Sometimes the lawyers are consulted before any claim document is prepared. In long and complicated cases, the claim documents can be of great use, not only to provide the architect and quantity surveyor with the information they need to perform their functions but also to append to the pleadings.

Claim documents are almost invariably prepared by persons qualified or experienced as quantity surveyors. It is usually not possible or practicable for the lawyers to write or extensively rewrite such claims but it is often useful for the lawyers to go through the claim documents and make suggestions before they are presented or incorporated into pleadings. The importance of well thought out claim documents has increased in the light of the decision of the Privy Council in *Wharf Properties v Eric Cumine* (1984) 45 BLR 72. This case has a number of important implications for the preparation of a claim in establishing liability and in the actual quantification of a claim. In this case, the plaintiff's claim for delay was struck out on the basis that it did not disclose a reasonable cause of action. In giving judgment, Lord Oliver stated as follows: 'Failure even to attempt to specify any discernible nexus between the wrong alleged, and the consequent delay, provides, to use the phrase of counsel for Eric Cumine "no agenda" for the trial'.

Therefore, when preparing a claim for delay rather than adopting the 'global' approach used in the past, to be certain of avoiding any possible application to strike out a claim, a lawyer should endeavour to demonstrate clearly the individual events causing delay, how those events caused delay and the actual amount of the delay so caused. It is thought that in relation to quantification of a claim, a global approach can still be adopted. Further guidance as to the preparation of claims by way of a Scott Schedule in High Court proceedings has been given by the Official Referee in *ICI v Bovis Construction* [1992] CILL 776.

See Chapter 21 for further discussion of establishing liability for delay.

(g) Retention money

Where the contractor is concerned as to the solvency of the employer, he may be well advised to insist on the retention money being paid into a separate bank account and if necessary apply for a mandatory order to that effect (*Rayack Construction Ltd v Lampeter Meat Co Ltd* (1979) 12 BLR 30, *Wates Construction (London) Limited v Franthorne Property Limited* [1991] CILL 655 and *J F Finnegan Limited v Ford Seller & Morris Developments Limited* [1991] CILL 672). If the contractor does not do this he will not generally have a prior claim for the retention money if the employer goes into liquidation (Re *Jartay Developments Ltd* (1982) 22 BLR 134).

3 Claims by sub-contractors for payment

From a sub-contractor's point of view the main contractor stands in the position of employer and, generally, the same considerations as set out above apply. Additionally, there are two circumstances where a sub-contractor may be entitled to look to the employer for payment directly where the JCT contract is used.

First, there is a procedure under Clause 35.13 of the main contract whereby the main contractor is obliged to provide the architect with reasonable proof that he has paid every nominated sub-contractor the amount he is directed so to do. If the contractor is unable to provide such proof, the nominated sub-contractor may be entitled to direct payment under Clause 35.13.5. This provision is expressed in the main contract in permissive and not mandatory terms, but if the nominated sub-contractor has entered into a form of direct warranty with the employer (NSC/2) the terms of that direct warranty will usually require the employer to operate the provision.

Secondly, where the main contract is determined by the employer under Clause 27 then the employer *may* pay any supplier or sub-contractor, whether nominated or not, for any materials or goods delivered for works executed for the purposes of the contract insofar as the price thereof has not already been paid by the contractor (Clause 27.4.2.2). This position does not apply where the determination occurs by reason of the bankruptcy of the contractor or of a winding up order being made (Clause 27.4.2.1).

It is sometimes the case that where a contractor disputes the validity of a determination notice he may wish to elect to continue with the contract and remain on site for that purpose. Can the employer force the contractor to leave site by means of an injunction in these circumstances? In *Hounslow v Twickenham Garden Developments Ltd* [1970] 3 All ER 326 the court refused the employer an injunction on the grounds that the contractor had a subsisting licence to be on site for the purpose of carrying out the works. That case was however decided before the House of Lords decision in *American Cyanamid Co v Ethicon Ltd* [1975] AC 396, from which the 'balance of convenience' test in interlocutory injunction cases emerges. The balance of convenience in cases where the parties are in serious dispute will ordinarily be for the contractor to leave site, and this is indeed the line taken by the court in recent cases; see for example *Tara v Moorfield* (1989) 46 BLR 72.

4 Claims by architects for payment

Usually, the first matter to consider in these claims is whether the architect was engaged either expressly or by reference under the standard RIBA terms, set out in a blue book called 'Architects' appointment' (or the shorter version of this for small works). These terms are not to be implied as a matter of custom or necessary implication (*Re Sidney Kaye, Eric Firmin & Partners* (1973) 4 BLR 1). A new version of these terms has recently been published. This is known as the Standard Form of Agreement for Appointment of Architects, July 1992 and commonly called the 'Black Book'.

It is not uncommon for an employer to refuse to pay the whole or part of his architect's fees because of some complaint about the architect's performance. It is useful to bear in mind that if an architect fails to recover the whole or part of his fee, then that is money out of his own pocket. If he recovers his fee but is also liable in damages for some breach of contract, then those damages will, subject to any questions of indemnity or excess, often be met by the architect's insurers.

Where an architect's retainer has been determined before the completion of a project then the entitlement to payment will depend greatly upon whether the RIBA conditions have been incorporated. If so, then the architect will be entitled to be paid according to which Work Stage has been reached. These are as follows:

A Inception
B Feasibility studies
C Outline proposals
D Scheme design
E,F,G Detailed design, production drawings, specifications and bills of quantities
H Tender action to completion.

If the employer has terminated the architect's services in an engagement where RIBA terms do not apply, then the employer may be liable to the architect for damages for wrongful termination.

There is an interesting and important decision of the Court of Appeal in *Nye Saunders v Bristow* (1987) 37 BLR 92; the architects were held not to be entitled to any fees in respect of their work because they failed to warn their client (who in this case was an experienced businessman and helicopter operator) of the likely effect of inflation.

An architect may also be deprived of all or part of his fee if his design is faulty, or if he fails to supervise the contractor, or if he fails to certify in accordance with the contract terms. For an example of such claims see *Townsend v Stone Toms & Partners (No 2)* (1984) 27 BLR 26.

5 Performance bonds

Performance bonds are common in construction projects and their existence can have a significant impact on the bargaining position of the parties, particularly at the early stages of a dispute.

There are two forms of bond which are quite distinct. The traditional form of bond may often be recognised by its time-honoured language: 'Know all men by these presents'. Its feature is that the bond is subject to conditions, typically that the bondsman will only pay upon presentation of either a signed admission that a sum of money is due or a court or arbitrator's award. Sometimes the bond is conditional upon presentation of a certificate from the architect of a sum due. It may be required by the employer of the contractor or *vice versa*. The main purpose and effect of these bonds is to protect one party against the risk of the other going into liquidation or otherwise disappearing. It is common for them to be subject to a maximum figure of ten or 15 per cent of the value of the contract in question. Ordinarily, the presence of such a bond does not much affect the contractual process.

The other and very much more vicious variant is the 'on demand' bond. This form of bond first became common in international contracts where one party or the other wished to safeguard its position in a way that does not involve the courts at all. The procedure under the bond is as follows. The party with the benefit of the bond (the 'beneficiary') can demand the money at any time during its currency, regardless of whether the money is actually due. The demand is made by the beneficiary on his own bank (the 'local bank') and the local bank will then seek payment from the paying party's bank (the 'correspondent bank'). The policy of correspondent banks in England is that they will pay on the bond regardless of whether their customer wants them to pay or not; and if the customer seeks to obtain an injunction against either its own bank or the beneficiary the application will be refused unless there is evidence of a fraud (*Edward Owen Engineering Ltd v Barclays Bank International Ltd* [1977] 1 WLR 764). For these purposes, 'fraud' means fraud to which the correspondent bank is a party, or at any rate of which it must have been aware (*GKN Contractors Ltd v Lloyds Bank plc* (1985) 30 BLR 48 CA). Neither will the court ordinarily freeze the proceeds of the call in the hands of the receiving party (*Potton Homes Ltd v Coleman Contractors Ltd* (1984) 28 BLR 19 CA). The refusal of an injunction by the court does not of course mean that the customer is deprived of his remedies for breach of contract or in tort for wrongful call, but the inevitable delay in pursuing those claims obviously affects the tactical position greatly.

For these reasons it is generally most unwise for either party to a building contract to provide an on demand bond. If a party has given one it may sometimes be prudent to wait until the expiry of the bond before taking any legal or other action that might provoke the calling of the bond.

For the sake of completeness it may be helpful to mention that there is a third type of performance bond which is sometimes provided on behalf of contractors, particularly in the United States, whereby the bondsman undertakes that he will himself complete the contract works if the contractor fails to do so. Such bonds are occasionally provided in this country by parent companies in respect of the contracts of their subsidiaries, but otherwise are not in common use.

6 Papers

Building contract litigation frequently involves paper-work on a huge scale. Even comparatively small contracts — in the region of say £50,000 — can produce enough paper-work to fill several lever-arch files; in larger cases the paper-work can run into many dozen such files.

At what stage in litigation should the parties and their advisers read the documentation? It is often a counsel of perfection to read all the papers before taking any steps in contemplation of litigation. That is frequently impractical and in large cases it may be impractical for any one person ever to read all of the papers; but it is essential to separate the important items.

Where the dispute concerns defects, it is likely to be important to read the following documents:

(1) the documents that set out the basic contractual obligation;
(2) the specification, drawings and/or bills of quantities which set out and describe the work which the contractor was obliged to do;
(3) correspondence between the parties or their agents with regard to the defects;
(4) any reports upon the defects; and
(5) the Building Regulations or any other requirements (which may or may not be included in the contract papers) as to the standard of the works. (It is often extremely relevant whether the defects alleged satisfy such statutory requirements, and it may well be worthwhile obtaining and reading the relevant parts of these documents.)

Where the claim is a claim for payment upon a certificate made under a building contract, it is usually sufficient merely to look at the contract documentation and the certificates themselves in the first instance. The form of pleading in such a case is simple, and there is frequently little point in wasting time considering the matters that the architect and/or surveyor would have considered before making their certificate.

The case of a claim by a builder for sums due under a contract where there is no certificate upon which he relies can pose much more difficult problems. The claim frequently contains elements relating to extra work, delay, loss of profit, liability to sub-contractors and so on. The documents that are likely to be material to the claim are often very substantial, and would include:

(1) the contract documentation;
(2) the specification, drawings and/or bills of quantities which set out the original contract work;
(3) architect's instructions and confirmations of verbal instructions;
(4) day work sheets;
(5) the site diary;
(6) the correspondence;
(7) interim applications, interim certifications and payments;
(8) prime cost records;
(9) materials invoices;
(10) sub-contractor claims;
(11) profit and loss accounts; and
(12) site meeting minutes.

The list goes on. It is often impractical to read all of these documents before proceeding to make a claim and to embark upon litigation or arbitration. It is frequently necessary to make an assessment of the position and then hope that the assessment will in due course be supported if necessary by the paper-work. How much can reasonably be taken on trust has much to do with the legal expertise of the person making the assessments but it is often well worthwhile making sample excursions into the above sources of paper-work in order to form a view as to the support that it would give at trial. This is often unnecessary before issuing the writ where some form of claim document has already been prepared; it may well be wiser to get proceedings in motion as soon as possible; but there are three dangers arising out of not reading the papers in such a case.

(1) It is almost impossible to make reliable practical decisions as to the interlocutory steps to be pursued without having read the material papers. Most cases have strengths and weaknesses and the ability of a party to play upon its strong points and distract attention from its weak points is paramount.

(2) There is a limit to which a party can rely safely upon its right to amend. Where there is an Ord 14 claim, the pleadings ought to bc in reasonable order from the outset. Where a case is going to trial, a party will suffer real prejudice if it has not got its pleadings reasonably in order, say, a month before trial when it delivers its papers to counsel to advise upon evidence.

(3) The vast majority of building contract cases are settled. It is extremely difficult to settle a case effectively without knowing the likely result at trial with some degree of certainty, and this almost always involves reading a substantial part of the material paperwork.

7 Bar charts

A bar chart is a diagrammatic illustration showing the order and duration of different operations with a project. Where a bar chart shows the *intended* sequence of operations it is usually known as a programme. Where it shows the *actual* sequence it is usually known as a progress chart. Where it contains an analysis of which delays have caused an overall delay it is usually known as a critical path analysis.

Figure 1 shows a programme for a hypothetical project to be completed within twelve weeks. It has the following hypothetical features.

Operation 1: *Foundations*. The foundations require to be completed before the rest of the work can proceed.

Operation 2: *Car park*. The car park may be constructed at any time independently of the rest of the building works. Because the construction of the car park requires the use of some of the same plant as the foundations, it follows on immediately after the foundations work.

Operation 3: *Framework*. The frame of the building cannot be commenced until the foundations are complete, and itself needs to be completed before either the roofing or the brickwork and blockwork can be commenced.

Figure 1 : Programme

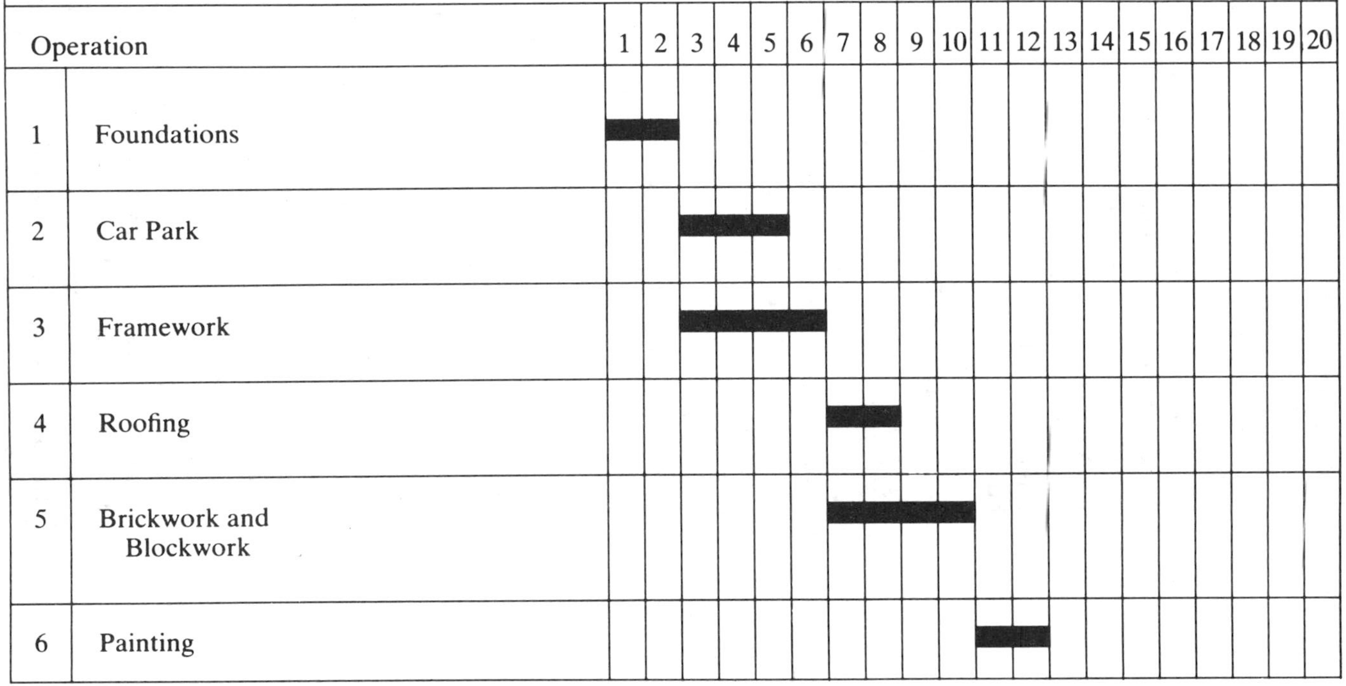

Operation		1	2	3	4	5	6	7	8	9	10	11	12	13	14	15	16	17	18	19	20
1	Foundations	■																			
2	Car Park				■																
3	Framework						■														
4	Roofing								■												
5	Brickwork and Blockwork										■										
6	Painting												■								

Operation 4: *Roofing.* The roofing cannot be commenced until the framework is complete, but may be carried out at the same time as the brickwork and blockwork. The roofing must be completed before the painting work can commence.

Operation 5: *Brickwork and blockwork.* The brickwork and block-work cannot be commenced until the framework is complete, and must itself be complete before the painting can start.

Operation 6: *Painting.* Because of its nature, the painting work cannot be started until all the other work within the building is complete.

It can be seen that the programme represents a plan for the execution of the work as quickly as possible. There are some operations which are envisaged as being on the critical path, that is to say that any delay in those operations will, *prima facie*, lead to a delay in the completion of the project as a whole. In this case, the critical operations are founda-tion, framework, brickwork and blockwork and painting. The car park is an example of an operation that is not critical; it would not delay completion if it were delayed (for example) from weeks three to five inclusive to weeks nine to 11 inclusive.

Figure 2 is a hypothetical progress chart. The black bars show the programmed sequence and the white bars show the actual time of the carrying out of the operation. The explanation for the delays is as follows.

Operation 1: *Foundations.* The plant which the contractor required to execute the foundation was late in arriving on site and a week was wasted as a result. Once the foundations were started they took two weeks as envisaged.

Operation 2: *Car park.* The car park took nine weeks instead of the three weeks envisaged. The reason for this was partly exceptionally heavy rainfall in weeks nine, ten and 11, and partly because the contractor did not have enough workmen on that operation.

Operation 3: *Framework.* This operation took five weeks instead of four weeks, because in week five the architect issued a variation requiring certain changes in the details of the framework.

Operation 4: *Roofing.* This operation took ten weeks instead of the two weeks envisaged. Of the additional eight weeks, six weeks were attributable to the contractor not having enough men on the operation, and two weeks were attributable to the exceptionally heavy rain in weeks nine to 11.

Operation 5: *Brickwork and blockwork.* This operation took five weeks instead of the four weeks envisaged. The reason

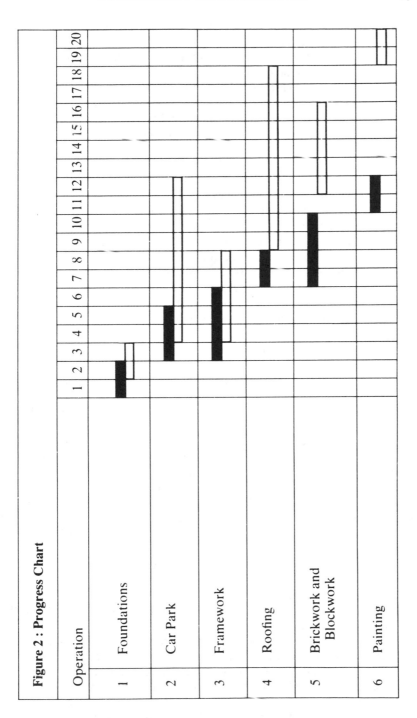

Figure 2 : Progress Chart

for this was the delay by the architect in giving the necessary instructions as to detailing.

Operation 6: *Painting*. The painting work took two weeks as envisaged.

It can readily be seen that, without the aid of a bar chart, it would be extremely difficult to show which of these delays had contributed and to what extent to the overall delay of eight weeks. In a complex case, where there may be 50 separate operations bearing relationships to each other, the problems of working without a bar chart would be greatly amplified.

Figure 3 shows a typical critical path analysis. The dotted line traces the critical path from commencement to completion. It shows that the delay in the construction of the car park was irrelevant to the time of completion, and it also shows that roofing has taken the place of brickwork and blockwork as the critical operation between the completion of the framework and the commencement of painting.

Critical path analyses are sometimes adorned with glorious polychromatic representations of such concepts as critical delay, non-critical delay, delay carried forward, float periods, and so on. The important representation is the apportionment of the total delay between various quarters. In *Figure 3* the hatched bar makes such an apportionment as follows:

Operation 1:	Foundations — Delay in arrival of plant	1 week
Operation 3:	Framework — Architect's instruction	1 week
Operation 4:	Roofing — Bad weather	2 weeks
	Contractor's delay	4 weeks
		8 weeks

It is often remarkably difficult in critical path analyses to make the individually analysed delays add up to the total delays. This difficulty often arises out of 'float periods', an example of which occurs in this example in the roofing operation. It can be seen from *Figure 1* that the roofing operation had a float period of two weeks, that is to say that the roofing operation could be delayed by two weeks before it would delay the commencement of painting and thereby delay completion as a whole. Accordingly, two weeks out of the total delay of eight weeks in Operation 4 was not critical. In the analysis at *Figure 3*, this two weeks has been deducted from the contractor's delay of six weeks, but arguably it could in whole or in part be deducted from the delay caused by bad weather in that operation.

If the contract were in the standard JCT form, the result of the analysis would be as follows.

Extension of time — The contractor is entitled to an extension of time of one week for the architect's instruction with regard to the framework and a further extension of two weeks having regard to the exceptionally adverse weather conditions affecting the roofing work. The contractor is accordingly entitled to a total extension of time of three weeks but must pay liquidated damages upon the balance of delay of five weeks.

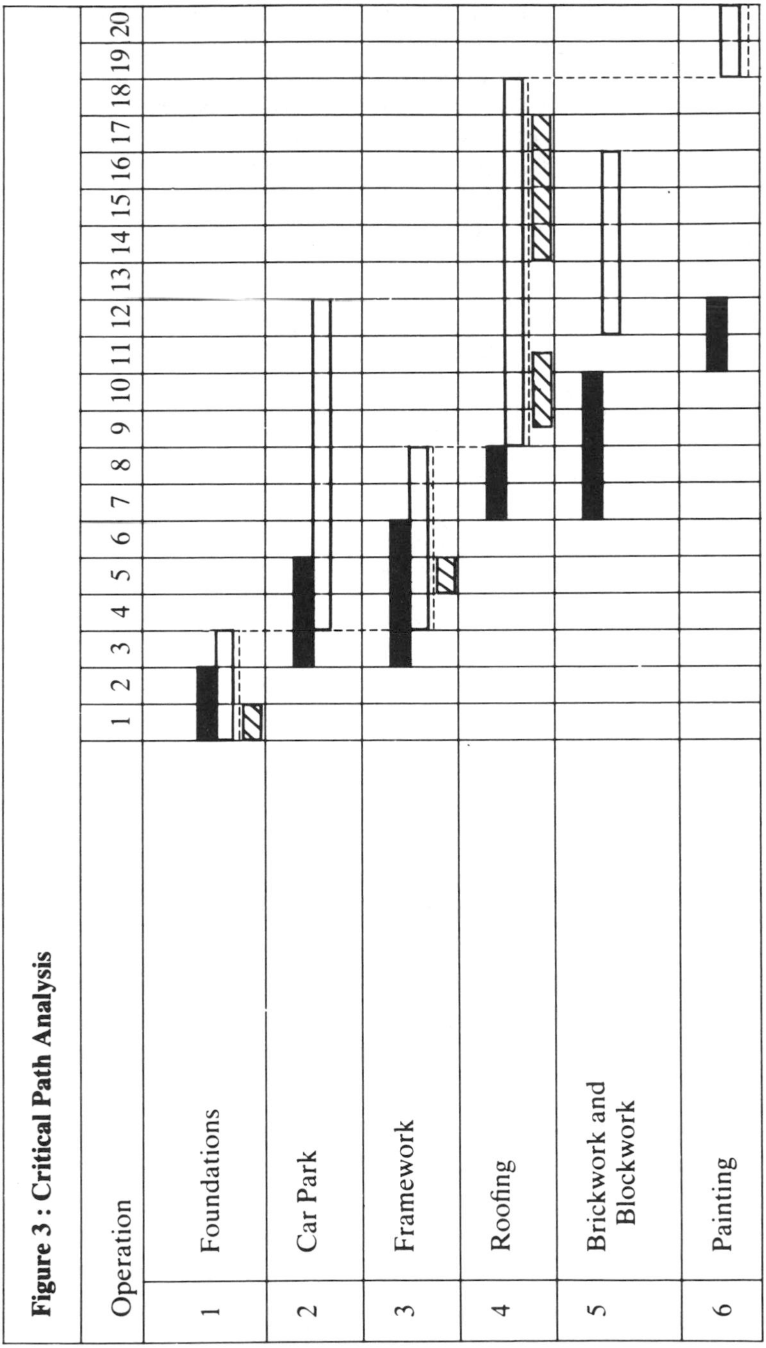

Figure 3 : Critical Path Analysis

Loss and expense — The contractor has a prolongation claim for the one week delay incurred by reason of the architect's instruction as to framework. Although it did not delay completion, the contractor may also have a disruption claim resulting from the delay by the architect in giving instructions with regard to brickwork and blockworks. The contractor is not entitled to any loss and expense caused as a result of bad weather.

See Chapter 21 for a more extensive treatment of the methods available for retrospective delay analysis.

Chapter 6

Who to sue

The list of *dramatis personae* in building contract litigation can be lengthy. Apart from the employer and the contractor, there is often an architect and/or surveyor and a number of sub-contractors. Sometimes there are specialist designers, receivers, bondsmen and insurers. The local authority is charged with enforcing the building regulations. There may be suppliers whose products are at fault.

In the past, all these bodies have been capable of attracting liability; now, with the collapse in tortious liability, it is necessary in most cases to have some form of direct contractual link in order to be able to bring an action successfully. These changes in the law of tort have led to a proliferation of collateral warranties throughout the construction industry. On a large development it is not uncommon for there to be a complex web of contractual relationships where a developer obtains collateral warranties from sub-contractors and suppliers, and contractual warranties are given by members of the design team and the contractor to the ultimate purchaser and tenants of the development. The following analysis is not intended to provide a code for making such a choice, nor is it intended to be exhaustive. It is, however, intended to assist in an orderly review of some of the more common causes of action that may now be founded in contract.

1 Claims by contractors for payment

(a) Against the employer

Most commonly, of course, the contractor's claim for payment will be against the employer with whom he has entered into the contract. The claim may be for payment under the contract, in quasi-contract, or for breach of the contract by the employer.

Ordinarily, there is no difficulty in identifying the employer, whether the employer be an individual, a company or a partnership. The ordinary rules of contract law apply. It sometimes happens, however, that the contractor's claim is for *quantum meruit* where, for example, the terms of the proposed contract are never settled with sufficient certainty as to create a binding contract. In these circumstances, the contractor's

77

quantum meruit claim may be against a different person from the person who proposed to enter into the contract. The person who is liable upon a claim for *quantum meruit* is the person for whom and at whose request the works are carried out, or perhaps the person who has benefited from the work. The position is far from clear, and may depend upon a fundamental schism in *quantum meruit* law.

Traditionally, the view of the courts has been that *quantum meruit* claims in these circumstances are founded in quasi-contract. Even though the parties may not have entered into any express contract, a contract between them is to be implied, it being a term of the implied contract that the contractor should be paid a *quantum meruit* or reasonable sum for his work.

The competing theory, which has gained ground in recent years and is expounded in Goff & Jones, *The Law of Restitution*, is that the entitlement arises out of the equitable doctrine of restitution.

The choice between these competing theories is not merely of academic interest, but raises fundamental questions. If the claim is in quasi-contract, does the quasi-contract contain implied terms as to the quality of the contractor's work, and the time within which he will do it? If not, what responsibility does the contractor have for bad work or delay? If the claim arises only in equity, does the contractor have to come with clean hands? And if founded on the equitable doctrine of unjust enrichment, what is the position where the person asking for the work to be done has no proprietary interest in the land, and obtains no benefit for himself as a result of the work? There are currently no definitive answers to these questions, although whichever competing theory is adopted, the time and manner of the contractor's performance might affect the amount of the *quantum meruit*.

(b) Against the architect

It frequently happens that the negotiations for building works are carried out by either an architect, a surveyor, an estate agent, or by some other professional person. In such circumstances it sometimes happens, more usually by accident than by design, that such a person himself incurs a contractual liability. Such a liability can arise where the architect or other professional person personally enters into the contract without disclosing the existence of a principal, or without expressly excluding his liability (*Beigtheil & Young v Stewart* (1900) 16 TLR 177). An architect may further be liable for breach of warranty of authority on the basis that one who expressly or impliedly warrants that he has the authority of another is liable for breach of warranty of authority to any person to whom the warranty is made and who suffers damage by acting on the faith thereof, if in fact he had no such authority (*Collen v Wright* (1857) 8 E & B 647). It is not necessary for a contractor to show fraud or negligence to found such a claim; in *Collen v Wright* it was said:

The fact that the professed agent honestly thinks that he has authority affects the moral character of his act; but his moral innocence, so far as the person whom he has induced to contract is concerned, in no way aids such person or alleviates the inconvenience and damage which he sustains. The obligation arising in such a case is well expressed by saying that a person, professing to contract as agent for another, impliedly if not expressly, undertakes to or promises the person who enters into the contract upon the faith of the professed agent being duly authorised, that the authority which he professes to have does in point of fact exist.

In practice it is often difficult for a contractor to know what measure of damage flows from a breach of warranty of authority by an architect, especially where the lack of authority represents a part only of the contractor's claim for payment. Where there is doubt as to whether and to what extent an employer will seek to defend himself by pointing to lack of authority in the architect, the contractor's prudent course is to join both the employer and the architect as joint defendants.

In a formal building contract, where the architect is appointed as a certifier, the architect has a duty both to the employer and to the contractor to act fairly, and it is clear that the architect may be liable to the employer in damages if he fails to do so (see *Sutcliffe v Thackrah* [1974] AC 727 HL). It used to be thought that the contractor might also be able to bring a claim in tort against a certifier and indeed in *Michael Salliss & Co Ltd v E C A & F B Calil and William Newman & Associates* (1988) 4 CLR 125, the court found on a preliminary issue that a contractor under JCT63 may recover damages on negligence from an architect who has certified unfairly. The *Michael Salliss* case was, however, doubted by the Court of Appeal in *Pacific v Baxter* [1989] 2 All ER 159. In that case, the contract was based on the FIDIC Form of Contract, including a provision that 'neither . . . the engineer nor any of his staff . . . shall be in any way personally liable for the act, but for acts or obligations under the Contract'. That exclusion may have been sufficient to have negatived liability in that case, but the Court of Appeal went further, concluding as a matter of principle that there can be no basis on which a duty of care to prevent economic loss can be imposed on a certifier in favour of the contractor. The *Pacific v Baxter* decision was at least partly founded on the existence of an arbitration clause ('important if not decisive') and the general applicability of the decision is not entirely clear. The decision does seem to be part of a trend in which the courts are unwilling to allow certificates to be challenged. See also *Northern Regional Health Authority v Crouch* [1984] 2 All ER 175, in which the Court of Appeal refused to review a certificate as between employer and contractor, and *Lubenham v South Pembrokeshire District Council* (1986) 33 BLR 39, where, in the context of determination, the employer was able to rely upon an architect's certificate that had been issued in good faith notwithstanding that it was actually wrong.

(c) Against an insolvent employer and limited companies

There are three main insolvency procedures.

(1) *Receivership*

Where a receiver is appointed to an employer company there is no prohibition on a contractor bringing a claim against a company for a pre-existing debt, although the contractor may wish to consider carefully whether the cost of instituting or continuing proceedings is worthwhile. A contract made by a company and current at the date of the appointment of a receiver is not binding on the receiver personally unless it becomes binding by a novation (*Moss Steamship Co v Whinney* [1912] AC 254).

(2) *Liquidation*

Where a company enters into a voluntary winding up, this has no effect upon the commencement or continuation of proceedings. However, where there is a compulsory winding up, proceedings cannot be commenced or continued against the company except by leave of the court (Insolvency Act 1986, s 130(2)). Where the contractor has a claim for payment against the company it should prove in the winding up for such a claim.

Where, notwithstanding s 130, an employer company in liquidation brings an action against a contractor, the contractor may, without the leave of the court, set up a cross demand for liquidated or unliquidated damages as a set-off to reduce or extinguish the company's claim (*Langley Constructions (Brixton) Limited v Wells* [1969] 1 WLR 503).

(3) *Administration*

Where an Administration Order is made and an administrative receiver of the company appointed, the Insolvency Act 1986, s 11(iii)(d) confirms that no proceedings or other legal process may be commenced or continued against the company without the consent of the administrators or the leave of the court.

(d) Against sub-contractors and suppliers

Where part of the contractor's cost of carrying out building works results from the defaults of his sub-contractors or suppliers, the terms of the contract usually prevent the contractor from recovering such part of the cost from the employer. He must look to the sub-contractors or suppliers in default.

2 Claims by employers for defects

Sometimes an employer's claim in respect of building defects is entirely straightforward and there is no doubt as to the liability of the contractor and the contractor's ability to meet that liability. In many other cases, however, the contractor may be able to raise some form of defence, or there may be doubts as to his solvency. In these circumstances the employer should consider whether to make a claim against some other party either alone, or as a co-defendant.

In addition to a claim for breach of contract against the contractor, the employer may also be able to bring claims for breach of contract against members of the professional team for breach of their design and supervision obligations and possibly a claim for breach of statutory duty or a claim under the Defective Premises Act 1972. The employer may also, as a result of collateral warranties with sub-contractors and suppliers, have direct claims against these parties. Now, unless the subsequent owner has the benefit of direct collateral warranties with the parties involved in the design and building work, then his remedies are likely to be limited as a result of the demise of tortious liability. These other avenues may be available not only to the original employer under the building contract but also to a subsequent owner of the building. The comments that follow are also of relevance with regard to the position of a subsequent owner.

(a) Against landlords and tenants

The employer is sometimes in the position of landlord and/or tenant of the site. If there is a lease involved, it is worthwhile considering the terms of the lease to see who is responsible for the physical state of the building. This consideration not only affects the issue of whether an employer should take it upon himself to enforce any rights against any party but also the question of in whose name the proceedings should be brought.

In a contract for the lease of a building to be erected, it is not unusual for the landlord to undertake that the building should be constructed properly (this undertaking may be formulated in any of a number of ways). Such an obligation does not become merged into the lease subsequently granted, even if that lease imposes repair obligations on the tenant.

(b) Against the contractor

The liability of a contractor under a contract is usually absolute. In the past if, for some particular circumstance such as limitation, the employer was unable to pursue the contractor in contract, then the employer could endeavour to show negligence on the part of the contractor. As a result of the restrictions in the type of damages now recoverable in negligence where an employer has sold on to a subsequent owner, the ability of the subsequent owner to pursue any claim against the contractor will depend upon the existence of some form of collateral warranty between the contractor and the subsequent owner. Alternatively, the subsequent owner may sue the employer direct and the employer can then join the contractor into proceedings. Employers and subsequent owners may also have a claim against the contractor under the Defective Premises Act 1972.

(c) Against sub-contractors and suppliers

The basic rule is that an employer has no direct contractual nexus with a sub-contractor, and the chain of liability flows 'down the line'. There are, however, various inroads into this general rule. First, the building owner may have a claim in tort against the sub-contractor under the principle of *Donoghue v Stevenson* [1932] AC 562, if he has suffered personal injury or damage to some property other than the building itself as a result of the sub-contractor's negligence (for some years, following *Anns v Merton* [1978] AC 728 it was thought that a building owner might also recover the cost of rectifying the defect under this lead, but that line of authority has been overturned by *DOE v Bates* [1990] 3 WLR 457).

Secondly, in the cases where it applies, the Defective Premises Act 1972 is capable of providing an employer with a direct cause of action against a sub-contractor.

Thirdly. where there are negotiations between a sub-contractor or supplier and the building owner or his architect, there may arise upon the facts a collateral warranty on the part of the sub-contractor or supplier as to his ability to perform. The consideration in such a case is usually the employer causing the nomination of that sub-contractor or supplier as in *Shanklin Pier Co Ltd v Detel Products* [1951] 2 KB 854. The continuing importance of the collateral warranty was vividly illustrated by the Court of Appeal in *Esso v Mardon* [1976] QB 801.

Under the JCT system, that collateral warranty is reduced to a formal agreement between the employer and the nominated sub-contractor in the standard form of agreement NSC/2. That warranty relates to design matters, the selection of materials and goods and the satisfaction of any performance specification or requirement; the warranty does not extend to workmanship in the ordinary sense of the word.

(d) Against the architect

Where a building owner employs an architect, the architect usually has obligations that include, *inter alia*, the design of the works and the supervision of the work carried out by the builder. Very often, the architect stipulates that the conditions of his employment should be RIBA Conditions of Engagement, but these conditions do not throw any great light upon the nature of these duties. In ordinary cases, the duties of design and supervision are not absolute, but are merely duties to exercise a reasonable degree of professional care and skill.

In practical terms, it is often very difficult for a building owner to know whether a building defect arises out of a failure of the architect to make a proper design, or out of the failure of the contractor properly to execute the design. Likewise, it is often difficult to know whether a workmanship failure by the contractor could have been prevented by proper supervision by the architect. This difficulty can have special importance in that a building owner often needs to know whether to regard the architect as friend or foe in litigation against the contractor. A course that building owners sometimes take in these circumstances is to obtain the agreement of the architect not to plead limitation and to make plain to the architect that, if litigation against the contractor proves unsuccessful by reason of the contractor showing the default to be that of the architect, the building owner reserves his right to pursue a claim against the architect. Usually, the architect will be insured through a professional indemnity policy, and such arrangements require the consent of the architect's insurer if the policy is not to be avoided.

In exceptional circumstances, the architect may be liable in a general way for the failures of the contractor. In *Pratt v Swanmore Builders Ltd* (1980) 15 BLR 37 the architect recommended contractors as being 'very reliable'. In fact the contractors were a total disaster. The plaintiff was able to recover from the architect all her resulting losses including the costs of her litigation with the contractor prior to their insolvency.

The above remarks also apply to the position of engineers and quantity surveyors who undertake the same functions as architects.

(e) Against the local authority

The position of local authorities has been radically altered following the decision in *Murphy v Brentwood District Council* [1990] 3 WLR 414. The position now is that in general a local authority will not be liable to the original owner or subsequent owners for the cost of repair to a defective building that has been constructed in breach of building regulations. The local authority's liability in such circumstances is limited to physical injury to persons or physical damage to other property. Further, *Murphy* establishes that the actual approval of plans by the local authority and the inspection of a building by the local authority and performance of their duties is still insufficient to found any action in negligence for a subsequent owner.

(f) Against the vendor or developer

Where a person has acquired his property from a vendor, especially if that vendor is a developer, a liability may conceivably attach to the vendor on account of the particular circumstances (*Batty v Metropolitan Property Realisations* [1978] QB 554), although that liability will now be limited to personal injury and damage to property other than the building itself (*Murphy v Brentwood* [1990] 3 WLR 414).

(g) Against a bondsman

Employers sometimes require that the contractor procure the issue of a performance bond or other guarantee from an insurance company or other financial institution. Such bonds are frequently required in the case of engineering contracts in the ICE form.

These bonds or guarantees are frequently limited in amount, often to 10 per cent of the contract price, and they are in the nature of a guarantee on the part of the bondsman that the contractor will perform his contractual obligations.

(h) Against the contractor's architect

In the case of a design-and-build contract, where the employer does not employ his own professionals to design the work, the contractor is responsible for the design of the work as well as the execution of that design. Frequently, the main contractor sub-contracts a part of the design work, sometimes together with a part of the construction work, to his own professional agent or specialist sub-contractor. In such a case, the designer is under an obligation in contract to the main contractor. In some circumstances this obligation may be an absolute obligation for fitness of purpose independently of whether or not the designer is negligent (*Greaves v Baynham Meikle* [1975] 1 WLR 1O95) although this will not usually be the case; *George Hawkins v Chrysler (UK) Ltd* (1986) 38 BLR 36 CA. In addition to this contractual liability the designer may possibly also have a liability in negligence to thc employer; *Independent Broadcasting Authority v EMI Electronics Ltd* (1981) 14 BLR 1, although that liability will now be limited to personal injury and damage to property other than the building itself (*Murphy v Brentwood* [1990] 3 WLR 414).

(i) Against the pre-purchase surveyor

Where an owner has bought a building following a survey or valuation upon which he has placed reliance, and he subsequently finds that the building contains defects which the surveyor failed to identify, then he has a *prima facie* case against that surveyor in contract. In the past, where a surveyor has been engaged by some other party, for example a building society, an action could still have been brought for negligence, but again in line with the developments in recent years, in general it is no longer possible to found such an action in negligence, although the cases of *Smith v Bush*; *Harris v Wyre Forest District Council* [1990] 1 AC 831 have established important exceptions to this general rule. In both these cases, surveyors had agreed to carry out, on the instruction of a mortgagee, a survey of an ordinary residential property where the survey fee was being paid by the purchasers of the properties and in circumstances where the surveyors knew that it was likely that the purchasers would rely upon the survey when deciding whether or not to purchase the properties. In these cases, it was held that the surveyors were responsible for the losses suffered by the purchasers as a result of the surveyors' negligence. If, however, the prospective purchasers had been of substantial means and were buying particularly expensive houses, or alternatively a commercial property, then it is unlikely that such a duty of care would have arisen as it would have been unreasonable for the prospective purchasers to rely solely upon the building society valuation. Further, in these cases, it was held that the surveyors could not rely upon the terms of their standard disclaimers as they were unreasonable within the meaning of the Unfair Contract Terms Act 1977.

Where an owner has bought a building following a survey or valuation upon which he has placed reliance, and he subsequently finds that the building contains defects which the survey negligently failed to identify, then he has a *prima facie* case against that surveyor. That case may either be in contract, if the owner has engaged the surveyor himself, or in tort where the surveyor has been engaged by some other party (usually a building society or other body lending money against the security of the property).

A number of issues arising in such cases have been tested in the courts in recent years. The following questions and cases provide some examples.

Does a surveyor engaged by a building society owe a *prima facie* duty of care to a purchaser? Yes; *Yianni v Edwin Evans & Sons* [1982] 1 QB 438.

Can a building society be vicariously liable for the negligence of its own staff surveyor? *Prima facie*, yes; *Stevenson v Nationwide Building Society* (1984) 272 EG 663.

A building society may, however, be entitled to rely upon the terms of a disclaimer; *Stevenson v Nationwide Building Society* (1984) 272 EG 663. In *Smith v Eric S Bush* (1987) 282 EG 326 the surveyor was not entitled to rely on his disclaimer because it was unreasonable within the meaning of the Unfair Contract Terms Act 1977.

A valuation is not negligent if the value given is accurate, regardless of whether it contains a warning that an identified defect might make resale difficult; *Sutcliffe v Sayer* (1987) 281 EG 1452 CA.

How much time should the surveyor put into the survey? As long as it takes. In *Roberts v J Hampson & Co* [1989] 2 All ER 504, the court found that the surveyor was under a duty to follow a trail of suspicion. The court said:

The fact that in an individual case he may need to spend two or three times as long as he would have expected, or as the fee structure would have contemplated, is something that he must accept . . . If in a particular case, the proper valuation of a £19,000 house needs two hours work, that is what he must devote to it.

The usual feature of these cases is that the survey is carried out before the owner contracts to buy the property. There are two reasons for this. Firstly, the period immediately prior to a purchase is by far the most common time for surveys to be carried out. Secondly, there is frequently little or no loss to the owner if a post contract survey negligently fails to identify a defect. Suppose, for example, an owner instructs a surveyor to identify the cause of apparently damp walls. The surveyor accurately identifies a lack of proper ventilation but negligently fails to identify a breakdown in the damp proof course. What is the owner's measure of loss? The surveyor has not caused the failure of the damp proof course, and the owner is only likely to have a substantial claim if the delay in identifying the defect has caused further deterioration to the fabric of the building, or if he has proceeded with decoration or refurbishment which is then affected by the defect. See p 203.

Chapter 7

To arbitrate or to litigate?

Contrary to popular belief in the construction industry, arbitration in building contract matters is generally slower, more expensive and less certain than High Court litigation. Many people in the industry take the view that it is essential to have their dispute heard by someone with a working knowledge of building contracts and the practices that are prevalent in the industry. They often lean towards arbitration as a means of achieving that end. They frequently fail to take account of the Official Referees Court, which is almost invariably the court within the High Court that takes building contract matters, at any rate in London. The Official Referees are appointed from leading counsel and spend a great deal of their time hearing disputes about building contracts. They have therefore come to acquire a detailed working knowledge of the construction industry in much the same way as the professional arbitrators, who are almost always qualified architects.

There is another common view in the industry that arbitrators are able to bring to bear more common sense than High Court judges and are able to 'cut through the red tape'. This is also largely fallacious. Where an arbitrator takes it into his head to 'cut through the red tape' his decision will very frequently be appealable in the courts. Sometimes it will go further. For example, in *Modern Engineering (Bristol) Ltd v C Miskin & Son Ltd* [1981] 2 Lloyd's Rep 135 the arbitrator was faced with a point of law as to whether an architect's certificate could be reviewed. The arbitrator evidently thought that he knew the answer to that point, and he made an interim formal award without listening to full legal argument. That attempt to shortcut the proceedings backfired. The arbitrator was removed for misconduct under the Arbitration Act 1950, s 21(1), and his award was set aside under s 23(2). A similar result also arose in the case of *Damond Lock Grabowski & Partners v Laing Investments (Bracknell) Limited* [1992] CILL 762.

Notwithstanding these matters, many building contracts contain an arbitration agreement, whereby the parties pre-agree to refer any disputes that may arise to arbitration.

It is a mistake for a claimant to assume that because the contract contains an arbitration clause he is necessarily bound to pursue his claim in arbitration rather than in the courts. Likewise, a defendant to High Court proceedings should consider whether to attempt to have the High Court proceedings stayed under the Arbitration Act 1950, s 4 so that the matter may proceed in arbitration. Similarly, a respondent who is served with an arbitration notice ought to consider whether he would be better off if the matter were dealt with in the courts.

This chapter then will provide guidance both for the pursuer and the pursued. In High Court litigation the parties are known as plaintiff and defendant; in arbitration proceedings the parties are known as claimant and respondent. In this chapter the terminology is used interchangeably according to the context.

Before examining the detailed considerations that are likely to influence the choice between arbitration and litigation, there are five points of major importance relating to: alternative dispute resolution (ADR), jurisdiction, limitation, Ord 14 and taking a step in the action. Failure to have regard to these points may seriously prejudice a party's position.

(1) *Alternative Dispute Resolution*: The case may be one in which it would be worthwhile trying an ADR solution; either the potential plaintiff or the potential defendant can suggest it but (subject to the wording of the contract) neither can insist on it. See page 190.

(2) *Jurisdiction*: The Court of Appeal decision in *Northern Regional Health Authority v Crouch and Crown* [1984] 2 WLR 676 has cast much doubt on the jurisdiction of the court in cases where certificates or decisions of the architect are in issue. In some cases, this factor will dominate the choice between litigation and arbitration.

(3) *Limitation*: If a plaintiff has reason to believe that the limitation period may expire before the determination of the dispute, then he must remember that for limitation purposes in arbitrations the test is whether the arbitration is commenced before the expiration of the limitation period, be it six years or 12 years. For these purposes, the arbitration commences when one party serves on the other a notice requiring him to appoint, or agree to the appointment of an arbitrator or (where the arbitration agreement names or designates the arbitrator) requiring him to submit the dispute to the persons so named or designated (Limitation Act 1980, s 34). Accordingly, for protective purposes it is necessary not only to issue a writ but also to commence arbitration proceedings by the service of a formal arbitration notice, which can be so worded as to make it clear that it is merely protective and without prejudice to a contention that the dispute ought to be dealt with in the court (see p 164). If the plaintiff merely issues a writ without serving an arbitration notice, then there is a danger that the defendant may successfully take out a summons staying the court proceedings under the Arbitration Act 1950, s 4. By that

time, an arbitration notice may already be out of time. Likewise, if a claimant merely pursues the arbitration without issuing a writ, then he may subsequently find that, for all sorts of reasons, he is later compelled to proceed in the court and it may be too late for him to issue a writ.

(4) *Order 14*: The third central point to bear in mind is that litigation and arbitration are not mutually exclusive. If a part of the claim is within the scope of Ord 14, then it is open for the claimant first to sue and recover under Ord 14 the indisputable part of the claim, and to pursue the balance in arbitration (see p 113).

(5) *Taking a step in the proceedings*: A party who is served with an arbitration notice usually has some time in hand if he wants the proceedings to be heard in the court. The arbitration does not commence (except for limitation purposes) until an arbitrator is appointed, and (unless both parties agree upon a mutually acceptable arbitrator) it usually takes some time for the claimant to procure that appointment. Arbitrators rarely accept any appointment until their identity is known to both parties. On the other hand, a defendant to High Court proceedings must move swiftly if he wishes to have the action stayed for arbitration. He must issue his summons under the Arbitration Act 1950, s 4, before delivering any pleadings or taking any other steps in the proceedings. Even a time summons can be fatal. Such a defendant must, therefore, decide very rapidly whether he wishes to issue a section 4 summons, and if he does he should not delay. A further discussion of the Arbitration Act 1950, s 4, and what constitutes a step in the proceedings appears in Chapter 10.

It is beyond the scope of this book to consider in detail the wording of the arbitration clauses in current use. Suffice it to say that arbitration clauses of the type in *Scott v Avery* (1856) 5 HLC 811 are rare in building contracts (ie it is rare to see provision in a building contract arbitration clause that the making of an award by an arbitrator is to be a condition precedent to the right to bring an action in the courts). It is also worth noting that the usual arbitration clauses are widely drawn and in particular the JCT arbitration clause (which appears at Article 5 of the 1980 Edition) is likely to cover almost any dispute between the parties to a building contract that relates to the works.

1 Jurisdiction

In February 1984 the Court of Appeal handed down a decision in the case of *Northern Regional Health Authority v Derek Crouch Construction Ltd and Crown House Engineering Ltd* [1984] 2 WLR 676. The particular facts of the case are not of any very general application. A series of disputes arose between an employer, a main contractor and a nominated sub-contractor, some of which were the subject of court proceedings, some of which were the subject of arbitration proceedings and some of which had been settled. The Court of Appeal decision arose out of some further arbitration proceedings instituted by the sub-contractor in the main contractor's name pursuant to its rights under the Green Form. The employer sought an injunction restraining that arbitration, which injunction was refused by an Official Referee. That refusal was upheld by the Court of Appeal.

The significant aspect of the decision is that the Court of Appeal dealt at length with the issue of whether the courts have power to open up, review, or revise any certificate, opinion or decision of the architect under a JCT contract. The Court of Appeal said that the courts did not have such power, although they indicated the following exceptions:

(1) Where the parties agree that an Official Referee should act as arbitrator under s 11 of the Arbitration Act 1950 (which is most unusual).

(2) Where a certificate or opinion was legally invalid because given, for example, in bad faith or in excess of the architect's powers.

(3) Where the machinery in the arbitration clause had broken down and was incapable of operating.

The *Crouch* decision caused very substantial difficulties. In particular it left some plaintiffs who had commenced proceedings before, or without knowledge of the decision in an extremely uncomfortable position. It is very common for there to be some part of the case on any JCT contract that is inconsistent with certificates, decisions or opinions of the architect. If it were to be held that such matters are the exclusive jurisdiction of an arbitrator, then a plaintiff would not only be deprived of all his investment in his chosen forum, but might be prevented from commencing an arbitration by reason of limitation.

The decision has been much criticised; see for example Duncan Wallace QC 'Construction Contracts: The Architects the Arbitrator and the Courts' (1986) 2 Const LJ 13 and the commentary in *Keating*. In particular:

(1) The decision does not lie happily with what the contract itself says. It is plain both from the final certificate provision and from the VAT Supplemental Agreement that the contract envisages certificates being reviewed by the courts as an alternative to arbitration. It seems that the Court of Appeal did not consider these provisions before finding that the contract excludes review by the courts.

(2) The decision undermines what has been taken for granted in many previous cases.

(3) The practical reality is that there are many disputes, particularly multi-party disputes, that simply cannot be dealt with conveniently without an effective third party procedure, which does not exist in arbitrations.

In February 1985 the principle was somewhat surprisingly extended to the JCT Minor Works agreement (*Oram Builders Ltd v Pemberton* (1985) 29 BLR 23), even though the Minor Works agreement arbitration clause contains no power for the arbitrator to open up and review certificates. Read on its face value and taken together with the *Crouch* decision, the position in Minor Works agreements appears to be that the court has no power to deal with certification disputes but that an arbitrator would be no better placed. It is difficult to imagine that this is what the court intended.

In November 1985 the matter came before His Honour Judge Davies in *Partington & Son (Builders) Ltd v Tameside Metropolitan Borough Council* (1985) 32 BLR 150. The court observed that the observations of the Court of Appeal in the *Crouch* case were *obiter* and declined to follow them, awarding a declaration that the court would have the same powers as an arbitrator under the JCT63 contract.

A few days later another official referee, His Honour Judge Lewis Hawser, heard *Reed v Van der Vorm* (1985) 35 BLR 136, a case in which there was no arbitration clause at all. On this occasion the court felt compelled to follow *Crouch*.

It was not until June 1987 that the Court of Appeal saw the issue again. In *Benstrete Construction Ltd v Angus Hill* (1987) 38 BLR 115 CA, Sir John Donaldson MR (who was one of the members of the Court of Appeal which heard the *Crouch* case) delivered a very short and curious judgment in which he referred to 'an internal arbitration clause' in the main contract which does not appear in the Minor Works contract. He did not refer to the *Oram* decision, and he may well have overruled it, since he found that the county court did have jurisdiction to determine a dispute under the Minor Works agreement. He did not appear to consider whether or not the resolution of the dispute would involve the opening up of the certificates. The position is far from clear, and has been further complicated by s 43A of the Supreme Court Act 1981, inserted by s 100 of the Courts and Legal Services Act 1990, to the effect that the High Court may exercise specific powers conferred on an arbitrator if all the parties to the agreement agree. It is worth questioning what effect this section is supposed to have on the usual case of not all parties agreeing.

2 Agreements relating to existing disputes

In building contract matters, arbitrations arise in one of two ways. Usually they arise out of a pre-agreement between the parties to refer to arbitration any disputes that may rise out of their dealings. Arbitration clauses containing such a pre-agreement appear (usually at the end) in practically every standard form of building contract and very frequently appear at the end of builders' standard terms and conditions. Very frequently, the parties to the contract will not even notice the existence of the arbitration clause. If they do, and if it is then their desire for any dispute to be promptly resolved by arbitration proceedings, there is still no guarantee that desire will subsist once a dispute has become apparent. More likely, the respondent would prefer to put off the resolution for as long as possible. Arbitrations are particularly suitable for respondents who wish to avoid the resolution of a dispute.

Alternatively, contracting parties who encounter a *bona fide* dispute during the course of their dealings may agree to refer that dispute to arbitration. Usually in such cases neither party is seeking to evade its liabilities. The parties simply disagree as to some matter and wish their disagreement to be resolved as quickly as possible by an independent person so that they can resume their business. The contract may yet be in progress and the parties may not wish to sour their working relationship by court proceedings. Note, however, that parties in this mood might well be better served by ADR.

Agreements to refer existing disputes are generally likely to involve different principles from the principles involved in pre-agreements to arbitrate. Agreements to arbitrate existing disputes are frequently accompanied by further agreement as to the choice of arbitrator, the time by which the arbitrator will be asked to make his award, and so on. If there is a genuinely reciprocal desire to resolve the dispute, the arbitration is likely to be efficient and successful as a forum. Many of the factors referred to in this chapter do not apply, but there are some particular dangers that a party in dispute should be warned against. In particular:

(1) Parties in dispute should be warned against selecting an inexperienced arbitrator. It is frequently thought by non-lawyers that the main requirement of an arbitrator is knowledge of the subject matter of the dispute. In fact, it requires experience of arbitrations to act effectively as an arbitrator and, except in the very simplest of cases, it is a dangerous practice to appoint as arbitrator a person who does not have adequate experience as such.

(2) There is a difference between experts and arbitrators, and clients may require advice as to which is preferable.

(3) If the dispute relates only to the construction of a document (and the standard contracts are full of scope for this) remember that that dispute can be resolved pursuant to the issue of a construction summons or by Order 14A in the High Court. The parties may not wish to involve the court at all, but it may be that they are simply unaware that it is possible to have a High Court judge construe a document without all the palaver of pleadings and discovery.

3 Costs

Some people fondly imagine that arbitrations are free of the enormous legal costs that court actions involve. This is not true. It is almost certain that each side in a building contract arbitration of any substance will require legal representation in exactly the same way as if the matter were proceeding in the courts. Furthermore, the arbitrator almost always has the power to order payment of the costs in the same way as if the matter were proceeding in the High Court (Arbitration Act 1950, s 18(1)) and the arbitrator must exercise that power in accordance with judicial principles (*Donald Campbell & Co v Pollack* [1927] AC 732 HL).

On the whole (and there is no hard and fast rule) the costs of an arbitration tend to be higher than the costs of a similar High Court action. There are two main reasons for this.

First, the costs of the arbitration itself (as opposed to the costs of the parties) are likely to be greater. Court fees are very modest, and no additional fees are paid for the time spent by the judge, the use of the court office, the use of the court room or the tape recording of proceedings by the mechanical recording department. In the case of arbitration proceedings, however, the parties must pay the arbitrator for his time spent on the arbitration (the current rate for a senior experienced arbitrator is about £200 per hour), must pay the hire charge for an arbitration room (which is likely to be at least £300 per day or part of a day), and may feel it necessary for a record of the proceedings to be kept by mechanical tape recording or by shorthand writers. These expenses (or a proportion of them) are frequently payable even if they are not used because of a last minute settlement.

Secondly, arbitrators generally do not exercise the same control over arbitrations, either at interlocutory stages or at a trial, that the High Court exercises in litigation. This is partly because of a wariness, understandable in a non-lawyer, and partly because they do not enjoy the same inherent jurisdiction as does the High Court. This means (a) that arbitration proceedings are frequently more protracted, which plainly involves greater cost for the parties, and (b) the more complex procedure of applying to the court in relation to an arbitration can involve additional expense.

4 Speed

There is a variety of factors that affect whether arbitration is likely to be quicker or slower than litigation in the courts.

There are some arbitrators who are particularly conscious of the need to resolve disputes speedily, especially in cases where the parties remain actively in contract and need their disputes resolved rapidly in order to proceed with their dealings. In those cases, arbitration can be substantially quicker. Likewise, where the only substantial point in issue is a short technical point, then again arbitration can frequently be substantially quicker than High Court litigation.

In cases where the parties are no longer actively in a contractual relationship with each other, as for example where there is a long list of alleged defects, or a complex loss and expense or damages claim, then litigation is generally more rapid than arbitration. Experienced arbitrators frequently have diaries booked many months in advance, and where a lengthy trial of weeks rather than days is required, then the trial date which they will give is frequently more distant than would be the case in the Official Referees' Court.

Where it is in the interests of one party to procrastinate, that party will have a greater opportunity for procrastination in arbitration than in the High Court. The procedure for enforcing orders as to discovery and as to the pleadings is more cumbersome in arbitration and takes correspondingly longer.

5 Third parties

It is a feature of arbitrations that they result from an agreement between two parties to submit differences *inter se* to an arbitrator. That arbitrator does not have the same jurisdiction as would the High Court over any other party.

Multi-party litigation is particularly common in building contract disputes. Where an employer alleges delay as against a main contractor, the main contractor will very frequently want to pass on the whole or part of the delay claim to one or more of his sub-contractors. Likewise, where an employer alleges that a main contractor's work is defective, the main contractor may well claim that the error originated from the architect, the structural engineer, or from one of his sub-contractors. Where a contractor claims entitlement or further entitlement to be paid from the employer, it may be because of an existing or anticipated claim by a sub-contractor. It is not unknown for the number of parties in substantial High Court building contract litigation to pass into double figures.

There are many advantages of joining all the relevant parties in the same action, as is only possible in the courts. It avoids duplication of cost, it reduces the possibility of different findings upon the same subject matter, and it reduces the risk of a party being called upon to meet a substantial claim before he is able to recover in respect of the same subject matter.

Arbitration agreements sometimes contain complex machinery designed to go some way to overcoming this defect in the arbitration process. Clause 41.2 of JCT80 contains such a provision. The terms of such a provision should be carefully considered in appropriate circumstances; at first sight provisions for multi-partite arbitrations look as if they give rise to difficulties, and indeed they do.

6 Limitation

It is possible for an action to be statute barred for the purpose of court proceedings but not for the purpose of arbitration, or *vice versa*. For

High Court proceedings the test is whether the plaintiff has issued his writ within the limitation period. For the purposes of an arbitration, however, the test is whether or not the claimant has, within the limitation period, served on the respondent a notice requiring him to appoint or agree to the appointment of an arbitrator or (where the arbitration agreement names or designates the arbitrator) requiring him to submit the dispute to the persons so named or designated (Limitation Act 1980, s 34).

The limitation consideration when choosing between litigation and arbitration is often complex. Limitation in building contract matters is almost always an imprecise science (see Chapter 17) and frequently the effect of limitation is to erode a party's case in stages rather than at one fell swoop. Furthermore, a plaintiff who has issued proceedings within the limitation period, but continues to litigate after that time, is in a vulnerable position in at least two respects.

(1) It is very common for building contract matters to be inadequately pleaded in the first case; to amend pleadings after the expiry of the limitation period is rather more difficult than to amend prior to the expiry of the limitation period; see the notes in the *White Book* at para 20/5–8/7.

(2) A complexity of building contract matters (and their comparative unfamiliarity to many general practitioners) results, in many cases, in delay in their prosecution. In *Renown Investments (Holdings) Ltd v F Shepherd & Son* (1976) 120 SJ 840 it was established that the complexity did not of itself render plaintiffs immune from the danger of being struck out for want of prosecution. *Birkett v James* [1977] 3 WLR 38 has rendered it very difficult indeed successfully to strike out an action for want of prosecution prior to the expiry of the limitation period, but after that time the plaintiff is vulnerable to such an application and in building contract matters the success rate of those applications is unusually high (see Chapter 15, section 2).

Where a complex matter is nearing the expiration of the limitation period, these two factors may encourage a plaintiff to choose arbitration and a defendant to choose litigation in the court. An arbitrator does have power to disallow amendments (*Crighton and Law Car and General Insurance Corpn, Re* [1910] 2 KB 738), but it is a brave arbitrator who will do so. More importantly, the House of Lords has now decided that arbitrations may continue notwithstanding inordinate and inexcusable delay by a claimant, and claimants are accordingly now in the fortunate position of not having to concern themselves unduly about the danger of losing their claims through want of prosecution (*Bremer Vulkan v South India Shipping* [1981] 1 All ER 289).

7 Commercial considerations

Arbitration is by its nature less aggressive than High Court proceedings. In the minds of many commercial men the service of a High Court writ represents something tantamount to a declaration of war and arbitration is frequently seen as far more in keeping with the commercial image of many business organisations.

Where a claimant has in mind the possibility of further contracts with a respondent but nonetheless wishes to pursue a particular dispute, then that can be an overwhelming consideration which would cause that party to choose arbitration rather than High Court litigation.

8 Privacy

Parties to building contract litigation are sometimes keen to keep the litigation out of the courts because they are sensitive to the possibility of publicity. On other occasions they may feel that their opponent is sensitive to publicity and regard this as a good reason to keep the matter in the court.

The distinction between court proceedings and arbitration in terms of the privacy they afford to the litigants is probably exaggerated in many cases. Although the theory of the matter is that trials in the High Court are open to the public, in practice it is rare for a building contract trial in the Official Referees' corridor to attract any publicity at all. Where the trial is in one of the courtrooms near to the main hall in the Royal Courts of Justice there may be the occasional group of bemused tourists who 'look in' for a few minutes before wandering off in search of something more interesting. In reality, the supposed advantage of arbitration proceedings to a sensitive party is often illusory in building contract cases. If a party does suffer from publication of its affairs it is very frequently as a result of gossip in the construction industry and the City, and that gossip will be no more or less than in arbitration proceedings. That said, parties are sometimes nervous of court proceedings where the subject matter is sensitive and this nervousness of itself is sometimes successfully exploited by the other party.

One advantage that arbitration may have over litigation is in the area of law reporting. Decisions of the courts are public property, whereas decisions of arbitrators are private. Would you be put off the idea of Stevenson's ginger beer? Remember that Mrs. Donoghue never established that there was a snail in the bottle in the first place.

9 International element

In the case of international contracts, particularly contracts with foreign governments or bodies sponsored by foreign governments, very different considerations apply. Where the parties to a contract are in different countries each is unlikely to want any disputes resolved on the home territory of the other. It is plainly a great advantage in many respects to be able to fight on one's home ground. Further, foreign governments are frequently most reluctant to submit to the jurisdiction of the court of any other country as it is an affront to their dignity.

For these reasons, arbitration agreements in contracts with an international element are of particular importance. They frequently provide that disputes should be settled under the Rules of Conciliation and Arbitration of the International Chamber of Commerce (the ICC). The standard form of building contract most widely used for international building contracts, the FIDIC contract, contains such an arbitration clause.

Where court proceedings are commenced despite a domestic arbitration agreement, the other party may apply to the court under the Arbitration Act 1950, s 4, and the court may order a stay of the court proceedings pending the arbitration. The court has a discretion as to whether the matter should go to arbitration. Where, however, a party issues proceedings and there is a 'non-domestic' arbitration agreement within the meaning of the Arbitration Act 1975, s 1, then the other party *may* apply to the court under the 1975 Act and the court *must* then stay the court proceedings. It has no discretion.

From the point of view of an English claimant, litigation in the court is very likely to be preferable to arbitration under the rules of the ICC. In the English courts he would have a natural advantage over an overseas opponent. See Chapter 16, section 11 for a description of the ICC Court of Arbitration.

10 Insolvency and impecuniosity

Legal aid is not available for arbitration, and if a party is within the financial limits for legal aid then that may be a conclusive reason for him preferring the court, whether he be plaintiff or defendant. Likewise, because it is extremely difficult for an unassisted party to obtain an order for the payment of costs where his opponent is an assisted party (see the Legal Aid Act 1974, s 13). A party whose opponent is, or may be within the financial limits is more likely to prefer arbitration, where s 13 has no application.

As to the legal aid consideration in section 4 summonses, it was held in *Smith v Pearl Assurance Co* [1939] 1 All ER 95 that the poverty of a litigant is not a ground for keeping the dispute in the court. It was for a time thought that *Smith v Pearl Assurance* had been extinguished in *Fakes v Taylor Woodrow Construction Limited* [1973] 1 QB 436. However, this issue came before the Court of Appeal more recently in the case of *Edwin Jones v Thyssen & Taylor Woodrow* [1991] CILL 697. Impecuniosity was again ruled not to be a reason for keeping a dispute with the court when there is a valid arbitration clause even though a party is deprived of the benefit of the Legal Aid system.

If a party is in danger of becoming insolvent, then that is a matter which is likely to encourage him towards arbitration and his opponent towards litigation in the court. The High Court exercises control over arbitrations in respect of such matters as security for costs, preservation of property and appointment of receivers under the Arbitration Act 1950, s 12(6), but these remedies are more conveniently available where the whole action is in the High Court, and in any event the High Court probably takes a more robust view than do arbitrators of the effect of potential insolvency of one of the parties.

11 Technical complexity

It is rare for building contract disputes to contain points of such technical complexity that they are beyond the wit of a High Court judge or Official Referee. There are, however, recurring building problems (in particular those relating to the design of foundations, the frames of buildings and condensation) where the technical issues are, to say the least, difficult and where an arbitrator may be better able to understand the issues fully. That can be a consideration to lean a party in favour of arbitration.

Technical complexity should not be confused with understanding of building contract practices and quantity surveying practices. These issues tend in the end to be legal issues and the Official Referees are familiar with the practices of the building industry.

A somewhat more complex issue arises concerning delay and disruption claims. Following the *Wharf Property* line of cases (see Chapter 21) the courts are tightening up the detail of proof required of a plaintiff. In response, it is becoming increasingly common for plaintiffs to prepare computer-assisted network analyses as the vehicle for calculating and demonstrating their entitlement. There will often be real doubt as to the reception that these analyses will get; most judges are more familiar with the language of Tacitus than DOS. Conversely, many arbitrators themselves have considerable experience of preparing and presenting delay and disruption claims, and the concepts now used in delay and disruption analysis are likely to be familiar to them.

12 Pleadings and evidence

Parties sometimes wish to have their dispute dealt with in arbitration because they imagine that this will obviate the need to prepare lengthy and unnecessary pleadings. In fact, pleadings in arbitrations tend to be little different from pleadings in High Court litigation. Arbitrators normally make orders at the preliminary meeting for delivery of points of claim, points of defence and counterclaim, and points of reply and defence to counterclaim which correspond more or less with the time scale one would expect in the High Court. The arbitrator may make further directions for the delivery of submissions or contentions; the terminology does not matter greatly and all these documents are in the nature of pleadings in the sense generally understood in High Court litigation.

There is an implied provision in arbitration agreements under the Arbitration Act 1950, s 12(1), that the parties are deemed to have agreed to 'do all other things which during the proceedings on the reference the arbitrator or umpire may require'; and this provision is construed to authorise an arbitrator to direct delivery of pleadings and exercise his discretion as to allowing or disallowing amendment of these (*Edward Lloyd Ltd v Sturgeon Falls & Co* (1901) 85 LT 162; *Crighton and Law Car and General Insurance Corpn, Re* [1910] 2 KB 738). Despite this, an arbitrator probably does have more flexibility than the High Court with regard to pleadings and where a party already has the benefit of a 'non-legal' but carefully researched and lengthy claim document it may be easier for that party to use the claim document with comparatively little amendment in an arbitration.

As far as evidence is concerned, the difference between arbitration and High Court litigation is principally procedural. The Arbitration Act 1950, s 12, contains provision for parties to the arbitration (s 12(1)) and other witnesses (s 12(2)) to give evidence on oath. If necessary, that evidence can be brought pursuant to a writ of *subpoena ad testificandum* (s 12(4)) and the court has further wide powers under s 12(6). It seems that perjury committed in an arbitration is tantamount to perjury at common law and punishable as such (*R v Crossley* (1909) 100 LT 463 CA)

It should in particular be noted that an arbitrator should not (except in the rare case of a 'look-sniff' arbitration) try to short-circuit the presentation of expert evidence. If he takes expert evidence from himself, so to speak, without giving the parties proper opportunity to be heard, then he will be liable to be removed by the court on the ground of misconduct (*Fox v Wellfair* (1981)19 BLR 52).

Accordingly, evidence will only rarely be a consideration which will influence the choice between arbitration and litigation in the High Court.

13 Discovery of documents

It is normal for the discovery process in arbitration to be conducted in much the same way as in the High Court. It is provided in the Arbitration Act 1950, s 12(1):

Unless a contrary expression is expressed therein, every arbitration agreement shall, where such a provision is applicable to the reference, be deemed to contain a provision that the parties to the reference, and all persons claiming through them respectively, shall, subject to any legal objection, submit to . . . produce before the arbitrator or umpire all documents within their possession or power respectively which may be required or called for, and do all other things which during the proceedings on the reference the arbitrator or umpire may require.

There is further provision in s 12(4) which provides that any party to a reference under an arbitration agreement may issue a writ of *subpoena duces tecum* (but not so as to compel any person to produce any document which he could not be compelled to produce on the trial of an action in the court); and there is a further general power under s 12(6) for the High Court to make orders in respect of discovery of documents.

The significant difference between arbitration and High Court litigation as regards discovery is, accordingly, as to enforcement only. It is the common practice of arbitrators to make original orders in respect of discovery in exactly the same way as in the High Court and the form of the list of documents is normally the same. However, the old provision under s 12 (6)(b) of the Arbitration Act 1950 has now been repealed by s 103 of the Courts and Legal Services Act 1990, thereby removing the power that could otherwise be conferred on the court to enforce discovery. This marks a further step towards the independence of arbitrators from the interference of the courts although, it has to be said, the judges still jealously maintain a watchful eye over arbitrations on points of law.

Accordingly, discovery is not generally a major consideration in the choice between arbitration or litigation in the High Court, but if severe problems are expected at discovery it marginally assists to have the action heard in the High Court.

14 Can the substantive law be different?

The general rule was stated in *David Taylor and Son Ltd v Barnett Trading Co* [1953] 1 WLR 562 at 568:

> The duty of an arbitrator is to decide the questions submitted to him according to the legal rights of the parties, and not according to what he may consider fair and reasonable under all the circumstances.

That is the theory. In practice, arbitrators frequently are heavily influenced by what they see as a just solution, and that vision of justice may differ from that of the High Court.

There may well be occasions where an arbitrator departs from the law; certainly non-legal arbitrators are less likely than the High Court to be convinced by complex legal arguments which might apparently fly in the face of what seems to be common sense on the particular facts.

In respect of arbitration commenced after 1 August 1979 the appeals procedure in the Arbitration Act 1950, s 21, has been replaced by the procedure in the Arbitration Act 1979, s 1. Under the 1979 Act appeal lies to the High Court on any question of law arising out of an award made on an arbitration agreement (s 1(2)), and the court may require the arbitrator to state the reasons for his award in sufficient detail to enable the court to consider the question of law (s 1(5)). It is, however, necessary for one of the parties to give notice to the arbitrator concerned that a reasoned order would be required *before* the award was made (s 1(6)).

15 Getting into the right forum

Having made a decision as to whether it is better to be in arbitration or in the court, how is a party to have his dispute heard in that forum? This question is considered below.

(a) A plaintiff who prefers the court

If it is comfortably less than six years since the date of the contract, the plaintiff should simply issue a writ and proceed in the court. As soon as the defendant takes a step in the action (see Chapter 10, section 1), the litigation is firmly established in the courts. Some plaintiffs attempt to force the defendant into taking a step in the action as soon as possible (eg by refusing to grant an extension of time, however short) in the hope that the defendant will lose the opportunity of arbitration before having a chance to consider it fully. A plaintiff will sometimes delay issuing his Ord 14 summons until after the defence is due specifically with this point in mind.

If the defendant does serve a section 4 summons then the plaintiff must oppose it as best he can. Where the plaintiff has reason to believe that the defendant will successfully take out a section 4 summons, then that is an especially good reason for the plaintiff to take out an Ord 14 summons in respect of as much of the claim as he can, since that part of the claim will be immune from the stay to arbitration (*Ellis Mechanical Services Ltd v Wates Construction Ltd* (1976) 2 BLR 57).

If six years have passed since the date of the formation of the contract (or will have passed by the time the defendant is forced to take a step in the action), there may be a limitation risk, and if the contract contains an arbitration clause the plaintiff would be well advised to serve a protective arbitration notice. It is possible for such a notice to be drafted making it quite plain that the plaintiff regards the High Court as the proper forum for the dispute (see p 165); and, although the notice will protect the position for the purpose of limitation in a subsequent arbitration, it will not of itself operate actually to put any arbitration into being.

If the defendant himself serves an arbitration notice, the plaintiff can simply ignore it and proceed with the High Court action unless and until prevented from doing so by an order under the Arbitration Act 1950, s 4, or in the case of a non-domestic arbitration agreement, under the Arbitration Act 1975, s 1.

(b) A plaintiff who prefers arbitration

Unless there is a limitation risk, the claimant first serves a notice requiring the respondent to concur in the appointment of an arbitrator. This will protect him for the purposes of limitation (Limitation Act 1980, s 34). If the respondent responds to the notice and it is possible to agree upon who should be the arbitrator, the claimant approaches the agreed arbitrator with a view to persuading the arbitrator to accept the appointment as rapidly as possible. If it is not possible to agree upon an arbitrator, generally the arbitration clause provides that the arbitrator shall be appointed by the president for the time being of the RIBA or sometimes the RICS (or similar body). The claimant requests such a nomination and then approaches the nominated person with a view to persuading him to accept the reference as soon as possible. In certain cases the court has power to appoint an arbitrator (Arbitration Act 1950, s 10, as amended by the Arbitration Act 1979, s 6(3)).

The arbitration does not commence until an arbitrator has been appointed and has accepted the appointment.

Where there is or may be a limitation risk a cautious claimant will often regard it as desirable also to issue but not serve a writ in the High Court. It is possible for the court to restrain an arbitration by injunction in exceptional circumstances and to revoke the authority of the arbitrator where the arbitrator is or may be partial (Arbitration Act 1950, s 24(1)) or the arbitration involves a question of fraud (Arbitration Act 1950, s 24(2)), or where the arbitrator is guilty of misconduct (Arbitration Act 1950, s 23(1)), or where the arbitrator himself fails to use all reasonable dispatch (Arbitration Act 1950, s 13(3)). Where an arbitrator is removed or his authority is revoked, then the court has power under the Arbitration Act 1950, s 25, to appoint an alternative arbitrator, but it also has power if it thinks fit to order that the arbitration agreement shall cease to have effect with respect to the dispute referred. A claimant will, therefore, be better protected in cases of limitation risk where he has a High Court writ upon file in the court. Unless renewed the writ will only remain valid for four months beginning with the date of its issue (Ord 6, r 8(1)), and accordingly it is counter-productive in the circumstances to issue the protective writ before there is any limitation risk.

(c) A respondent who prefers the court

Once an arbitration has commenced, it may be very difficult for the respondent to resist the matter proceeding by arbitration. He may be able to apply to the court if the dispute is or may be outside the terms of the arbitration agreement; the High Court will restrain an arbitration in certain circumstances (see the cases cited in Part 2 of the *White Book* at para 5742); and 'if one thing is quite plain, it is that an arbitrator cannot give himself jurisdiction by deciding in his favour some preliminary point upon which his jurisdiction depends' (*Smith v Martin* [1925] 1 KB 745). However, the grounds upon which the court will restrain an arbitration by injunction are limited and a party who wishes to have the dispute heard in the court will usually have a far better chance of fulfilling that wish if he fights upon the ground of a section 4 summons. Accordingly, the defending party will in many cases be well advised to issue a writ prior to the appointment of an arbitrator (and if necessary in the short intervening period between notice to concur in the appointment of an arbitrator, and the actual appointment of an arbitrator).

If the party who wishes litigation in the court has a money claim, then a writ with statement of claim indorsed may be issued and served claiming that sum. It is immaterial that it may be met by a far greater counterclaim. If the defending party does not have any money claim at all, he can nonetheless issue a writ claiming a declaratory judgment that he is not liable to meet the other's claim. The Rules of the Supreme Court, Ord 15, r 16, provides:

No action or other proceedings shall be open to objection on the ground that a merely declaratory judgment or order is sought thereby, and the Court may make binding declarations of right whether or not any consequential relief is or could be claimed.

An application for a declaratory judgment should not be made prematurely since the person against whom no claim has been made may not obtain a declaration that no such claim exists (*Re Clay* [1919] 1 Ch 66 CA)

In the circumstances, the defendant to the declaratory writ (ie the party who has the major claim) is very likely to issue a section 4 summons. However, the plaintiff will be entitled to all arguments normally available on a section 4 summons and of particular importance in building contract matters is the effect of *Taunton-Collins v Crombie* [1964] 1 WLR 63 CA (see p 127), where a stay was refused because there were more than two parties.

It would be unusual for an arbitrator to accept an appointment in a case where he knew that a High Court writ had been issued and served and was being actively pursued. The plaintiff in the High Court proceedings (ie the potential respondent in the arbitration) should accordingly put any proposed arbitrator on notice of the position, and in an extreme case, where a proposed arbitrator threatens to try to shortcut the section 4 procedure, the plaintiff should carefully consider the possibility of obtaining an injunction restraining the prospective arbitrator.

(d) A defendant who prefers arbitration

A party who is potentially a respondent to an arbitration is sometimes well advised to commence the arbitration himself and so become a claimant. There are two reasons for this.

First, a claimant in an arbitration has marginally more control over the proceedings than a respondent. In particular, a claimant can often dictate the pace of the arbitration proceedings more effectively than a respondent.

The second reason is that once he has obtained the appointment of an arbitrator he has substantially closed the door to an opponent who would prefer the High Court. Usually, the only prospect that such an opponent will have will be to move quickly and issue proceedings prior to the appointment of the arbitrator.

If a plaintiff has issued and served a writ, a defendant who prefers arbitration must, before taking any step in the proceedings, issue a summons either under the Arbitration Act 1950, s 4, or under the Arbitration Act 1975, s 1, depending upon whether the arbitration agreement is a domestic arbitration agreement within the meaning of the Arbitration Act 1975, s 1.

Chapter 8

Litigation in the High Court

1 Commencement of litigation

In principle, building contract litigation is like other litigation at common law. In the High Court, it is properly commenced as Official Referees' Business in the Queen's Bench Division and the Rules of the Supreme Court apply. In practice, it tends to differ in certain material respects. In particular:

(1) Very frequently building contract disputes involve a multiplicity of issues. The pleadings often involve lengthy tabulations and calculations concerning the cost of building works which the lawyers are not usually in a position to evaluate without the assistance of experts. The contracts are often long and complicated and can give rise to as many legal points as the parties choose to identify; but within the complexities there are often undeniable truths that can be made to stand out.

(2) Almost all building contract litigation, if it goes to trial, is tried before the Official Referee. The Official Referees' Court is in fact most sensible and helpful but it is unfamiliar to many lawyers.

(3) The Official Referees' Court is, in effect, a specialist court for building contract litigation. There is also a specialist building contract bar, and there are firms of solicitors that specialise in building contract law. The existence of these specialists can create a hostile environment for the unequipped stranger.

The source of most knowledge of High Court procedure is the Supreme Court Practice, commonly known as the *White Book*. The *White Book* is published in two volumes every two years and a cumulative supplement is released every few months. Volume 1 of the *White Book* contains not only the Rules of the Supreme Court but also lengthy and very useful commentaries. The Rules themselves have the force of statute in matters of procedure, being made under the Supreme Court Act 1981 and other statutes. The notes, which are printed in slightly smaller type, do not have any formal force of law, but they do provide very useful cross references and guidance and are taken to have a persuasive value. It is often difficult when looking at precedent books of court forms to distinguish between what is required by the rules, and what is suggested by the editor of such books. Part 2 in Volume 2 of the *White Book* contains all the forms which it is *necessary* to follow.

The function of the court is, or ought to be, to assist the parties in the matter of formal requirements. Where possible, the court officials are usually prepared to give advice as to formal requirements over the telephone (the telephone number of the Central Office is 071-936 6000).

In the Queen's Bench Division, hearings are either in open court or in chambers. In building contract cases, practically all hearings are in chambers except the trial itself. Solicitors have rights of audience in proceedings in chambers, and so do their legal executives and managing and other responsible clerks (*Vimbos v Meadowcroft* (1902) 46 SJ 2). Neither counsel nor solicitors appear robed at proceedings in chambers.

The substantial majority of building contract cases are settled. Indeed, the view is often expressed that the trial of a building contract case is of itself an indication of the failure of the legal advisers of one or both parties. In practice, the terms of settlement are usually very heavily influenced by the result of interlocutory hearings in chambers, and it is usually unreasonable for a solicitor to expect general common law barristers to be able to match the advice of specialist barristers.

Particular aspects of building contract litigation in the High Court are considered elsewhere in this book. Some of the more important features are summarised below.

It is a mistake to assume that a party is bound to accept his opponent's choice to go to arbitration, even if the contract contains an arbitration clause. If a claimant serves an arbitration notice it may be possible for the other party to get the dispute before the courts by issuing a writ, and if the plaintiff sues in the courts it may be possible for the defendant to obtain a stay of proceedings under the Arbitration Act 1950, s 4.

It is often a mistake to assume that an 'expert' will be able to deal with all of the detailed facts, especially where those facts relate to the valuation of work. Surveyors, and particularly quantity surveyors, provide an invaluable service to the building industry by adopting pragmatic attitudes to complex matters but they are not lawyers and many of their most adamant assertions will wilt under the judicial gaze. The parties' lawyers should check the legal basis of the expert's figures, particularly where terms like 'preliminaries', 'claims' or '*contras*' are used.

It is sometimes thought that the interlocutory proceedings of litigation are merely formal, and that the court will be able to do justice at trial. This is frequently a mistake. Even if a case is not settled before trial, the conduct of the interlocutory stages will usually have caused one party materially to improve his position, and may have practically guaranteed him a judgment which he could not possibly have relied upon at the outset of proceedings.

The plaintiff begins by issuing a writ usually marked 'Official Referees' Business'. Sometimes the statement of claim is endorsed on the writ or served with it; on other occasions it can be served at another time but no later than 14 days after the defendant has given notice of intention to defend the action unless time is extended either by agreement or by the courts. In practice, it may be some weeks before the statement of claim is served.

If the writ is issued out of a district registry there may be a skirmish as to whether the action be tried in the district registry or in the central office in London.

Once the statement of claim has been served then it is not uncommon for the plaintiff to take out an Ord 14, Ord 14A or Order 29 summons, or for the defendant to take out a section 4 summons. If one or both of these summonses is opposed it can take six months or more for both summonses to be disposed of.

The parties then resume the process of pleadings. Commonly, the statement of claim is followed by a defence and counterclaim which is in turn followed by the plaintiff's reply and defence to counterclaim. In theory, these pleadings ought to follow within 14 days of each other (Ord 18, rr 2 and 3) but in practice this time is almost never sufficient in a building case, and time for the service of pleadings is extended by consent or pursuant to the issue of a time summons under Ord 3, r 5. In practice, the time to close of pleadings in building contract cases in the High Court is more usually counted in months than in weeks.

In many cases, there are further summonses before trial often based upon failure or alleged failure of one or other party to give proper discovery, or to give particulars in the form requested or ordered by the Official Referee. It is comparatively rare for the parties to fail to settle before trial.

It is misleading to regard building contract litigation as following preordained steps. To adopt a 'check list' approach can be particularly disastrous and lead to great delay and expense. Skilfully conducted, the litigation is in some respects like a game of chess. Each party tries to take the initiative where it can, and is constantly adjusting its position in the light of the other party's position. During the proceedings, the confidence of one party usually grows at the expense of the confidence of the other. It becomes clear who is likely to win and the parties settle. Sometimes a party can achieve an overwhelming advantage quite early, at the Ord 14 stage for example. Sometimes, he gradually builds up an advantage, and by continually seeking particulars and admissions he at last persuades his opponent that the latter is not going to be able to put up a good enough case.

There are some sorts of litigation, such as actions by landlords for possession of premises, where it is at trial that the action is won or lost. It is rare for the trial of a building contract case to represent an attractive prospect for either party. Ordinarily, the underlying purpose of each step in the litigation is to force the other party into a mood for settlement on the right terms.

2 Information technology in High Court proceedings

There are a number of respects in which the conduct of building contract litigation has become affected by the increasing availability of computer technology.

Most solicitors in the field gave up the use of typewriters a long time ago in favour of word processors. When serving lengthy pleadings, statements, requests for particulars, etc, it is now common also to provide a floppy disk containing the text of the document being served.

In large cases, lists of documents are now usually prepared in the form of databases instead of word processed documents. This can considerably ease the task of preparing the list of documents, and can considerably assist in the task of keeping track of the documents as the case progresses. Again, it is good practice for the parties to exchange these databases in data form.

In 1992, the Official Referees' Solicitors Association published a 'Protocol on Information Technology' (the ORSA Protocol), which not only contains some guidance for solicitors as to how to use information technology, but also sets out some suggested procedures as to how information should be exchanged (see Appendix C).

The courts have generally shown themselves to be receptive to the opportunities afforded by information technology. By way of example, in *Hastie & Jankerson v McMahon* (1990) *The Times* 3 April, the courts held that service by fax constituted good service provided that the document was complete and legible and that it had been received by the person for whom it was intended. The court of one of the Official Referees — His Honour Judge Peter Bowsher QC — had been fitted out with video camera equipment which enables a document being shown to a witness to be simultaneously broadcast on to television screens around the court. During trials, the Official Referees have shown themselves to be tolerant of solicitors and counsel operating notebook computers in court. Armed with a notebook computer and some text retrieval software, it is possible for a solicitor or barrister to locate very rapidly the instance of any given word within the data contained on the notebook computer. Because of this, parties will often, in a complex case, scan the important documents into a computer using Optical Character Recognition (OCR) equipment in order to provide a body of data that may be searched in these circumstances. Those unused to the process are sometimes surprised by the ability of counsel, when cross-examining, to pick up references scattered among thousands of documents; this trick is often performed with the assistance of text retrieval software.

In lengthy cases, a transcript of proceedings is often necessary, and again modern methods offer considerable advantages over the traditional transcriber. A few companies offer the facility of a transcript that is prepared in electronic form virtually instantaneously. At the end of every day, a transcript can be provided of the day's proceedings in hard copy and/or floppy disk form. Again, the latter will enable text retrieval systems to locate, within a few seconds, any occurrence of a given word. In a lengthy trial, where the transcripts will soon occupy several lever arch files, this facility is extremely useful.

In delay claims, a Retrospective Delay Analysis is often carried out with the assistance of computers — see Chapter 21. The project in question may well have been planned with the assistance of project planning software such as 'Open Plan' or 'Artemis'; obtaining electronic copies of the datafiles used on the project can provide a good springboard for the necessary analysis work.

The text of the ORSA Protocol is reproduced at Appendix C.

Chapter 9

Summary judgment and interim payment

It has always been the case that building contract litigation tends to take a substantial period of time to come to trial. It is not uncommon for a case to take a year or more before the pleadings are complete, and even waiting for a trial date can, in a substantial case, mean a delay of as much as three years.

Plaintiffs have occasionally sought to force the pace by making demand for their claims pursuant to s 123 of the Insolvency Act 1986; the Companies Court has consistently prevented plaintiffs from allowing winding up petitions from being used as a form of pressure in this way.

Prior to the extension in 1980 of Ord 29 to commercial cases, Ord 14 provided the only substantial means of avoiding delay on the part of a defendant. Ord 14 and Ord 29 now provide a double-barrelled weapon which is of some importance in building cases. The recent addition of Ord 14A enabling points of law, or the construction of documents, to be considered summarily in certain circumstances adds another weapon to the armoury.

1 The importance of Ord 14 and Ord 29

Judgment under Ord 14 for the whole of the sum claimed amounts to a final determination of the plaintiff's claim, subject to an appeal. Such a judgment has considerable advantages in terms of speed and cost. Experience shows that, as a very rough guide, the cost of obtaining an Ord 14 judgment might be about one-fifth or one-sixth of the cost of obtaining a judgment at trial. The time saving varies from case to case, but might be something in the order of two years.

There are other advantages of Ord 29 and/or Ord 14 for a plaintiff that are less widely recognised. In particular, Ord 29 and/or Ord 14 can be an effective way of bringing the minds of the defendant and his advisers to bear upon the issues of the litigation. It is very common for defendants to put from their minds in the early stages of litigation precisely how they will defend a claim. Although pleadings are intended to set out the issues, they all too often represent nothing more than a catalogue of assertions and points of law that might or might not avail the party putting them forward. Once they are served, the pleadings are often ignored by the parties until trial itself, when the parties finally decide how to present their respective cases. Different considerations apply to the defendant's affidavit to show cause against an Ord 29 and/ or Ord 14 application. It is not sufficient for the defendant to deny the claim generally (*Wallingford v Mutual Society* (1880) 5 App Cas 685). A defendant who raises transparently spurious matters in his defence at Ord 29 and/or Ord 14 will merely irritate the court and increase the chances of an order being made or a judgment being given against him. The realism induced in a defendant's mind by an Ord 29 and/or Ord 14 application can not only discourage him from subsequently raising spurious matters in his defence but can also force him to consider more carefully whether or not he ought to make an early realistic offer of settlement.

These considerations can sometimes be sufficient to make an Ord 29 and/or Ord 14 application attractive to a plaintiff in circumstances where there is only an outside prospect of the plaintiff being awarded a substantial order or judgment.

In broad terms, the factors influencing the decision whether or not to make an Ord 14 application are the same whether the contract in question contains an arbitration clause or not. Generally, where a claim or a part of a claim is within the scope of Ord 14, then the court will give judgment under Ord 14 and refer the balance of the dispute, if any, to arbitration (*Ellis Mechanical Services Ltd v Wates Construction* (1976) 2 BLR 57), also *Imodco v Wimpey and Taylor Woodrow* (1988) 40 BLR 1. The court has similar powers in respect of Ord 29 applications (*Scobie v Clayton* [1900] CILL 565 but they will be used less readily. Order 14 can sometimes have a particular attraction for plaintiffs where there is an arbitration clause, if the plaintiffs would benefit from some point of law being put before the court rather than before an arbitrator without legal qualifications.

The court may give an Ord 14 judgment for a part only of the plaintiff's claim; and if there is a part of the plaintiff's claim that is within the scope of Ord 29 and/or Ord 14, then it is usually in the plaintiff's interest to seek a judgment or order in respect of that part, even if it is a comparatively minor part of the total claim. This not only accelerates the time when the plaintiff can receive some of the money but also often represents a tactical advantage. In an area of law where the rate of settlement is so high, it is important for the plaintiff to try to sap the enthusiasm and confidence of the defendant as quickly as possible. A defendant will often resist a summons for a minor part of the claim without any real thought, as though this were a reflex reaction. If such a defendant loses an early skirmish under Ord 29 and/or Ord 14 he will often form a less sanguine view of his overall prospects.

A word of warning, however. The courts, and particularly the Court of Appeal, have in recent years shown a marked shift of attitude, now discouraging Ord 14 and Ord 29 applications that would hitherto have succeeded. Much depends, of course, on the facts and the individual judge, but bear in mind that a higher threshold now applies than was the case during the 1970s and 1980s. See for example, *Home and Overseas v Mentor* [1989] 3 All ER 74.

2 The grounds for summary judgment

Order 14, r 1, prescribes the ground upon which the plaintiff may apply to the court for summary judgment, namely that 'the defendant has no defence to a claim included in the writ, or to a particular part of such claim, or has no defence to such claim or part except as to the amount of any damages claimed'. Further, the application must be supported by an affidavit verifying the facts upon which the claim, or the part of the claim to which the application relates, is based and stating that in the deponent's belief there is no defence to that claim or part, as the case may be, or no defence as to the amount of any damages claimed (Ord 14, r 2).

It seems that the test as to whether there is a defence is objective for the purposes of Ord 14, r 1; and that the test of whether there is a defence for the purposes of Ord 14, r 2, is a subjective one (ie does the plaintiff believe that there is no defence?). That subjective test, however, only goes to the question of whether it is proper for the plaintiff to swear his affidavit in support in the required form. For the purpose of determining whether or not the Ord 14 application is a proper one, the court will decide not whether the plaintiff or the defendant believes there is a defence but whether there is in fact a defence. The court must decide this without trying whatever matter the defendant seeks to put forward by way of defence, and accordingly the word 'defence' has been construed as meaning '*bona fide* defence', 'fairly arguable defence', 'reasonable ground of defence', or 'good defence on the merits'.

In theory, it is only half the battle under Ord 14 for the plaintiff to show that the defendant has no defence. Ord 14, r 3, envisages that the defendant might satisfy the court that there is an issue or question in dispute which ought to be tried or that there ought, for some other reason, to be a trial of the claim or part of the claim. Ord 14, r 4, permits a defendant to 'show cause against an application under r 1'. In practical terms, r 3 and r 4 add little in commercial building contract cases to the 'no defence' test save to strengthen the element of discretion inevitably present at Ord 14 hearings. The court operates a single test: is it abundantly plain from the evidence on affidavit that the defendant is going to lose and is merely playing for time or being hopelessly optimistic about his prospects at trial?

The degree of proof required from the plaintiff varies from case to case. In the case of a claim by a contractor for payment, the certificate of the architect that the sum claimed is due is usually regarded as very cogent evidence, and is generally sufficient unless the defendant is able to put forward a *bona fide* set-off or counterclaim. Where there is no certification procedure, the court will usually accept the contractor's valuation of work done unless the defendant can show that there are good grounds to suggest that the claim is, in fact, excessive. In the absence of something convincing from the defendant, the court does not require a plaintiff contractor to adduce expert evidence as to the reasonableness of the sum claimed.

The courts look at the surrounding circumstances as they appear from the affidavit evidence. Where, for example, a contractor does work for an employer it sometimes happens that the employer makes no payment at all and raises no complaint as to the work until he makes his affidavit in reply to an Ord 14 summons, where he alleges defects to a value slightly exceeding the cost of the works. The employer in such circumstances has an uphill task in attracting the sympathy of the court under Ord 14, but may nevertheless be able to do enough to escape judgment.

A notable feature of building contract litigation is the preponderance of cross-claims.

A set-off is a defence, and is treated as such for Ord 14 purposes. To be fully successful, however, it must at least match the amount of the claim. If the defendant establishes a set-off for a lesser amount of the claim, then the plaintiff has judgment for the balance (*Hanak v Green* [1958] 2 QB 9). It is not sufficient, however, for a defendant merely to allege the existence of a set-off; he must, subject to express contractual provisions, set up a plausible and properly quantified cross-claim if he is to extinguish or reduce his liability under Ord 14. The authority frequently quoted in support of this proposition is *Modern Engineering v Gilbert-Ash* [1973] 3 WLR 421, but this case must be read in the light of the express provision in the contract in the case entitling the defendants to raise any '*bona fide*' set-off, and the court held this provision to allow the defendants a subjective test. In *Stewart Gill Limited v Horatio Myer & Co. Ltd* [1992] 2 All ER 257, a clause in a contract disallowing any set-off against sums due was held to be unreasonable under s 13 of the Unfair Contract Terms Act 1977.

It was once thought, following *Dawnays v F G Minter and Trollope & Colls* [1971] 1 WLR 1205, that there could be no set-off against an architect's certificate for payment but that such a certificate was to be treated like a bill of exchange. The *Minter* case was, however, overruled on this point by *Modern Engineering v Gilbert-Ash* [1973] 3 WLR 421, and there is now no rule precluding a defendant from resisting judgment under Ord 14 upon the ground of a sufficiently established set-off or counterclaim. In *Enco Civil Engineering Ltd v Zeus International Development Limited* (1991) 28 CLR 25, judgment under Ord 14 was refused in a situation where an engineer's certificate had been challenged and therefore could be cancelled.

There has been some speculation as to whether the position has altered following *Northern Regional Health Authority v Derek Crouch Construction Co Ltd* [1984] 2 All ER 175. It seems that for Ord 14 purposes it has not. In C *M Pillings v Kent Investments Ltd* (1985) 30 BLR 80 CA, it was common ground that the counterclaim raised issues that were the exclusive province of an arbitrator. The plaintiff contractor sought Ord 14 judgment on an interim payment certificate. The defendant employer challenged that certificate and sought a stay under s 4 of the Arbitration Act 1950. The court found as follows:

(1) payment of the certificate was not a condition precedent to the defendant's right to arbitration;

(2) the defendant was entitled to set off its claim challenging the certificate against the plaintiff's claim under the certificate.

The court did, however, look at the nature of the defendant's challenge to the certificate, and found that it was not 'clear-cut'. As a condition of granting the stay the defendant was required to give security as to some 70 per cent of the certified sum.

It is not entirely established what degree of proof is required from a defendant seeking to resist an Ord 14 judgment by reference only to a set-off or a counterclaim. In practice, it seems to be much less than the degree of proof required by the plaintiff upon his claim and, although this proposition cannot be stated with any certainty, it may be that the result depends upon the court's view of the set-off or counterclaim as follows:

(1) if the court thinks that there is a genuine cross-claim, the cross-claim will operate to extinguish or reduce the defendant's liability under Ord 14 and leave to defend will be given accordingly;

(2) if the court is less convinced as to the validity of the cross-claim, it will give judgment for the plaintiff, stay execution upon that judgment and give directions as to the trial of the counterclaim;

(3) if it suspects, but cannot be sure, that the cross-claim is a sham it will order the defendant to pay the amount of the plaintiff's claim into court, and give directions for the trial of the counterclaim.

A defendant cannot defend himself in Ord 14 proceedings by pointing to an arbitration clause in the contract. If the defendant has good grounds for a stay of proceedings under the Arbitration Act 1950, s 4, then the court will give judgment under Ord 14 for such part of the claim as falls within the scope of Ord 14, and only then grant the stay. In *Ellis Mechanical Services Ltd v Wates Construction Ltd* (1976) 2 BLR 57 Lord Denning said:

There is a point on the contract which I might mention upon this. There is a general arbitration clause. Any dispute or difference arising on the matter is to go to arbitration. It seems to me that if a case comes before the Court in which, although a sum is not exactly quantified and although it is not admitted, nevertheless the Court is able, on an application of this kind, to give summary judgment for such sum as appears to be indisputably due, and to refer the balance to arbitration. The defendants cannot insist on the whole going to arbitration by simply saying that there is a difference or a dispute about it. If the

Court sees that there is a sum which is indisputably due, then the Court can give judgment for that sum and let the rest go to arbitration . . .

It is plain from the terms of Ord 14, r 1, that it is not necessary for the plaintiff to have quantified his claim if he is to obtain judgment under Ord 14. If he is able to establish the fact of the defendant's liability but not the amount of it then the court can give judgment for damages to be assessed. In such a case interest is payable from the date of the summary judgment even though the amount of the damages is not then known (*O'Connor v Amus Bridgman Abattoirs Ltd* (1990) *The Times*, 13 April). But see also *Putty v Hopkinson* [1990] 1 All ER 1057, where the judge exercised his discretion such that judgment was given in a form which did not attract interest.

It is also not necessary for a plaintiff to seek an Ord 14 judgment against all of several defendants. It is provided by Ord 14, r 8, that where a plaintiff obtains judgment against one defendant he may proceed with the action against any other defendant. This rule does not, however, overrule the cases summarised in the notes in the *White Book* at para 14/8/2. A plaintiff must exercise especial care when obtaining judgment against a joint (cf joint and several) contractor, or an agent or principal.

It is, of course, no answer for a defendant merely to say that he has the right to be indemnified by some third party (*Thorne v Steel* [1878] WN 215 CA).

Conflicting decisions have been given in the past as to whether or not the courts will consider difficult points of law under Ord 14. This conflict has now been solved by the introduction of Ord 14A which specifically provides that the courts may now determine any question of law, or construction of any document, at any stage in the proceedings where it is suitable for determination without a full trial and where such determination will finally determine the entire cause or matter or any claim or issue in connection with it. Thus, either party may now apply for summary judgment on a point of law provided that the conditions set out in Ord 14A are fulfilled. In this regard 'suitability' means that it is essential that the relevant facts relating to the subject matter of the question should not be in dispute and that it can be dealt with without a full trial.

The courts do not have any wider powers at Ord 14 to grant relief than are stated in the rules, nor any residual or inherent jurisdiction to grant relief where it would be just to do so (*C.E. Heath v Ceram* [1988] 1 All ER 203).

3 The availability of Ord 29

The relevant parts of Ord 29, r 11 and Ord 29, r 12 are as follows:

11 — (1) If on the hearing of an application under rule 10 in an action for damages, the Court is satisfied:
(a) that the defendant against whom the order is sought (in this paragraph

referred to as 'the respondent') has admitted liability for the plaintiff's damages, or
(b) the plaintiff has obtained judgment against the respondent for damages to be assessed, or
(c) that, if the action proceeded to trial, the plaintiff would obtain judgment for substantial damages against the respondent or, where there are two or more respondents, against any of them,
the Court may, if it thinks fit . . . order the respondent to make an interim payment of such amount as it thinks just, not exceeding a reasonable proportion of the damages which in the opinion of the Court are likely to be recovered by the plaintiff after taking into account any relevant contributory negligence and any set-off, cross-claim or counterclaim on which the respondent may be entitled to rely.
12 — If, on the hearing of an application under rule 10, the Court is satisfied —
(c) that if the action proceeded to trial the plaintiff would obtain judgment against the defendant for a substantial sum of money apart from any damages or costs, the Court may, if it thinks fit, and without prejudice to any contentions of the parties as to the nature or character of the sum to be paid by the defendant, order the defendant to make an interim payment of such amount as it thinks just, after taking into account any set-off, cross-claim or counterclaim on which the defendant may be entitled to rely.

These words should be wide enough to include virtually every sort of money claim in relation to a building contract dispute if the evidence is strong enough. Among the sorts of claim that may be within the scope of Ord 29 are the following:

(1) payment for work done under a building contract (under Ord 29, r 12(c));
(2) the cost of remedial work where the defendant is palpably in breach of contract or liable in negligence (under Ord 29, r 11(1)(c)).

The rules do not say what standard of proof is required under Ord 29, r (11)(1)(c), or Ord 29, r 12(c) but the courts have shown themselves inclined to demand a similar standard of proof to that required in Ord 14 cases. Indeed the Court of Appeal appeared to take this for granted in *Rapid Building Group Ltd v Ealing Family Housing Association Ltd* (1984) 29 BLR 5.

In *Shanning v Wimpey* [1988] 3 All ER 475, it was said that the test was a balance of probabilities but to a high standard. In *British & Commonwealth v Quadrex* [1989] QB 842, the Court of Appeal said that interim payment will not be ordered where unconditional leave to defend is given on an Ord 14 application, but may be so ordered where only conditional leave to defend is given.

It is not a bar to an order for interim payment that a previous application has been made for interim payment, whether successfully or not (Ord 29, r 10(5)).

It is not clear what is the position where the plaintiff's claim, or the defendant's answer to it, is wholly or partly within the certification scheme of a contract containing an arbitration clause (which is the case with most claims under formal building contracts such as the JCT contracts). The point was considered at first instance in *Derek Crouch Construction Co Ltd v Northern Regional Health Authority* (1983) 24 BLR 60. In that case, Judge Sir William Stabb QC found that he was not barred from awarding an interim payment either by the absence of certification or by the fact that he was dealing with an interim claim under a contract which was still current, although he recognised that an award by the court concurrent with the architect's continuing administration of the contract might well be undesirable. However, the Court of Appeal decision arising out of the same contract, in *Northern Regional Health Authority v Crouch and Crown* (see p 87) overturned the first of these findings.

It is not any bar to an order for interim payment that a claim appears by counterclaim (Ord 29, r 18). The order is also available for third party claims. In practice the sheer volume of material may operate as a bar to recovery of an interim payment. In the *Crouch v Northern Regional Health Authority* case, Judge Sir William Stabb QC had before him a claim by the plaintiffs particularised in great detail in an exhibit of some 100 pages together with the defendant's detailed commentary running to over 150 pages. The judge said 'No doubt I might be able to arrive at a useful estimate by a prolonged consideration of the many issues which will be the subject matter of a future hearing, but that is not what an application for an interim payment should properly require'. In declining to make an order for interim payment, it seems that the judge was also influenced by the long period of time that had elapsed before the claim was made.

It is not appropriate to make an interim payment order in cases where the plaintiff is unable to show which of a number of defendants will be liable (*Breeze v McKinnon & Son Ltd* (1985) 32 BLR 41 CA; *Ricci Burns Ltd v Toole* [1989] 3 All ER 478).

4 Procedure

Neither the Ord 14, Ord 14A nor the Ord 29 procedure can commence until the plaintiff has served the writ and the defendant has acknowledged service of the writ. In the case of Ord 14 the plaintiff must have served the statement of claim (which may or may not have been endorsed on the writ).

The procedure is commenced by the plaintiff issuing a summons. If the plaintiff is seeking judgment under Ord 14 only (not usually wise, as indicated at the beginning of this chapter) he should follow the form of either Queen's Bench Master's practice form PF11 or PF12, according to whether the plaintiff seeks judgment for the whole of this claim or for part only.

It is expressly provided by Ord 29, r 10(2) that an application under Ord 29 may be included in a summons under Ord 14. The wording for the summons will vary from case to case but a typical form of application is as follows:

Let all parties attend the Official Referee in Chambers
on   day the   day of   199, at   o'clock in the noon on the hearing of an Application by the Plaintiff for
- (i) judgment in this action against the Defendant for the sum of £   , being one of the claims, namely the claim appearing at paragraph   of the Statement of Claim herein, together with interest, or
- (ii) final judgment in this action against the Defendant for damages to be assessed, and/or
- (iii) for an order requiring that the Defendant do make an interim payment to the Plaintiff of £   or such other sum as may be just

Take notice that a party intending to oppose this application or to apply for a stay of execution should send to the opposite party or his solicitor, to reach him not less than three days before the date above mentioned, a copy of any affidavit intended to be used.

Dated the   day of   199

This Summons was taken out by   of

Solicitors for the Plaintiff.

To:

In cases where proceedings are originally brought as Official Referees' Business (usually the sensible course) the Ord 29 and/or Ord 14 summons may be taken out as soon as the defendant has given notice of his intention to defend the action. Applications under Ord 29 should be made before an Official Referee other than the one assigned, the practice being for the applicant to mention the point to the judge's clerk when taking out the summons so that use can be made of the transfer machinery provided by Ord 36, r 7(3), (see *Fay*, para 71). This practice reflects Ord 29, r 15, whereby it is prohibited to communicate the fact of an order for interim payment to the court at trial until all questions of liability and quantum have been determined. The note in the *White Book* at paragraph 29/10/1 to the effect that applications for interim payment must be made before the Master or district judge does not apply to Official Referees' Business.

Where for some reason proceedings are commenced but not marked 'Official Referees Business', the plaintiff's proper course is generally to issue an Ord 29 and/or Ord 14 summons and application to the Official Referee returnable on the same date. The practice of the Queen's Bench Masters is to transfer the case together with the outstanding Ord 14 summons to the Official Referee. This should be done by consent or upon short appointment. The Queen's Bench Division Masters are not now usually prepared to hear Ord 29 and/or Ord 14 summonses in building cases.

It is usually in the plaintiff's interest to issue the summons as soon as the defendant has given notice of his intention to defend the action. If the summons is to be heard by an Official Referee then it must be served within three days of its issue. The service of an Ord 14 summons suspends the obligation on the defendant to serve a defence (Ord 18, r 2(2)). Indeed, if the plaintiff serves an Ord 14 summons, not only need the defendant not serve his defence but he should not serve his defence until the summons is heard (*Hobson v Monks* [1884] WN 8).

The summons is not required to be served personally but may be served by pre-paid post, at the address for service given by the defendant in the acknowledgment of service. The plaintiff's solicitor should, however, be careful to make a contemporaneous note as to the posting of the summons since an affidavit of service may later be required if the defendant does not acknowledge service or appear at the hearing of the Ord 14 summons.

If a summons is an Ord 14A summons, then the court will not determine the question of law or construction unless satisfied that both parties have had an opportunity of being heard on the question, or that both parties have consented to an order or judgment on such determination. Thus, great care must be employed in the service of a summons under this Order so that the court can be satisfied that the other party has had the opportunity of being heard.

In the Official Referees' Division standard directions are now endorsed on all Ord 14 and Ord 29 summonses requiring that:

(1) within three days of the issue of a summons, a summons and the evidence in support must be served on the defendants; and

(2) if the defendants wish to contest the summons, they must within 24 days of its issue, serve evidence on the plaintiffs; and

(3) the plaintiffs must not less than two days before the date fixed for the hearing of the summons, file with the court a paginated bundle of affidavits and exhibits (or copies); and

(4) any party wishing to obtain changes in the standard directions, including time limited, or additional directions, must issue a summons for directions.

The purpose of these directions is to prevent summonses having to be adjourned because of the late delivery of evidence.

In order to comply with the directions it is necessary to serve the affidavit in support of the summons within three days of the issue of the summons. In practical terms this will mean that the summons and the affidavit in support will be served at the same time, although this is not strictly necessary. In other divisions of the High Court, the requirement under Ord 14, 2(3) applies, namely, that a summons, a copy of the affidavit in support and of any exhibits referred to therein must be served on the defendants not less than ten clear days before the return day. In neither case is there a specific requirement that all these documents must be served together.

Where the summons or affidavit is served by first class post there is a rebuttable presumption that it will have been delivered on the day after posting (Master's Practice Direction No 26A).

The affidavit should not be sworn before any solicitor or commissioner for oaths from the plaintiff's firm of solicitors (Ord 41, r 8).

5 The order under Ord 14

The most common orders made under Ord 14 are to the following effect:

(1) that the plaintiff should have judgment for the whole of his claim;
(2) that the plaintiff should have judgment for a part of his claim, directions for trial being given as to the balance;
(3) that the defendant should have leave to defend the action but that the action be tried as a short cause;
(4) that the defendant's leave to defend the action should be conditional upon payment of the whole or part of the claim into court;
(5) that the plaintiff should have judgment upon his claim, but that execution be stayed pending trial of the defendant's counterclaim; or
(6) that the defendant should have leave to defend the whole action. It can be seen that there is a variety of orders possible which fall between outright success for one or other of the parties.

6 The order for interim payment under Ord 29

The Court of Appeal considered the appropriate amount of an interim order in a claim for damages in *Newport (Essex) Engineering v Press & Shear Machinery* (1981) 24 BLR 71. The court summarised the principles as follows:

The plaintiffs particularised their claim for damages under five heads:

(i)   consequential loss of profits;
(ii)   installation costs;
(iii) irrecoverable overheads;
(iv)   lost tax advantages;
(v)   damage to floor.

Before I examine these claims and consider how they were dealt with by the learned Official Referee, I think it desirable to make some general observations.

The power to make or refuse an order is discretionary so that this court will only interfere on the well established principles. An interim payment is defined by rule 9 as 'a payment on account of any damages the defendant may be held liable to pay to the plaintiff'.

Rule 11(1) provides that the payment on account is not to exceed 'a reasonable proportion of the damages which, in the opinion of the court, are likely to be recovered by the plaintiff'.

Lastly, if the court decides to make an order, the amount is to be such 'as it thinks just'.

The court has to make an estimate of the damages which are 'likely to be recovered'; that is, when the issue is finally determined. The ease or difficulty in making such an estimate will vary enormously from case to case. In some cases it is quite impossible to make a useful estimate without hearing the case out. Are plaintiffs in such cases to be excluded from obtaining an interim payment? I think not, for, on the material available to the court hearing the application, the court may be in a position to say 'the plaintiff should recover at least £x and is likely to recover more or a great deal more'.

In such a case, I do not think it would be wrong to say that £x itself is a reasonable proportion. In contrast, if the court can say 'the plaintiff should recover at least £x, but is unlikely to recover more', then £x itself becomes the likely award and a reasonable proportion should be something substantially less than £x.

I do not think it desirable that applications for interim payments should turn into long drawn out investigations into the very issues which are to form the subject matter of a future hearing. The wide discretion given to the court, coupled with the safety net for the defendants in rule 17, show that these applications should be decided on a fairly broad approach, with a minimum of expense to the parties.

Rule 17 authorises the court at any stage in the proceedings, including the giving of a final judgment, to order repayment of all or any part of an interim payment.

Chapter 10

Section 4 summonses

Building contracts frequently contain an arbitration clause which provides, in broad terms, that if there is a dispute between the parties then that dispute should be referred to arbitration. If there is such a clause, a party may nonetheless issue a writ in the High Court or take proceedings in the county court. If he does so, the defendant may, however, apply to the court for an order staying those court proceedings so that an arbitration may take place. If the arbitration agreement is a domestic arbitration agreement, he does so under the Arbitration Act 1950, s 4(1), which provides as follows:

If any party to an arbitration agreement, or any person claiming through or under him, commences any legal proceedings in any court against any other party to the agreement, or any person claiming through or under him, in respect of any matter agreed to be referred, any party to those legal proceedings may at any time after appearance, and before delivering any pleadings or taking any other step in the proceedings, apply to that court to stay the proceedings, and that court or a judge thereof, if satisfied that there is no sufficient reason why the matter should not be referred in accordance with that agreement, and that the applicant was, at the time when proceedings were commenced, and still remains, ready and willing to do all things necessary to the proper conduct of the arbitration, may make an order staying the proceedings.

The court has a certain discretion under s 4, and there is substantial case law upon the circumstances in which the court will exercise that discretion. The plaintiff has a number of potential grounds upon which to resist a section 4 summons, and thereby keep the matter in the court. Those grounds are considered at pages 124 et seq.

The burden of proof is twofold. In the first place, the defendant must show that he is within the scope of s 4. In practical terms, this means that he must show:

(1) the existence of a valid arbitration agreement covering the dispute;

(2) that he has not delivered any legal pleadings or taken any other steps in the proceedings; and

(3) that he was, at the time when the proceedings were commenced, and still remains ready and willing to do all things necessary to the proper conduct of the arbitration.

121

In the second place, if the defendant can satisfy the court as to these matters, the burden of proof shifts to the plaintiff to show that there is a material reason why the matter should not be referred to arbitration.

Where there is an international element in the arbitration agreement, such that it is not a domestic arbitration agreement within the meaning of the Arbitration Act 1975, s 1(4), then the position is different. Whereas under the Arbitration Act 1950, s 4, the court *may* stay the court proceedings, under the Arbitration Act 1975, s 1, the court *must* stay the court proceedings. The relevant parts of the Arbitration Act 1975, s 1, are as follows:

1 — (1) If any party to an arbitration agreement to which this section applies, or any person claiming through or under him, commences any legal proceedings in any court against any other party to the agreement, or any person claiming through or under him, in respect of any matter agreed to be referred, any party to the proceedings may at any time after appearance, and before delivering any pleadings or taking any other steps in the proceedings, apply to the court to stay the proceedings; and the court, unless satisfied that the arbitration agreement is null and void, inoperative or incapable of being performed or that there is not in fact any dispute between the parties with regard to the matter agreed to be referred, shall make an order staying the proceedings.

(2) This section applies to any arbitration agreement which is not a domestic arbitration agreement; and neither s 4(1) of the Arbitration Act 1950 nor s 4 of the Arbitration Act (Northern Ireland) 1937 shall apply to an arbitration agreement to which this section applies.

(3) . . .

(4) In this section 'domestic arbitration agreement' means an arbitration agreement which does not provide, expressly or by implication, for arbitration in a State other than the United Kingdom and to which neither:

(a) an individual who is a national of, or habitually resident in, any State other than the United Kingdom; nor

(b) a body corporate which is incorporated in, or whose central management and control is exercised in, any State other than the United Kingdom; is a party at the time the proceedings are commenced.

For the effect of the Arbitration Act 1975, s 1, see p 172 and the case of *Associated Bulk Carriers v Koch Shipping* (1977) 7 BLR 18.

In addition to its powers under the Arbitration Act 1950, s 4, and the Arbitration Act 1975, s 1, the High Court has an inherent jurisdiction to stay proceedings under the Supreme Court Act 1981, s 49(3) (*Roussel-Uclaf v G D Searle & Co Ltd* [1978] 1 Lloyd's Rep 225). Section 49(3) provides as follows:

Nothing in this Act shall affect the power of the Court of Appeal or the High Court to stay any proceedings before it, where it thinks fit to do so, either of its own motion or on the application of any person, whether or not a party to the proceedings.

A commentary upon the Supreme Court Act 1981, s 49(3), appears at paras 5204 et seq of Part 2 of the *White Book*. It is not usual to rely upon this section when seeking a stay upon the ground of a domestic arbitration agreement since the court has a wide discretion under the Arbitration Act 1950, s 4. A commentary to s 4 appears at para 571 et seq of Part 2 of the *White Book*.

1 Practice

If a defendant is sued in relation to a contract containing an arbitration clause, he should decide as quickly as possible whether he is content to have the matter heard in the court or whether he wishes to have the matter referred to arbitration. If the latter is chosen, he should issue his section 4 summons as soon as possible after acknowledging service of the writ. The reference in s 4 to 'appearance' should now be regarded as a reference to 'acknowledgment of service' (Ord 12, r 10).

The application under s 4 is made by summons. There is no prescribed form for this summons; a typical wording is:

... for an order that these proceedings be stayed pursuant to s 4 of the Arbitration Act 1950, and that the plaintiffs do pay the defendants the costs of these proceedings, including the costs of this application.

Although not prescribed, an affidavit is also required in practice from the defendant, and the affidavit should include the matters in respect of which the burden of proof rests upon the defendant (see page 121).

Save that there is a general rule that summonses should be served two clear days before the return day (Ord 32, r 3), there is no express guidance in the court rules as to when the summons and the affidavit should be served. In practice, however, it is generally thought that a minimum of several days is appropriate and it is reasonable to allow the plaintiff time to prepare and serve an affidavit in reply.

It is an anomaly of the rules of the Supreme Court that there is no provision for an automatic extension of time for service of a defence where a defendant issues a section 4 summons. It is, however, universally accepted that the issue of a section 4 summons does have this effect.

It frequently happens that a defendant issues a section 4 summons after the plaintiff has issued an Ord 14 summons, or that a plaintiff issues an Ord 14 summons after the defendant has issued a section 4 summons. In these cases, it is appropriate for both summonses to be heard at the same time, and an *ex parte* application should be made to the court for leave to make the second summons returnable at the same time as the first. Further, it is common for a plaintiff to make a single affidavit in support of his Ord 14 application and in opposition to the defendant's section 4 summons, and for the defendant to make a single affidavit in opposition to the Ord 14 summons and in support of his section 4 summons.

In an appropriate case, the court can order a stay upon the condition that the whole matter should be referred to a legally qualified arbitrator (*John Mowlem v Carlton Gate* [1990] CILL 584.

2 No step in the proceedings

The defendant should issue his section 4 summons 'before delivering any pleadings or taking any other steps in the proceedings'. If he has taken a step in the proceedings, that is usually fatal to him.

The question of what is and what is not a 'step' has been the subject of much litigation; the leading cases are reviewed at para 5718 of Part 2 in the *White Book*. The taking out of a time summons by the defendant does constitute a step in the action (*Fords Hotel v Bartlett* [1896] AC 1), but it is clear that it is not a step in the action for a defendant merely to write to the plaintiff asking for an extension of time and obtaining it (*Brighton Marine etc Co v Woodhouse* [1893] 2 Ch 486). It is not unknown for a plaintiff's solicitor to refuse an extension of time with the specific hope that the defendant will take out a time summons and thereby lose the chance of having the action stayed under s 4. Opposition to an Ord 14 summons may constitute a step in the action, but a defendant does not take a step in the action by serving an affidavit in reply to an Ord 14 summons after or at the same time as issuing a section 4 summons (*Pitchers Ltd v Plaza (Queensbury) Ltd* [1940] 1 All ER 151). Such an affidavit is, however, a step in the action if not preceded or accompanied by a section 4 summons, even if the affidavit invites the court to consider whether the matter should be dealt with by way of arbitration (*Turner & Goudy v McConnell* (1985) 30 BLR 108 CA).

The article at para 5718 of Part 2 of the *White Book* suggests:

The distinction seems to be that negotiation or correspondence between parties or their solicitors does not constitute a step in the action, but an application by summons or motion, or the service of a pleading, does.

It appears, however, that the courts are now drawing the dividing line in a different way. In *Eagle Star Insurance Co Ltd v Yuval Insurance Co Ltd* [1978] 1 Lloyd's Rep 357, the defendants' application to strike out the plaintiffs' endorsement on the writ was found not to constitute a step in the action. Lord Denning said:

What then is a 'step in the proceedings'? It has been discussed in several cases. On principle it is a step by which the defendant evinces an election to abide by the Court proceedings and waives his right to ask for an arbitration. Like any election, it must be an equivocal act done with knowledge of the material circumstances.

A 'step in the proceedings' must be one which impliedly affirms the correctness of the proceedings and the willingness of the defendant to go along with a determination by the courts of law instead of arbitration.

Similarly, in *Blue Flame Mechanical Services Limited v David Lord Engineering Limited* [1992] CILL 760 it was held that a step in the action which bars a defendant from staying proceedings to arbitration is a significant procedural act, done or acquiesced in by the defendant, with the intention, objectively viewed, of electing to litigate rather than arbitrate.

Again, in *Roussel-Uclaf v G D Searle & Co Ltd* [1978] 1 Lloyd's Rep 225 it was found that the defendants had not taken a step in the action by defending an application for an interlocutory injunction; in *Skopos v Home Life* (1988) 5 CLD 03 22 the defendant did not take a step in the action by ticking a box on a printed form saying he wished to transfer the proceedings to London.

3 Ready and willing

The defendant must show that he was, at the time when the proceedings were commenced, and still remains, ready and willing to do all things necessary to the proper conduct of the arbitration. This should appear from his affidavit in support (*Piercy v Young* [1879] 14 Ch D 209).

There is a point upon limitation which has been argued more than once. It is as follows. It sometimes happens that a plaintiff issues a writ in the High Court at the last moment. The writ is sometimes not served for some time, and the limitation period has expired by the time the defendant issues a section 4 summons. The plaintiff then realises that he has overlooked the Limitation Act 1980, s 34, which provides that for the purposes of arbitration proceedings, the test is whether or not the claimant has served a notice upon the respondent requiring him to concur in the appointment of an arbitrator. The claim would therefore be statute barred in any arbitration proceedings. The plaintiff then asks the defendant whether he would waive any limitation point in arbitration proceedings, and the defendant declines to make any such waiver. The plaintiff then argues at the hearing of the section 4 summons that the defendant, by declining to make that waiver, is not ready and willing to do all things necessary to the proper conduct of the arbitration. This argument generally fails upon the authority of *W Bruce Ltd v J Strong* [1951] 2 KB 447. The authority of the *Bruce* case is, however, weakened partly by the fact that the Court of Appeal declined to follow it upon another point in *Taunton-Collins v Crombie* [1964] 1 WLR 633, and partly because of the terms of the particular arbitration clause in question. Indeed, it seems that *Bruce v Strong* was not followed by Bean J in *County and District Properties v Jenner*, although the point is not entirely clear from the report of the later judgment of Swanwick J, reported at [1976] 2 Lloyd's Rep 728.

A defendant may well be unable to show his willingness to do all things necessary to the proper conduct of the arbitration if he has declined to execute the RIBA's standard form of application for the appointment of an arbitrator; see p 166. A defendant should not be so keen to show his readiness and willingness to proceed with the arbitration as to encourage an arbitrator to proceed with an arbitration pending the hearing of a section 4 summons (*Doleman & Sons v Ossett Corporation* [1912] 3 KB 257).

4 No dispute

The defendant cannot insist on a matter going to arbitration where there is no dispute between the parties as to that matter (*Nova (Jersey) Knit Ltd v Kammgarn Spenneri GmbH* [1977] 1 WLR 713). There is authority for the proposition that this principle is widely applied in building contract cases. In *Ellis Mechanical Services Ltd v Wates Construction Ltd* (1976) 2 BLR 57 Lord Denning discussed this point (see the quotation on p 113).

The test as to whether there is a dispute for the purposes of s 4 is essentially the same as the test under Ord 14.

It is clear from the judgments that if appropriate the courts will give Ord 14 judgment for part of the claim, and refer the balance to arbitration (eg *Achital Luxfer v A J Dunning* (1989) Const LJ 47). In *Associated Bulk Carriers v Koch Shipping* (1977) 7 BLR 18 (a case under the Arbitration Act 1975) the Court of Appeal found itself unable to split the claim in this way. Differing views have been expressed as to this case; the editors of *Building Law Reports* suggest that it illustrates the limits of the principles enunciated in the *Ellis* case whereas Keating, at p 399, suggests that the position is different under the Arbitration Act 1975.

The court also has jurisdiction to order an interim payment under Ord 29 before granting a stay for the balance of the claim (*Imodco v Wimpey and Taylor Woodrow* (1988) 40 BLR 1 and *Scobie & Macintosh v Clayton Bowmore* (1990) 49 BLR 119).

5 The arbitration agreement

A defendant will succeed in obtaining a stay of the court proceedings under s 4 only if the court is satisfied that there is a valid arbitration agreement, and further that all (or all but a small part) of the relief claimed is within the scope of the arbitration agreement (*Ives & Barker v Willans* [1894] 2 Ch 478).

If there is a genuine dispute as to whether the contract (or the part of the contract which contains the arbitration clause) has ever regulated the legal position between the parties, the courts will not generally stay the court proceedings. In *Heyman v Darwins Ltd* [1942] AC 356, the House of Lords said:

If the dispute is whether the contract which contains the clause has ever been entered into at all, that issue cannot go to arbitration under the clause, for the party who denies that he has ever entered into the contract is thereby denying that he has ever joined in the submission. Similarly, if one party to the alleged contract is contending that it is void *ab initio* (because for example, the making of such a contract is illegal), the arbitration clause cannot operate for on this view the clause itself is also void.

Whilst these principles remain the law, there is something of a shift in climate towards arbitration. In *Harbour Assurance Co (UK) Limited v Kansa General International Insurance Co Ltd* [1992] 1 Lloyd's Rep 81, Steyn J held that whilst there were undoubtedly strong policy reasons for holding that an arbitration clause was capable of surviving initial invalidity, or illegality of the contract, he was bound to follow the decision in *Taylor & Son Limited v Barnett Trading Co Ltd* [1953] 1 WLR 562 to hold that an issue of illegality *ab initio*, ie from the very beginning, as opposed to invalidity of the contract subsequent thereto, was always a matter beyond the jurisdiction of an arbitrator. This decision is in keeping with the earlier case of *Heyman v Darwins Limited* (1942). The judge in the *Harbour Assurance* case did, however, go on to expound upon the policy advantages there would be in extending a separability principle — ie a principle that the arbitration clause is a separate and severable agreement from the contract in which it is contained.

The position is, however, clear where one party alleges (or both allege) that the contract has been repudiated, for an arbitrator does have jurisdiction to decide upon this point (*Heyman v Darwins Ltd*).

6 Jurisdiction to decide the dispute

It seems from the reasoning of the Court of Appeal in *Northern Regional Health Authority v Crouch & Crown* [1984] 2 WLR 676 that a defendant will ordinarily be able to succeed in a section 4 summons, thereby having the disputes heard by an arbitrator, if he can show that it is a necessary part of his case that any certificates issued under a JCT contract should be reviewed. This is because the *Northern Regional Health Authority* case decided that the court does not ordinarily have power to look behind the face of a certificate in a JCT contract and only an arbitrator appointed under the contract has that jurisdiction.

It is not uncommon for arbitration clauses to prevent the arbitration being commenced before a certain stage (see, for example, Clause 41.3 of JCT80). A party cannot, however, go to the court in the meantime (*Enco v Zeus* [1992] CILL 719; *Eurotunnel v TML* [1992] CILL 754 CA).

7 Multiplicity of proceedings

Where the facts give rise not only to a dispute between the plaintiff and the defendant, but also to disputes involving third parties, then that is a factor that tilts the balance of convenience against arbitration, since it is rarely possible to have all the disputes heard effectively in the same arbitration. The court recognises the increased cost and danger of split findings if these claims cannot be heard together, and the involvement of more than two parties in a dispute generally dissuades the court from ordering a stay of the court proceedings (*Taunton-Collins v Crombie* [1964] 1 WLR 633).

8 Question of law

Where the dispute involves or substantially involves a question of law, that may be a factor to influence the court to refuse to stay the court proceedings. There are conflicting decisions upon this point. It has been said that a point upon the construction of a clause in a civil engineering contract should be tried by an arbitrator because of the relevance of custom and technical terms (*Metropolitan Tunnel etc Ltd v London Electric Railway* [1926] Ch 371). Conversely, it was said in *Martin v Selsdon (No 2)* (1950) 67 RPC 64 that it may be bad practice to permit matters of construction of building contracts to go to arbitration; and in *Bristol Corporation v John Aird Ltd* [1913] AC 241 the House of Lords said:

Everybody knows that with regard to the construction of an agreement it is absolutely useless to stay the action because it will only come back to the court on a case stated.

The practical effect of these conflicting decisions appears to be that the court has a free hand in each case to decide whether a point of law ought to be tried in the courts or by arbitration.

9 Fraud

Where a dispute arises as to whether a party has been guilty of fraud, then the High Court has express power under the Arbitration Act 1950 s 24(2) and (3) to refuse to stay any court proceedings. Where it is the party alleging fraud who seeks to resist a stay, it is a matter for the court's discretion whether to grant or refuse one (*Cunningham-Reid v Buchanan Jardine* [1988] 1 WLR 678).

10 Professional reputation

Where allegations of incompetence, negligence and impropriety are made so that a man's professional reputation is at stake, he is entitled to the benefit of a trial in the High Court (*Turner v Fenton* [1982] 1 WLR 52).

11 Impartiality of arbitrator

Where the arbitration agreement names or designates the arbitrator, the High Court has an express power under the Arbitration Act 1950, s 24(1) and (3), to refuse to stay the High Court proceedings upon the ground that the arbitrator is not or may not be impartial.

12 Legal aid

Where a plaintiff does not himself have the necessary funds to pay the legal costs of an action, and requires legal aid, it can mean great hardship on him if his claim is referred to arbitration since legal aid is not available in arbitrations. It was held in *Smith v Pearl Assurance Co* [1939] 1 All ER 95 that the poverty of a litigant is not a ground for keeping the dispute in the court. That principle has been affirmed in *Edwin Jones v Thyssen & Taylor* [1991] CILL 697 CA.

13 Delay

The courts are often alive to the fact that defendants sometimes take out section 4 summonses with a view to taking advantage of the delay inherent in arbitration proceedings. As to the court's view of the merits of that tactic, see *Associated Bulk Carriers Ltd v Koch Shipping Inc* (1977) 7 BLR 18.

Where the court finds that the object of the defendant in issuing the section 4 summons is indeed to delay the plaintiff, a stay of the court proceedings may be refused (*Lury v Pearson* (1856) 1 CB (NS) 639).

Clause 41.3 of the JCT contract provides that a reference to arbitration must not be 'opened' prior to completion without the consent of both parties. Differing views have been expressed as to the meaning of this obscure wording, and different views have been expressed as to whether a party loses his right to arbitration if he withholds his consent (see *Gilbert-Ash Ltd v Modern Engineering (Bristol) Ltd* [1974] AC 689 and *Mitchell Construction Ltd v East Anglian Regional Hospital Board* (1966, unreported)).

Chapter 11

Official Referees' Business

Strictly speaking, the office of 'Official Referee' was abolished by the Courts Act 1971. The term 'Official Referee' is, however, universally used to describe such judges as the Lord Chancellor has from time to time determined are to discharge the functions conferred on Official Referees in accordance with the Rules of the Supreme Court, Ord 36.

There are six Official Referees in London:

(1) His Honour Judge John Newey QC (Clerk: Ms J Cooper)
(2) His Honour Judge Esyr Lewis QC (Clerk: Mr A Lee)
(3) His Honour Judge James Fox-Andrews QC (Clerk: Ms W Taylor)
(4) His Honour Judge Peter Bowsher QC (Clerk: Ms S Powell)
(5) His Honour Judge Thayne Forbes QC (Clerk: Ms J Morgan)
(6) His Honour Judge John Lloyd QC (Clerk: Mr T Green)
(7) His Honour Judge John Hicks QC (Clerk: Ms J Mulholland)
(8) His Honour Judge Richard Havery QC (Clerk: Ms H Packer).

The Official Referees are assisted by Circuit Official Referees, provided by circuits normally for 10–15 days at a time, and by 19 Official Referee Recorders who sit when they are available and required, but not normally for more than 10 days at a time.

The Official Referees' Department is located in St Dunstan's House, 133–137 Fetter Lane, London, EC4A 1HD (this is located at the south end of Fetter Lane). The main switchboard number is 071-936 6022, and it is possible and often helpful, to speak to the Clerk to the Official Referee assigned to the claim in question.

There are eight large and two small courts situated on the third to sixth floors of St. Dunstan's House and the Registry is on the third floor.

In practice, the Official Referees' Court is usually regarded as a subdivision of the Queen's Bench Division, although a few cases are taken from the Chancery Division. The Official Referee assigned to the case normally takes all hearings, and therefore acts as both master and judge. The clerk to the assigned Official Referee performs substantially all the administrative functions with regard to the case, such as maintaining the court file, issuing summonses, sealing orders and acting as the court's associate during hearings.

Proceedings in the Official Referees' Court are marked by an informality as though they were a hybrid between arbitration proceedings and other proceedings in the Queen's Bench Division. The clerks are able, because of their extensive functions, to be particularly helpful.

The Official Referees are addressed as 'Your Honour' whether sitting in chambers or in open court. Solicitors and their clerks do have, and often exercise, rights of audience at hearings in chambers, and indeed it is quite common at interlocutory hearings for solicitors and counsel to appear facing each other. Neither the Official Referees nor the advocates appear robed at interlocutory hearings, but they do at trial.

Once an action has been transferred to the Official Referee, no further applications are normally to be made in the Queen's Bench corridor.

1 Origination of Official Referees' Business

Appropriate types of litigation, which includes all building litigation, may be commenced in the Official Referees' Division from the outset. If, for any reason, it is not, it may be transferred there either from the Queen's Bench Division, or more rarely, from the Chancery Division.

Official Referees' Business is defined (Ord 36, r 1) as:

including any cause or matter which includes a prolonged examination of documents or accounts, or a technical, scientific or local investigation such as could more conveniently be conducted by an Official Referee, or for which trial by an Official Referee is desirable in the interest of one or more of the parties on grounds of expedition, economy or convenience or otherwise.

This somewhat circular definition is helpfully expanded upon in the notes to the *White Book* at 36/1–9/13 as including the classes of action which are concerned with the following matters, namely:

(1) civil or mechanical engineering;
(2) building and other construction work generally;
(3) claims by and against engineers, architects, surveyors, accountants, and other such specialised professional persons or bodies;
(4) claims by and against local authorities relating to their statutory duties concerning the development of land or the construction of buildings;
(5) claims between neighbouring owners and occupiers of land in trespass, nuisance and liability under *Rylands v Fletcher*;
(6) claims between landlord and tenant for breaches of repairing covenants;
(7) claims relating to the quality of goods sold or hired;
(8) claims relating to work done and materials supplied or services rendered;
(9) claims involving the taking of accounts especially where these are complicated;
(10) claims arising out of fires;
(11) claims relating to computers; and
(12) claims relating to the environment.

Business may be commenced as Official Referees' Business under Ord 36, r 2 simply by marking the writ in the top left hand corner with the words 'Official Referees' Business'. There are provisions at Ord 36, r 3 enabling the Official Referee to transfer such an action to the Chancery Division or Queen's Bench Division if he considers that it may more appropriately be tried by a master or judge, and conversely an action pending in the Chancery Division or Queen's Bench Division may be ordered to be transferred to the Official Referees' Court upon application by one of the parties. The business is assigned among the Official Referees in rota.

The writ is issued at St. Dunstan's House, even if it is chancery business (Practice Direction [1989] 1 All ER 896.)

2 The application for directions

Unlike the Queen's Bench Division practice, the application for directions should be made by the plaintiff within fourteen days of the giving by the defendant of notice of intention to defend (or, in the case of a transfer, within fourteen days from the date of the order of the transfer) (Ord 36, r 6(1)). The Official Referees like to look at the action first in order to set a realistic timetable from the outset as to the conduct of the action. It is advisable for the parties to be properly represented at these hearings. An unprepared or unintelligent approach to the application for directions will not impress the Official Referee, and it is not advisable for a solicitor to delegate appearance at the application to an inexperienced clerk. Indeed, it is not uncommon for counsel to appear on this application.

The following issues are likely to arise on the application for directions, and it is worth giving thought to them before the summons:

(1) The 'main' pleadings. Where the reference to the Official Referee is made on the hearing of an application for judgment under Ord 14, then the only pleading served may be the statement of claim. If so, then the Official Referee will normally make orders for the time for service of subsequent pleadings.

(2) Schedules. In addition to the main pleadings, the Official Referee frequently orders preparation of a Scott Schedule (see section 3 below). The Official Referee frequently makes orders as to the form and timing of the schedule on this first summons before him.

Sometimes, the precise form of the schedule is of particular importance, and it may be in the interests of one party to make sure that the headings are prescribed by the court rather than left to the other party. For example, an employer defending a disruption claim may be able to get an order requiring the contractor to particularise in schedule form precisely which loss and expense results from precisely which matter complained of. This may be an impossible task for the contractor where all the contractor can do is point to the totality of his loss. Likewise, where an employer makes complaint of a very large number of defects, the contractor may seek to require the employer to particularise in schedule form the probable cause of every defect alleged. Again, this can sometimes be an unanswerable question. For these reasons, it is highly desirable that each party's representative at the summons should know what particulars his client can give, and with what difficulty, and should also have a view as to what his opponent's clients will be able to particularise, and with what difficulty.

(3) It is usually at this summons that the Official Referee makes orders for discovery and inspection of documents. It is not usually fatal to a party if he fails to meet the first deadline for discovery and inspection. Indeed it is fairly rare for him to do so. It is however worth bearing in mind that the court is not impressed where the representatives of the parties cannot or do not make realistic estimates for the time necessary for discovery at the outset.

Particularisation of building claims, especially claims for disruption or delay, whether in further and better particulars or in Scott Schedules, has recently increased in importance, since the case of *Wharf Properties Limited v Eric Cumine Associates* (1991) 52 BLR 10 where Lord Oliver of Aylmerton referred to the obligation of a plaintiff to plead his case with such particularity as is sufficient to alert the opposite party to the case which is going to be made against him at trial, and stated that 'The failure even to attempt to specify any discernible nexus between the wrong alleged and the consequent delay provides, to use the phrase of counsel for Eric Cumine Associates, "No agenda for the trial"'. That case concerned some further and better particulars, but in *Imperial Chemical Industries v Bovis Construction and Others* (1992, unreported), the court referred to this decision in connection with a Scott Schedule and gave guidance as to the nature and extent of the obligation to plead in its Scott Schedule. It stated that the 'case against each defendant must be properly particularised, and each defendant must set out their positive case in response to the extent that they blame the plaintiff or another defendant. This, too, must be properly set out and particularised . . . The Scott Schedule must be pleaded with sufficient particularity as to sufficiently alert the opposite party to the case he will have to meet at the trial'. In this case, although the judge did not debar the plaintiffs from pursuing their claim, he ordered that a fresh schedule had to be observed.

(4) Experts. It is often premature at the time of the first summons to reach a final view as to the desirability of expert evidence. Nevertheless, orders are frequently made at this stage and the representatives of the parties should arm themselves with the answers to the following questions:

(a) might my clients wish to call expert evidence?

(b) if so, how many experts will be necessary?

(c) when will those experts' reports be ready, bearing in mind the need to consider them after receipt from the expert and before delivery to the other side? The parties should also bear in mind that leave to call expert evidence at trial is usually made conditional on their reports being furnished to the other parties at a fixed date before trial.

(5) Trial date. The practice of the Official Referees' Court is to set a trial date at the hearing of the first summons before it. Where the parties are represented by solicitors, it is well worthwhile for those solicitors to establish from counsel's clerk the state of counsel's diary over the next year. Many specialist counsel have trial dates marked in their diaries for a year or even two years hence and indeed for some periods may be double-booked or even treble-booked. Many of those dates will become inoperative by reason of settlements of other cases and it is rarely possible to form an accurate picture of when any individual counsel will be available. Usually, however, some dates are plainly more difficult than others, and where a party's counsel has difficulty with a trial date put forward by the court then he should say so to the court immediately. The parties' representative should, of course, be in a position to estimate as accurately as possible the likely length of trial.

In the Official Referees' Courts the trial will be listed for hearing at the same time as anything between one to five other trials. This is done on the basis that most actions settle before trial. Notwithstanding the number of cases fixed for hearing at the same time, it is in practice rare for the court not to be able to hear the matter on the trial date originally given, provided that the estimate of length was reasonably accurate. If the Official Referee before whom it has been listed is not available, it may be transferred either to another Official Referee or heard by one of the Official Referee Recorders.

(6) Pre-trial review. An Official Referee will also normally fix a date for a pre-trial review at which solicitors and counsel representing the parties will attend before him, shortly before the trial is due to commence, for a short hearing to discuss how the trial should proceed, and to ensure that all parties are ready for trial and to deal with any outstanding matters.

(7) Other matters. This summons is the appropriate time for the parties to raise any other matter with the court which they would have raised at the summons for directions in an ordinary case in the Queen's Bench Division. It is also the time at which the court will make an order for exchange of witness statements (see section 4 below) and consider such matters as meetings of experts (see

Chapter 14, section 4) and whether or not a view is required.

Official Referees have also begun to include a new direction informing the parties that disputes may be disposed of by Alternative Dispute Resolution, rather than by litigation, at a saving in costs. They have provided that, should the parties lodge with the court a statement that they have agreed to try the mediation process, all directions are suspended for, say, four weeks, save for the pre-trial review and trial date and all direction dates then apply as if they had been ordered to be four weeks later than actually ordered.

Under the rules of the Supreme Court there are certain things which must be done within a certain period after setting down for trial. In particular, a notice to admit facts under Ord 27, r 2, should be served not later than 21 days after the action is set down for trial. Likewise, a notice of desire to give hearsay evidence under Ord 38, r 1, ought to be given within 21 days after setting down. The rules are not explicit about when an Official Referees' matter is deemed to be 'set down' for these purposes and in any event, the 21 days are not usually regarded as a rigid time limit.

The notice to admit facts, in particular, can be a powerful weapon and the time to consider using it is not later than the first summons before the Official Referee.

As soon as possible after the hearing it is the responsibility of the party who made the application (usually the plaintiff) to draw up the order. This is done by drawing up the order made and taking two copies of this plus the summons itself to the clerk to the Official Referee, who usually will have been in court at the time the order was made. The clerk then seals the order and retains one copy. It is for the party drawing up the order to serve copies of it on the other parties after it has been sealed.

3 Scott Schedules

Apart from the 'main' pleadings it is very common for the Official Referee to order further pleadings in the form of an Official Referees' Schedule, or 'Scott Schedule' as it is popularly known. Scott Schedules should be seen as ancillary to the main pleadings and are in the nature of further and better particulars set out in tabular form.

Scott Schedules can take various forms. They are usually pleadings in tabular form (often typed on large sheets of paper) where the contentions of the plaintiff and the defendant and the comments of the Official Referee can all be marked side by side in columns. The case of *Imperial Chemical Industries v Bovis Construction and Others* (referred to in paragraph 2(3) above) has recently emphasised the necessity for Scott Schedules to particularise the claims which each party has against the other party or parties, so that each party is aware of the case that will have to be met at trial. Whilst failure to do so will not necessarily result in the pleading being struck out, as it did in *Wharf v Eric Cumine Associates*, it will undoubtedly lead to costs being wasted.

Scott Schedules are used both in respect of claims by contractors for payment, and in respect of claims by employers for defects. In the former case, a typical layout for the columns, from left to right, is as follows:

1 paragraph number;
2 description of item of work;
3 plaintiff's comments;
4 amount of plaintiff's claim;
5 defendant's comments;
6 price (if any) conceded by the defendant;
7 Official Referee's comments:
8 Official Referee's price;
9 VAT.

    In the case of a claim by an employer for defects, a typical layout is as follows:

1 paragraph number;
2 defect alleged by plaintiff;
3 sum claimed by plaintiff;
4 defendant's comments;
5 defendant's estimate of the cost of remedial work;
6 Official Referee's comments;
7 damages awarded.

The form of these Schedules can vary considerably. The Official Referee usually specifies in his order which party is responsible for preparing the first part of the Schedule, and which party must reply to that. He does not usually prescribe the form of the Schedule but leaves it to the good sense of the parties. Sometimes, however, it is appropriate to ask the Official Referee to specify in his order the precise form of the Schedule. Certainly, the form of the Schedule can make a party's task in preparing his part of the Scott Schedule comparatively easy or comparatively difficult. For example, it would often be extremely difficult for a contractor to set out a claim for an extension of time under the JCT contract if he were required to complete the following columns:

1 paragraph number;
2 cause of delay alleged;
3 date of notice under clause 25.2. 1.1 ;
4 date of delivery of notice to nominated sub-contractors under clause 25.2.1.2;
5 date of particulars under clause 25.2.2.1;
6 date of estimate under clause 25.2.2.2;
7 dates of further notices under clause 25.2.3;
8 particulars of contractors best endeavours under clause 25.3.4.1;
9 subclause of clause 25.4 relied on by the contractor.

A contractor would be strongly advised not to agree to prepare his part of the Scott Schedule in this form, for in doing so he would take upon himself a burden of proof so heavy that the mere research needed for the pleading would, in a complex case, be almost impossible.

Conversely, it is often in an employer's interest to press hard for particulars of notices of this sort, especially since it is commonly and erroneously thought that such notices do not much matter, especially where the employer's professional advisers know what is happening. In *John Laing Construction v County and District Properties* (1982) 23 BLR 1, for example, it was held that the quantity surveyor has no right to waive the requirement for written notice as a pre-condition to fluctuations under clause 31 (D)(2) of the Green Form.

Precedents for Scott Schedules can be found in Fay, Keating, and in the standard court precedent books.

4 Witness statements

The recent amendment of Ord 38, r 2(a) introduces the system for exchange of witness statements which was pioneered by the Official Referees. Now, in every action commenced by writ, simultaneous exchange of witness statements *must* be ordered at the summons for directions, to take place within 14 weeks (or such other period as the court may specify). Further Ord 3, r 5(3) which allows time limits to be extended either by the court or upon application or by consent, does not apply to this time limit. It remains to be seen whether the court will entertain any application for extension of this time limit.

The witness statements must be dated and signed and include a declaration that the contents are true to the best of the maker's information and belief. Any documents referred to must be sufficiently identified.

This procedure is similar to the exchange of experts' reports, also required by Ord 38, which was also pioneered by the Official Referees.

The Official Referees also now frequently order that such statements should stand as the evidence in chief. This effectively does away with the need for examination in chief by a party of his own witnesses, with the advantage of considerably shortening the time taken for oral evidence to be given at trial. In circumstances where such a direction is given, a Queen's Bench Division *Practice Direction* ([1992] 4 All ER 679) has been made enabling the judge to direct that such statements should be certified and made open to inspection by the public, with provisions for copies to be obtained, for seven working days after the end of trial. Conversely, the statements are confidential and may not be referred to until verified by the witness on oath (*Fairfield-Mabey v Shell* [1989] 1 All ER 576).

The system of exchanging proofs sometimes means that two versions of a witness's statement will have to be prepared. The first will be a preliminary statement for use by the solicitors and counsel for the party calling that witness. The second will contain only what is required in the evidence in chief for exchange. Indeed, it may further be necessary to prepare two versions of the statement exchanged, one with annotations for the use of the solicitors and counsel who prepared it, and the other without annotations.

Given that the average length of a trial in the Official Referees' Courts was about 12 days and that, previously, much of that time was taken up by examination in chief of witnesses of fact, the introduction of this system not only in the Official Referees' Courts, but in the High Court generally, can only assist in speeding up trials and thus enable cases to be heard more quickly.

5 Appeals from the Official Referee

(a) Interlocutory orders

Appeal does not lie from interlocutory orders or judgments of an Official Referee without the leave of either the Official Referee himself or the Court of Appeal, which is the appellate court if leave is given; Supreme Court Act 1981, s 18(1)(h).

(b) Final orders and judgments

In 1988, a new Ord 58, r 4, was introduced which states that an appeal is to lie to the Court of Appeal from a decision of an Official Referee:
  (1) On a question of law (no leave is required here); and
  (2) With the leave of the Official Referee or the Court of Appeal, on any question of fact.

This alters the previous law under which there was an appeal as of right against decisions of Official Referees on certain questions of fact (fraud and breach of professional duty), but no appeal at all against other findings of fact. Now it is possible to appeal against any finding of fact by an Official Referee, but only if leave to appeal is granted either by the Official Referee or by the Court of Appeal. In *Hoskisson v Moody* (1989) 5 Const LJ 205 the Official Referee refused to give leave to appeal on fact because the prospect of success would be slight.

Appeal does lie from the exercise of discretion by an Official Referee, since this is a point of law (*Instrumatic Ltd v Supabrase Ltd* [1969] 1 WLR 519). Leave is not necessary to appeal against an Ord 14 judgement (s 18(2)(a), Supreme Court Act 1981).

As to procedure before the Court of Appeal the usual rules apply. In view of the propensity of construction cases to generate large bundles of documents it may, however, be helpful to draw attention to the *Practice Direction* of 22 October 1986 ([1986] 3 All ER 630). In *Fairclough Building Ltd v Rhuddlan Borough Council* (1985) 30 BLR 26 CA the Court of Appeal warned that failure of the solicitors to prepare a 'master' bundle of principal documents may lead to an order for costs against the solicitors personally.

Chapter 12

Pleadings

Pleadings do not, perhaps, have the importance they once had. Nevertheless, the decision in *Wharf Properties v Eric Cumine* (1991) 52 BLR 10 has revived much of their original importance; an inadequately pleaded case may be struck out as embarrassing. Further, if a party does not have his pleadings in order until the last moment before trial he may be forced into a lengthy adjournment and/or face cost penalties.

Pleadings of complexity are usually settled by counsel. That said, it is of great importance for those instructing counsel to understand thoroughly any pleadings settled by counsel. Counsel do overlook points, and solicitors are at a grave disadvantage at subsequent interlocutory stages if they do not fully understand the case that has been put forward on their client's behalf in the pleadings. In simple cases, it is common for the pleadings to be settled by solicitors. That has the advantage of being quicker and cheaper, but care should be taken to ensure that the pleading comprehends the true nature of the case being put forward.

1 Precedents

There follow four precedents which set out the typical form of statements of claim in certain straightforward circumstances.

Precedent 1
Statement of Claim for payment under quantum meruit

The Plaintiff's claim is for £5,000[1], being the price of work done and materials supplied by the Plaintiff for and at the request of the Defendant at 10 Ironside Villas, Upton, Somerset in or about June 1992.

PARTICULARS

Demolishing existing coal bunker	£500.00
Construct new 5′×3′×4′ coal bunker in fair faced brick	£2,500.00
Supply and fix 'Blackamoor' coal bunker cover	£2,000.00
	£5,000.00

AND THE PLAINTIFF CLAIMS

(i) £5,000

(ii) Interest pursuant to Section 35A of the Supreme Court Act 1981 at 15 per cent p.a. of

    (a) £   calculated from 30th June 1992 to the date hereof, and

    (b) £   per day from the date hereof to Judgment or sooner payment[1].

Precedent 2
Statement of Claim for payment under quantum meruit
by reference to invoice, part paid

The Plaintiff's claim is for £4,000[1], being the balance of the price of work done and materials supplied by the Plaintiff for and at the request of the Defendant at 10 Ironside Villas, Upton, Somerset in or about June 1992.

PARTICULARS

Invoice No 9992 dated 1st August 1992 full particulars of which have been delivered to the Defendant on or about 2nd August 1992	£5,000.00
Less Paid by the Defendant on or about 15th August 1992	£1,000.00
Balance outstanding	£4,000.00

AND THE PLAINTIFF CLAIMS

(i) £4,000

(ii) Interest pursuant to Section 35A of the Supreme Court Act 1981 at 15% p.a. of

    (a) £   calculated from 2nd August 1992 to the date hereof, and

    (b) £   per day from the date hereof to judgment or sooner payment[2].

Precedent 3
Statement of Claim for payment under
informal lump-sum contract with extra work

1 By a contract between the Plaintiff as Contractor and the Defendant as Employer the Plaintiff agreed to execute and the Defendant agreed to pay for certain building work at 10 Ironside Villas, Upton, Somerset. The terms of the said contract are contained in, alternatively evidenced by the Plaintiff's letter to the Defendant of 1st June 1992.

2 The agreed price for the said work was £5,000.00.

3 The Plaintiff has duly executed the said work together with certain further work ordered by the Defendant to a value of £3,000.00. The total sum due to the Plaintiff under the said contract is accordingly £8,000.00, particulars of which appear by the Plaintiff's invoice no 9992 dated 1st August 1992 delivered to the Defendant on or about 2nd August 1992.

4 The Defendant has failed to pay the whole or any part of the said sum of £8,000.00.

AND THE PLAINTIFF CLAIMS

(i) £8,000.00

(ii) Interest pursuant to Section 35A of the Supreme Court Act 1981 at 15 per cent p.a. of

  (a) £   calculated from 2nd August 1992 to the date hereof, and

  (b) £   per day from the date hereof to judgment or sooner payment[2].

Precedent 4

Statement of Claim for payment under an interim architect's certificate

1 By contract in writing dated 1st June 1992 between the Plaintiff as Contractor and the Defendant as Employer, the Plaintiff agreed for the consideration therein mentioned to carry out certain building works at 10 Ironside Villas, Upton, Somerset. The said contract was in the Standard Form of the Joint Contract Tribunal, Private Edition, With Quantities, 1980 Edition.

2 There was an express term, inter alia, by clause 30.1.1 of the said Contract that the Architect should from time to time issue Interim Certificates stating the amount due to the Plaintiff from the Defendant and that the Plaintiff should be entitled to payment therefore within 14 days from the date of issue[4] of each Interim Certificate.

3 Pursuant to the said term the Architect named in the said Contract, L da Vinci, issued Interim Certificate No 2 on 15th August 1992 in the sum of £5,000.

4 The Defendant has failed to honour the Certificate within 14 days or at all.

AND THE PLAINTIFF CLAIMS

(i) £5,000

(ii) Interest pursuant to Section 35A of the Supreme Court Act 1981 at 15 per cent p.a. of

(a) £   calculated from 29th August 1992 to the date hereof, and

(b) £   per day from the date hereof to judgment or sooner payment.

Notes to precedents
(1) Dates, sums and other numbers must be expressed in a pleading in figures and not in words (Ord 18, r 6(3)).
(2) Section 35A does not itself specify an interest rate. These precedents claim interest at 15 per cent (being the rate currently payable on judgment debts) so that the claim for interest is treated as a claim for a liquidated demand and thus qualifies for a default judgment to be entered in respect of such interest under Ord 13, r 1(1), without the assessment of interest. Section 35A of the Supreme Court Act 1981 only applies to High Court proceedings; in arbitrations the corresponding provision is s 19A of the Arbitration Act 1950 introduced from 1st April 1983 by the Administration of Justice Act 1982.
(3) Where it is necessary to give particulars of debt, expenses or damages and those particulars exceed three folios, they must be set out in a separate document referred to in the pleading and the pleading must state whether the document has already been served and, if so, when, or is to be served with the pleading (Ord 18, r 12(2)). 'Folio' means seventy-two words, each figure being counted as one word (Ord 1, r 4(1)).
(4) Under Clause 30(1) of the 1963 Private Editions of the JCT Contract, interim certificates were payable within fourteen days

from the presentation of the certificate by the contractor to the employer. Consequently. it was appropriate also to plead the fact and time of presentation.

2 Amendment

The same principles with regard to amendment apply in construction cases as apply in other litigation, but there are two particular remarks to make.

The first is that the propensity of construction cases to involve lengthy pleadings has led in the past to a somewhat relaxed view in the Official Referees' Courts to the question of amendment. The use of Scott Schedules often diverts attention away from the statement of claim and defence in any event, and it is not unknown for the Official Referees to allow fundamental amendments at a very late stage.

The second remark to make is that there seems to have been some movement away from the trend. In *Ketteman v Hansel Properties Ltd* (1987) 36 BLR 1 the House of Lords held that leave should not have been given to the defendants to amend during trial to plead limitation. Lord Griffiths considered the old rule in *Clarapede & Co v Commercial Union Assurance* (1883) 32 WR 262 that:

however negligent or careless the first omission, and however late the proposed amendment, the amendment should be allowed if it can be made without injustice to the other side. There is no injustice if the other side can be compensated by costs . . .

but said:

. . . whatever may have been the rule of conduct a hundred years ago, today it is not the practice to allow a defence which is wholly different from that pleaded to be raised by amendment at the end of the trial even on terms that an adjournment is granted and that the defendant pays all the costs thrown away. There is a clear difference between allowing amendments to clarify the issues in dispute and those that permit a distinct defence to be raised for the first time . . . a judge is entitled to weigh in the balance the strain litigation imposes on litigants, particularly if they are personal litigants rather than business corporations, the anxieties occasioned by facing new issues, the raising of false hopes, and the legitimate expectation that the trial will determine the issues one way or the other . . . Another factor that a judge must weigh in the balance is the pressure on the courts . . . We can no longer afford to show the same indulgence towards the negligent conduct of litigation as was perhaps possible in a more leisured age.

The House of Lords also considered in the *Ketteman* case the line of authority in support of the 'relation back' theory, that when an additional defendant is added to an action by amendment, that additional defendant is deemed for limitation purposes to have been sued at the time of the issue of the original writ. That line of cases was overruled and it is now clear that for limitation purposes the action is not brought against an additional defendant until he is served.

3 Financing charges

Increasing attention has been focused over the last few years upon the question of interest. Under the Law Reform (Miscellaneous Provisions) Act 1934 the court had power to award interest upon a judgment, but that Act forbade the award of interest upon interest (compound interest) and it did not apply to allow a plaintiff in litigation to obtain interest where a debt was paid late but before the issue of proceedings. Under s 35A of the Supreme Court Act 1981 these limitations remain (although the old requirement for the proceedings to be 'tried' has been dispensed with).

In *F C Minter Limited v Welsh Technical Services Organisation* (1980) 13 BLR 1 the Court of Appeal vindicated the principle that interest may be recoverable as loss and/or expense under the express terms of a building contract, and in *Techno-Impex v Gebr van Weelde Scheepvaart-kantoor BV* [1981] Com LR 82, Lord Denning held that it is open to arbitrators in the City of London to award interest by way of damages where claimants had suffered loss by being denied their money. In this case, Lord Denning expressly said that this principle applies where the principal sum is paid before the commencement of the arbitration and interest is claimed for the period of delay. In that case, a shipping case, the principal claim was for demurrage, and the court was, therefore, expressly sanctioning the award of interest upon interest since, although interest upon interest was forbidden by the 1934 Act, arbitrations are not subject to it. In *President of India v Pintada* [1984] 3 WLR 10, however, the House of Lords reaffirmed the general principle of *London, Chatham and Dover Railway v South Eastern Railway* [1893] AC 429 that interest is not payable as damages at common law for the late payment of money.

Where interest is being claimed not under the 1934 Act but as damages for breach of contract or loss and expense, it is now common to refer to it as finance charges, or financing charges.

In the case of small claims where it is intended to proceed under Ord 14 there is little material advantage in pleading financing charges. In a more substantial case, however, where a lengthy delay is anticipated, then it is always worthwhile to consider making a claim for financing charges.

4 Particulars

Where a case is destined for the Official Referees' Court, the Official Referee will, in an appropriate case, order the preparation of a Scott Schedule (see Chapter 11, section 3). In these circumstances there is often little point in the parties giving or requiring further and better particulars in the ordinary form where to do so would lead only to duplication.

Where a plaintiff knows that he will have to give extensive particulars, for example on a lengthy claim for extra work or in respect of many defects, it is often convenient for him to particularise these matters by an appendix to his statement of claim in a form that can itself be used as a Scott Schedule. By doing this, he can save time and avoid duplication.

That said, it is often of great importance to obtain proper particulars of an opponent's pleading under Ord 18, r 12. In particular, it is quite common for a claim on a lump sum contract not to give particulars as to how the sum claimed is to be reconciled with the pre-agreed lump sum or as to the basis of each and every item of the extra work. It will rarely give an opponent an advantage to wait until trial before pointing to the inadequacy of such a pleading, and provided it is properly timed an interlocutory attack upon such a pleading, which usually involves seeking those particulars, can have a devastating effect. Likewise, a party making a claim in respect of defects in negligence frequently particularises the defects complained of but not the negligence relied upon. Being required to particularise that negligence can often give such a party cause for doubt as to his prospects of success.

5 Notice to admit facts

Notices to admit facts are certainly of value in assisting a party to know what facts he is expected to prove at trial and what facts are not seriously in dispute. In practical terms, however, the notice to admit facts is probably even more valuable as a means of encouraging settlement. Order 27, r 2(1), provides as follows:

A party to a cause or matter may not later than twenty-one days after the cause or matter is set down for trial serve on any other party a notice requiring him to admit, for the purpose of that cause or matter only, the facts specified in the notice.

Notices to admit facts are often very lengthy, and set out to dissect issues of fact into individual parts. It is a feature of the present pleading system that a party can plead his case generally, and thereby reach an advanced stage in litigation without applying his mind to the question of precisely which facts he is going to be able to prove or resist in evidence at trial. In practice, notices to admit facts are capable of being used to good effect in a rhetorical way as well as in a genuinely inquisitorial way.

Chapter 13

Discovery and inspection of documents

The same principles as to discovery and inspection of documents apply in building contract matters as in other litigation and arbitration, and the extensive notes to Ord 24 are as helpful as always.

Under Ord 24, r 2, the parties must exchange lists of documents within 14 days after the close of pleadings. In practice, this rule is frequently disregarded, and in many cases where the documentation is heavy, compliance with it would be entirely impracticable. The Official Referees do not usually expect discovery to have taken place when the matter first comes before them, and orders for discovery are usually made at that stage. In *McVeigh v Tarmac* (1981) 78 LSG 633 the Court of Appeal said that the practice of waiting for an express order for discovery ought to cease, but it has not in fact done so.

In arbitrations, an order for discovery is usually made at the preliminary meeting, and the typical form of order for directions, given in *The Architect as Arbitrator* (RIBA publication), contains the following precedent:

That after the close of pleading the Claimant and Respondent do respectively within . . . days deliver to the other a list of the documents which are or have been in their possession or power relating to the matters in question in this arbitration and that inspection be given within . . . days thereafter.

Where the documentation is weighty, it is frequently impracticable to list each and every document, and the parties resort to bundling (see Ord 24, r 5(1), and the note at 24/5/4). Where the litigation involves particularly contentious issues it is normal to list individually the documents relating specifically to those issues, and to list by bundles the other documents. Where documents are listed by bundles, particular care must obviously be taken to ensure that documents are not removed from the bundles and it is often appropriate for each page of the discovered documents to be separately marked with a mechanical numbering machine, a process that is much quicker than page-by-page description in a list of documents. When this is done the parties sometimes reach an arrangement whereby, for example, the plaintiff uses numbers from 1 to 499,999 and the defendant uses the numbers from 500,000 onwards.

These days, it is much more efficient, in a case involving many documents, to prepare the list of documents in the form of a database, rather than on a word processor. Where this is done, it is appropriate to use the field structure suggested in the ORSA Protocol that is reproduced at Appendix C. One of the advantages of preparing a list of documents in this form is that, in respect of each document, useful information may be entered into a computer that need not be printed out as part of the list of documents, but which will be readily accessible to the computer user. By way of example, it is useful to record the name of the individual author of any given letter, as well as the company on behalf of which it is written; this process makes it much easier to locate it in the future.

Likewise, it is common to include provision for a few key words from the document, or even the whole text of the document which might be scanned by Optical Character Recognition equipment, and also fields identifying where the document can be found in the core and/or named trial bundle. Techniques such as these not only enhance one's ability to cope with the documents (especially if the lawyers are prepared to learn how to operate the database themselves), but also potentially reduce the cost of litigation, because they make it practicable for the clients to do much of the routine work in preparation of the list of documents. A word of warning, however, is necessary. The larger the number of documents, the more difficult it is to prevent privileged documents slipping through the net. It should always be ensured that there is a field to signify whether the document in question is privileged (a logical field will do for this purpose), and that that field is entered by someone suitably qualified for the task — if this is done it is very easy to filter such documents out of the full information on computer.

It is sometimes said that building contract litigation can be won or lost at discovery. It is certainly the case that it is very common for a party not to disclose all the documents that ought to be disclosed at discovery, and much can hinge upon the steps taken by that party's opponent to obtain all the documents. The documentation obviously varies from case to case, but the following comments are frequently of relevance.

1 Reports upon the defects and third-party correspondence

Typically, a party obtains a report upon defects in the work soon after they appear and before litigation is contemplated. Those reports are only privileged from production if the purpose of preparing for litigation is either the sole reason for the preparation of the report, or at least the dominant purpose of it (*Waugh v British Railways Board* [1979] 3 WLR 150 HL).

In the case of a dispute between an employer and a contractor as to defects, there will often be correspondence between the employer and the architect. This correspondence is sometimes marked 'without prejudice'. Unless that correspondence falls within the privilege rules enunciated in *Waugh v British Railways Board*, it will generally be discoverable to the contractor.

Likewise, in the case of a dispute between the employer and the contractor, correspondence between the contractor and the sub-contractor upon the defects is usually discoverable to the employer, and in the case of a dispute between a contractor and a sub-contractor as to defects, correspondence as to the defects between the employer and the contractor is usually discoverable to the sub-contractor.

It seems that the courts will have regard to policy considerations in applying these rules to insurers, and in *Guinness Peat Properties Ltd v Fitzroy Robinson Partnership* (1987) 38 BLR 57 CA the Court of Appeal found that the notification of claim written by the defendants to their insurers was a privileged document despite the evidence of the defendants that their purpose in writing the notification was not at all with a view to legal advice, but simply to comply with the terms of their insurance policy. The court, however, took a wider view that the notification procedure is required by insurance companies generally in order to enable them to obtain legal advice on claims made against their insured. By the same token it seems that subsequent correspondence between an insured and his insurers will be privileged. In *Buttes Oil v Hammer (No 3)* [1981] 1 QB 223 Brightman LJ said:

... if two parties with a common interest and a common solicitor exchange information for the dominant purpose of informing each other of the facts, or the issues, or advice received, or of obtaining legal advice in respect of contemplated or pending litigation, the documents or copies containing that information are privileged from production in the hands of each.

Similarly, in *Re Highgrade Traders Ltd* [1984] BCLC 151 reports procured by insurers from specialists in fire investigation were privileged.

2 Architect's documents

It is usually thought that an employer has the right to delivery up of the architect's plan and other documents, at any rate unless the architect has a lien on them for non-payment of fees (see *Hudson*, p 188). Accordingly, the architect's documents are usually regarded as within the power of the employer, and therefore discoverable by the employer in litigation between the employer and the contractor.

In the case of litigation between the employer and the architect, the employer is entitled to his usual rights of discovery against the architect notwithstanding the existence of a lien on the documents (*Woodworth v Conroy* [1976] QB 884).

3 Contractor's documentation

In the case of a dispute between the employer and the contractor as to payment for the works, the employer will frequently be entitled to see at discovery many documents that he has not seen before.

Most contractors keep prime-cost records, often on computer. This is so even in the case of lump sum contracts where the contractor is not entitled to be paid the prime cost of the works as such: the records are kept by the contractor *inter alia* so that eventually he can see whether he has made a profit on the contract or not. In all but the simplest cases, these prime-cost records do relate to the issues in question, and are discoverable by the contractor to the employer. Contractors usually keep a site diary on site containing contemporaneous notes as to the works, and this site diary is usually discoverable.

Where the contractor makes a claim for a profit element on works he has undertaken, or where the Hudson Formula is relevant (see p 52), the employer can sometimes press for discovery of the contractor's profit and loss accounts since these documents will disclose the profit usually earned by the contractor.

4 Sub-contractor's documentation

Where a dispute arises between the employer and the contractor as to payment, the employer will often be entitled to discovery of all correspondence and other documentation passing between the contractor and the sub-contractor. The employer is not, however, usually entitled to discovery of the sub-contractor's own documentation since this is not usually within the power of the contractor.

Chapter 14

Expert evidence

It is particularly common for expert evidence to be necessary in building contract litigation.

The purpose of expert evidence is to prove fact, not to advocate law. Accordingly, expert evidence is not generally appropriate to assist the court to construe the terms of the contract, nor is it appropriate to adduce expert evidence as to whether a particular head of claim is admissible. These are matters of law and, however unfamiliar they may be to a general practitioner lawyer, it is the function of the lawyers and not of the expert witnesses to unravel the terms and effect of the contract.

Expert evidence can, however, be indispensable both for the purpose of ascertaining what sum is due to the contractor, and for the purpose of establishing the responsibility for, and extent of, building defects.

1 Expert evidence upon payment for the works

There are various matters upon which expert evidence may be appropriate in this area.

First, disputes sometimes arise as to whether work undertaken by a contractor is properly to be regarded as extra work, or whether it is properly to be regarded as being within the scope of the work originally undertaken by the contractor. Where there are formal bills of quantities, those bills of quantities are usually to be interpreted in accordance with the Standard Method of Measurement. The JCT contract expressly so provides in Clause 2.2.2.1, and even if there is no express provision a similar effect may be incorporated by implication. In some cases, it can be appropriate to adduce expert evidence as to whether a description in the bills of quantities is sufficient to include all the work actually carried out by the contractor.

It is comparatively rare for a building contract dispute as to price to turn upon the quantity of work actually carried out by the contractor. Where such a dispute does arise it can be appropriate to adduce expert evidence upon this.

More commonly, disputes arise as to the rate of payment to which the contractor is entitled. Such disputes arise not only with regard to the whole contract works where the contract is for a reasonable sum, but also with regard to the valuation of extra work. In some cases, much of the evidence at trial consists of the experts for both sides being taken through a lengthy Scott Schedule and expressing views upon the value of many items of work.

Where there are defects in the works, the contractor can sometimes fall into the trap of adducing evidence as to the defects without adducing evidence as to the credit to be given to the contractor in respect of work that he has done which does not require replacement.

In all these cases, the person best able to give the expert evidence is usually a quantity surveyor, although in small cases the evidence of an architect or building surveyor may suffice.

2 Expert evidence as to delay

In claims for liquidated damages, extensions of time and damages or loss and expense for delay or disruption, there is frequently a multiplicity of possible causes and a court or arbitrator may benefit from evidence from a claims consultant or other suitably qualified expert (*James Longley & Co Ltd v South West Thames Regional Health Authority* (1983) 127 SJ 597). See Chapter 21.

3 Expert evidence as to defects

There are three main issues in this area where expert evidence is frequently necessary.
(1) Is there a defect in the works?
(2) If so, whose responsibility is that defect? (This issue frequently turns upon whether the defect arises out of a design fault or bad workmanship.)
(3) Where the obligation of the person responsible for the defect is not an absolute one, but merely an obligation to use proper skill and care, did that person exercise proper skill and care?
It is not uncommon for a plaintiff to be able to satisfy the court as to issues (1) and (2) above, but to fail to adduce proper evidence in respect of (3). In some cases, this oversight can be fatal. In *Worboys v Acme Investments Ltd* (1969) 4 BLR 133, Sachs LJ had this to say:

To my mind the architect's duty was limited to one of showing reasonable competence in an attempt to produce saleable houses at around the price which the defendants had in mind.
Now [plaintiff's counsel] urges that this is a class of case in which the court can find a breach of professional duty without having before it the standard type of evidence as to what constitutes lack of care on the part of a professional man in the relevant circumstances. There may well be cases in which it would not be necessary to adduce such evidence — as, for instance, if an architect omitted to

provide a front door to the premises. But it would be grossly unfair to architects if, on a point of the type now under consideration, which relates to a special type of dwelling, the courts could without the normal evidence condemn a professional man . . . In those circumstances I have come to the conclusion that there was simply no evidence that there was any breach of duty on the part of the plaintiff in this instance.

It is, therefore, highly desirable that a plaintiff should form a realistic assessment as soon as possible as to whether or not the defendant's obligation is absolute or whether he must show negligence. If negligence is an indispensable part of his claim, the sooner he obtains expert evidence upon that issue the better. It is entirely unreliable for the plaintiff to hope for assistance from the doctrine *res ipsa loquitur*.

Where there is an issue as to limitation, then expert evidence may well be necessary as to the date upon which the damage occurred, which is ordinarily the date upon which the limitation period began to run. In cases where the limitation period may be postponed by reason of fraudulent concealment under the Limitation Act 1939, or deliberate concealment under the Limitation Act 1980, then expert evidence may be necessary as to the date of discoverability. The importance of expert evidence is illustrated by *Ketteman and Others v Hansel Properties Ltd and Others* [1984] 1 WLR 1274, where it appears that the defendants failed to bring forward expert evidence that subsidence is a gradual process, and in the absence of such evidence the Deputy Official Referee found the occurrence of the damage to be contemporaneous with its discovery.

4 The rules as to expert evidence

The rules as to expert evidence in civil proceedings were substantially changed following the Civil Evidence Act 1972 and now appear in Ord 38, Pt IV, beginning at Ord 38, r 35.

The function of expert witnesses is (*inter alia*) to explain words, or terms of science or art appearing on the documents which have to be construed by the court, to give expert assistance to the court (eg as to the laws of science, or the working of a technical process or system), or to inform the court as to the state of public knowledge with regard to the matters before it (see *Crosfield & Sons Ltd v Techno-Chemical Laboratories Ltd* (1913) 29 TLR 379; *British Celanese Ltd v Courtaulds Ltd* (1935) 152 LT 537 HL). In building contract cases expert evidence is not infrequently used in relation to such matters as the reasons for the failure of a building, the factual matters necessary to determine whether a particular failure was negligent and the practice of the building industry with regard to various matters such as the practices embodied in the Standard Method of Measurement. It is not open to parties to give expert evidence as to matters of English law, and accordingly expert evidence is not used to assist the court as to the construction of contracts.

The restrictions on adducing expert evidence appear at Ord 38, r 36, which provides as follows:

36 — (1) Except with the leave of the Court or where all parties agree, no expert evidence may be adduced at the trial or hearing of any cause or matter unless the party seeking to adduce the evidence has applied to the Court to determine whether a direction should be given under rr 37, 38 or 41 (whichever is appropriate) and has complied with any direction given on the application.

(2) Nothing in paragraph (1) shall apply to evidence which is permitted to be given by affidavit or shall affect the enforcement under any other provision of these Rules (except Ord 45, r 5) of a direction given under this Part of this Order.

It is apparent from the terms of Ord 38, r 36, that a party seeking to adduce expert evidence must, unless he obtains the leave of the court or the agreement of all parties, not only obtain a direction as to that evidence, but must also comply with that direction.

Order 38, r 37, deals with medical evidence in action for personal injuries.

Order 38, r 38, applies to expert evidence in other actions, and is the rule usually applicable in building contract litigation.

Order 38, r 41, relates to expert evidence of engineers in motor accident cases.

Order 38, r 38, provides as follows:

38 — (1) Where an application is made under r 36(1) in respect of oral expert evidence to which r 37 does not apply, the Court may, if satisfied that it is desirable to do so, direct that the substance of any expert evidence which is to be adduced by any party be disclosed in the form of a written report or reports to such parties and within such period as the Court may specify.

(2) In deciding whether to give a direction under para (1) the Court shall have regard to all the circumstances and may, to such an extent as it thinks fit, treat any of the following circumstances as affording a sufficient reason for not giving such a direction:

(a) that the expert evidence is or will be based to any material extent upon a version of the facts in dispute between the parties; or

(b) that the expert evidence is or will be based to any material extent upon facts which are neither:

(i) ascertainable by the exercise of his own powers of observation, nor

(ii) within his general professional knowledge and experience.

The whole purpose of Ord 38 is, in relation to expert evidence, to save expense by dispensing with the calling of experts where there is in reality no dispute and, where there is a dispute, by avoiding parties being taken by surprise as to the true nature of the dispute and thereby being obliged to seek amendments or adjournments; and in either case, will probably lead to the settlement of the action. Therefore, the court should in practice ordinarily make an order for the exchange of non-medical expert reports (*Ollet v Bristol Aerojet Ltd* (*Practice Note*) [1979] I WLR 1197).

The ordinary practice of the Official Referees' Court is to consider with the parties the need for expert evidence on the first occasion that the matter comes before the Official Referee. In theory, the onus of satisfying the court to give a direction for the disclosure of expert evidence is upon the party applying for such disclosure to be made, but in practice the onus is not a heavy one (*White Book* paragraph 38/37–39/1). The court does not usually give one party the right to call expert evidence without giving a similar right to the other party; the court usually directs that the parties simultaneously exchange their experts' reports on or before a fixed date, which is usually some months before the trial date. The court sometimes directs that the experts' reports be agreed if possible. The court also has power under Ord 38, r 4, to limit the number of expert witnesses who may be called at trial.

Where a party fails to apply for or comply with a direction of the court to adduce expert evidence at trial, he runs the risk that evidence will be excluded at trial. Parties are often a few days late in complying with an exchange date contained in a direction and provided that this is well before trial no harm is caused. The court tends to take a more serious view where an expert's report is not delivered until the month of trial, or where a party seeks to adduce evidence materially outside the terms of the report previously delivered. Sometimes, a party is penalised in costs: for example, where a defendant failed to serve on the plaintiff the report of his expert in breach of Ord 38, r 40, but nevertheless, in spite of its imperative terms, obtained the leave of the trial judge to admit the report under the powers conferred by the opening words of r 36(1), he was awarded his costs taxed up to the date of the hearing, but only half the costs of the trial of the action (*Cable v Dallaturca* (1977) *The Times*, 9 November).

By Ord 38, r 39, the court has power to direct that a part only of expert evidence sought to be adduced should be disclosed, and by Ord 38, r 44, the court has power to revoke or vary a previous direction as to expert evidence.

Expert evidence is normally only given on affidavit on interlocutory hearings, and at trial a party adducing disputed expert evidence is normally expected to call that expert so as to give the other party the opportunity of cross-examination.

The court has a further power under Ord 40 to appoint a court expert, but only rarely avails itself of this power.

In arbitrations, the arbitrator does in practice enjoy considerable latitude in the control of proceedings (*Star International v Bergbau-Handel* [1966] 2 Lloyd's Rep 16), but he is bound to follow as closely as possible the procedure adopted by the courts. In many cases, the arbitrator will have been chosen by reason of his own specialist knowledge, but such specialist knowledge should be used to understand and appreciate the evidence before him, not to provide his own (*Fox v Wellfair* (1981) 19 BLR 52).

5 Meeting of experts

The traditional way in which differing expert opinions are judged is for each expert to be cross-examined by counsel upon his pre-disclosed report. This procedure is not always regarded as satisfactory; expert witnesses are frequently impatient of our adversarial system of trial and if they are permitted to communicate with each other it is common for them to form, so far as they are able, a joint view. In order to encourage this practice, the Official Referees now direct that the experts meet by a given date.

Ord 38, Rule 38 specifically gives the Court the power to direct that there be a 'without prejudice' meeting of experts either before or after the disclosure of their reports. It further provides that the purpose of such meeting is to identify those parts of their evidence which are in issue and that where such meeting takes place, the experts may prepare a joint statement indicating those parts of their evidence on which they are in agreement and those parts on which they are not. The practice of making such orders is now widespread since such an order tends to save costs.

The rules as to meetings of experts are somewhat bizarre. In *Richard Roberts Holdings v Douglas Smith Stimpson* (1989) 47 BLR 113, it was held that agreements reached at such meetings prior to trial are not binding and may not be referred to the court. Meetings after the commencement of trial, however, are different; there agreements are binding and may thus be referred to the court. Conversely, in *Murray Pipework v UIE* [1990] 8 CLD 06 16 it was found that pre-trial agreement between experts had the effect of ending the 'without prejudice' protection. These two cases are very difficult to reconcile.

6 The payment of experts

A solicitor instructing an expert on behalf of a client should make it plain whether he does so as principal or agent. Unless he makes it plain to the expert that it is the client who is responsible for the payment of fees, the solicitor may have a responsibility to pay them. The solicitor's responsibility may arise not only in contract but also as a matter of professional conduct. The Law Society's *Guide to the Professional Conduct of Solicitors* gives the following guidance:

In all cases where a solicitor has not clearly disclaimed personal liability to pay witnesses and other persons advising him in their professional capacity, he is obliged to pay them their proper fees and accordingly failure to do so will amount to unbefitting conduct which may lead to disciplinary action.

For the purposes of taxation of standard basis costs, both the fees of expert witnesses and the costs of solicitor and counsel in obtaining and considering their reports or advices are recoverable in a proper case. The court has an over-riding discretion regarding costs, however, and *Cable v Dallaturca* (1977) *The Times*, 9 November) illustrates the power of the court to penalise the party in costs in an appropriate case. In *F Rigolli v Lambeth* (5 December 1977) (unreported) Donaldson J, sitting with assessors, held that the Taxing Master was wrong to disallow the costs incurred in calling a second expert witness whose evidence was, in his view, unnecessary. If a witness was called the cost involved should not be disallowed unless the judge so ordered.

An issue frequently arises as to whether a party may include the cost of his claims consultant within his party and party costs. The cost of a claims consultant preparing a claim is not ordinarily allowable, but the preparation of proper expert evidence may be. In *James Longley v South West Thames Regional Health Authority* (1983) 127 SJ s 97, for example, the claimants were allowed £6,452 of their claim consultant's bill of £16,022 for preparing for, and for the first 16 days of, an expected 16 week hearing.

Chapter 15

Dismissal for want of prosecution

There are various rules of the Supreme Court which empower the court to dismiss an action for want of prosecution: Ord 19, r 1 (where the plaintiff is in default of service of statement of claim); Ord 24. r 16(1) (default in the discovery and production of documents); Ord 25, r 1(4) (default in taking out a summons for directions); Ord 26, r 6(1) (default in answer to interrogatories); and Ord 34, r 2 (default in setting down). In addition, the court has an inherent jurisdiction to dismiss an action for want of prosecution where there is default in compliance with an order of the court, or where the plaintiff is guilty of excessive delay in the prosecution of the action.

In *Birkett v James* [1977] 3 WLR 38 the House of Lords reviewed the principles upon which the jurisdiction of the court to dismiss an action for want of prosecution is exercised. Lord Diplock said that:

the power should be exercised only where the court is satisfied either
(1) that the default has been intentional and contumelious, eg, disobedience to a peremptory order of the court or conduct amounting to an abuse of the process of the court, or
(2) (a) that there has been inordinate and inexcusable delay on the part of the plaintiff or his lawyers; and
    (b) that such delay will give rise to a substantial risk that it is not possible to have a fair trial of the issues in the action or is such as is likely to cause or to have caused serious prejudice to the defendants either as between themselves and the plaintiff or between each other or between them and the third party.

The application of these rules to building contract litigation is of special importance because of the great difficulty that plaintiffs frequently have in adhering to the time scale set out in the rules of the Supreme Court.

The principles lying behind the cases upon dismissal for want of prosecution are reviewed in the notes to the *White Book* at Paras 25/1/4 et seq. There are two cases that are of particular importance to building contract cases: *Renown Investments (Holdings) Ltd v F Shepherd & Son* (1976) 120 SJ 840 and *Birkett v James* [1977] 3 WLR 38. Different principles apply in arbitrations.

1 *Renown Investments v Shepherd*

The flood of applications by defendants for dismissal for want of prosecution began in the late 1960s. After a few years the Court of Appeal heard *Renown Investments (Holdings) Ltd v F Shepherd & Son* (1976) 120 SJ 840. In that case the plaintiff claimed damages for breach of contract and for alleged negligence against contractors, engineers and architects arising out of building defects. The pleadings were closed in December 1971 and by July 1974, when there had been no summons for directions and no discovery, the defendants issued a summons to strike out the action for want of prosecution.

It was urged for the plaintiff that building contracts were so complicated and detailed that they were in a special category, and a great deal of time could be spent in preparing them for litigation. The court rejected that contention and held that building contract litigation was not in any special category and should be prosecuted expeditiously in compliance with the RSC time scale, particularly where it involved charges of negligence against professional men.

2 *Birkett v James*

In *Birkett v James* [1977] 3 WLR 38 the House of Lords has put two very important limits upon the power of the court to dismiss actions for want of prosecution.

First, the power will not usually be exercised where the limitation period has yet to expire. Lord Diplock said:

For my part, for reasons that I have already stated, I am of opinion that the fact that the limitation period has not yet expired must always be a matter of great weight in determining whether to exercise the discretion to dismiss an action for want of prosecution where no question of contumelious default on the part of the plaintiff is involved; and in cases where it is likely that if the action were dismissed the plaintiff would avail himself of his legal right to issue a fresh writ, the non-expiry of the limitation period is generally a conclusive reason for not dismissing the action that is already pending.

Where there is doubt as to whether the limitation period has expired, the court may consider the likelihood of fresh proceedings (*Barclays v Miller* [1990] 1 All ER 1040).

The second limit relates to the time which elapses before the issue of a writ. It had been settled law even before *Birkett v James* that a plaintiff who left it until the last moment before issuing a writ was in greater danger of being struck out. In the words of Lord Diplock:

A late start makes it all the more incumbent upon the plaintiff to proceed with all due speed and a pace which might have been excusable if the action had been started sooner may be inexcusable in the light of the time that has already passed before the writ was issued.

However, in order to justify dismissal of an action for want of prosecution, the House of Lords in *Birkett v James* held that the defendant must, if he is to succeed, point to time which the plaintiff allows to elapse unnecessarily *after* the writ has been issued, and must further show that delay in prosecuting the action after that time has added to the prejudice which the defendant would have sustained in any event from the late issue of the writ. The additional prejudice need not be great compared with that which may have been caused by the time elapsed before the writ was issued, but it must be more than minimal.

The House of Lords returned to the point in *Department of Transport v Chris Smaller* [1989] AC 1197. The action was to be tried nearly 11 years after the original accident, of which 13 months was attributable to inexcusable delay. The defendants submitted that this delay had prejudiced them because it had hindered them in raising finance to expand their business. The court did not accept this as sufficient prejudice for striking out purposes.

For an example of sufficient prejudice, see *Lowfield v Modern Engineering* (1988) 15 CLR 27, where the plaintiffs delayed for four years. Documents were destroyed, experts did not meet and proofs were not exchanged.

3 The position in arbitration

Until recently, a respondent in arbitration had a much more difficult task than a defendant in High Court litigation in taking action to bring to an end arbitrations which have proceeded slowly. Now, however, section 102 of the Courts and Legal Services Act 1990 introduces a new section 13A to the Arbitration Act 1950 which provides as follows:

13a (1) Unless a contrary intention is expressed in the arbitration agreement, the arbitrator or umpire shall have power to make an award dismissing any claim in a dispute referred to him, if it appears to him that the conditions mentioned in subsection (2) are satisfied.

(2) the conditions are —

(a) that there has been inordinate and inexcusable delay on the part of the claimant in pursuing the claim, and

(b) that the delay —

(i) will give rise to a substantial risk that it is not possible to have a fair resolution of the issues in the claim; or

(ii) has caused, or is likely to cause or to have caused, serious prejudice to the respondent.

. . .

This section is to come into force on 1 January 1992, and gives arbitrators identical powers to the court to dismiss claims for want of prosecution. It remains to be seen how it will operate in practice.

4 Practice

It is very common for building contract litigation to take a long time, and a plaintiff is often quite unable to adhere to the time scale for taking various steps laid down by the rules of the Supreme Court. A plaintiff's real risk begins once six (or twelve) years have passed since the date of the accrual of the cause of action.

Of course, the safest course for a plaintiff is to pursue the litigation as rapidly as possible. Where, however, it is not possible for the plaintiff to take any particular step within the time laid down by the rules, he should obtain an extension of time either by agreement or from the court. Where, for example, the plaintiff wishes to postpone a hearing, or to defer the fixing of a hearing so that without prejudice discussions may take place, then he should obtain the agreement of the defendant to that postponement. An agreement between the parties that the hearing should be adjourned generally with leave to restore when both parties are ready, or an agreement to the like effect, will preclude the defendant from applying to strike out for want of prosecution without, at any rate, giving reasonable notice of his own readiness and requiring the opposite party to be ready (*Banca Popolare di Novara v John Livanos & Sons Ltd* (1973) *The Times*, 22 June, CA). If a plaintiff is in genuine difficulties in meeting the time limit, and cannot obtain an extension from the defendant, he may apply to the court for an extension of time, and the court has power to extend the period within which a plaintiff is required to do any act in any proceedings (Ord 3, r 5(1)).

There is no prescribed stage at which the defendant may apply to the court to exercise its inherent jurisdiction to dismiss a plaintiff's action for want of prosecution. Sometimes, the defendant will issue his summons upon receipt of notice of intention to proceed under Ord 3, r 6. Sometimes the application will be coupled with an application for, or following, an 'unless' order.

In support of his application, the defendant will almost always need an affidavit in support, and the affidavit must generally show three things:

(1) that the limitation period has expired;
(2) that there has been inordinate and inexcusable delay since the date of the issue of the writ, referring particularly to any delay immediately preceding the issue of the summons; and
(3) that the defendant has suffered some real prejudice by reason of that delay. Examples of prejudice are that the memories of the main witnesses have faded, or that witnesses have died or left the employ of the defendant and cannot be traced, or that the passage of time has rendered it impossible or difficult to obtain necessary evidence from an inspection of the building in question. Prejudice may sometimes be caused by the loss of opportunity to pursue remedies against third parties, although the proper time for issuing third party notices is prior to the service of the defence and

it may be necessary to show exceptional circumstances (such as the intervening insolvency of a third party) in order to show prejudice.

The affidavit must, to be effective, be made by a deponent who can actually prove the facts (*Kue v Tretol* [1991] CILL 657).

Ordinarily, the plaintiff should file an affidavit in reply endeavouring to explain all the circumstances relied upon as excusing the delay and, where appropriate, making proper comment upon the prejudice referred to in the defendant's affidavit.

Chapter 16

Arbitration

Arbitration arises out of a written agreement to submit present or future differences to arbitration, whether an arbitrator is named therein or not (Arbitration Act 1950, s 32). That is to say, it arises as a matter of contract. It is, however, a contract that is much affected by the provisions of the Arbitration Acts and by common law.

It is a mistake to think of arbitration as an option open to save the trouble of litigation. Arbitration is akin to litigation except that the parties have chosen their own judge (or a means of appointing their own judge). There are usually pleadings, interlocutory applications, discovery, inspection, briefs, witnesses, subpoenas, trials, taxation of costs and appeals, and the arbitrator is bound to reach his decision according to the legal rights of the parties and not according to what he may consider fair and reasonable under all the circumstances (*Taylor (David) & Son Ltd v Barnett Trading Co* [1953] 1 WLR 562).

There are three relevant Arbitration Acts.

(1) The Arbitration Act 1950 — This Act was a consolidation of the previous law and sets out the main body of arbitration law.

(2) The Arbitration Act 1975 — This Act deals with arbitrations with a foreign element. Section 1 removes the court's discretion to stay court proceedings. For claims within a non-domestic arbitration agreement, the court *must* now stay such court proceedings. Sections 2 to 6 give effect to the New York Convention on the Recognition and Enforcement of Foreign Arbitral Awards.

(3) The Arbitration Act 1979 — This Act replaced s 21 of the 1950 Act (which provided for appeal by way of case stated) with a new appeals procedure and a new procedure for taking preliminary points in the High Court. By s 5 it also provided for the High Court to empower an arbitrator to make 'unless' orders.

The Courts and Legal Services Act (CLSA) 1990 has introduced some changes to this legislation. For example, s 11 of the Arbitration Act 1950 has been modified by s 99 of the CLSA, which provides that Official Referees are not permitted to take arbitrations unless the Lord Chief Justice so authorises, such decision to be based on the formal workload the Official Referee could otherwise be undertaking in the lists.

Furthermore, arbitrators now have added power under s 13 of the Arbitration Act 1950 to strike out for want of prosecution. Lastly, but not least, the High Court's power to order discovery has now been repealed, removing the power that was previously available under s 12(6)(b) of the 1950 Act.

As to the procedure in arbitration, there is no comprehensive set of rules comparable to the rules of the Supreme Court, the Matrimonial Causes rules or the County Court rules. The Arbitration Act 1950 contains what are in effect a number of terms to be implied into the arbitration agreement but these do not go into great detail.

For this reason, the conduct of arbitration tends to be at times haphazard in comparison with court proceedings. The standard works on arbitration are *Russell on Arbitration* (A Walton (Ed)), 20th edn (Stevens and Son Ltd, 1982) and *Mustill & Boyd*. In practice, arbitrations conducted before experienced arbitrators are generally conducted according to established customs which were set out with clarity in the RIBA publication, *The Architect as Arbitrator* (revised edition 1987).

This chapter deals only with arbitration pursuant to arbitration clauses in building contracts. In particular, it does not relate to arbitrations under statutes, nor does it relate to arbitrations within the meaning of the County Court rules.

1 The jurisdiction of the arbitrator

The arbitrator derives his powers from the arbitration clause in the contract, and in building contracts these are usually drawn extremely widely. In Article 5 of JCT 80, for example, the parties refer to the arbitrator:

any dispute or difference as to the construction of this Contract or any matter or thing of whatsoever nature arising hereunder or in connection herewith . . .

Unless the parties otherwise agree, the arbitrator has no jurisdiction to determine whether or not the contract came into being or not, because that would necessarily entail his deciding whether the arbitration clause, and hence his own appointment was valid. The arbitrator does, however, have jurisdiction to decide a claim for rectification (*Ashville v Elmer* (1987) 37 BLR 55).

The arbitrator's jurisdiction goes much further than that of merely resolving disputes (the arbitral function), since Clause 41.4 of JCT 80 goes on to provide that the arbitrator has power:

to ascertain and award any sum which ought to have been the subject of or included in any certificate and to open up, review and revise any certificate, opinion, decision, requirement or notice and to determine all matters in dispute which shall be submitted to him in the same manner as if no such certificate, opinion, decision, requirement or notice had been given.

In *Northern Regional Health Authority v Derek Crouch Construction Co Ltd* [1984] 2 All ER 175 it was decided by the Court of Appeal that this gave to an arbitrator powers that a court would not have (save in the exceptional circumstances of a High Court judge being appointed an arbitrator). The arbitrator's role is thus a dual one, not only to decide the rights of the parties as arbitrator but also to create rights in the review process. The primary effect of this decision is that it is only an arbitrator (and not a court) who may enforce the contract terms themselves (as opposed to the certificates) in the many areas where the contract calls for certification. It also seems that the duality of the arbitrator's role may have some side effects. Presumably, it is only the arbitral function and not the review function which is subject to the Arbitration Acts. There are a number of as yet unanswered questions which arise out of this. Is the arbitrator subject to judicial review as well as or instead of the appeal procedure insofar as he performs his review role? Might he even be susceptible to an action in negligence if he fails in his review procedure? May the review function proceed even if the arbitral function is stayed by order of court?

The arbitration clause does not give the arbitrator power to order the contractor to undertake remedial work as an alternative to paying damages, and the court has said that such an order is not only clearly outside the powers of an arbitrator but also quite impracticable of implementation; *BFI Group of Companies Ltd v DCB Integration Systems Ltd* [1987] CILL 348.

2 The arbitration notice

The term 'arbitration notice' is usually used to describe the notice from one party to a contract requiring the other party to agree to submit a dispute between them to an arbitrator. Its significance arises out of the Limitation Act 1980, for under s 34 of that Act it is the service of an arbitration notice that is regarded as the commencement of the arbitration for limitation purposes, and thus equivalent to the issue of a writ in the High Court for that purpose. It should be noted that although the arbitration notice marks the commencement of the arbitration for limitation purposes, it does not represent the commencement of the arbitration in any other sense, and an arbitration is not regarded as having been commenced until such time as an arbitrator has accepted a proper appointment.

An arbitration notice need not be in any prescribed form and it is usual for it simply to contain a notice of dispute and a request of the other party to concur in the appointment of an arbitrator. The terms of the notice generally depend upon the terms of the arbitration clause in the contract relied upon. A typical wording of an arbitration notice written by a solicitor where the contract is in the standard JCT form is as follows:

Dear Sirs,

We are instructed by Messrs X in relation to their contract with you for works at X.

We hereby give you notice on behalf of our clients of disputes or differences that have arisen between you and them and hereby request that you concur in the appointment of an arbitrator.

Yours faithfully,

It is usually unwise to try to particularise the nature of the dispute in the notice to concur.

An arbitration notice is not usually regarded as an offer capable of acceptance, nor does it operate to activate any arbitration machinery.

The arbitration does not commence until an arbitrator is actually appointed. Further, there is nothing to prevent a claimant from serving an arbitration notice before, at the same time as or after issuing a writ in the court. However, the service of an arbitration notice by a party who is already a plaintiff is frequently regarded as adding fuel to the fire of a defendant who takes out a s 4 summons to stay any parallel proceedings in the court. For this reason, it is common practice in appropriate cases to make the position entirely plain in the arbitration notice, by adding a further paragraph along the following lines:

Please take note that our clients take the view that the proper forum for the hearing of this dispute is the High Court. This notice is accordingly served in order to protect our clients' position for limitation purposes.

It is sometimes said that this paragraph should be contained in a separate letter dispatched contemporaneously with the arbitration notice, but it is open to doubt whether this procedure carries with it any advantage. In any event, doubts have been expressed as to whether such a paragraph deprives the arbitration notice of its effect for limitation purposes; notwithstanding those doubts it probably represents the best available course in an unsatisfactory area of law.

Arbitration notices are sometimes typed up as formal legal documents with words like 'In the matter of the Arbitration Act, 1950 and 1979' at the top of the page. There is no harm in this practice but a letter is quite sufficient.

3 Choosing an arbitrator

The arbitration provisions in the JCT form of contract (Article 5 and Clause 41) provide that the arbitrator is to be a person agreed between the parties to act as arbitrator, or failing agreement within fourteen days after the arbitration notice, a person to be appointed on the request of either party by the president or vice president for the time being of the Royal Institute of British Architects. Forms of contract published by other professional bodies generally provide for appointment by their own president for the time being failing agreement by the parties. Some other forms of building contract simply provide that disputes are to be referred to arbitration without providing the machinery for selection of an arbitrator where the parties cannot agree; in such a case the High Court has power to appoint an arbitrator under the Arbitration Act 1950, s 10 as amended by the Courts and Legal Services Act 1990, s 101.

The question arises, how should a party select an arbitrator whom he seeks to have appointed? This is a matter of experience and knowledge of the many names to choose from, but it is possible to give certain guidelines.

(1) In the case of substantial disputes where the sum in dispute exceeds say £100,000, then it is normal to appoint one of the few senior building contract arbitrators in the country. There is no substitute for the personal experience of these people in making a choice between them. In any event, great caution should be exercised before appointing an arbitrator who is not a member of the Chartered Institute of Arbitrators. Assistance may be obtained from the Society of Construction Arbitrators whose secretary is Francis Goodall, 37 Molyneaux Street, Marylebone, London, W1H 5HW, telephone 071-262 6651.

(2) Specialist counsel generally know by reputation, if not by personal experience, of arbitrators who habitually arbitrate in building contract disputes.

It is not normal to seek the consent of a proposed arbitrator before suggesting his name to the other party. The suggestion is generally made subject to that arbitrator consenting to act.

When suggesting the arbitrator to the other party, it is frequent practice to suggest two names. Often the party making the suggestion will put his first choice second in the belief that the second-placed suggestion is more likely to be acceptable than the first.

It goes without saying that to attempt to have appointed an arbitrator who is not or may not be impartial is a recipe for disaster. It does no harm, however, when considering the other party's proposals as to choice of arbitrator, to ask for warranties that the proposed arbitrator does not have, so far as the other party is aware, any interest or potential interest in the dispute or connection with the parties.

4 The appointment of the arbitrator

Where the parties are able to agree upon a suitable arbitrator, one or the other of them should write to the proposed arbitrator asking whether he is prepared to accept the appointment. It is customary to enclose copies of the correspondence following the arbitration notice and wise to ask for details of the remuneration that the arbitrator will require. The arbitrator's authority does not commence until he has accepted the appointment.

Even before the appointment of the arbitrator it is customary to follow the normal rules as to communications with the arbitrator as follows:

(1) neither party should exchange any oral communication with the proposed arbitrator concerning the arbitration except in the presence of the other party;

(2) telephone messages should only be relayed through the arbitrator's secretary; and

(3) each party should immediately send a copy of any written communication with the arbitrator to the other party.

Where it is not possible to agree the proposed arbitrator with the other party, it is necessary to apply to the RIBA or other professional body, or to the court.

To obtain the appointment of an arbitrator by the RIBA it is necessary to write to the RIBA at 66 Portland Place, London, WlN 4AD requesting a form of application. The RIBA will then provide a standard form of application for appointment which needs to be executed by one or both of the parties. One or both of the parties is required (jointly and severally) to agree as follows:

(1) to provide adequate security for the due payment of the fees and expenses of the arbitrator if he so requires;

(2) to pay the fees and expenses of the arbitrator whether the arbitration reaches a hearing or not; and

(3) to take up the award (if any) within ten days of receipt of notice of publication.

Arbitrations frequently involve a claimant who is keen to proceed with the arbitration and a respondent who is considerably less eager. Sometimes the respondent declines to sign the application form. The RIBA will not appoint an arbitrator unless the claimant himself signs and returns the form, thus making him primarily liable to provide any required security and to pay the arbitrator's fees and expenses. What can the claimant do? It is plain from the Arbitration Act 1950, s 12(1), that it is an implied term of arbitration agreements that each party will do all things required by the arbitrator for the proper conduct of the arbitration, but it is not clear what effect the section has before the arbitrator is actually appointed. In theory it might perhaps be possible to obtain an injunction requiring the respondent to execute the form of appointment, but in practice this is likely to be unrealistic and the claimant must choose between accepting responsibility himself for the arbitrator's fees and expenses, or instituting or returning to proceedings in the court. A defendant who has refused to execute the standard RIBA form of appointment may well have difficulty in showing that he is and remains ready and willing to do all things necessary to the proper conduct of the arbitration, as he would be required to show under the Arbitration Act 1950, s 4.

The standard RIBA form of appointment contains a space for the signed acceptance of the appointed arbitrator.

Where there is no machinery for appointment by the president of a professional body and it is necessary to apply to the court under the Arbitration Act 1950, s 10 as amended by the Courts and Legal Services

Act 1990, s 201, then application is made to the High Court by originating summons (Ord 73, r 3(3)).

5 The preliminary meeting

It is customarily the arbitrator's first step upon appointment to call the parties to a preliminary meeting, which is analogous to an immediate summons for directions. It is suggested in *The Architect as Arbitrator* that the directions may be given in a form which sets out a timetable for the delivery of pleadings, a timetable for discovery, for agreement of figures etc, as to the number of experts, that communications to the arbitrator should be simultaneously copied to the other party, and as to costs and liberty to apply.

It is normal for the parties to be represented at the preliminary meeting by their solicitors, although representation is sometimes by counsel in more complex cases.

It is customary (but by no means universal) for the arbitrator to be handed the original contract at the preliminary meeting.

6 Interlocutory matters

In practice, arbitrators in building contract matters usually follow High Court procedure as closely as possible.

In respect of arbitrations commenced after 1 August 1979, the potential powers of the arbitrator have been augmented by the Arbitration Act 1979, s 5(1) and (2), which provide as follows:

5 – (1) If any party to a reference under an arbitration agreement fails within the time specified in the order or, if no time is so specified, within a reasonable time, to comply with an order made by the arbitrator or umpire in the course of the reference, then, on the application of the arbitrator or umpire or of any party to the reference, the High Court may make an order extending the powers of the arbitrator or umpire as mentioned in subsection (2) below.

(2) If an order is made by the High Court under this section, the arbitrator or umpire shall have the power, to the extent and subject to any conditions specified in that order, to continue with the reference in default of appearance or of any other act by one of the parties in like manner as a judge of the High Court might continue with proceedings in that Court where a party fails to comply with an order of that court or a requirement of the rules of court.

The effect of s 5 is that, where necessary, the High Court may clothe the arbitrator with the power to make 'unless' orders, but in practice the section is unwieldy. It enables one party to the arbitration to say to the other, 'I am going to get an order from the arbitrator about this procedural point, and if you do not comply with it I am going to issue High Court proceedings and ask the judge to tell the arbitrator to tell you that if you do not comply with the order, then we are not going to ask you again!'.

In the case of arbitration commenced before 1 August 1979, or where the arbitrator is unduly hesitant in the exercise of his powers, the High Court has power to make direct orders under the Arbitration Act 1950 s 12(6), which provides as follows:

(6) The High Court shall have, for the purpose of and in relation to a reference, the same power of making orders in respect of —
   (a) security for costs;
   (b) discovery of documents and interrogatories;
   (c) the giving of evidence by affidavit;
   (d) examination on oath of any witness before an officer of the High Court or any other person, and the issue of a commission or request for the examination of a witness out of the jurisdiction;
   (e) the preservation, interim custody or sale of any goods which are the subject matter of the reference;
   (f) securing the amount in dispute in the reference;
   (g) the detention, preservation or inspection of any property or thing which is the subject of the reference or as to which any question may arise therein. and authorising for any of the purposes aforesaid any persons to enter upon or enter into any land or building in the possession of any party to the reference, or authorising any samples to be taken or any observation to be made or experiment to be tried which may be necessary or expedient for the purpose of obtaining full information or evidence; and
   (h) interim injunctions or the appointment of a receiver; as it has for the purpose of and in relation to an action or matter in the High Court.
Provided that nothing in this subsection shall be taken to prejudice any power which may be vested in an arbitrator or umpire of making orders with respect to any of the matters aforesaid.

7 Sealed offers

There is no formal procedure in arbitrations equivalent to payment into court, and accordingly there has evolved the practice of making sealed offers in appropriate cases. The following helpful guidance appears in *The Architect as Arbitrator* (1987 edn):

In arbitrations such an offer is made in writing, a copy of the letter being placed in a sealed envelope and handed to the arbitrator for him to open after he has made his award, but before he comes to consider the question of costs. In this way the arbitrator's decision about what ought to be paid is not influenced by knowing what has been offered.

The arbitrator may find the very existence of a 'sealed offer' from one of the parties slightly to prejudice his consideration of the amount to be awarded as it could be interpreted as an admission of liability. This can be overcome by agreeing with both the parties at the outset (without their disclosing which of them would be making the offer) that he will issue an interim award after the hearing dealing finally with the subject matters in dispute but reserving his decision on costs to his final award. After the publication of the interim award, the arbitrator can hear submissions from the parties on the question of costs when the existence of any open offer can be announced and the liability for costs adjusted accordingly.

If the arbitrator is not informed sufficiently early, after making his substantive award, that a sealed offer has been made so that costs can be dealt with separately, the cost benefit and protection could be lost (*MF King Holdings plc v Thomas McKenna* [1991] 2 QB 480).

It should be noted that a sealed offer is the arbitral equivalent of making a payment into court (*Tramountana Armadora SA v Atlantic Shipping* [1978] 1 Lloyd's Rep 391) and so the withdrawal of a sealed offer may nullify its effect as to costs; see the Court of Appeal decision in *Garner v Cleggs* [1983] 1 WLR 862.

8 Trial

Reference was made in Chapter 7 to the unsuitability of the arbitration process for multi-partite disputes. This unsuitability cannot be resolved by the arbitrator or arbitrators ordering related arbitrations to be heard at the same time unless all parties consent (*Oxford Shipping Co Ltd v Nippon Yusen Kaisha* [1984] 2 Lloyd's Rep 373).

Unless many people need to be present, interlocutory hearings in arbitrations are very frequently held at the offices of the arbitrator. It is usually necessary, however, to hire a room for the trial itself, and it is frequently left to the solicitors for the parties to perform this function.

In some arbitrations it is regarded as desirable to have a transcript record of the proceedings, which can be done by shorthand writers or mechanical recording. Again, it is usually left to the parties' solicitors to arrange this if appropriate.

In major building contract litigation the proceedings at trial are scarcely distinguishable from trial in the courts, save that the advocates do not appear robed and the arbitrator is addressed as 'Sir' rather than 'Your Honour' or 'My Lord'. The usual rules apply as to evidence, and the court has powers under the Arbitration Act 1950, s 12, to make orders with regard to subpoenas and such matters. It should not be forgotten that a Bible is necessary to swear in the witnesses.

9 Appeals

The rules as to appealing from the decision of arbitrators were radically changed by the Arbitration Act 1979, ss 1–4. Before that Act came into force, the position as to the statement of cases by arbitrators for a decision of the High Court was governed by the rules of the Arbitration Act 1950, s 2, which were widely regarded as unsatisfactory.

If an appeal is contemplated then reference must be made to the terms of the Arbitration Act 1979, but in any event it is important to have regard to the Arbitration Act 1979, s 1(6)(a), which provides that if a party contemplates the possibility of an appeal he should give notice to the arbitrator that a reasoned award is required.

Under the Arbitration Act 1979, s 2, the High Court now has power to determine any question of law arising in the course of the reference in an appropriate case. The section replaces the previously unsatisfactory position whereby preliminary points of law, if to be tried before the court, had to be tried by way of case stated upon a preliminary point.

The courts do not encourage appeals from arbitration, even appeals on points of law under s 1(2) of the Arbitration Act 1979. In *Pioneer Shipping v B T P Tioxide*; *The Nema* [1981] 3 WLR 292, the House of Lords laid down some principles upon which leave to appeal should ordinarily be granted or refused; one of those principles was that leave to appeal should not ordinarily be given as to the construction of 'one off' clauses. Rather less strict criteria are appropriate where questions of construction of contracts in standard terms are concerned. The principles laid down by the *Nema* case are applicable in building cases in the same way as in other cases (*Higgs and Hill Building v University of London* (1983) 24 BLR 139).

10 Compulsory arbitration rules

There is already an arbitration procedure, which has been prepared by the Institution of Civil Engineers, which may govern the conduct of arbitration of ICE contracts.

11 The ICC Court of Arbitration

The International Chamber of Commerce Court of Arbitration has been in existence for more than fifty years, and is established as the major international 'independent' arbitration service. Compared with domestic arbitrations, international arbitrations are necessarily expensive and troublesome. In practical terms, that is inevitable and in major contracts between parties resident in different countries (particularly where one party is a government), arbitration before the ICC Court of Arbitration represents the only acceptable means of resolving disputes since only the ICC Court of Arbitration can offer a sufficient guarantee of neutrality.

In the building contract world, international contracts are frequently entered into in the FIDIC form, which is prepared by the Fédération Internationale Des Ingénieurs-Conseils, and is in effect an adaptation from the ICE form of contract. The FIDIC contract contains an arbitration clause referring disputes which cannot be settled by the engineer to the ICC Court of Arbitration.

Where the ICC Court of Arbitration has been nominated in the arbitration agreement, it is unlikely that the arbitration agreement will be a 'domestic arbitration agreement' within the meaning of the Arbitration Act 1975. In the case of a non-domestic arbitration agreement, the court does not have a *discretion* under the Arbitration Act 1950, s 4, to stay any proceedings commenced in the court. It *must* stay the court proceedings under the Arbitration Act 1975, s 1(1), which provides as follows:

1 — (1) If any party to an arbitration agreement to which this section applies, or any person claiming through or under him, commences any legal proceedings in any Court against any other party to the agreement, or any person claiming through or under him, in respect of any matter agreed to be referred, any party to the proceedings may at any time after appearance, and before delivering any pleadings or taking any other steps in the proceedings, apply to the Court to stay the proceedings; and the Court, unless satisfied that the arbitration agreement is null and void, inoperative or incapable of being performed or that there is not in fact any dispute between the parties with regard to the matter agreed to be referred, shall make an Order staying the proceedings.

It can be seen that although the court does not have its discretion in non-domestic cases, there are three circumstances where the court will allow court proceedings to continue:

(1) Where the defendant takes a step in the proceedings, which he may do by accident or design (see Chapter 10, section 2).

(2) Where the court is satisfied that the arbitration agreement is null and void, which will usually hinge upon whether the whole of the contract is null and void.

(3) It will be seen that the Arbitration Act 1975 expressly preserves the principle enunciated in *Ellis Mechanical Services Ltd v Wates Construction Ltd* (1976) 2 BLR 60; that is to say, that it is for the court to decide whether or not there is a dispute. It seems that the words of Lord Denning MR in that case at p 61 are applicable in non-domestic cases as well as in domestic cases:

The defendants cannot insist on the whole going to arbitration by simply saying that there is a difference or dispute about it. If the court sees that there is a sum which is indisputably due, then the court can give judgment for that sum and let the rest go to arbitration . . .

Indeed, this passage was cited by Geoffrey Lane LJ in *Associated Bulk Carriers v Koch Shipping* (1977) 7 BLR 18, a case decided under the Arbitration Act 1975. In that case, the *Ellis* decision was distinguished upon the ground that, although liability was admitted by the defendants and it was clear that the plaintiffs would recover substantial damages, there was no definable or quantified part of the plaintiffs' claim which was not in fact in dispute. The defendants were able to avoid an Ord 14 judgment by putting up various different calculations as to the minimum sum due. All the judges in the case found that the defendants were devoid of any merits, and were seeking arbitration in order to take advantage of the long delays involved in arbitration. Although it does not appear from the judgment, it may be that the conclusion to be drawn from *Associated Bulk Carriers v Koch Shipping* is that the court adopts a more cautious and less robust approach to Ord 14 cases where there is a non-domestic arbitration agreement than it does where there is a domestic one.

Even if one of the above three circumstances appertain, an English claimant is likely to have other difficulties apart from the Arbitration Act

1975 which he must overcome in order to proceed in the English courts. If he wishes to serve the proceedings upon a defendant outside the jurisdiction, he must obtain the *ex parte* leave of the court under Ord 11, r 1. If the court grants leave to serve the writ out of the jurisdiction, the defendant can apply to set aside the writ on the ground of want of jurisdiction under Ord 12, r 8.

Where the claimant does not wish or cannot have the matter dealt with by the English courts, then he will generally serve his opponent with a formal arbitration notice for limitation purposes, and then approach the International Chamber of Commerce.

The head office of the International Chamber of Commerce is at 38 Cours Albert-1er, 75008 Paris. ICC United Kingdom, the British affiliate of the ICC, has offices at Centre Point, 103 New Oxford Street, London WC1A 1QB (tel 071-240 5558) and it is possible to obtain from that address the thirty-two page booklet which sets out the Rules for the ICC Court of Arbitration. The Rules provide for pleadings, submission of all relevant documents, hearings, amendments and costs.

Chapter 17

Limitation of actions

Limitation issues in construction cases have not been an easy topic over the last few years. There are a number of reasons for this.

First, the courts went through a long period of uncertainty and change as to what period of limitation ought to be applied to a claim for defects in tort. Those doubts began with *Dutton v Bognor Regis* [1972] 1 All ER 462 and continued until *Pirelli v Oscar Faber* [1983] 1 All ER 65.

The *Pirelli* case contained a suggestion by Lord Fraser that the decision might not apply if a building were 'doomed from the start'. These words sparked off a further line of cases. Not to be outdone, Parliament introduced massive complications in the Latent Damage Act 1986.

The following discussion will endeavour to summarise the present position.

1 Defects claims for breach of contract

The Latent Damage Act 1986 is worded so as to introduce three new provisions, ss 14A, 14B and 28A, into the Limitation Act 1980. Section 28A deals with persons under a disability; it will be rare for these provisions to be relevant in construction cases and they will not be discussed here. Sections 14A and 14B are each applicable to actions 'for damages for negligence'. Although the Act is not explicit on the point it seems that this means the tort of negligence and is not intended to include actions where the negligence is in breach of a contractual duty. The Latent Damage Act 1986, therefore, is thought not to affect the existing law on limitation in contract cases.

An employer's action in contract against a contractor for defects generally becomes statute-barred about six years after the date when the contractor was obliged to complete the works. If the contract was under seal, the period is twelve years. In the case of contracts where there is an express defects liability period, it is sometimes said that the employer's action in contract becomes statute-barred six (or twelve) years from the expiry of the defects liability period. This rule is subject to the important exception under the Limitation Act 1980, s 32, under which the limitation period can be extended if the contractor has deliberately concealed the defect. This section is now construed widely in building contract cases and may apply even where the employer had the benefit of agents overseeing the works (*Lewisham Borough Council v Leslie & Co* (1979) 250 EG 1289). It is, however, incumbent upon the plaintiff to lead evidence to establish deliberate concealment so that, where he employed his own expert supervisors he can establish that, in exercising reasonable skill, the supervisors could not have been expected to have observed the defects (*William Hill v Bernard Sunley* (1982) 22 BLR 1). Merely getting on with the work does not necessarily give rise to a legal reference of concealment (*E Clarke & Sons v Axtell Yates Hallett* [1989] CILL 532).

2 Defects claims in tort — the old law

The Latent Damage Act 1986 does not apply to actions that had been commenced prior to 18 September 1986, nor to any subsequent action that was already statute barred as at that date (Latent Damage Act 1986, s 4(1)). It will therefore be some considerable time before the Act will take full effect.

Neither does the Act apply to cases of deliberate concealment under s 32(1)(b) of the Limitation Act 1980. For reasons which appear below it will usually be in a defendant's interest to deny deliberate concealment; occasionally it will be in his interests to allege it.

In an employer's action in negligence against a builder for defects, the claim becomes statute-barred six years from the date on which the cause of action accrued (Limitation Act 1980, s 2).

In *Pirelli General Cable Works Ltd v Oscar Faber & Partners* (1982) 21 BLR 99 the House of Lords was asked to determine when the cause of action accrues. Lord Fraser said:

It seems to me that, except perhaps where the advice of an architect or consulting engineer leads to the erection of a building which is so defective as to be doomed from the start, the cause of the action accrues only when physical damage occurs to the building.

The *Pirelli* decision did not lay the debate to rest. There has, in particular, been almost total confusion as to when a building or part of a building is to be regarded as 'doomed from the start'. Much attention has been focused upon the meaning of the reference in the *Pirelli* case to the 'doomed from the start' cases. In *Ketteman and Others v Hansel Properties Ltd* [1984] 1 WLR 1274, the Court of Appeal found that the reference was *obiter* and no more than a cautionary dictum. On further appeal the House of Lords was more direct; it found that the houses in question were doomed from the start but nevertheless the limitation period still began when the damage occurred (see *Ketteman and Others v Hansel Properties Ltd* (1987) 36 BLR 1). It therefore seems that cases in which the limitation period will run from the time of construction by reason of being doomed from the start are so extraordinary as to be virtually non-existent. Two matters were, however, made plain by the *Pirelli* decision, both of them over-ruling the previously important decision of *Sparham-Souter v Town & Country Developments (Essex) Ltd* [1976] 1 QB 858.

(1) There is no rule that time begins to run again every time the property is transferred from owner to owner.

(2) There is no postponement of the limitation period until the defects appear, or could with reasonable diligence be discovered. This aspect of the decision relates, of course, to the position at common law and does not effect any extension of the limitation period under the Limitation Act 1980, s 32.

In a contractor's action in contract against a sub-contractor in respect of defects, the position appears to depend upon whether the sub-contract contains an express clause indemnifying the contractor against breaches of contract. If so, the contractor's action upon the indemnity clause is not statute-barred until six (or twelve) years from the date when the liability of the main contractor to the employer has been established (*County and District Properties v Jenner* [1976] 2 Lloyd's Rep 728).

In the case of a claim under the Defective Premises Act 1972, the claim becomes statute-barred six years after the time when the dwelling was completed or when remedial work was finished (Defective Premises Act 1972, s 1(5)).

3 Defects claims in tort — the new law

The scheme of the Latent Damage Act 1986 is that negligence claims are to become statute-barred either:

(1) six years from the date on which the cause of action accrued (such date falls to be established in accordance with the old rules, ie *Pirelli*); or

(2) three years from the date when the plaintiff knew he had an action ('the starting date');

whichever is the later (Limitation Act 1980, s 14A), but subject in either case to a 'long stop' of fifteen years from the date of the negligence complained of (Limitation Act 1980, s 14B).

The Act is explicit about what knowledge is required for the starting date. The plaintiff must know the material facts about the damage itself (ie 'such facts as would lead a reasonable person who had suffered the damage to consider it sufficiently serious to justify his instituting proceedings for damages against a defendant who did not dispute liability and was able to satisfy a judgment') and also certain other facts (ie that the damage was attributable to the negligence, the identity of the defendant, and in cases of vicarious liability, the identity of the person for whom the defendant is vicariously liable). Knowledge includes not only actual knowledge but the knowledge that the defendant might reasonably be expected to acquire with the benefit of expert advice.

If past experience of limitation disputes is any guide, this statutory definition of knowledge is capable of proving a Pandora's box of issues. Will plaintiffs regularly be able to plead lack of knowledge because they did not know the identity of the defendant's employees, for whom the defendant is vicariously liable? What person would not issue proceedings against a defendant who does not deny liability and who is good for the money, even if the damage is comparatively modest? On the other hand, why should it be necessary to issue proceedings in these hypothetical circumstances? If a defendant did not deny liability, would he not pay up? Is it inherent that there must be some sort of dispute as to quantum for these circumstances to apply at all? What is the meaning of 'expert advice'? Does it mean expert advice obtained for the purpose of remedial work, or the expert advice obtained for the purpose of litigation? Some light is shed on these issues by the decided cases on the comparable provisions in s 14 of the Limitation Act 1980 (personal injuries). In that context, the court has found that a plaintiff's solicitor is not an 'expert' (*Fowell v National Coal Board* [1986] CILL 294), but nevertheless the knowledge that a party's solicitor has, or could reasonably have had, is to be imputed to the party himself (*Simpson v Norwest Holst Southern Ltd* [1980] 2 All ER 471).

As a guide through the legislation, a questionnaire appears at Appendix D.

4 Other considerations in defects claims

Special rules apply to claims for contributions under the Law Reform (Married Women and Tortfeasors) Act 1935 or the Civil Liability (Contribution) Act 1978.

The period here is two years from the date of judgment in or settlement of the main action. The effect of these rules is that a party may be brought into an action as a third party long after the plaintiff's claim against that third party directly would be statute-barred. It was sometimes thought that a similar position might arise where an additional defendant was introduced to the action by amendment, but the 'relation back' theory was disapproved by the House of Lords in *Ketteman v Hansel Properties Ltd* (1987) 36 BLR 1 HL.

5 Claims for payment

It is rare for a plaintiff to leave a claim for payment outstanding for long enough for limitation issues to arise, but it occasionally happens in cases where there are very lengthy negotiations. It is common for there to be some sort of acknowledgment of the debt or part payment of it, which will have the effect of restarting the limitation period under s 29(5)(a) of the Limitation Act 1980. This section applies even if the plaintiff's claim is in *quantum meruit* and there is no agreement as to the amount of the liability (*Amantilla v Telefusion* (1987) 9 CLR 139).

A contractor's claim against an employer for payment frequently becomes statute-barred piecemeal. Much depends upon the precise terms of the contract but sometimes the first parts of the claim will become statute-barred six years after the commencement of work and the last part of the claim will become statute-barred about seven years after the completion of the work.

6 Limitation in arbitrations

For the purpose of proceedings in the High Court, the action will be statute-barred unless the plaintiff has issued his writ within the limitation period. For the purposes of arbitration proceedings, an action is statute-barred unless the claimant has, within the limitation period, served upon the respondent a notice requiring the respondent to concur in the appointment of an arbitrator (Limitation Act 1980, s 34). There is no provision whereby a plaintiff in the High Court can rely upon the date of an arbitration notice, nor any provision whereby a claimant in an arbitration can rely upon the date of the issue of a writ. Unless and until a party knows with certainty in which forum the dispute will be heard, his only safe course in order to stop time running is both to issue a writ and serve an arbitration notice. For a suggested form of words, see p 165.

For the limited purposes set out in the clauses themselves, arbitration clauses in JCT contracts contain provision for finality of final certificates if not challenged by litigation or arbitration within 28 days. There is power for the High Court to extend this period under s 27 of the Arbitration Act 1950, but only if refusal of the order would cause the applicant undue hardship. See *Emson Contractors Ltd v Protea Estates Ltd* [1987] CILL 366 for an example of such an application being refused.

Chapter 18

Settlement and Alternative Dispute Resolution

The vast majority of building contract cases are settled, reflecting the complexity and cost of bringing a building action to trial.

Some commercial lawyers and general practitioners take the view that litigation or arbitration is the end of the line. If they fail to achieve a commercial settlement without proceedings, they sometimes assume that they can delegate the file for the purpose of the interlocutory stages, and then instruct eminent leading counsel for the trial. This attitude is based upon the premise that the case will go to trial. But it is far more likely that the case will be settled, and the terms of settlement are usually very heavily influenced by the interlocutory process. For this reason, the *raison d'être* of many interlocutory steps in well-conducted building contract litigation is often to improve the climate for settlement, as well as to prepare for trial.

Thus, it has been the case for many years that solicitors conducting a building contract litigation or arbitration for their clients will be continually conscious of the prospects for settling the case. In recent years, it has been increasingly common for the parties to go further and embark upon an Alternative Dispute Resolution process, the only purpose of which is to obtain a settlement without court or arbitral proceedings.

The litigation process and the settlement process should not be regarded as separate as though the one excludes the other. On the contrary, it is often sensible to take steps in litigation which do not of themselves enhance one's prospects of success at trial, but which are calculated to increase the prospects of settlement. A particularly common example is where a defendant has to make a decision as to whether to seek further and better particulars of a flawed case. Counsel will often advise a defendant that it is better not to seek these particulars, on the basis that they will of themselves cause the plaintiff to put his house in order before trial. He may, however, insist on serving such a request in order to emphasise to the plaintiff the difficulties that the plaintiff would face if he went on to trial.

Conversely, it is sometimes sensible to attempt an Alternative Dispute Resolution process, even if it is thought unlikely to succeed in the first instance, because it might focus the minds of the parties on what are the essential issues, thus permitting subsequent litigation to be conducted much more economically and with a significantly enhanced prospect of settlement.

This interaction between litigation and negotiation is particularly complex in that class of case that is sometimes described as 'untriable'. These are cases which are so enormously complex that the time and cost that would be needed in trial is unthinkable. But beware; one man's shambles can be another man's triumph. It occasionally happens that a party will, in the final preparation stages of a case, engage the other party in 'dummy' settlement discussions. He may have no intention of settling the case along the lines he is discussing, but is simply trying to dissuade the other party from preparing for trial properly. In particular, this tactic is favoured by defendants who are simply trying to win time. The best response for a plaintiff in these circumstances is to split his negotiator or negotiators from his trial preparation team. The trial preparation team will continue to prepare for trial, completely separated from the negotiation process, unless and until settlement is achieved.

It is important that no-one should be afraid to negotiate, nor should anyone negotiate out of fear.

1 Achieving the climate for settlement

Before looking at the detailed techniques that can be used to achieve a climate for settlement, it is worth pausing to consider why parties litigate. *Prima facie*, litigation will almost always be counter to the aggregate interests of the parties; it distracts them from their real business and is extremely expensive. One needs to ask, therefore, what it is that typically stands in the way of the parties settling their disputes by agreement.

(a) Factors militating against settlement

In building cases, there are probably four main factors which keep the parties apart in the early stages. In three out of these four cases, the equation will typically change at some stage during the litigation process, making settlement easier.

Cash flow The defendant may not have the money that the plaintiff is claiming. Even if he has got the money, he will want to retain it for as long as possible.

The advantage for a defendant of holding out tends to disappear as trial gets closer. Legal costs rise very steeply at the trial stage, and the defendant not only has to write some very hefty cheques for his own lawyers, but faces the prospect of an imminent judgment against him and liability for the plaintiff's costs.

Similarly, as the plaintiff approaches trial, and finds himself making substantial payments to his lawyers instead of recovering anything, he is very likely to reconsider his position.

The enormous cost of litigation represents a crude but ultimately very powerful mechanism to encourage settlement.

Internal politics   Most litigation arises from mistakes having been made within an organisation, and there is often an enormous reluctance on the part of the individuals involved to admit those errors within their own company. This mechanism applies to plaintiffs and defendants equally. Thus, where a contractor has made a substantial loss on a project, the contract manager will often want to tell his directors that this was because of failures by the architect or sub-contractors. The architect will not usually want to admit to the employer that the job was held up by his own delay in issuing drawings.

Again, this effect tends to reverse as trial approaches. From an architect's point of view it is bad to have to recommend an extension of time for late instructions, but the imminent prospect of being taken apart in cross-examination, or being castigated in a court judgment, is even worse.

Ignorance   Litigation often proceeds because the parties do not yet know what result to expect. This ignorance might be ignorance of the facts, or uncertainty about the law, or both.

The factual problem is often very real for insured defendants; the insurance company may be faced with a substantial claim about which it initially knows nothing, and its advisers may have real difficulty in the early stages of litigation in giving any helpful advice about whether, and if so what, settlement would be wise. Litigation and arbitration are an extraordinarily crude and expensive way for the parties to find out about the strength and weaknesses of each other's cases but, nevertheless, by the time a case reaches the stage of counsel's advice on evidence, the parties should be able to form a view on the factual matrix of the dispute.

Legal uncertainty is somewhat different. There are many cases where one or the other party has marched on towards trial armed with what any specialist would describe as an absurd legal notion. Those cases are sometimes very difficult to settle until the party in question briefs leading counsel for trial, and that leading counsel explains to his client that he is on a loser. At the other end of the spectrum, building contract litigation abounds with interesting and difficult points of law which could easily go either way. Although well advised, the parties there may feel that they need to see which way the point is decided before deciding upon the terms upon which they would settle. And just occasionally, of course, the courts will cause an upset by deciding in favour of some legal proposition that all the 'experts' had hitherto regarded as absurd.

Again, this is a factor which will sometimes reverse as trial becomes imminent. The closer the parties get to trial, the more likely they are to weigh up the odds of succeeding on any particular issue, and to factor those odds into their negotiating position.

Aggression Some decision makers tend, when faced with a challenge, to harden their position. The more they are challenged, the more determined they become. Such confrontational types often do rather well in construction companies. Where the decision makers for both parties in a dispute have this characteristic, settlement can be extremely difficult. Unlike the preceding three factors, this factor does not automatically tend to reverse with the approach of trial.

(b) Practical steps to find a settlement

Against these four main background considerations, what practical steps can be taken to achieve a suitable climate for settlement?

By their nature building contract disputes often involve many issues. Some of those issues will usually assist one party and some will assist the other. An experienced litigator will select those issues that highlight his opponent's weaknesses, and at interlocutory stages he will seek to fight upon those issues. If he can, he will rely upon them in his Ord 29 affidavit, or to show that his opponent has disclosed no cause of action, or he will take them as a preliminary point or concentrate on them at discovery.

Sometimes, a party can find two or three issues upon which he can base interlocutory applications. If that party can achieve two or three successes upon interlocutory hearings, that can give him an extremely good climate for settlement. If his opponent sees himself worsted on two or three issues in a row, he is unlikely to be consoled by the thought that there are another dozen issues to go.

The best time for settlement depends upon the particular circumstances of the case. For a plaintiff this often occurs shortly after obtaining an Ord 14 judgment for part of the claim or an order under Ord 29; for a defendant, it is often when the plaintiff's task of preparing for trial appears to be most long and difficult, which is often part way through the discovery process.

It is comparatively rare for correspondence between the parties' solicitors during the course of the litigation to be referred to at trial, *a fortiori*, if the correspondence is marked 'without prejudice'. The inter-solicitor correspondence can, however, have a marked effect upon the climate for settlement. A party can often improve the chances of a favourable settlement by repeatedly making unanswerable rhetorical points, even if those points relate to comparatively minor issues. The correspondence can further be of importance in keeping the door open for settlement discussions. It is not necessarily a sign of weakness for a party to suggest settlement; for example, where a defendant sued for £100,000 suggests settlement at £1,000, that suggestion is a sign of confidence and yet can force the plaintiff to think in terms of what settlement might be possible.

The effectiveness of correspondence often depends upon the extent to which it is circularised. Where a party has got into procedural difficulties, the solicitor for that party will often be reluctant to pass onto his clients copies of correspondence which identify those procedural difficulties. What should the other party do in those circumstances? It is unprofessional for a solicitor to communicate with his opponent's client merely because he suspects that his opponent is reporting to his client less than fully. There is, however, nothing improper about direct client to client contact. Indeed, it is often sensible for one party to write directly to his opposite number to say 'Has your solicitor told you about these letters?'. Nor is it in any sense improper for a client to go above the head of his opposite number, particularly where his opposite number is one of the competitive types described above. Indeed, it can sometimes be helpful for a client to write to the chief executive of his opponent along the lines of 'I do not want to have to continue to litigate against your company, but the unreasonable and unrealistic attitude of your people is making settlement impossible.' Almost inevitably, the written response, if any, to such letters is to support the manager on the ground; behind the scenes, however, approaches such as this can often help in removing an impasse.

The limitation to rhetorical correspondence is that it lacks the impact of face to face meetings. Without prejudice meetings between parties and their solicitors can sometimes cause very considerable shifts in parties' expectations. Some general guidelines can be provided on such meetings.

(1) They are often beneficial where the lay opponent is a dominant personality and the professional opponent is ineffectual, or otherwise falls short of his client's expectations as a champion.

(2) When acting for a main contractor, making a claim based upon failings of the architect or engineer, it is often desirable to get both the architect/engineer and a representative of the employer present at without prejudice meetings. This can be the best way of allowing the employer to see for himself how his architect/engineer has performed. Employers will sometimes themselves encourage or insist upon such meetings where they suspect that they are being told less than the complete story by their professional advisers.

(3) Where the success of a case is going to depend largely upon the evidence of one individual, it may be a good idea to get that individual to attend a without prejudice meeting if he is going to be a strong witness; otherwise it is advisable to keep him well clear.

(4) It is not usually realistic to expect any agreement about any disputed point of law at such a meeting. It is possible to turn up armed with chapter and verse if it is thought that a professional opponent is failing to deliver sufficiently informed advice to his client as to the legal position.

Where these solicitor and client without prejudice meetings are successful in obtaining settlement (and they often are), the success usually comes not at the meeting itself but in follow up discussions between the solicitors or the lay clients.

Where there are matters of fact which assist, then it is often desirable to set out those matters of fact in a notice to admit facts under Ord 27, r 2(1), which provides as follows:

A party to a cause or matter may not later than 21 days after the cause or matter is set down for trial serve on any other party a notice requiring him to admit, for the purpose of that cause or matter only, the facts specified in the notice.

If a party is served with a notice to admit facts, and neglects to admit a fact which ought properly to have been admitted, he will ordinarily be ordered to pay the other party's costs of proving that fact regardless of the result of the trial as a whole. Accordingly, a notice to admit facts can force a party to consider what facts are certain to be proved against him, and this can have a material effect upon the climate for settlement. It is surprisingly common for a party not to settle only because he has not properly considered the strength of the case against him.

Multipartite litigation is frequently more difficult to settle than bipartite litigation, especially where there are several defendants and/or third parties who are in doubt, not only as to the extent to which the plaintiff will succeed but also as to the way in which the burden will be borne. Payment into court is often unsatisfactory, but a defendant can often make co-defendants think hard about a settlement proposal by marking it 'without prejudice save as to costs' (see Ord 22, r 14, and *Cutts v Head* [1984] 2 WLR 349).

2 Without prejudice funding agreements

There is a special case where it is sometimes appropriate to reach a partial settlement.

Defects sometimes appear in building work that the employer alleges are the responsibility of the contractor. The contractor denies that they are his responsibility but both the employer and contractor are at one that there are defects and that the employer will suffer a substantial loss if the defects are not rectified without delay. In those circumstances it can be in the interests of both the employer and the contractor to reach a without prejudice funding agreement. The terms of such an agreement are usually along the following lines:

(1) the contractor agrees that, without prejudice to the question of his liability to do so, he will execute the necessary remedial work;

(2) the employer agrees on a cash flow basis to pay x per cent of the cost of the remedial work, such payment to be made without any set-off except arising out of the remedial work itself; and

(3) it is agreed that both the employer and the contractor have the right to refer the question of liability to litigation or arbitration

and in particular the employer is entitled to claim repayment of the sum paid by him, and the contractor is entitled to claim the balance of the cost (plus a reasonable percentage for profit) of the remedial works.

Such an agreement is not usually regarded as without prejudice in the sense of a without prejudice offer since it represents a concluded agreement (*Tomlin v Standard Telephones & Cables Ltd* [1969] 1 WLR 1378). Accordingly, the agreement may be referred to in court, but the court is not to regard the agreement as tantamount to an admission of liability for the defects by either side.

It may be appropriate for a party making an offer of this sort to reserve the right to draw the offer to the attention of the court or arbitrator, and this may be effective even if the offer is marked 'without prejudice' (see *Computer Machinery Co Ltd v Drescher* [1983] 1 WLR 1379 and *Cutts v Head* [1984] 2 WLR 349).

It is good practice expressly to exclude the employer's right of set-off against his obligation to make the funding payment. The exclusion may well be implied if not expressed but it should be made clear that the employer is not permitted to enter into a without prejudice funding agreement, have the remedial work done, and then refuse to pay the agreed percentage upon the ground that he thinks the defects were the contractor's responsibility anyway.

The time of making a without prejudice funding agreement is, of course, also the time to consider whether to appoint an expert to inspect the work before the physical evidence of the defects is lost for all time.

3 Risk formula calculation

Some litigation in the High Court concerns a single issue. As soon as the parties have a feel for the strength of their respective cases, they have a feel as to the area within which they look for settlement.

Building contract litigation frequently involves a multiplicity of claims. The parties often have a feel about the respective strengths and weaknesses of these claims but that does not of itself provide a feel for the area of settlement. A calculation is sometimes necessary for this purpose.

It is rarely possible to be entirely confident of any item of claim in a building action. There is usually some risk that the item will not succeed. In crude terms, the claim can be valued by applying its percentage prospect of success to the sum in issue. A simple example may be given as shown overleaf.

Suppose a contractor sues an employer for £60,000. Of this, £10,000 relates to payment for the work which has been certified by the architect and the balance of £50,000 is a claim for loss and expense which the architect has not certified. Of the latter figure, £30,000 is a prolongation claim and £20,000 is a disruption claim. By way of set-off the employer

	Sum Claimed £	Percentage Prospect	Value of Claim £
Contractor's claim:			
Certified sums	10,000	90%	9,000
Loss and expense			
Prolongation	30,000	70%	21,000
Disruption	20,000	40%	8,000
			38,000
Employer's claim:			
Patent defects	15,000	80%	12,000
Foundations	200,000	5%	10,000
			22,000
Balance:			
Value of contractor's claim			38,000
Less			
Value of employer's claim			22,000
BALANCE:			16,000

brings a claim against the contractor for £215,000, of which £15,000 relates to clearly visible defects and £200,000 relates to a speculative claim that the foundations are defective. The parties can crudely calculate the settlement area by valuing these claims and cross-claims as shown in the table above.

By means of a risk formula calculation such as this, the parties might accordingly come to the view that a reasonable settlement might be for the employer to pay the contractor £16,000. If either party feels that it is in a strong position in the litigation, it can aim for a more ambitious settlement. Risk formula calculations can be very sophisticated, and take into account cost orders already made, cost orders liable to be made, irrecoverable standard basis cost element, interest and so on. However sophisticated they are, they should, however, be treated with circumspection. The result is as likely to prove correct at trial as a family is to have 2.83 children.

4 Terms of settlement

In general terms, the same considerations apply to the settlement of building contract cases as other litigation. There are, however, one or two matters worthy of comment.

It is usually dangerous to limit the terms of settlement to the particular contract since parallel causes of action may exist in tort, in quasi contract, or under a collateral contract. Accordingly, the terms of settlement frequently include wording along the following lines:

... in full and final settlement of all the plaintiff's claims of whatsoever nature (including without prejudice to the generality of the foregoing all future claims, costs and interest) against the defendant relating to or connected with the works executed by the plaintiff/defendant at ... on or about ...

Care should be given to whether the terms of settlement include future actions. It was said in *Sparham-Souter v Town and Country Developments (Essex) Ltd* [1976] 1 QB 858 that for the purpose of an action in negligence no cause of action arises unless and until the plaintiff can show some actual injury. Accordingly, unless the settlement refers to future claims, it may not operate to settle a claim by an employer in negligence in respect of defects where no actual injury had been suffered at the time of the settlement.

Sometimes a settlement is intended to be a compromise of only certain defects, and is not intended to compromise the employer's rights in respect of other defects which have yet to appear. If that is the intention, particular care needs to be exercised because there is authority in *Conquer v Boot* [1928] 2 KB 336 to the effect that in a claim for defects in an ordinary lump sum contract there is only one cause of action in contract in respect of all the defects. Accordingly, the terms of settlement should specify with particularity which defects are within the scope of the settlement and care should be taken before consenting to any court order embodying the terms of settlement lest future claims should become *res judicata*.

Where the claim being settled is a claim by a contractor in respect of which the architect has not issued certificates, it may be appropriate in the terms of settlement to preclude the contractor from bringing any subsequent claim against the architect in negligence for under-certification.

5 Complications in multipartite disputes

Settlement tends to be much more difficult to achieve in multipartite disputes. There are a number of reasons for this, not least the tendency for defendants, particularly those represented by insurers, to sit back in the hope that some other defendant will meet the plaintiff's claim. Even where all the defendants wish to settle the plaintiff's claim, the disputes between themselves as to apportionment of blame will often have the effect of hindering them in making a joint approach to the plaintiff. What can be done to overcome the difficulties presented by an intransigent defendant? Different methods are available.

A straightforward approach is for the settling defendant to make a payment into court in satisfaction of the plaintiff's claim against him.

This approach, however, is subject to a number of disadvantages.
(1) It may rid neither the plaintiff nor the settling defendant of the litigation. Unless the payment is so generous as to satisfy the plaintiff in respect of his claim against the intransigent defendant as well as the settling defendant the plaintiff will have to continue with his action against the intransigent defendant. Acceptance of the payment in will not necessarily prevent the intransigent defendant from continuing or commencing third party or contribution proceedings against the settling defendant.
(2) At trial, the intransigent defendant will be able to obtain the benefit of the payment in, if accepted, in diminution of the damages that would otherwise be awarded against him (*Townsend v Stone Toms & Partners* (1984) 27 BLR 26 CA).
(3) The parties will also have to consider whether, depending on the pleadings, the acceptance of the payment in would not have the effect of releasing the intransigent defendant from the action.

These difficulties cannot easily be overcome by making a *Calderbank* offer under Ord 22, r 14. In somewhat unusual circumstances in *Corby District Council v Holst* (1984) 28 BLR 35 the Court of Appeal declined to find that it had jurisdiction to say that a *Calderbank* offer could operate in the same way as a payment into court.

In *Victoria University of Manchester v Hugh Wilson & Lewis Womersley* (1984) 2 CLR 43 the following agreement was reached on the fifth day of trial between the plaintiff and the settling defendant:
(1) the settling defendant should have judgment against the plaintiff;
(2) the plaintiff should proceed against the intransigent defendant at the settling defendant's cost;
(3) the settling defendant should indemnify the plaintiff against any shortfall in recovery below the agreed level, including interest and costs, of £1.3m;
(4) in the event of the intransigent defendant obtaining sums by way of contribution from the settling defendant, the plaintiff would indemnify the settling defendant, providing the plaintiff still recovered £1.3m;
(5) the settling defendant should pay interest to the plaintiff on the £1.3m from the date of the settlement until it was received by the plaintiff.

The inherent difficulty in such a scheme is the problem of preventing the intransigent defendant from obtaining a contribution from the settling defendant. The agreed dismissal of the action against the settling defendant does not give the settling defendant any immunity as regards the claims of the intransigent defendant. The scheme may be of limited practical use in cases where the damage occurred after 1 January 1979, because then the Civil Liability (Contribution) Act 1978 will generally open the door to a contribution claim. Likewise, the scheme of a *Victoria University* settlement may be defeated if the intransigent defendant has a direct cause of action against the settling defendant. Such a direct cause of action was alleged by the intransigent defendant in *Victoria University* but was not successful, and the scheme was successful in limiting the exposure of the settling defendants.

In *Lovell v South East Thames Regional Health Authority* (1985) 32 BLR 127 a different but broadly similar approach was taken. Again, agreement was reached by all the parties except one intransigent defendant. One of the settling defendants (the 'sponsoring defendant') was prepared to take over the costs involved in proceeding against the intransigent defendant. The terms of the agreement reached were as follows:

(1) the sponsoring defendant should take over and continue in the plaintiff's name the plaintiff's action against the intransigent defendant;

(2) the sponsoring defendant should likewise take over the other settling defendants' third party claims against the intransigent defendant;

(3) if the action failed against the intransigent defendant, the sponsoring defendant should pay the plaintiff £325,000 and other defendants should pay £325,000 between them, making a total of £650,000;

(4) any recovery in the plaintiff's action should be credited against the sponsoring defendant's contribution;

(5) any recovery in the third party proceedings should be retained by the sponsoring defendant;

(6) any costs payable by the intransigent defendant should be paid to the sponsoring defendant, who would indemnify the plaintiff and the other settling defendants against any costs order obtained by the intransigent defendant;

(7) pending determination of the plaintiff's claims against the intransigent defendant the settling defendants should make an interest free loan to the plaintiff of £650,000.

The settlement was unsuccessfully attacked by the intransigent defendant; it was found not to be void for champerty. The scheme thus appears to have been successful. It is thought that the intransigent defendant under this scheme would not, as in the *Townsend* case, be entitled to have the £650,000 taken into account in reduction of any damages award.

It is noticeable that in both the *Victoria University* case and the *Lovell* case the terms of the settlement were put before the court. The obligation of disclosure does in fact go further than that, and the intransigent defendant is entitled to discovery of the without prejudice correspondence that precedes the settlement between the plaintiff and the settling defendant: *Rush and Tomkins Ltd v Greater London Council* [1988] 1 All ER 549 CA.

If it is possible it is desirable in the interest of saving costs for the settlement to include all of the parties to the action. One of the impediments to this, particularly in actions with a very long history and perhaps many parties, is that the parties take entrenched positions with regard to each other. The main contractor, for example, may be determined not to pay the sub-contractor a penny piece. The uninsured architect may be ready to die for the principle of not paying any more compensation to the client than the engineer pays. It is sometimes possible for these impasses to be resolved by the solicitors for one party (not necessarily the plaintiff) acting as broker and arranging a pool into or out of which each party pays or receives a sum of money, including any entitlement to interest or costs. Sometimes such settlements are arranged on the basis that each party's contribution is kept confidential from the other parties.

Where a case is settled between the employer and the contractor, and there remain outstanding claims by or against sub-contractors, then great care needs to be taken in the terms of settlement. There is particular difficulty where the sub-contract contains a 'pay-when-paid' clause or where the sub-contractor's entitlement is related to architects' certificates, as under NSC/4. It is a matter of great uncertainty what effect a settlement between an employer and a contractor has upon the sub-contractor in such circumstances, and the terms of settlement sometimes contain elaborate provisions including indemnity clauses.

In the settlement of defect claims, it is now sometimes appropriate for the building owner to indemnify the contractor or other claimee against any subsequent claim by any subsequent building owner (see *Sparham-Souter v Town & Country Developments (Essex) Ltd* [1976] 1 QB 858).

Following the Civil Liability (Contribution) Act 1978 a prudent paying party will often insist on the plaintiff giving an indemnity against contributions, for if the plaintiff goes on to make a claim in respect of the same damage against some other party then that other party may be able to recover a contribution from the paying party, notwithstanding that the paying party had already settled with the plaintiff (*Logan v Uttlesford District Council* (1984) *The Times*, 21 February).

6 Alternative Dispute Resolution (ADR)

It has already been mentioned that the vast majority of building contract disputes are resolved by settlement as opposed to court judgment. All too often, however, the settlement process has been treated as an incidental adjunct to the process. One does not, these days, expect nations to resolve their disputes by declaring war on each other; it is expected that they will endeavour to resolve their disputes amicably by means of diplomacy, if necessary under the auspices of the United Nations or some similar body. ADR is the equivalent of diplomacy in this context.

There are a number of key respects in which ADR fundamentally differs from litigation and arbitration.

(1) It is non-binding. ADR agreements typically provide that either party may withdraw from the ADR process at any time. This might, of itself, be seen as an overwhelming disadvantage; what is the point of a dispute resolution system in which the loser is free to ignore an adverse result? ADR's recently good track record to date shows, however, that the parties often are prepared to abide by the result, not least because the whole process is consensual. The great advantage of the non-binding nature of the process is that it enables the process to go very much more quickly.

(2) There is in ADR an independent third party, usually called the Neutral or Neutral Adviser, who 'holds the ring'. Unlike a judge in litigation or arbitrator in arbitration, however, the Neutral is not primarily concerned to do justice between the parties in any absolute sense; his role is simply to obtain a resolution of the dispute between the parties. Suppose, for example, that the dispute is about the contractor's entitlement to payment. The contractor's true legal entitlement is £100. The contractor claims £200. The employer is prepared to pay £150, but no more. The function of an ADR Neutral is to find a solution acceptable to both parties which will, in practice, mean a solution between £150 and £200.

(3) The rules as to communication are quite different. In litigation and arbitration, the rule is that neither party may communicate with the judge or arbitrator in the absence of the other save in exceptional circumstances (eg, ex parte applications). In ADR processes, however, the parties are free, and are encouraged, to confide in the Neutral things that they would not say to the opposite party. Where formalised, these are known as 'caucus sessions'.

(4) ADR is designed to be, and generally is, much quicker and cheaper than litigation or arbitration.

(5) Unlike arbitration, ADR is at the time of writing entirely free from control or interference by the court. There is no equivalent of the Arbitration Acts, whereby the parties can call upon the courts in order to disqualify or remove a Neutral, or to hear preliminary points of law, or to overturn his findings on appeal, or anything of that sort. Indeed, ADR agreements usually contain provisions designed to prevent any part of the ADR proceedings ever being referred to a court.

(6) ADR agreements usually provide that each party bears their own costs and half of the Neutral's costs regardless of the outcome.

A feature which distinguishes ADR from informal settlement discussions is the range of techniques which have been established. Because of these techniques, it is common for the parties to choose, as a Neutral, someone who has been trained in the techniques available. There are a number of organisations which are involved in training Neutrals and/or suggesting suitable appointments, including the following:

(1) CEDR, 100 Fetter Lane, London, EC4A 1DD.
(2) The Chartered Institute of Arbitrators, International Arbitration Centre, 24 Angel Gate, City Road, London, EC1V 2RS.
(3) The British Academy of Experts, 90 Bedford Square, London WC1.

The individuals who have been approved by those organisations as Neutrals often have a background as lawyers or arbitrators, and a number of them are well acquainted with the construction industry. In the case of comparatively simple disputes, the technique usually adopted will be either mediation or mini-trial; in complex cases a combination of the two is more often adopted.

Mediation essentially consists of the following process. A meeting is arranged between the Neutral and both parties. Each party will make a short presentation of its position in the presence of everybody. The parties might instruct their solicitors for this purpose, or might make the presentations themselves. Following these presentations, the parties go into separate rooms, and the Neutral shuttles between them in caucus sessions, exploring the areas in which the parties might be willing to compromise and endeavouring to find a solution acceptable to both parties. In this, he acts essentially as a go-between. Some Neutrals think it is very important never to express an opinion to either party as to the relative strengths and weaknesses of their cases. Other Neutrals adopt a more proactive stance, and will, in the caucus sessions, take it upon themselves to tell a party in no uncertain terms if that party is being unreasonable. Whichever approach is adopted, this 'shuttle diplomacy' carries on until a solution is found. The parties are very much encouraged to open their hearts to the Neutral and disclose their 'bottom line' for settlement; the Neutral is not permitted to pass on to the other party anything which he has heard in caucus without the consent of that disclosing party.

The mini-trial procedure works on a rather different basis. Here, the centrepiece is a hearing at which the parties put forward their respective cases. The hearing is called a mini-trial because it is designed to be very short; for a case in which trial might take several months, the mini-trial hearing would be perhaps one day. The parties are usually represented by their internal or external solicitors for this process. The mini-trial takes place before a 'bench' of three: the independent Neutral plus one senior executive from each side who has not been personally involved in the matters which led to the dispute. Following the hearing, these executives are supposed to get together and openly discuss and agree the relative strength of the cases that their people have made.

In both of these variations, the emphasis is on trying to get agreement rather than indulging in a legal trial of strength. Thus, any written submissions are generally kept fairly short; unlike pleadings, they are supposed to go to the central issues rather than to cover every conceivable way that a case might be put. There is generally little or no discovery. At no stage are the rules of evidence applied. Members of the Bar are not ordinarily involved in the process. Official robes are not worn and meetings are usually conducted on first name terms.

Although the focus is on agreement, the ADR agreement will often provide for the Neutral to make a recommendation to the parties if, at the end of the day, there remains a gap between the parties which has not been bridged. The recommendation is non-binding, and indeed the agreement may prevent either party referring to the content of the recommendation in the event of subsequent litigation or arbitration. Nevertheless, in practical terms, a recommendation may carry very powerful commercial weight, particularly where those who have been engaged in the process are in turn answerable to someone else, such as a main board of directors, a holding company, or a funder.

When should ADR be used? There are those who are very enthusiastic about the ADR process and others who are implacably sceptical. It is possible to give some guidelines to those who fall into neither category:

(1) ADR works best where both parties are keen to resolve the dispute; it is of limited use where the defendant is simply trying to delay payment. Even in those circumstances, however, it may work, particularly where the defendant is a part of a large organisation, or is dependent upon external funding.

(2) ADR may be particularly suitable where one or both parties is insured. ADR provides good opportunities for insurers to participate in the process.

(3) ADR is generally unattractive to trustees or other people who want or need to enforce their legal rights in full. The ADR process is concerned with compromise, not vindication.

At the time of writing, ADR plays a small but significant part in the resolution of building contract disputes. In some other common law jurisdictions, such as Hong Kong, ADR plays a much larger part, and it remains to be seen to what extent ADR will grow in the United Kingdom. One of the Official Referees, His Honour Judge James Fox-Andrews QC, now includes a standard direction in cases informing the parties of the possibility of ADR and offering a stay of proceedings whilst ADR is attempted.

Chapter 19

Value Added Tax

It is beyond the purpose of this book to deal exhaustively with the charge to Value Added Tax (VAT) as it applies to the construction industry. There are, however, two significant questions to consider when looking at the impact VAT has upon building contract litigation.

(1) How much VAT can the contractor claim from the employer?

(2) Can VAT be included in a claim for damages or costs?

Before considering either of these issues it is appropriate briefly to review the charge to tax.

1 The charge to Value Added Tax

Unless specifically zero-rated, supplies of construction services are now subject to VAT at the standard rate, currently 17.5 per cent. The exceptions are to be found in Sched 5 to the Value Added Tax 1983:

(1) the construction of a building designed as a dwelling or intended for use solely for a 'relevant residential purpose' or a relevant charitable purpose;

(2) civil engineering work necessary for the development of a residential caravan park;

(3) approved alterations to a protected building;

(4) certain works for the use or benefit of handicapped persons;

(5) the supply to a person of materials, hardware, sanitary ware or other articles usually supplied by builders as fixtures by a supplier who also supplies the building services to that same person.

In order to zero-rate construction works, the works must not amount to a conversion, reconstruction, alteration or enlargement of an existing building. HM Customs & Excise have produced guidelines as to their interpretation, contained in VAT leaflet number 708/2/89.

2 The contractor's right to reimbursement of VAT

Payment of VAT is, of course, primarily the responsibility of a VAT registered contractor. Legislation relating to VAT is surprisingly unforthcoming as to whether, in the absence of express agreement, the contractor is entitled to be paid VAT by his employer in addition to any agreed price. In *Franks and Collingwood v Gales* (1983) 1 CLR 2 it was held that, in the absence of any mention of VAT in the contract, a private employer is entitled to assume that a quoted price is inclusive of VAT. In such circumstances it is accordingly immaterial to the employer whether, or to what extent, VAT is chargeable on the works; insofar as VAT is payable, it is payable by the contractor.

JCT contracts contain Supplemental Agreements with regard to VAT. The procedure under JCT80 is that the contractor gives the employer an assessment of the VAT chargeable in respect of each certificate (the certificates issued by the architect are VAT exclusive) and the employer pays the contractor the VAT calculated, subject to the rights of objection in clauses 1.2 and 3.1. The contractor is obliged to provide a VAT invoice upon receipt of any amount paid under the certificates and of any tax (clause 1.4).

The obligation of the employer under the Supplemental Agreement is to pay 'any tax properly chargeable'. If the employer and the contractor cannot agree as to the VAT that is due on interim payments, then the effect of clause 1.2.2 is apparently that the contractor can appropriate whatever money he does receive to the VAT he claims.

If the employer disagrees with the final statement of VAT issued by the contractor, he can require the contractor to obtain the decision of the Commissioners of Customs & Excise and then, upon giving security, require the contractor to appeal (clause 3.1). If the contractor must pay or account for the VAT in the meantime the employer is required to put the contractor in funds (clause 3.2).

The Supplemental Agreement expressly provides that the arbitration clause in the contract does not apply to any matters to be dealt with under clause 3 of the Supplemental Agreement. It therefore seems that an arbitrator does not, in the absence of any further agreement, have any jurisdiction to determine the amount of VAT finally payable by the employer to the contractor where this is in dispute.

It is expressly provided by clause 2 of the Supplemental VAT Agreement that liquidated and ascertained damages are not to be taken into account for the purposes of the VAT calculation (liquidated damages are not the consideration for a supply and are outside the scope of VAT).

More difficult issues arise with regard to whether VAT is payable by the employer to the contractor on sums recovered by the contractor in respect of:

(1) fluctuations;
(2) loss and expense attributable to additional work;
(3) loss and expense attributable to other causes;
(4) damages for breach of contract.

Probably, the proper test is to ask whether these sums are recovered in respect of supplies within the meaning of the VATA 1983. There is some ground for believing that categories (1) and (2) are chargeable to VAT, and that categories (3) and (4) are not. It is common for contractors to cut the Gordian knot by charging VAT on whatever they invoice or whatever is certified, and not charging VAT on any further sum that they recover by means of a judgment, award or negotiated settlement.

3 VAT on damages or costs

It is a very common mistake for a defendant to agree to pay the VAT element on damages awarded or agreed to be paid to a trading plaintiff.

As an example, take the case of a trading company for whom defective work is carried out. Suppose that the trading company has remedial work executed at a cost of £100 plus VAT of £17.50. In this example, the sum initially paid out by the plaintiff is £117.50 but in the following financial quarter he will be entitled to a credit of £17.50 for the sum which he had to pay HM Customs and Excise in respect of his own 'supplies'. In other words, the net loss suffered by the plaintiff is £100 and the defendant should not agree to pay £117.50. The defendant is not, of course, entitled in his own VAT return to credit for the VAT on the repair works supplied to the plaintiff.

The same principle applies to the award of costs. Whether the paying party should pay VAT depends upon whether the party benefiting from the order will be entitled to a VAT credit on those costs.

Apart from payment a frequent question is whether VAT is added to any award. If an award is made against an employer for the cost of work carried out then, except for specific classes of work which are zero-rated, VAT should be claimed in addition because the contractor will be obliged to account for it as a general rule.

Less easy are awards which do not relate directly to work carried out. The nature of the claim must be considered. VAT is a tax on the supply of goods and services. A supply is anything done for a consideration, and a consideration is any form of payment in money or in kind, whether from the recipient of the supply or a third party.

Chapter 20

Quantum of damages

Generally, the same principles apply to the quantification of damage in building cases as in any other case. Accordingly, it is useful before looking at the particularities of building claims to review the general principles.

(1) 'Where two parties have made a contract which one of them has broken the damages which the other party ought to receive in respect of such breach of contract should be such as may fairly and reasonably be considered either arising naturally, ie according to the usual course of things from such breach of contract itself, or such as may reasonably be supposed to have been in the contemplation of both parties at the time they made the contract, as the probable result of the breach of it' (*Hadley v Baxendale* (1854) 9 Ex 341).

(2) In cases of breach of contract, 'the governing purpose of damages is to put the party whose rights have been violated in the same position, so far as money can do, as if his rights had been observed' (*Victoria Laundry Ltd v Newman Ltd* [1949] 2 KB 528).

(3) In cases of negligence, 'the essential factor in determining liability is whether the damage is of such a kind as the reasonable man should have foreseen'. The foreseeability must be of 'damage which in fact happened — the damage in suit' (*Overseas Tankship (UK) Ltd v Morts Docks & Engineering Co Ltd, The Wagon Mound (No 1)* [1961] AC 388).

Claims by a building owner (or lessee) may be either for breach of contract or in tort, or both. Since the case of *Murphy v Brentwood District Council* [1990] 3 WLR 414 economic loss is, in the words of Lord Bridge at p 435, 'no longer recoverable in tort in the absence of a special relationship of proximity imposing on the tortfeasor a duty of care to safeguard the Plaintiff from economic loss'. Consequently, the measure of damages in contract is once again more generous than the measure of damages in tort.

1 Remedial work

Where the plaintiff's claim is based upon breach of an obligation of the defendant with regard to building work, the main head of damage is usually the cost to the plaintiff of having the work remedied or completed, or otherwise obtaining what he has a right to expect from that defendant. In breach of contract cases the plaintiff must give credit for any sums which he has not paid, but which he would have been obliged to pay had the defendant completed his contractual obligations.

It should be stressed that this rule applies where the plaintiff has a right to the proper execution of work. Different rules apply to negligent survey cases where the defendant's only obligation is to advise upon an existing building: a surveyor who negligently fails to identify dry rot is not the cause of that dry rot and is liable only for such loss as arises subsequently.

The basic rule is subject to occasional exceptions. For example in *Newton Abbott Development Co Ltd v Stockman Brothers* (1931) 47 TLR 616 it was held that a property development company was entitled to recover the diminution in value of houses that it had sold in their defective state. It is thought that there is an exception to the basic rule where remedial work would be wholly inappropriate. In *Cory v Wingate Investments* (1980) 17 BLR 104 the Court of Appeal said:

There may be cases where the carrying out of remedial work to bring the building into line with the specification may be so entirely out of line with what the cost of those works would be and the nature of those works having regard to the nature of the building as a whole that the Court would gladly accept some other basis for the assessment of damages.

The cost of repair was once thought to be assessed as at the date of the breach. It is now clear that this so called rule is merely a mitigation point, so that if repairs are undertaken at the first time they can reasonably be undertaken then the plaintiff is entitled to damages assessed at that time, even if that time does not arise until trial (*Dodd Properties Ltd v Canterbury City Council* [1980] 1 WLR 433). The court will consider either the actual cost of remedial work, or its estimated cost if the work has not been done at the time the damages are assessed.

In claims against an architect for failure to supervise it may be relevant whether the employer employed a clerk of works (*Kensington and Chelsea and Westminster v Wettern Composites* [1985] 1 All ER 346).

2 Recovery from others

To what extent should the court take into account recoveries that the plaintiff may be able to obtain from others? Ordinary principles apply, but there are some decisions particularly applicable to building contracts.

It is not uncommon in building cases for an employer to have parallel cases against a number of parties. Such a case arose in *Townsend v Stone Toms & Partners (No 2)* (1984) 27 BLR 26 where the employer sued the contractor and accepted a payment into court of £30,000. He then proceeded against his architects for defective design, inadequate supervision and wrongful certification. It was found that he must give credit for the sum which he recovered from the contractors.

Conversely, in *Design 5 v Keniston Housing Association Ltd* (1986) 34 BLR 92 it was found as a preliminary issue that the counterclaiming defendants were entitled to all the increased costs incurred by the alleged negligence of the architects notwithstanding that those losses were being made good to the housing association by the Department of the Environment through housing association grants. Likewise in *Treml v Ernest W Gibson & Partners* (1984) 272 EG 68 the court declined to take into account by way of reduction of damages the amount of an improvement grant paid by a local authority under Sched 12 of the Housing Act 1980. The principle appears to be that wherever money is received by the plaintiff from public funds by way of grant (as opposed to by way of damages or compensation) then the grant is to be disregarded, just as the proceeds of a claim under an insurance policy are to be disregarded.

In *Jones v Stroud* (1986) 8 CLR 23 an interesting point arose with regard to the plaintiff's loss. The plaintiff obtained estimates for the necessary remedial work but did not in fact accept any of them, instead rectifying the defects as part of a wider scheme of improvement to the property. There was no difficulty about that in itself, but the wider scheme was carried out by Marlothian Ltd, a company controlled by the plaintiff. The plaintiff failed to provide any evidence, apart from an unsupported general assertion, that he had paid Marlothian Ltd anything for the work. In these circumstances, could it be said that the plaintiff himself (as opposed to his company) had suffered the loss? The Court of Appeal found that it could, on the authority of *The Endeavour* (1890) 6 Asp MC 511, in which it was said:

> If somebody out of kindness were to repair the injury and make no charge for it, the wrongdoer would not be entitled to refuse to pay as part of the damages the cost of the repairs to the owner.

3 Economic loss

Where remedial work is carried out by a commercial enterprise upon its premises, that remedial work may prevent or inhibit the enterprise making use of its premises, so that it may suffer a loss of profit, have to pay rent for temporary accommodation, or suffer some other form of economic loss. It has always been the case that such loss is *prima facie* recoverable in breach of contract under the first and usually also the second limb of the rule in *Hadley v Baxendale* (above). It is no longer recoverable in tort (*Murphy v Brentwood* [1990] 3 WLR 414) except in negligent misstatement cases pursuant to *Hedley Byrne v Heller* ([1964] AC 465).

4 Physical inconvenience and mental suffering

Where a person is unable to live in his home, or is caused inconvenience or mental suffering in his home by reason of breach of contract by another, damages may be awarded for distress following the principles established in *Jarvis v Swan Tours* [1973] 1 QB 233. The amount awarded is a modest amount (*Perry v Sydney Phillips* [1982] 3 All ER 705 CA). However, there is evidence to suggest that, until recently, awards under this head were increasing faster than inflation:

1977 *Batty v Metropolitan Property Realisations* [1978] 2 All ER 445: £250 (agreed quantum) where there was a landslip causing danger to the plaintiff's house.

1980 *Haig v London Borough of Hillingdon* (1980) 19 BLR 143: £1,000 following failure of plaintiff's bedroom floor.

1983 *Franks & Collingwood v Gates* (1983) 1 CLR 21: £500 following delay of some months in work to plaintiff's holiday home; plaintiff lost at least three weekends in the house and had to spend Christmas in a hotel.

1984 *Hooberman v Slater Rex* (1984) 1 CLR 63: £600 where the plaintiff had to endure building works in his house for six months amid dust and scaffolding.

1988 *Roberts v Hampson* [1989] 2 All ER 504: £1,500 following a negligent survey. Plaintiffs had to move into wife's mother's house whilst repairs were carried out.

1988 *Cloggre v Sovro* (Scottish case, unreported): £2,000 in a rising damp case where £17,400 worth of remedial work was necessary.

1990 *Syrett v Carr and Neave* [1990] CILL 619: £8,000 where remedial works in a farmhouse were totally disruptive of family life for 2½ years; only two bedrooms habitable.

In 1991, however, the Court of Appeal in *Watts v Morrow* (1991) 54 BLR 86 went some way to reverse this trend of increasing awards under this head. The plaintiffs had to endure eight months of their weekend home being a building site. Their marriage had broken down by the time of trial, and at first instance they were awarded £4,000 damages each. The Court of Appeal reduced this award to £750 each, and summarised the position as follows:

A contract-breaker is not generally liable for any distress, frustration, anxiety, displeasure, vexation, tension or aggravation which his breach of contract may cause to the innocent party . . . But the rule is not absolute. Where the very object of a contract is to provide pleasure, relaxation, peace of mind or freedom from molestation, damages will be awarded if the fruit of the contract is not provided . . . A contract to survey the condition of a house for a prospective purchase does not, however, fall within this exceptional category. In cases not falling within this exceptional category, damages are in my view recoverable for physical inconveniences and discomfort caused by the breach and mental suffering directly related to that inconvenience and discomfort. If those effects are foreseeably suffered during a period when defects are repaired I am prepared to accept that they sound in damages even though the cost of the repairs is not recoverable as such. But I also agree that awards should be restrained.

No damages are awarded where the plaintiff suffers distress in the course of a business such as where the plaintiff intended to let the property (*Hutchinson v Harris* (1978) 10 BLR 19).

There are two excellent analyses of these and other cases on inconvenience and distress by Kim Franklin at (1988) Const LJ 264 and (1992) Const LJ 318.

5 Interest

A plaintiff is entitled to interest upon his damages in the ordinary way: 'to explore the actual cost to a plaintiff of borrowing would be in some cases to find them too low because he could finance the work out of his own resources and in other cases to find them high because he had little or no security to offer' (*Haig v Hillingdon* (1980) 19 BLR 143 at 159).

Subject to that principle, it is, as a matter of arithmetic, sometimes convenient for a plaintiff to present his claim for interest on the basis of what he has been charged by his bank, particularly when he has maintained a separate bank account for the purpose of remedial works and made several payments from that account over an extended period, or where he has been placed at the mercy of the bank by the defendant's wrong (see *Archer v Brown* [1984] 3 WLR 350).

6 Insurance premiums

If the plaintiff has to pay increased insurance premiums because, eg, of the failure of a sprinkler system, those increased premiums may be recoverable but only for such period as is reasonable (*Rumbelows v AMK* (1980) 19 BLR 25).

7 Exploration

Where discovery of some defects leads a plaintiff reasonably to suspect that other similar defects may be concealed elsewhere in his building, then he is entitled to recover the cost of appropriate investigation even if that further investigation does not in fact reveal further defects.

8 Tax

The position as regards VAT is considered in Chapter 19. There are occasionally circumstances in which the rule in *British Transport Com-*

mission v Gourley [1956] AC 185 (reduction in damages to account for tax) will operate to reduce the amount payable by the defendant to the plaintiff. The application of the rule in *Gourley's* case is beyond the scope of this book, save to say that if it appears that the plaintiff might escape capital gains tax, corporation tax or income tax on damages awarded then the defendant should consider as to whether the rule might apply.

9 Surveyors' negligence

The liability of a surveyor who has failed properly to survey, or value, property or work depends upon the loss actually suffered by the plaintiff. Some common examples of this are listed below.

(1) The plaintiff has his own property surveyed because he is concerned by an unfamiliar smell. The surveyor negligently fails to diagnose the existence or extent of a dry rot attack. In these circumstances the surveyor is not usually liable for all the cost of remedying that attack, but he is liable for the part of the cost attributable to the growth of the attack pending its eventual diagnosis and eradication. He is also liable for the reinstatement of any work such as decoration carried out after the time of his survey.

(2) The plaintiff employs a surveyor to see that work is properly carried out by a contractor. The surveyor negligently fails in that duty and approves defective work causing the plaintiff to pay or commit himself to some contractual arrangement. The surveyor may be jointly and severally liable with the contractor for the full cost of remedial works (*Raybeck Properties Ltd v County & Nimbus Estates Ltd* (1983) 268 EG 1205).

(3) The plaintiff buys a property upon the strength of a negligent survey. There has been much confusion upon this subject, part of which arises from a failure to distinguish between cases where the defendant is under a duty to produce a result (such as a builder's duty to build) and cases where the defendant's duty is merely to take reasonable care in advising (such as a surveyor reporting upon a proposed purchase). It is desirable to regard the cases on surveys for intending purchasers as distinct from the cases where the defendant is under a duty to produce a result.

In example (3) above the measure of damage is usually assessed on a diminution of value basis. Even this basis is not, however, free from difficulty. There seem to be at least four relevant figures to consider. They are (in approximately descending order):

Figure A — the market value that the property would have had if it had been free of the defect upon which the defendant negligently failed to report;

Figure B — the price actually paid by the plaintiff for the property;

Figure C — the market value of the property;

Figure D — the price that the plaintiff would have been prepared to pay for the property had the survey report been properly made.

The leading case is the Court of Appeal decision in *Philips v Ward* [1956] 1 WLR 471, in which the court found that the proper measure of damage is (A) minus (C). This approach was followed in *Hooberman v Slater Rex* (1984) 1 CLR 63, where the court refused to make any additional award for the further cost of eradicating the dry rot which spread from the time of the purchase to the time that it was eventually discovered. However, in *Ford v White & Co* [1964] 1 WLR 885 it was said that a more accurate measure of damage is (B) minus (C). The matter came back before the Court of Appeal in *Perry v Sidney Phillips & Son* (1982) 22 BLR 120 and *Franks & Collingwood v Gates* (1983) 1 CLR 21. In this case, Lord Denning found that the proper measure of damage is (B) minus (D) while Oliver & Kerr LJJ agreed with the decision in *Ford v White* that the proper measure is (B) minus (C). This is also the opinion as to the correct measure expressed in *McGregor on Damages*, 14th edn (Sweet & Maxwell Ltd, 1980), para 979, and was the agreed measure in *Treml v Ernest W Gibson & Partners* (1984) EG 68. It was the measure found by the Court of Appeal in *Watts v Morrow* [1991] CILL 687. On balance, it seems that (B) minus (C) is indeed the correct measure.

The court may award damages for physical inconvenience and discomfort and related mental suffering in addition to the diminution of value head to be found in *Watts v Morrow*, but such damages should be 'restrained'.

Parties preparing evidence should carefully consider on which basis they contend and what evidence they will need. In general, the evidence they will require will be:

For Figure A — expert evidence;

For Figure B — evidence from the documents;

For Figure C — expert evidence;

For Figure D — evidence of fact from the plaintiff.

As matters stand, Figures (A) to (D) are all to be assessed as at the date of the survey, which will usually be the same thing as assessing damages as at the date of the purchase by the plaintiff, and not as at the date of the trial. This principle was set out in *Philips v Ward* (above) and confirmed in *Perry v Sidney Phillips* (above). The plaintiff's loss in terms of rising prices will be compensated by an interest award.

There have been occasional cases where the liability of surveyors for negligent survey preceding purchase has been measured by the cost of remedial work (eg *Hipkins v Cotton* [1989] 2 EGLR 157 and *Syrett v Carr and Neave* [1990] 2 EGLR 161) but in *Watts v Morrow* the Court of Appeal found that those cases were wrongly decided.

Chapter 21

Retrospective delay analysis

Much building contract litigation is concerned with delay. Delay cases takc various forms. The main contractor may be seeking an extension of time in order to obtain relief from liquidated damages. The employer may be seeking to prove that his construction manager or professionals have mismanaged the project, so that the project has taken longer than it should have. The main contractor may be seeking to demonstrate that delay has been caused by a nominated sub-contractor, so that he may get an extension of time on that ground and be enabled to proceed with a claim for loss and expense against that sub-contractor (under the JCT80 form, the main contractor is not entitled to make any claim against a nominated sub-contractor without a certificate of the architect under Clause 35.15 of the main contract).

Claims for extensions of time under main contracts are subject to special difficulty. Frequently the main contractor will need to seek an extension of time from the architect in respect of late instructions or late information; these matters often arise from shortcomings in the original design, and so the contractor is, in effect, asking the architect to certify his own — the architect's — failings. Not surprisingly, the architect is often unwilling to do this, and this frequently leads to a dispute requiring litigation or arbitration.

It is very rare for delay on building contracts to arise from a single cause; typically, there are a large number of delays which, in aggregate, far exceed the delay to the completion of the contract as a whole. There are various methods which can be adopted to determine the question of fact: which of the delays was causative, and to what extent, of the overall delay to the contract. The task of making this assessment, sometimes referred to as Retrospective Delay Analysis, is one that straddles three distinct areas:

(1) Extensive factual detail is required. This usually comes from the people who were involved with the contract whilst it was proceeding.

(2) 'Planning' expertise is required in order to operate the time analysis — although see below as to the danger of assuming that

those proficient in planning will necessarily have any expertise in the different task of Retrospective Delay Analysis.

(3) Legal expertise is generally required to ensure that the time analysis is carried out in a way which is acceptable to the courts or arbitrator.

In recent years, a number of time claims have failed entirely, and the main reason for this seems to be that the task has fallen between the above three positions. All too often, those preparing the time analysis do not understand the legal requirements and the lawyers do not understand the planning techniques which are being used.

In the past these failings did not generally matter too much; time claims were pursued on a 'global' basis without any systematic time analysis. It was sometimes referred to as the 'scattergun' technique; the plaintiff would make myriad complaints of things which delayed him. Such claims were often accompanied by bar charts showing the dates on which information was supposed to be received according to information release schedules, and the dates on which information was actually received. Generalised complaints were made about the number of variations, and the time of the instructions. There was sometimes talk of a 'critical path' but the matters complained of were not restricted to the matters that were on that critical path. Thus, in a contract which was delayed by 50 weeks, the contractor would typically claim an extension of time for all of that overrun. The employer might concede only, say, five weeks. During the hearing, there would be very little information on the facts of the delays, and the judge or arbitrator was expected to pluck a figure out of the air according to how he thought the parties had done — he might, for example, award the contractor an extension of time of a further 25 weeks. It was not generally expected that the amount of that award would be the result of any arithmetical calculation; it was just a matter of 'feel' having heard the parties argue.

Much has changed, however, largely because of the Privy Council decision in *Wharf Properties v Eric Cumine* (1991) 8 CLD 02 02. In order to understand the current legal position it is necessary to look briefly at the legal history.

1 The History of the '*Wharf*' cases

The first case is *Crosby v Portland UDC* 5 BLR 133. This was an ICE case which had gone to arbitration; it was the classic case of a contractor seeking extensions of time for a variety of things. The arbitrator eventually made his award on a 'rolled-up' basis, that is to say he made his award in favour of the contractor without identifying precisely how much extension of time he was awarding in respect of that matter. The employer challenged the award in court, on the basis, they said, that the arbitrator should not make an award in that form. The court found for the contractor. Donaldson J (as he then was) stated that:

Extra costs are a factor common to all these clauses, and so long as the arbitrator does not make any award which contains a profit element, this being permissible under Clauses 51 and 52 but not under Clauses 41 and 42, and provided he ensures that there is no duplication, I can see no reason why he should not recognise the realities of the situation and make individual awards in respect of those parts of individual items of the claim which can be dealt with in isolation and a supplementary award in respect of the remainder of these claims as a composite whole.

Note that these words relate only to the form of the arbitrator's award. It was, however, universally assumed that the decision was approving global claims as well as global awards. This was an assumption which in due course proved unreliable.

Some people thought that the *Crosby* decision might be limited to ICE contracts, but the issue came back before the court in *Merton v Leach* (1985) 32 BLR 51. Again, the case arose out of a claim by a main contractor for extensions of time but this time the form of contract was JCT. The court upheld the *Crosby* decision, Vinelott J said:

The position in the instant case is, I think, as follows. If application is made (under Clause 11(6) or 24(1) or under both sub-clauses) for reimbursement of direct loss or expense attributable to more than one head of claim and at the time when the loss or expense comes to be ascertained it is impracticable to disentangle or disintegrate the part directly attributable to each head of claim then, provided of course that the contractor has not unreasonably delayed . . . the architect must ascertain the global loss directly attributable to the two causes, disregarding . . . any loss or expense which would have been recoverable if the claim had been made under one head in isolation and which would not have been recoverable under the other head taken in isolation. To this extent the law supplements the contractual machinery which no longer works in the way in which it was intended to work so as to ensure that the contractor is not unfairly deprived of the benefit which the parties clearly intended he should have.
Like the arbitrator, I do not think it appropriate at this stage . . . to endeavour to define in more precise terms the circumstances in which a rolled up award can be made. I think I should nonetheless say that it is implicit in the reasoning of Donaldson J, first, that a rolled up award can only be made in a case where the loss or expense attributable to each head of claim cannot in reality be separated and secondly, that a rolled up award can only be made where apart from that practical impossibility the conditions which have to be satisfied before an award can be made have been satisfied in relation to each head of claim.

Thus, the matter lay until the case of *Wharf Properties v Eric Cumine*. The case arose out of the Harbour City development in Hong Kong; the employer engaged Eric Cumine Associates as his architects. The work became subject to very considerable cost overspends and time overruns, and the employer sued for some HK$600 million — equivalent to about £60 million. The plaintiff gave a fair amount of detail in the Statement of Claim (it originally ran to over 400 pages) but the defendants attacked the form of pleading. The matter eventually came before the Privy Council, who struck the action out in its entirety on the basis that the pleading was embarrassing. The essential criticism of the Statement of Claim was that it was a global, or a rolled up, claim. Lord Oliver said:

As has already been observed, the pleading is hopelessly embarrassing as it stands and their Lordships are wholly unpersuaded by Mr Butcher's submission that the two cases of *J Crosby & Sons v Portland Urban District Council* and *London Borough of Merton v Stanley Hugh Leach Limited* provide any basis for saying that an unparticularised pleading in this form ought to be permitted to stand. The cases establish no more than this, that in cases where the full extent of extra costs incurred through delay depend upon a complex interaction between consequences of various events, so that it may be difficult to make an accurate apportionment of the total extra costs, it may be proper for an arbitrator to make individual financial awards in respect of claims which can conveniently be dealt with in isolation and a supplementary award in respect of the financial consequences of the remainder as a composite whole. This has, however, no bearing upon the obligation of a plaintiff to plead his case with such particularity as is sufficient to alert the opposite party to the case which is going to be made against him at trial. ECA are concerned at this stage not so much with quantification of the financial consequences — the point with which the two cases referred to were concerned — but with the specification of the factual consequences of the breaches pleaded in terms of periods of delay. The failure even to attempt to specify any discernible nexus between the wrong alleged and the consequent delay provides, to use Mr. Thomas' phrase, 'No agenda' for the trial.

In some respects *Wharf* was an unusual case and the Privy Council warned about assuming its universal applicability, Lord Oliver said: 'It has become apparent that the case, whilst of obvious importance to the parties because of the sums involved raises no question of any general importance'. Nevertheless, it was inevitable that the decision would cause a considerable stir, and it has indeed done so. Following the decision, there was some debate as to the effect of the passage quoted above. The rival interpretations are:

(1) that the House of Lords was drawing a distinction between the position of an arbitrator or judge (who may make a global award in certain circumstances) and the parties who are pleading (who must establish the nexus between cause and alleged effect);

(2) that the Court was distinguishing between claims for time (which may be pursued globally) and the claims for money (which may not).

Mid Glamorgan v J Devonald Williams [1991] CILL 722 appeared to support the second of these interpretations. Mr John Tackaberry QC summarised the rules as follows:

Paragraph 56.1: A proper cause of action has to be pleaded.

Paragraph 56.2: where specific events are relied upon as giving rise to a claim for monies under the contract then any preconditions which are made applicable to such claims by the terms of the relevant contract will have to be satisfied, and satisfied in respect of each of the causative events relied upon.

Paragraph 56.3: when it comes to quantum, whether time-based or not, and whether claimed under the contract by way of damages, then a proper nexus should be pleaded which relates each event relied upon to the money claimed.

Paragraph 56.4: where however a claim is made for extra costs incurred through delay as a result of various events whose consequences have a complex interaction that renders specific relation between event and time/money consequence impossible or impracticable, it is permissible to maintain a composite claim.

ICI v Bovis [1992] CILL 776, 10 CLD 06 16 was a case which was, in some respects, similar to *Wharf Properties*. The case was brought by an employer who had suffered substantial cost overspend and time overrun on his project; he sued his management contractor, his architect and his engineer. As in the *Wharf* case, the plaintiffs pleaded in considerable detail, but were unable to convincingly identify which of their losses were said to flow from which of their complaints. They tried pleading everything in the alternative.

In striking out the plaintiff's Scott Schedule His Honour Judge Fox-Andrews QC said this:

On the basis of the decision in *Merton* it is permissible in certain circumstances to plead that a large number of matters contributed to prolongation and therefore additional expense. I have already indicated ICI's notes that they do not seek in aggregate to recover more than their actual losses. The question arises whether, notwithstanding that, it is possible to plead that a relatively small breach gave rise to a claim in millions of pounds . . .

The defendants took as an example the factual consequences of two items, 6.1.B(i)(a) at P6/56, 'Circuit needed changing' and 6.1.C(i)(c) at P6/85 'Fire bell had to be repositioned'. Suppose the defendants considered that save for these two items they had a complete defence in respect of all the other items, how did they know what monetary consequences are alleged to flow from these two items?

Mr Seymour QC helpfully set out in writing his answer to these criticisms:

The plaintiff's case is that the various events set out in Section 6 all contributed to the sums claimed with no actual apportionment being possible. However, as the total cost claimed has in fact been paid, if any of the events is not proven at trial, the only consequence is that the actual sum paid will fall to be distributed between a lesser number of events, not that the total sum recoverable will be less.

But I find that it is palpable nonsense that £840,000 could be the cost of repositioning a fire bell.

It is worth noting that the Judge did not, in this case, strike out the plaintiff's claim of itself. Nevertheless, the requirements he identified for the Scott Schedule were such that the plaintiffs were unable to proceed further with the case.

It was also Judge Fox-Andrews who struck out the plaintiffs in *Trust Securities v McAlpine* (unreported). This extremely complex but ultimately futile litigation arose out of an office development in Croydon which was said to suffer from a variety of defects. The first writs were issued in 1985 — a time when there was still material causes of action in Tort in building defect cases. During the course of the litigation, British Airways Pensions — the co-plaintiff which had owned the building — had sold their interest in the building, and at the time of the striking out application their claim was for £3.1 million being the reduction in price which they said they were obliged to give by reason of the defects in the building. They could not, however, identify which of the alleged defects in the building was causative of what part of that diminution in value, and it was essentially on this basis that the claim was struck out. (The plaintiffs faced a further problem, in that Trust Securities was the only plaintiff which was in contract with the defendants. The plaintiffs said that Trust Securities had suffered a loss in that they had a liability to British Airways Pensions; they were, however, unable to particularise that liability.)

The above cases are all concerned with being struck out before trial and as such they would have only limited application to arbitrations because an arbitrator does not have the same inherent jurisdiction as a court has to strike claims out (see below as to the 'review' point). However, a plaintiff is not in the clear because he is able to escape a striking out application.

The Court of Appeal decision in 1992 in *McAlpine v McDermott* 58 BLR 1 represents, if anything, an even bigger problem for plaintiffs than the *Wharf* decision.

The facts in short were that McAlpine were subcontractors to McDermott for the construction of some pallets for the weather deck of a North Sea oil platform. There were large numbers of drawings, and McAlpine claimed £3.5 million.

At first instance, the case was heard by His Honour John Davies QC. He gave judgment in June 1980, finding that the issue of the drawings had indeed so distorted the substance and identity of the contract that McAlpine were freed from the obligation to complete within the contract period and were entitled to recover on a cost plus basis. Not surprisingly, McDermott appealed successfully to the Court of Appeal again instructing John Uff QC, and the decision in the appeal was given in March 1992.

The Court of Appeal's judgment reversed the first instance decision. It found that McAlpine had, during the 92 day trial, failed to establish an entitlement to any money at all, and delivered a judgment of general application upon the correct approach to 'theoretical' claims. There were four key points in the Court of Appeal's judgment:

(1) McAlpine presented their claim for extension by going through each of the variation orders, identifying how long it took to do that work, and adding up those delays. The Court of Appeal said that this method suffered from the major defect that it assumed that if one man was working for one day on a particular variation order, then the whole contract was held up for that day. The Court noted the absurdity of this assumption.

(2) For calculating its claim for additional labour costs, the plaintiff calculated the number of man hours allowed in the tender for each activity, and divided that by the number of days that the activity

was originally planned in order to arrive at the number of man hours per day that that activity absorbed. McAlpine then extrapolated that number of man hours per day for the whole period of delay, making adjustments for holidays, night work, etc. Again, the Court of Appeal threw out this approach. It said it assumed that the whole of the work force planned for a particular activity was engaged continuously on that activity from the day it started until the day it finished. The whole of McAlpine's claim therefore failed.

(3) The Court of Appeal went on to identify what sort of approach is needed in this sort of case, namely a retrospective and dissectional reconstruction of what actually happened.

(4) The Court considered the 'colour of the front door' argument, ie the suggestion sometimes made that a contractor is entitled to extensions of time, as of right, where instructions are late. The Court of Appeal firmly dismissed that approach, saying 'If a contractor is already a year late through his culpable fault, it would be absurd that the employer should lose his claim for unliquidated damages just because at the last moment, he orders an extra coat of paint.'

It is by no means uncommon to see delay claims where the methodology is indistinguishable from the methodology so roundly condemned in the *McAlpine* case.

This latter question was dealt with at length in *Balfour Beatty Building v Chestermount Properties* [1993] CILL 821, a decision of Mr Justice Colman in the Commercial Court. The contractors appealed from the arbitrator's finding in respect of two questions of law:

(1) Does Clause 25 confer upon the architect, jurisdiction to grant an extension of time for the completion of the works in respect of a relevant event occurring during a period of culpable delay?

(2) In granting an extension of time in respect of the relevant event occurring during a period of culpable delay, ought the architect to award a 'gross' extension (that is one which re-fixes the completion date at the calendar date upon which the work could reasonably be expected to be completed, having regard to the calendar date upon which it is instructed), or a 'net' extension (that is one which calculates the revised completion date by taking the date currently fixed and adding the number of days which the architect regards as fair and reasonable).

The arbitrator answered these questions as follows:

(1) Yes. The practical effect of this answer was that an architect may order extra work during a period of culpable delay without thereby setting time at large.

(2) In granting an extension of time in respect of the relevant event occurring during a period of culpable delay, the architect ought to award a 'net' extension of time, that is, one which calculates the

completion date by taking the date currently fixed and adding the number of days which the architect regards as fair and reasonable. The Commercial Court upheld the arbitrator on both points.

It is worth noting that the timing of a relevant event may still be relevant, and will always be relevant where the relevant event contended for is the lateness of necessary instructions. The Court said this:

> Before leaving this issue it is right to add that the application of the 'net' method to 'relevant events' occurring within a period of culpable delay may give rise to particular problems of causation. These were discussed at some length in the course of argument. In each case it is for the architect exercising his powers under Clause 25.3.2 to decide whether an adjustment of the completion date is fair and reasonable having regard to the incidence of relevant events. Fundamental to this exercise is an assessment of whether the relevant event occurring during a period of culpable delay has caused delay to the completion of the works and, if so, how much delay . . . For example, a storm which floods the site during a period of culpable delay and interrupts progress of the works would have been avoided altogether if the contractor had not overrun the completion date. In such a case, it is hard to see that it would be fair and reasonable to postpone the completion date to extend the contractor's time.

2 Time Analysis — The Nature of the Problem

In Chapter 5, we looked at simple hypothetical example of delay. Let us look again at the problems of making a Retrospective Delay Analysis in this hypothetical case. The progress chart at figure 2 chapter 5 shows that the project should have been complete at the end of week 12 but was not complete until the end of week 20 — a delay of eight weeks. How does one apportion that eight weeks? It does not, of itself, help to add up the delays to completion — that is to say the delays between the time that activities were supposed to start and the time when they actually started. These delays are as follows:

Table 1

Activity	Delay to commencement
Foundations	1 Week
Car Park	1 Week
Framework	1 Week
Roofing	2 Weeks
Brickwork and Blockwork	5 Weeks
Painting	8 Weeks
Total:	18 Weeks

There is no very ready way of reconciling that 18 weeks with the eight weeks of actual delay. Similarly, adding up the delays to completion does not help. These are as follows:

Table 2

Activity	Delay to completion
Foundations	1 Week
Car Park	7 Weeks
Framework	2 Weeks
Roofing	10 Weeks
Brickwork and Blockwork	6 Weeks
Painting	8 Weeks
Total:	34 Weeks

Nor is it any help, of itself, to look at the extended durations, that is to say the amount by which activity duration has exceeded the planned duration:

Table 3

Activity	Extended duration
Foundations	Zero
Car Park	6 Weeks
Framework	1 Week
Roofing	8 Weeks
Brickwork and Blockwork	1 Week
Painting	Zero
Total:	16 Weeks

It is clear that, in order to identify what matters were causative of the eventual eight weeks delay it is necessary to make some sort of Retrospective Critical Path Analysis. Before considering this, it is necessary to look at the way critical paths are used for planning purposes.

3 Contract planning

There are essentially three methods, of increasing complexity, which contractors use to plan building projects. The first is the traditional method of drawing a bar chart by hand. The planner will rely upon his general common sense and experience of building to hand draw a bar chart showing when the various operations are to take place. The second method is to network the contract programme. The networking is done by establishing the logical relationships between the activities. An example of a simple network appears at Figure 1; this is simply a diagrammatic representation of the logic described in words on page 71.

Figure 1: A simple network

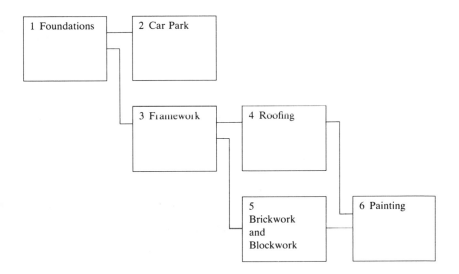

In substantial sized contracts, the planning operation will usually be carried out using a computer and planning software. There are two main files into which the data is inserted: the activity file and the relationship file.

In its simplest form, the data put into the activity file will be as shown in Figure 2. For each activity there is a unique activity number, a description, and a duration.

Figure 2: Activity listing

Activity number	Description	Duration (weeks)
1	Foundations	2
2	Car Park	3
3	Framework	4
4	Roofing	2
5	Brickwork and Blockwork	4
6	Painting	2

The information put into the relationship file is, in its simplest form, as in Figure 3. For each relationship it is necessary to identify the predecessor, the successor, and the type of relationship.

Figure 3: Relationship listing

Predecessor	Successor	Type
1	2	FSO
1	3	FSO
3	4	FSO
3	5	FSO
4	6	FSO
5	6	FSO

Given the two sets of data, and the date on which the project may start, the computer will work out the contract programme.

In a small hypothetical example like the one above, it would of course be quicker to draw the bar chart by hand. But in practice, a substantial building contract will involve anything between 100 and 2,000 activities and perhaps double that number of relationships. At those levels of complexity, the use of computers is regarded as indispensable.

The third level of sophistication involves resource scheduling. Some logical relationships are non-resource dependent, or primary. Thus, for example, it is physically impossible to paint a wall until it has been constructed. Other relationships are resource based. Thus a programmer may provide for the painter to finish painting the north face of a wall before starting to paint the south face of the wall. That relationship is a function of expecting to have only one painter. If the contractor were to bring on another painter, then both sides of the wall could be painted at the same time.

With this in mind, planning programmes generally include a resourcing capability. The contract planner will identify, in respect of each activity, what resources that activity will require, and the planner will also feed in information as to how much of each resource is available. In calculating the dates of each activity, the computer will calculate whether there are enough painters to paint the north side of the wall at the same time as the south side of the wall, and if not, whether it is more effective to paint the north side or the south side first.

Planning aficionados often say that resourcing is essential for sophisticated planning. Nevertheless, it is still comparatively rare for contractors to resource their contract programmes, and its technical complexities mean that it is rarely used in Retrospective Delay Analysis. Logical relations give rise to quite enough complication, and further discussion of resource scheduling is beyond the scope of this book.

(a) Types of relationship

In the simple example given above, only one type of relationship has been used — a simple finish–start relationship, which is shown diagrammatically in Figure 4. In that simple relationship, there is no lag between the time when the predecessor finishes and the successor starts.

Figure 4: Simple finish–start relationship

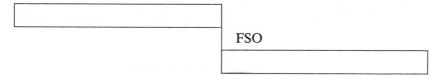

Figure 5 shows diagrammatically a lagged finish–start relationship. The predecessor may, for example, be the plastering of a wall, and the successor may be the painting of that wall. It may be necessary to wait for two days, to allow the plaster to dry, before the painting may commence.

Figure 5: Finish–start relationship with lag

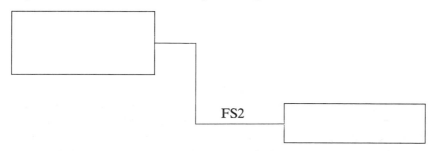

In practice, it is very common for there to be an overlap between the predecessor and the successor; this is typically the case where one trade follows anothcr around a building. One way to cope with the overlap is to insert negative lag, as shown in Figure 6.

Figure 6: Finish–start relationship with negative lag

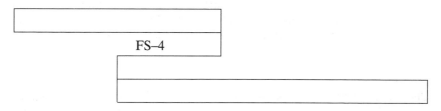

With such a relationship, the computer will place the second activity to commence four days before the finish of the succeeding activity. This is, however, somewhat artificial logic, and it is far more common for planners to use pairs of start–start and finish–finish relationships, as shown in Figure 7. Here the logical constraint is that the succeeding activity may not start until three weeks after the start of the preceding activity, nor may it finish before five weeks after the finish of the predecessor. Note that there is still considerable artificiality in these relationships, but they are nevertheless widely used for planning purposes.

Figure 7: Period start–start/finish–finish relationship

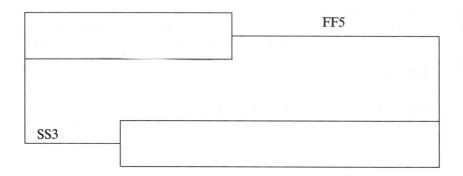

(b) Target Start Dates and Target Finish Dates

The ordinary way that the time analysis programmes work is to place each activity according to the logical relationships that are fed into the computer. Sometimes, however, a planner will wish to override that purpose, and to insist on a particular activity starting on a particular date regardless of what the logic would show. Similarly, he may provide that a particular activity must start not earlier or not later than a given date. Further, he can insist that any given activity must finish on or not earlier or later than any given date.

These start and finish target dates are generally stored in the relationship file, and must be treated with deep suspicion in Retrospective Delay Analysis. Where these start or finish target dates have been used, they 'overrule' the time analysis and thus enable the computer operator to get any answer he desires, even though a time analysis has apparently been run.

(c) Calendars

There are essentially two ways to count time, either in terms of calendar days or in terms of working days. Contract planners usually prefer to make their calculations in working days, and thus their computers will contain data as to which calendar days are working days, and which are not. Typically, the calendar will exclude Saturdays, Sundays, bank holidays and the standard construction holidays at Christmas and Easter. Sophisticated planning software contains provision for different calendars for different trades.

(d) Float

Float is a difficult concept, because the word is used to describe at least three different things.

The primary meaning of float is, in respect of any activity, the amount of time between the earliest and the latest start date. It usually follows this pattern:

(1) When the planning software runs its Time Analysis, it first runs a 'forward pass' in which it will work out the earliest start date and the earliest finish date for each activity. These are the first dates on which each activity may start, paying regard to the logical relationships and any start of finish target dates which may have been entered. The computer stores these dates in the activities file.

(2) Second, the computer looks to see what is the latest of these early finish dates — that becomes the project completion date.

(3) Third, the computer performs a 'backward pass', in which it calculates start and finish dates, by reference to the logical relationships and any target start dates or target finish dates, also bearing in mind the project completion date. These dates are known as the latest start dates and the latest finish dates.

The difference between the earliest start/finish dates and the latest start/finish dates is the float; activities where the float is zero are described as critical. When drawing the bar charts, the computer usually gives the option of showing this float period, typically in an empty bar immediately following the main bar, as a single line. Usually, the main part of the bar is shown in blue for non-critical activities, and in red for critical activities.

Lawyers do not usually regard criticality and float in this technical way, more often they will ask a generalised question in order to establish whether or not a particular activity is critical or is on the critical path such as: 'Suppose this activity were delayed by a single day. Would that have led to completion of the project as a whole being delayed by a day?' That is, essentially, the same test of criticality as the one described above (except that it does not deal with start or finish target dates).

The second sense in which the word 'float' is used is in the sense of 'local' float. That is to say the amount by which any activity could be delayed without delaying any other activity at all. It is, of course, possible that delay on one activity would impact on just one or a few activities, but not in such a way as to delay completion of the project as a whole.

Thirdly, float is sometimes used to describe a 'contractor's float'. The contract period may be, for example, for a year from 1 January to

31 December. The contractor may, however, decide that he wishes to complete the work by the end of October. The months of November and December are sometimes described as float. Consider another scenario where the employer's architect issued instructions, the result of which is that the contractor finishes at the end of November instead of the end of October. The position in this case under the JCT Contract is reasonably clear. The contractor is not entitled to an extension of time as such, because under Clause 25.3.1, extensions of time are only due if completion of the works is delayed beyond the completion date. In *Glenlion Construction v The Guinness Trust* (1987) 39 BLR 89, His Honour Judge Fox-Andrews found that there was no term to be implied into a JCT contract that, if and so far as the programme shows a completion date before the date for completion, the employer must enable the contractor to carry out the works in accordance with the earlier date. Nevertheless, if the contractor can show that he has been caused loss and expense by reason of the delay, he may be entitled to claim it under Clause 26 (The position may depend on the reason for the delay. If a contractor is delayed or disrupted by an instruction ordering additional work, he is entitled to loss and expense regardless of whether the additional work delayed the contractor in the completion of the works).

More difficult questions arise if the effect of the delays is to prevent the contractor from completing until after the contractual completion date. Is the employer entitled to make use of this float or, as the question is sometimes put, 'to whom does the float belong?' There is no unequivocal answer to this point. It is suggested that the answer is probably the same as in the preceding hypothesis, ie that the float belongs to the employer for the purposes of extensions of time, but to the contractor for the purposes of loss and expense.

(e) The Critical Path

The concept of a critical path was discussed in Chapter 5. The concept of a single critical path going from activity to activity through the job is an attractive one to lawyers, because it is a concept which can readily be grasped. Unfortunately, however, the concept of a critical path begins to break down when anything other than straightforward finish/start zero lag relationships (see Figure 4 above) are present. For example, where they are critical activities with paired start–start and finish–finish relationships, then the aggregate length of the activities on the 'critical path' will exceed the length of the project as a whole. For the purpose of Retrospective Delay Analysis, this problem may be solved either by splitting activities into several parts, or by the use of percentage relationships, see below.

(f) Hammocks

Looking at a bar chart containing 1,000 activities is tedious, for this reason, planning programmes usually contain provision for hammocking, whereby a number of activities may be grouped together and shown as a single bar on a bar chart.

(g) Multiple Starts and Multiple Finishes

For a simple project, there will generally be a single date on which the project can start, and a single date on which the project will be regarded as complete. In more complex projects, however, there may be separate start dates for different areas of the site, and different completion objectives as different areas of the project are handed over to the employer in turn. Sophisticated planning programmes are capable of planning accordingly. However in *Glenlion Construction v The Guinness Trust* (1987) 39 BLR 89, it was conceded by the contractor that 'a relevant fact is that both parties at the time of entering into the contract would have been well aware that contractors frequently produce programmes that were over-optimistic'. The judge quoted, apparently with approval passages to that effect from Hudson and Keating (pages 104–105).

(h) Available Planning Software

There are a number of commercially available planning software packages which are used by contractors for planning purposes. These packages include Open Plan, Artemis and Power Projects. Some of these packages, such as Open Plan, are based on databases on PCs, so that to operate them you will need:
  (1) the planning software, which will cost a few thousand pounds,
  (2) the host database, which will cost a few hundred pounds,
  (3) a computer.
The planning data on which the contract programme is put together are usually contained in a series of files with the same file name but different extensions. Therefore a contractor who has planned a contract at Toytown using Open Plan software may be expected to have the following datafiles:
TOYTOWN.ACT — The activities file
TOYTOWN.REL — The relationships file
TOYTOWN.CAL — The calendar file
If the project has been resourced, there will also be a TOYTOWN.RES file. In addition to that, there may be a number of index files; these are not essential and can be re-created from the data files with the correct software.

4 Retrospective delay analysis — the nature of the problem

The idea of feeding information into a computer and getting information out as to the cause of delay sounds straightforward but there are some key difficulties. The first objective of the Retrospective Delay Analysis must be to identify what matters were critical, and what matters were not critical. There is no point complaining about something which was not critical to completion. The first problem to consider is whether things critical on the contract programme may not have been critical in the actual event of the project as performed. This comes about in at least three ways, new activities, duration changes and logic changes.

(1) New activities

Consider a scenario where on a project as planned, the activity roofing is not critical. However, if the roofing materials, when they arrived on site as planned, just before they were needed, were the wrong size and had to be sent back to the manufacturer for adaption — a four week process. This process would have to be inserted into the project as an activity and the route of the critical path would change, flowing through this new activity and the roofing instead of through the brickwork and blockwork.

(2) Duration change

A similar result occurs if, without any new activity being required, an activity takes longer than anticipated. Therefore if the roofing work took ten weeks instead of the two weeks originally envisaged, then again the critical path flows through the roofing instead of through the brickwork and blockwork.

(3) Changes of Logic

It is very common for there to be changes in logic in building contracts; for example, a contract programme may require that the construction of one brick wall should be completed before the construction of another may commence. If the contract is in delay, a decision may be made to bring on more bricklayers and more scaffolding, such that both walls may be constructed at the same time. Similarly, someone may decide to bring on another crane or additional formwork, these matters can make a marked difference to the route of the critical path.

For all of the above reasons, the original contract logic will be inherently unreliable for the purpose of analysing what actually happened. Further, there is a serious technical problem where paired start–start/finish–finish relationships have been used, see Figure 7 above. Consider the example of two activities: the predecessor is laying underfelt in four rooms and the successor is laying carpet in the same four rooms. There is one man to lay the underfelt, and another man to lay the carpet, and they will each take one day per room. The true nature of the relationship is as per Figure 8; once the underlayer has finished in room A then the carpet layer can move into room A, and so on for each room.

Figure 8:   Planned

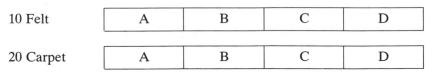

| 10 Felt | A | B | C | D |
| 20 Carpet | A | B | C | D |

The traditional planning technique will show a start-start relationship and a finish–finish relationship of one week. However, if the felt layer takes two days in room A (not an unlikely supposition — we would not analyse the project unless there were delays in it). The original contract logic is obviously no longer applicable. After one day, the felt layer is still only half way through room A, and so it would be impossible for the carpet layer to commence work in that room.

Figure 9:   Planned logic

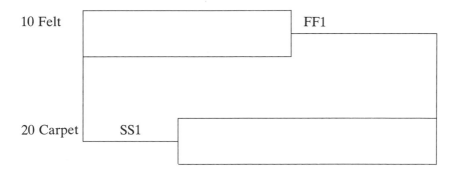

10 Felt

FF1

20 Carpet

SS1

There are at least three ways of overcoming this problem, each with its disadvantages.

The first method is to recalculate the lag *pro rata* to the increase in duration in the preceding activity. However, if the actual performance is as per Figure 10: the felt underlayer took two days to do room A and one day each to do rooms B, C and D; a total of five days instead of the originally planned four days. By method A, the start–start relationship would be increased from a one day lag to a 1.25 day lag. The disadvantage of this method, of course, is that it is not accurate. The carpet layer cannot start until two days after the felt underlayer has started.

Figure 10:   Actual

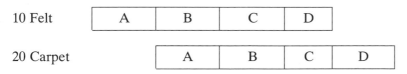

10 Felt | A | B | C | D |

20 Carpet | A | B | C | D |

The second method is to split each activity into its component parts so that the network would be as per Figure 11. This is logically sound, but it suffers from the disadvantage, in practice, of being unwieldy. In this simple example, it would quadruple the number of activities and the number of relationships. This does not necessarily create a problem in the printing of bar charts (since activities 10A, 10B, 10C and 10D could be grouped together to be shown as a simple bar, but it makes the explanation of the network enormously more complicated.

Figure 11:   Split activity network

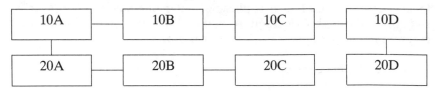

A third option is to use percentage relationships instead of the lags. These are exemplified at Figure 12. These relationships dictate that it is necessary to complete 25 per cent of the predecessor before commencing the successor. It is necessary to complete 50 per cent of the predecessor before proceeding beyond 25 per cent of the successor etc.

Figure 12:   Percentage relationships

10 Felt					
		25,0	50,25	75,50	100,75
20 Carpet					

This system provides a reasonably good approximation regardless of how activities are progressed, and avoids proliferation of activities. The disadvantage, however, is that it requires the use of purpose written software instead of an off-the-shelf planning package.

(a) Where to Start?

It can be seen from the above that the actual logic will be different from the planned logic. It is necessary to identify the actual logic in any analysis which endeavours to show what actually happened. The question which usually arises is where to start. The normal approach is to start with the contract programme. Where the contract programme was originally networked that logic will already be known. Where the original contract programme was hand drawn it is possible to synthesise that logic. It will then usually be necessary to make some changes to that logic before it can accurately be used to explain what actually happened. Every new activity, every extension to a duration of a particular activity, and every change in logic, is potentially causative of the delay to the project as a whole; the Time Analysis will show whether it was critical or not.

The alternative approach is to start with what actually happened. The delaying events are identified, and a comparison is made between what actually happened, and what would have happened but for the delaying event. There is a fundamental and philosophical difference between these two approaches; it hinges on the very nature of perceived cause.

Take the case of a school picnic in the country. Unseen by his teacher a boy leaves the picnic and goes to a nearby village where he finds an unattended motor garage, he gets into a car which had no effective brakes because the mechanic was part way through replacing the hydraulic brake fluid. The boy drives off in the car and is killed. What is the cause of his death? Different people may answer this question in different ways:

(1) A disciplinarian may say the cause was the teacher's neglect in not keeping an eye on the boy.

(2) The garage proprietor may say that it was his mechanic's neglect in leaving the workshop unattended.

(3) The moralist may say it is the boy's fault for doing something he must have known was wrong and dangerous.

It is unlikely that anybody would blame the fact that the car had petrol in it, although this cause would equally satisfy the 'but for' or *sine qua non* test. Perceived cause depends on what one expected to happen.

In building contracts, is one to expect that the contract would have run according to the contract plan if it had not been for the delaying events? In practice, it is generally assumed by courts and arbitrators that the contract would have been performed according to the contract programme unless the contrary is demonstrated.

(b) First Cause or Ultimately Critical?

It is often necessary to choose between competing causes. Competing causes may be either serial or parallel.

Parallel, or necessary causes are those which must all be present if a given state of affairs is to come about. An example is defective workmanship which should have been inspected. In order for any harm to occur it is necessary both for the work to be done badly and for the inspection system to fail to pick it up. There is a fair quantity of authority on serial causation; the general approach of the law is to ascribe part of the blame to each cause. In delay cases, where there are serial delays, no difficulty generally arises, each delay is ascribed to the responsible party. Thus, if an activity starts two weeks late because of late instructions, and once started is halted by a further three weeks because of the need to rectify bad workmanship, the total delay to that activity will be five weeks of which two weeks will ordinarily be blamed on the employer and three weeks will ordinarily be blamed on the contractor. Parallel, or necessary causes are more difficult. The most typical example is where the employer's architect is late in providing necessary information for an activity, in circumstances where the contractor, through his own fault, was not ready to start on time anyway. Here, the combined effect of the two causes is less than the aggregate of the two delays, and a choice needs to be made between the two.

Various tests have been propounded, but there is no clear authority upon which is right. In *Keating*, it is suggested that the appropriate test is the 'dominant cause' test, but however attractive this concept, it suffers from two problems:

(1) It does not, of itself, provide much assistance to whoever is carrying out a Retrospective Delay Analysis as to how to conduct that analysis.
(2) It was flatly rejected as the appropriate test in *Fairweather v Wandsworth* (1988) 12 BLR 40. Regrettably the court did not in that case explain what was the right test!

In essence, the choice facing the analyst is whether to adopt a first cause approach, or an ultimately critical approach.

On a first cause approach, the analyst will typically start from the position of the contract programme. He will then introduce the delaying events into the analysis bit by bit, altering the logic and durations as necessary, and noting at each step the amount by which the contract completion date is moved out. The amount of delay which is ascribed to each delaying event, or group of delaying events, is the amount by which that event or those events push out the completion date. This process starts at the beginning of the project, and proceeds through to the end, by which time the entire delay will have been accounted for.

By contrast, in an ultimately critical analysis, the analyser will look at all the delaying events at the same time, and will conduct a single *ex post facto* analysis to determine what in the event, turned out to be critical to completion.

These differing methods of analysis can produce startlingly different results, and there is no absolutely clear authority as to which is appropriate. There are few precedents in contract and there are conflicting decisions in tort. In principle, it is difficult to see why there should be any difference between the approach to be adopted in tort and the approach to be adopted in contract, and with this in mind it is worth considering the House of Lords decisions in *Baker v Willoughby* [1969] 13 All ER 1528 and *Jobling v Associated Dairies* [1981] 2 All ER 752.

(c) Baker v Willoughby

The plaintiff was involved in a car accident which led to permanent damage to his leg. Subsequently, the plaintiff, in a separate incident was shot in the same leg during an attempted robbery and his leg was amputated. The first tortfeasor was not relieved of his responsibility for loss of earnings.

(d) Jobling v Associated Dairies

The plaintiff injured his back by reason of his employer's breach of statutory duty. However, the plaintiff later developed a condition of the spine which rendered him totally unfit for work. As a result the employer was relieved of all responsibility.

Consideration of *Jobling v Associated Dairies* alone may suggest that an ultimately critical approach is generally correct, but it can lead to very unnatural results in building contract delay cases. Such absurdities are sometimes described as 'colour of the front door' arguments. This hypothesis is as follows:

> Suppose a contract to build a house has been massively delayed through the fault of the contractor. The external scaffolding is finally removed and the architect, surveying the building decides that the colour of the front door is a shade too dark. He instructs the contractor to repaint it. The contractor then argues that he is entitled to an extension of time in respect of the whole of the period of delay because he could not have complied with that final instruction until the date on which that instruction was given.

This, in essence, is the argument that the Court of Appeal described as 'absurd' in *McAlpine v McDermott* (1992) 58 BLR 1. Lloyd LJ said:

> If a contractor is already a year late through his culpable fault, it would be absurd that the employer should lose his claim for unliquidated damages just because, at the last moment, he orders an extra coat of paint.

How, should the analyst treat the architect's instruction to paint the front door, must he ignore it altogether?

It may be that the correct treatment of these events depends on the reason for their timing. There are two ways this might be dealt with:

(1) Suppose the final instruction to change the colour of the front door was given on 1 December and it took one day to do the work. There is a need to introduce a new activity into the analysis to 'repaint front door'. But what is the appropriate logic?

One approach of the analyst would be to 'lock' the date by the use of a target start date, dictating that it should be not earlier than 1 December. That will force the absurd result of ascribing all but one day of the delay to late receipt of that instruction, and the balance of one day to the repainting of the door.

(2) Alternatively, the analyst may explain why the repainting of the front door was done on 1 December by a different route. He may say that the architect was not in a position to decide about the colour of the front door until the scaffolding was down. Therefore, it introduces a finish–start relationship between the removal of the scaffolding and the instruction to repaint the front door. The analyst will also include the matters which delayed the contract through to the striking of the scaffold. In this case, the analysis will ascribe only the last day of delay to the painting of the front door. It is inherent in this approach that, had the scaffolding been struck much sooner, then the architect would have made his decision to change the colour of the front door that much sooner.

The moral of the above examples is to draw attention to the use of start or finish target dates in analysis.

(e) Adding new activities

Construction programmes are generally concerned with construction matters not design matters. Main contractors may be given or may prepare information release schedules, detailing the dates by which design information is required but they do not habitually include those matters in their programmes. Nor do they usually include in their contract programmes, lead times for the manufacture of materials or items fabricated off site such as secondary steelwork.

It follows from the above, however, that Time Analysis often needs to include such matters. Consider for example that the lead time for the manufacture of some secondary steelwork is six weeks and the architect does not provide details of that secondary steelwork, until two weeks before the secondary steelwork needs to start on site. All too often claims are put forward containing long schedules comparing the dates for information on the information release schedules with the dates on which information is received. Of itself, this is not sufficient, because it does not identify what effect, if any, the lateness of the information actually had on the project. The courts often know that information release schedules call for information to be provided substantially before it is actually needed by the contractor, especially if the project is already in delay.

A much better approach is for the analyst to include activities for the provision of design information and the lead time for manufacture in the programme with logical links between them. He will insert those activities into the original planned logic and check that they do not affect the timing of any existing bars. In the actual analysis, the analyst will introduce the delay in the design process, and show how this impacts on the construction programme.

(f) Watersheds

Some analysts carry out first cause analysis on an event by event basis, that is to say they analyse the impact of every single delaying event one by one. In order to keep a permanent record of this process, they usually take a copy of all the data files at each point. On a substantial project this can lead to an immense quantity of data and problems arise as to when to incorporate logic changes associated with reprogramming.

Accordingly, it is sometimes sensible for analysts to adopt a 'watershed' approach. The analyst will choose various points through the project — generally not more than half a dozen or a dozen at the most — which stand at the crossroads on the job, or points where decisions are made to change course in some way. Typical points are the completion of the ground floor slab (especially in 'top down' contracts), achieving a watertight envelope, 'power on' (ie the time when it is possible to activate the electricity supply to the building) etc.

These watersheds can often be helpful to keep the size of the analysis within manageable proportions, and often accords more closely than other methods with a 'commonsense' approach in terms of what the parties thought was important at the time. Depending on exactly how the analysis is carried out, the watershed approach will often be first cause from watershed to watershed, but ultimately critical within each watershed.

5 Seasonal effects

Builders can work more productively in the summer than they can in the winter. Builders therefore aim, if they can, to carry out work, particularly 'out of doors' work, during the summer months. If, through no fault of his own, the contractor is delayed so that work is carried out during a period of bad weather, to what cause is that additional delay ascribed? Is it ascribed to the bad weather or as a further consequence of the original delaying events?

6 The relationship between delay and disruption

Delay is something which causes a postponement of the contract as a whole, and disruption is something which does not, although it may cause the contractor loss. Others say that there is little difference and arguments along those lines tends to cause further delay to the contract and additional cost to the contractor. The truth is somewhere in between. Almost all disruption involves some sort of delay, generally non-critical. The way that it is put generally depends on what accelerative measures are taken by the contractor.

Take, by way of example, winter working. If the contractor is forced to carry out an activity during a period of winter working that will reduce his productivity. There is not as much daylight. People get cold and cross, and if it is during the festive season that takes its toll. If the contractor does not increase his resources he will generally suffer delay and will claim for it. If he is prepared to pay for it however, he can generally overcome these problems by means of more overtime, lighting, heating, and so forth. In those circumstances, he will probably make his claim for disruption.

The broad distinction between delay and disruption is useful; delay is something which delays completion of the project as a whole, and disruption is not. Retrospective Delay Analysis may, however, be relevant for some disruption claims. Take, for example, the case of a contract, without any sectional completion dates, but which nevertheless involves the construction of several buildings. There may be delays to the completion of one of those buildings, perhaps not critical to the project as a whole, but which nevertheless mean the contractor is forced to maintain time related expenses, such as craneage or scaffold on that structure for longer than would otherwise have been the case.

7 Features of Good Retrospective Delay Analyses

A good Retrospective Delay Analysis will provide a comprehensive explanation of what actually happened on the project. It will be typified by a bar chart containing two bars:

(1) What actually happened on site, as a matter of historical record, without any calculation or manipulation at all.

(2) The result of the analyst's 'actual' time analysis. This analysis should be free of any start or finish target dates, or of any other device whereby the dates are forced to correspond with what actually happened.

If these two bars more or less marry up then the analyst has succeeded in putting forward a credible explanation of how the contract went. Do not expect a perfect match; in practice it is impossible for analysts to achieve an accuracy better than within a day or so. If the match is exact the analyst is probably cheating. It should be clear from the above that the analysis should explain the actual delay on site neither more nor less.

A good Time Analysis will have fallback positions. It may well be that the court or arbitrator will not accept some element of the analysis put forward. In a good analysis, this should not be fatal to the claim, other items should be ready to step into criticality. In practice, this will often mean that the case should be put forward as a complete analysis, on floppy disks containing data if necessary. In this way a court or more particularly an arbitrator, can be given further information to consider should he find against a particular logical link or duration.

A good Time Analysis is something that a sensible advocate can explain. This is not merely a point about trials. Most claims are settled by negotiation of one form or another. The biggest failures of negotiation tend to occur where there is a failure of communication between lawyer and analyst. This may be the fault of the lawyer or it may be the fault of the analyst who is unable to communicate effectively what he has done and why. A good analysis will always trace through the effect, if any, of every matter complained of on completion. It may contain alternative cases as reserve arguments which include other matters. But every argument whether first line or reserve should be calculated and arguable.

8 Bad Analyses

There are so many types of bad analysis that a complete catalogue would be impossible. This work accordingly restricts itself to the defects in analysis which are most commonly seen in practice.

The worst time claims — those most certainly doomed to fail — are those claims which contain no analysis at all. The acid test is this: does the claim ascertain precisely which events are alleged to have caused how much delay? If not, the claimant will be at severe risk of being struck out (as in the *Wharf* cases) or of recovering nothing at trial (as in *McAlpine v McDermott*).

The extensions of time contended for should not exceed the actual delay. Under most standard contracts extensions of time are only due for matters which actually delay completion. Where a project is delayed by ten weeks there is no point in the contractor making a claim for extension of 50 weeks in the hope that he will be partially successful; the more likely result these days is that the claim will be dismissed in its entirety. The worst manifestation of this tendency is the 'entitlement' approach where the contractor claims that he is 'entitled' to an extension of time of, for example, 50 weeks, although he was actually only delayed by ten. If the truth of the matter is that he would have been delayed by 50 weeks but for its accelerative measures he should claim for ten weeks' extension of time and use the rest of his material in support of claim for disruption.

Appendix A

Glossary

Absolute obligation. An obligation come what may. Cf an obligation merely to use best endeavours or to exercise reasonable care.

Activity. Something which needs to be done in a building project, and which is separately identified for the purpose of planning or Retrospective Delay Analysis.

Actual cost. This expression is sometimes used as a synonym for prime cost in a cost contract: see Chapter 1, section 1.

Adjudicator. Creature of Clause 24 of the JCT nominated sub-contract form NSC/4 (formerly Clause 13B of the Green Form). An adjudicator is like an 'instant arbitrator' for the purpose of quantifying the contractor's set-off against a nominated sub-contractor. The adjudicator is appointed by agreement between the contractor and the sub-contractor, and is usually a quantity surveyor.

ADR. Alternative Dispute Resolution. A structured but non-binding method of associating settlement of a dispute, usually by means of mediation and/or mini-trial. See Chapter 18.

Application. This usually means an application by a contractor or sub-contractor for interim payment or for reimbursement of loss and expense, eg under Clause 26.1 of the JCT contract.

Arbitrator. (i) Generally, a person qualified to act as arbitrator, often an architect but sometimes an engineer, quantity surveyor or a barrister. Membership of the Institute of Arbitrators is common but not essential. (ii) In particular, a person appointed as arbitrator pursuant to an arbitration agreement within the meaning of the Arbitration Act 1950.

Architect. (i) Generally, a person entitled to practise or carry on business under any name, style or title containing the word 'architect', being registered in the Register of Architects: Architects Registration Act 1938, s 1(1). In broad terms, this means someone with the initials RIBA after his or her name. (ii) In particular, the architect with the contractual status under a contract to issue instructions and certificates as to various matters. He may or may not have designed the Works; his function is to exercise control over the Works as they proceed. Used loosely in this sense, 'architect' can sometimes include any engineer, surveyor or supervising officer with this contractual function.

Articles of agreement. Usually means the articles of agreement which are to be found in the opening pages of the JCT contract.

Artists and tradesmen. Expression used in the old JCT contract to mean persons who execute work not forming part of the main contract. The expression was dropped in the 1980 edition. The 'artists and tradesmen' clause can apply to statutory undertakers such as electricity or gas boards (see *Henry Boot v Central Lancashire New Town Development Corporation* (1980) 15 BLR 1).

230

Bills of quantities. A full description of the amount of work necessary for completion of building works. In major projects, there are likely to be several volumes, and the bills will respectively deal with such matters as preliminaries, foundations, framework etc. Bills of quantities have columns on the right hand side of the page to allow the contractor to price the work. *The Standard Method of Measurement of Building Works* (6th edn), published by the Royal Institution of Chartered Surveyors and the National Federation of Building Trades Employers, sets out rules for the preparation and interpretation of Bills of Quantities.

Bills of variations. An account prepared at the end of the contract showing the effect upon the pre-agreed lump sum of variations to the Works.

Bills. Abbreviation for bills of quantities.

Bondsman. Synonym for the surety (eg under the ICE Form of Performance Bond). Often a bank or insurance company.

Building employer. Synonym for employer.

Building inspector. Local authority officer charged with ensuring compliance with Building Regulations.

Building owner. This expression is sometimes used as a synonym for the employer.

Building surveyor. This expression is sometimes used to describe a surveyor in general practice, in contrast to a quantity surveyor.

CAR Policy. A Contractors' All Risks insurance policy.

Caucus sessions. Sessions within an ADR process in which the Neutral talks to one party in the absence of the other. See Chapter 18.

CEDR. The Centre for Dispute Resolution. See Chapter 18.

Certifier. The person named in a contract as having power to issue certificates which have a contractual effect. In the JCT contract the certifier is either the architect (Private editions) or the supervising officer (Local Authorities editions). In the ICE contract the certifier is the engineer.

Claims consultant. A quasi-professional person who carries on the business of drafting, negotiating and advising upon claims for the payment of money or extension of time under building contracts. Usually a quantity surveyor by training.

Clause 22 perils. A series of perils defined by Clause 22 of JCT80 including fire, explosion and flood.

Clerk of works. An appointee of the employer whose duty is to act as an on-site inspector. His powers to give instructions to the contractor are usually limited. Usually a builder by training.

Client. Synonym for employer.

Completion. The completion of the execution of the work.

Completion date. In JCT form of contract (1980 edition), the agreed date for completion as extended by the architect.

Consortium. In the building industry, this expression most commonly means a partnership between two or more contractors which subsists for the purpose of one project only. The expression is also sometimes used to describe a joint venture between contractors, whether or not that joint venture is strictly speaking a partnership in the legal sense of the word.

Construction management. A procurement system whereby the contractor acts as the employer's agent, assisting the employer to enter into a series of trade contracts, and managing the whole design and construction process.

Contract. In addition to its legal meaning, this expression is often used to describe the project as a whole.

Contract bills. Synonym for bills of quantities.

Contract sum. This expression is generally used to describe the pre-agreed price for lump sum building works. In the JCT contract it has a particular definition which excludes VAT. The expression is not usually used to describe the sum that the contractor is entitled to at the end of the day; this is called the 'adjusted contract sum' in Clause 30.6.3 of the JCT contract.

Cost contract. A contract where the contractor's final entitlement is calculated by reference to the actual cost of the Works, rather than by reference to a pre-agreed lump sum. See Chapter 1, section 1.

Cost plus contract. Synonym for cost contract.

Cost plus percentage contract. Synonym for cost contract.

CPA conditions. The model conditions for the hiring of plant of the Contractors' Plant Association. See Chapter 1, section 2(h).

Critical delay. A delay that causes or contributes towards a delay in completion of building works as a whole. See p 72.

Critical path. The path of those operations that are critical to completion. See p 72.

CVI. Confirmation of Verbal Instruction, ie the confirmation by the contractor in writing of a verbal instruction of the architect (eg under Clause 4.3.2 of the JCT contract).

Date for completion. In JCT form of contract, the date by which the contractor must complete if his time is not extended. Cf completion date.

Defects liability period. A 'guarantee' period from practical completion within which the contractor must remedy any defects appearing in the works without charge. The expression has a particular definition under Clause 1.3 of the JCT contract.

Delay. Sometimes means delay in the completion of the works that is the responsibility of the contractor.

Disruption. Loss and expense caused to a contractor by reason of breaches or failures by the employer or his agents that do not necessarily result in prolongation of the works as a whole.

Domestic sub-contractor. A sub-contractor other than a nominated sub-contractor.

Eiusdem generis. The rule that provides that general words are to be construed within the ambit of preceding particular words. Thus the expression 'lions, tigers, pumas and other animals' would not be construed to include ants, notwithstanding that an ant is an animal. The *eiusdem generis* rule was found not to apply to a clause in JCT63 in *Henry Boot Construction Ltd v Central Lancashire Development Corporation* (1980) 15 BLR 1.

Employer. A person who enters into a contract with a building contractor whereby he agrees to pay for building works. The expression is not usually used to include the employing party to a sub-contract.

Engineer. (i) Generally, a professionally qualified civil engineer, structural engineer, heating and mechanical engineer, etc. (ii) In particular, the person so named in an ICE or FIDIC contract.

Entire completion. Completion in every respect, exceptionally a condition precedent to payment. See p 2.

Estimator. A person employed by a contractor to estimate the cost of proposed building works.

Expert. (i) A person who gives expert evidence in litigation or arbitration. (ii) The expression is sometimes used to describe a person who decides some matter between two parties, but whose position is not that of an arbitrator within the meaning of the Arbitration Act 1950.

Extended preliminaries. Method of calculation of a contractor's on-site losses following prolongation. Widely thought to be fallacious. See p 49.

Extras. Synonym for extra work, that is to say extra work required to be carried out by the employer, or the architect on behalf of the employer, not included within the original contract work.

Final account. The calculation of the sum due to the contractor in respect of the contract as a whole. The expression is used as an abbreviation for the 'computation of the adjusted Contract Sum for the Works', referred to in Clause 30.6.3 of the JCT contract.

Financing charges. (i) Where the cost of being kept out of money is claimed, not as interest on a debt, but as a constituent part of the debt. It is now fashionable to refer to it as financing charges, or finance charges, following the language used in *F C Minter v Welsh HTSO* (1980) 13 BLR 1. See p 54. (ii) Less delicately, synonym for interest. (iii) The expression is sometimes used to refer particularly to delay in the release of retention money.

Fluctuations. Adjustments to a contract sum that fall to be made by reason of increases or decreases in the cost of the works. See Chapter 4, section 1*(b)*.

Foreman-in-charge. Designation in the old JCT Form of the contractor's on-site representative.

Formula rules. The formula rules issued by the Joint Contracts Tribunal for use with Clause 40 of the JCT contract, which is one of the alternative fluctuation clauses.

Frustration. 'Frustration occurs whenever the law recognises that without default of either party a contractual obligation has become incapable of being performed because the circumstances in which performance is called for would render it a thing radically different from that which was undertaken by the contract. *Non haec in foedera veni*. It was not this that I promised to do' (Lord Radcliffe in *Davis Contractors Ltd v Fareham Urban District Council* [1956] AC 696 at 729). Frustration of building contracts is very rare; see for example *Wates Ltd v Greater London Council* (1983) 25 BLR 1.

General contractor. Unfashionable synonym for main contractor.

Green form. The form of sub-contract for use where the sub-contractor is nominated under the 1963 edition of the JCT Form issued under the sanction of and approved by the National Federation of Building Trades Employers and the Federation of Association of Specialists and Sub-contractors and approved by the Committee of Associations of Specialist Engineering Contractors. Now supplanted by NSC/4 or NSC/4(a).

Hancock v Brazier terms. The three terms usually implied in a contract for the sale of a house to be erected. See pp 26 and 36.

Hudson Formula. Method of calculating a contractor's loss of gross profit following prolongation. See p 52.

ICE. The Institution of Civil Engineers.

IFC. The Intermediate Form of Contract published by the JCT. It bridges the gap between JCT80 and the Minor Works Agreement.

JCT. The Joint Contracts Tribunal. See Chapter 1, Section 2*(a)*.

JCT63. An abbreviation for the 1963 Edition of the JCT Standard Form of Contract.

JCT80. An abbreviation for the 1980 Edition of the JCT Standard Form of Contract.

Joiner. A carpenter, usually responsible for finer work.

Labour-only sub-contractor. In theory, a sub-contractor who enters into sub-contracts for the provision of labour but not materials. In practice, a workman taxed under Schedule D.

Latent defect. A defect that is hidden. Cf patent defect.

Letter of intent. A letter, usually written by or on behalf of an employer to a contractor evincing an intention to enter into a contract with the contractor at some time in the future. The usual features of a letter of intent are that it makes clear that the parties are not at this stage entering into contractual relations, and that the employer will pay for any work carried out by the contractor in reliance upon the letter.

List of rates. Usually, the pre-agreed rates in a re-measurement contract.

Lump sum. The pre-agreed consideration in a lump sum contract.

Lump sum contract. A contract to execute work for a pre-agreed lump sum. See Chapter 1, section 1.

M & E. Mechanical and electrical work, such as plumbing, ventilation, electrical and lift installations.

Maintenance period. Synonym for defects liability period.

Management contracting. This expression is now generally used to mean the procurement system whereby the main contractor, paid on a cost plus basis, will sub-contract the whole of the works.

Management contractor. (i) A party which does not undertake any part of the works itself, but which contracts with the employer to act as an organiser of other contractors.

(ii) A contractor who undertakes works, usually on a cost plus basis, with the intention of sub-contracting the whole of the works.

Measurement. Usually means the measurement of the amount of building work done .

Measurement and value contract. Synonym for re-measurement contract.

Mediation. An Alternative Dispute Resolution Technique whereby an independent third party, usually called a Neutral, facilitates a settlement between the parties by techniques including caucus sessions, in which the Neutral will talk to the parties independently of each other. See Chapter 18.

Method statement. A statement by the contractor as to the method he proposes to adopt for the carrying out of the works. The use of method statements is more common in civil engineering contracts than building contracts. For examples of the relevance of method statements see *Yorkshire Water Authority v Sir Alfred McAlpine & Son (Northern) Ltd* (1985) 32 BLR 114 and *Holland Dredging (UK) Ltd v Dredging and Construction Co Ltd* (1987) 37 BLR 1.

Mini-trial. An ADR technique whereby the parties make a short presentation of their respective cases, often before a panel consisting of a senior executive from each party plus an independent neutral chairman. See Chapter 18.

Minor Works agreement. The Agreement for Minor Building Works issued by the JCT. See p 14.

Nemo dat quod non habet. Legal principle that a transferee of property cannot acquire ownership of it unless the transferor himself owned it.

Nominated sub-contractor. Generally, a sub-contractor with whom a main contractor enters into contract pursuant to the instructions of the architect. The expression has a precise meaning in JCT contracts (at Clause 35.1 of the 1980 edition; a different definition appeared at Clause 27(a) of the 1963 edition).

NSC/4. The standard form of nominated sub-contract issued by the JCT, taking the place of the Green Form.

OCR. Optical Character Recognition. A technique whereby typed or printed documents may be 'read' by electronic equipment.

Official Referee. For practical purposes, one of the judges who hear building contract cases in the High Court. In theory, the post was abolished by the Courts Act 1971 and the function formerly exercised by the Official Referee is now exercised by designated circuit judges. See Chapter 11.

Official Referees' Schedule. A form of pleading commonly used in the Official Referees' Court, where the contentions of the parties appear in tabular form. See Chapter 11, section 3.

Omissions. Items of original contract work required not to be carried out by the employer or the architect on the employer's behalf.

Package deal contract. Synonym for design and build contract.

Patent defect. A defect that is not hidden. Cf latent defect.

Pay-when-paid clause. A clause in a sub-contract which provides that the main contractor need not pay the sub-contractor until the main contractor himself receives payment from the employer in respect of those works.

Performance bond. This expression has various meanings. In the building industry it does not usually mean the kind of 'on demand' banker's bond which stands on a similar footing to a letter of credit (*Edward Owen Engineering Ltd v Barclays Bank International Ltd* [1977] 1 WLR 764). It usually means a guarantee in the ordinary sense of the word by a surety, often a bank or insurance company, that the contractor will perform his obligations under the contract.

Performance specification. A specification which defines the physical characteristics required of building works, eg the air temperature to be attained by a central heating system given an ambient temperature or the rate of air change to be attained by a ventilation system.

Period of final measurement. The period referred to in Clause 30.6.1.2 of the JCT contract within which the quantity surveyor must prepare and deliver a statement of all the final valuations of extra work etc.

Person-in-charge. JCT jargon for foreman-in-charge.

Plant. (i) Equipment such as cranes, earthmoving equipment, generators, and other equipment used in the execution of building works. (ii) Machinery installed in a finished building.

Practical completion. Generally means the stage at which the works are sufficiently complete to be fit to hand over, albeit there may be minor defects or omissions.

Preliminaries. Work and materials necessary for the execution of building works, but not actually forming part of the completed works themselves. Examples are site huts, scaffolding, site clearance, plant and temporary lighting.

Prime cost. In broad terms, the cost to a contractor of executing building work, usually excluding overhead costs that are not exclusively referable to that work. Sometimes it is more exactly defined, eg in the JCT form of fixed-fee contract.

Prime cost contract. A contract where the price is fixed after the work is done by reference to the prime cost of the work. Synonym for cost-plus contract.

Prime-cost sum. In a bill of quantities, the price placed against an item requiring the contractor to enter into a nominated sub-contract. The expression is to be distinguished from other uses of the expression prime cost; the tenuous connection is that under the usual nomination system the main contractor is, in respect of that work, paid whatever he (the main contractor) must pay the nominated sub-contractor. See Chapter 4, section 1(c).

Programme. A diagrammatic representation of the intended sequence of building operations. See p 70.

Prolongation. (i) Usually delay in the completion of the Works that is the responsibility of the employer. (ii) Synonym for prolongation costs.

Prolongation costs. Loss and expense caused to a contractor by reason of prolongation.

Provisional sum. (i) An item in a bill of quantities designed to estimate approximately the cost of work yet to be particularised. See Chapter 4, section

1(*d*). (ii) The expression is sometimes loosely used to describe any approximate estimate of the cost of building work.

Quantity surveyor. A surveyor whose principal function is to measure and value building work.

RDA. Retrospective Delay Analysis — see Chapter 21.

Relationship. In planning or Retrospective Delay Analysis, a statement as to the way in which the work must be carried out, eg that a wall cannot be painted until a certain amount of time after it has been plastered.

Relevant event. In the JCT form of contract, an event which entitles the contractor to an extension of time in which to complete the works.

Re-measurement contract. Hybrid between lump-sum contract and cost contract. See Chapter 1, section 1(*d*).

Retention. The money deducted and retained by the employer from sums that would otherwise be due to the contractor, usually 5 per cent. The retention fund is usually released as to half upon practical completion and as to the other half upon the architect's certificate of completion of making good defects.

RIBA. Royal Institute of British Architects, whose headquarters are at 66 Portland Place, London W1N 4AD (not pronounced 'reeber', but RIBA).

RIBA contract. The forerunner of the JCT contract, now sometimes used as a synonym for the JCT contract. See Chapter 1, section 2(*b*).

Scott Schedule. Familiar synonym for Official Referees' Schedule. See Chapter 11, section 3.

Section 4 summons. Summons issued by a defendant to court proceedings under the Arbitration Act 1950, s 4, seeking a stay of those proceedings so that the dispute may be referred to arbitration. See Chapter 10.

Services. This expression is usually used to describe the installations that provide central heating, air conditioning, hot water, drainage, electric power, lifts, etc.

Small works agreement. Expression sometimes used to describe the agreement for minor building works issued by the JCT.

Snagging list. A list of minor defects and omissions usually prepared when works are nearing completion.

Specialist contractor. This expression is generally used to describe a sub-contractor (usually nominated) who is responsible for some specialised part of the works, such as services.

Specification. (i) Generally, any description of building works. (ii) The expression is sometimes particularly used to describe a document containing special requirements as to the works, eg as to which British Standards the materials are to conform. (iii) The expression is sometimes used to describe an informal or short document in lieu of a bill of quantities.

Spon's. A guide, edited by Messrs Davis Belfield and Everest, Quantity Surveyors, to the cost of building works.

Standby letter of credit. Synonym used in some Commonwealth jurisdictions to describe an 'on demand' performance bond.

Structural engineer. An engineer whose principal responsibility is the load bearing structure of building works.

Subbie. Contractor's jargon for labour-only sub-contractor.

Sub-let. Synonym for sub-contract as a verb.

Subrogation. The right of an insurer which arises in some circumstances upon payment of a claim to take over the rights of the insured and sue the party at fault. See *Petrofina (UK) Ltd v Magnaload Ltd* (1983) 25 BLR 37 for an example of an insurer under a Contractors' All Risks policy being refused the right of subrogation.

Substantial completion. That degree of completion which is ordinarily necessary

Substantial completion. That degree of completion which is ordinarily necessary for the contractor to recover anything under a lump-sum contract. It is usually a lesser degree of completion than practical completion or entire completion.

Supervising officer. Creature of the JCT Local Authorities contracts. A person other than an architect who fulfils the function of certifier.

Target contract. There are various forms of complex arrangements whereby the method of calculation of the contractor's final entitlement depends upon whether the final cost of the Works exceeds a pre-agreed target sum. The scheme is sometimes used where the employer and the contractor wish to share between them any saving in the anticipated cost of the Works.

Temporary disconformity. Something less than a breach of contract; see the speech of Lord Diplock in *P and M Kaye Ltd v Hosier and Dickinson Ltd* [1972] 1 WLR 146 at 165.

Tender. A formal written offer by a contractor to do work, usually (but not always) for a lump sum.

Turnkey contract. An expression sometimes used to describe a design and build contract where the contractor not only designs and builds the building but also designs and installs any plant necessary. The idea is that all the employer has to do is to turn the key to the front door and start using the building. The term, however, is not a term of art (*Cable (1956) Ltd v Hutcherson Ltd* (1969) 43 ALJR 321, High Court of Australia).

Uneconomic working. The disruptive effect upon the contractor of architect's instructions or interference via the employer. Often one head of a loss and expense claim by the contractor.

Valuation. This usually means the valuation of building work carried out by the quantity surveyor upon which the architect makes his interim certification of payment to the contractor, eg under clause 30.1.2 of the JCT contract.

Variation. This expression usually means a variation required by the employer or the architect on the employer's behalf. It rarely includes any unilateral change of plan by the contractor.

Work person. This expression has a precise definition under Clauses 38.6.3 and 39.7.3 of the JCT contract and Clauses 35.6.3 and 36.7.3 of NSC/4.

Works. An abbreviation for building works, meaning both the work and the materials required for the building.

Appendix B

Selected JCT and NSC/4 provisions

Note on the use of this Appendix: The text of the JCT conditions selected is that of the Local Authorities with Quantities 1980 Edition with Amendments up to and including number 5. The most important of the provisions of NSC14 are also included in this appendix. The notes on each case have been kept as brief as possible; they are designed only to give the reader an indication as to whether the case in question might be relevant to any particular situation.

The Main Contract — JCT80 Local Authorities with Quantities

Copyright of the following JCT provisions belongs to the Royal Institute of British Architects and they are reproduced with the kind permission of RIBA Publications Ltd.

2 Contractor's obligations

2.1 The Contractor shall upon and subject to the Conditions carry out and complete the Works shown upon the Contract Drawings and described by or referred to in the Contract Bills and in the Articles of Agreement, the Conditions and the Appendix (which Drawings, Bills, Articles of Agreement, Conditions and Appendix are in this Contract referred to collectively as 'the Contract Documents') in compliance therewith, using materials and workmanship of the quality and standards therein specified, provided that where and to the extent that approval of the quality of materials or of the standards of workmanship is a matter for the opinion of the Architect/Supervising Officer, such quality and standards shall be to the reasonable satisfaction of the Architect/Supervising Officer.

2.2.1 Nothing contained in the Contract Bills shall override or modify the application or interpretation of that which is contained in the Articles of Agreement, the Conditions or the Appendix.[1]

2.3 If the Contractor shall find any discrepancy in or divergence between any two or more of the following documents, including a divergence between parts of any one of them or between documents of the same description, namely:

2.3.1 the Contract Drawings,

2.3.2 the Contract Bills,

2.3.3 any instruction issued by the Architect/Supervising Officer under the Conditions (save insofar as any such instruction requires a Variation in accordance with the provisions of *clause 13.2*), and

2.3.4 any drawings or documents issued by the Architect/Supervising Officer under *clause 5.3.1. 5.4* or 7,

238

2.3.5 the Numbered Documents

he shall immediately give to the Architect/Supervising Officer a written notice specifying the discrepancy or divergence, and the Architect/Supervising Officer shall issue instructions in regard thereto.

---

[1] *English Industrial Estates Corporation v Wimpey* [1973] 1 Lloyd's Rep 118: Lord Denning followed the provisions of the bills of quantities in preference to the printed conditions despite the express words of this clause. See also the comments of Judge Fay QC who was astonished by the provision in *Henry Boot v Construction Central Lancashire New Town Development Corporation* (1980) 15 BLR 8. Conversely, the clause was followed in *M J Gleeson (Contractors) Ltd v London Borough of Hillingdon* (1970) 215 EG 165.

---

4 Architect's/supervising officer's instructions

4.3.1 All instructions issued by the Architect/Supervising Officer shall be issued in writing.

4.3.2 If the Architect/Supervising Officer purports to issue an instruction otherwise than in writing it shall be of no immediate effect, but shall be confirmed in writing by the Contractor to the Architect/Supervising Officer within seven days, and if not dissented from in writing by the Architect/Supervising Officer to the Contractor within seven days from receipt of the Contractor's confirmation shall take effect as from the expiration of the latter said seven days. Provided always:

(1) that if the Architect/Supervising Officer within seven days of giving such an instruction otherwise than in writing shall himself confirm the same in writing, then the Contractor shall not be obliged to confirm as aforesaid, and the said instruction shall take effect as from the date of the Architect's/Supervising Officer's confirmation; and

(2) that if neither the Contractor nor the Architect/Supervising officer shall confirm such an instruction in the manner and at the time aforesaid but the Contractor shall nevertheless comply with the same, then the Architect/Supervising Officer may confirm the same in writing at any time prior to the issue of the Final Certificate, and the said instruction shall thereupon be deemed to have taken effect on the date on which it was issued otherwise than in writing by the Architect/Supervising Officer.

5 Contract documents — other documents — issue of certificates

5.3.1 As soon as possible after the execution of this Contract:

(1) the Architect/Supervising Officer without charge to the Contractor shall provide him (unless he shall have been previously so provided) with two copies of any descriptive schedules or other like documents necessary for use in carrying out the Works; and

(2) the Contractor without charge to the Employer shall provide the Architect/Supervising Officer (unless he shall have been previously so provided) with two copies of his master programme for the execution of the Works and within 14 days of any decision by the Architect/Supervising Officer under *clause 25.3.1* or *33.1.3* [with decision by the Architect/Supervising Officer under *clause 25.3.1* or *33.1.3*] with two copies of any amendments and revisions to take account of that decision.

5.3.2 Nothing contained in the descriptive schedules or other like documents referred to in *clause 5.3.1*(1) (nor in the master programme or the execution of the Works or any amendment to that programme or revision therein referred to in *clause 5.3.1*(2)) shall impose any obligation beyond those imposed by the Contract Documents.

5.4 As and when from time to time may be necessary the Architect/Supervising Officer without charge to the Contractor shall provide him with two copies of such further drawings or details as are reasonably necessary either to explain and amplify the Contract Drawings or to enable the Contractor to carry out and complete the Works in accordance with the Conditions.[1]

5.8 Except where otherwise specifically so provided any certificate to be issued by the Architect/Supervising Officer under the Conditions shall be issued to the Employer, and immediately upon the issue of any such certificate the Architect/Supervising Officer shall send a duplicate copy thereof to the Contractor.

---

[1] *Holland Hannen & Cubitts (Northern) Ltd v Welsh Health Technical Services Organisation* (1981) 18 BLR 80: The obligation on the architect to provide further drawings or details arises *inter alia* where site conditions prove to be different from those which were anticipated, or specified materials are unavailable, or the design proves ineffective. *London Borough of Merton v Stanley Hugh Leach Ltd* (1985) 32 BLR 51: In addition to this express provision there are further terms to be implied; see p 39.

---

6 Statutory obligations, notices, fees and charges

6.1.1 Subject to *clause 6.1.5* the Contractor shall comply with, and give all notices required by, any Act of Parliament, any instrument, rule or order made under any Act of Parliament, or any regulation or byelaw of any local authority or of any statutory undertaker which has any jurisdiction with regard to the Works or with whose systems the same are or will be connected (all requirements to be so complied with being referred to in the Conditions as 'the Statutory Requirements').

6.1.2 If the Contractor shall find any divergence between the Statutory Requirements and all or any of the documents referred to in *clause 2.3* or between the Statutory Requirements and any instruction of the Architect/Supervising Officer requiring a Variation issued in accordance with *clause 13.2* he shall immediately give to the Architect/Supervising Officer a written notice specifying the divergence.

6.1.3 If the Contractor gives notice under *clause 6.1.2* or if the Architect/Supervising Officer shall otherwise discover or receive notice of a divergence between the Statutory Requirements and all or any of the documents referred to in *clause 2.3* or between the Statutory Requirements and any instruction requiring a Variation issued in accordance with *clause* 13.2, the Architect/Supervising Officer shall within seven days of the discovery or receipt of a notice issue Instructions in relation to the divergence. If and insofar as the instructions require the Works to be varied, they shall be treated as if they were Architect's/Supervising Officer's instructions requiring a Variation issued in accordance with *clause* 13.2.

6.1.4 (1) If in any emergency compliance with *clause 6.1.1* requires the Contractor to supply materials or execute work before receiving instructions under *clause 6.1.3* the Contractor shall supply such limited materials and execute such limited work as are reasonably necessary to secure immediate compliance with the Statutory Requirements.

(2) The Contractor shall forthwith inform the Architect/Supervising Officer of the emergency and of the steps that he is taking under *clause 6.1.4*(1).

(3) Work executed and materials supplied by the Contractor under *clause 6.1.4*(1) shall be treated as if they had been executed and supplied pursuant to an Architect's/Supervising Officer's instruction requiring a Variation issued in accordance with *clause* 13.2 provided that the emergency arose because of a divergence between the Statutory Requirements and all or any of the documents referred to in *clause* 2.3 or between the Statutory Requirements and any instruction requiring a Variation issued in accordance with *clause* 13.2, and the Contractor has complied with *clause 6.1.4*(2).

6.1.5 Provided that the Contractor complies with *clause 6.1.2*, the Contractor shall not be liable to the Employer under this Contract if the Works do not comply with the Statutory requirements where and to the extent that such non-compliance of the Works results from the Contractor having carried out work in accordance with the documents referred to in *clause* 2.3, or with any instruction requiring a Variation issued by the Architect/Supervising Officer in accordance with *clause* 13.2.

8 Materials, goods and workmanship to conform to description, testing and inspection

8.1.1 All materials and goods shall, so far as procurable, be of the kind and standard described in the Contract Bills, provided that materials and goods shall be to the reasonable satisfaction of the Architect where and to the extent that this is required in accordance with *clause* 2.1.

8.1.2 All workmanship shall be of the standard described in the Contract Bills, or, to the extent that no such standards are described in the Contract Bills, shall be of a standard appropriate to the Works, provided that workmanship shall be to the reasonable satisfaction of the Architect where and to the extent that this is required in accordance with *clause* 2.1.

8.3 The Architect/Supervising Officer may issue instructions requiring the Contractor to open up for inspection any work covered up, or to arrange for or carry out any test of any materials or goods (whether or not already incorporated in the Works), or of any executed work, and the cost of such opening up or testing (together with the cost of making good in consequence thereof) shall be added to the Contract Sum unless provided for in the Contract Bills, or unless the inspection or test shows that the materials, goods or work are not in accordance with this Contract.[1]

8.4 If any work, materials or goods are not in accordance with this Contract the Architect, without prejudice to the generality of his powers[2] may;

8.4.1 issue instructions in regard to the removal from the site of all or any of such work, materials or goods; and/or

8.4.2 after consultation with the Contractor (who shall immediately consult with any relevant Nominated Sub-Contractor) and with the agreement of the Employer, allow all or any of such work, materials or goods to remain and confirm this in writing to the Contractor (which shall not be construed as a Variation) and where so allowed and confirmed an appropriate deduction shall be made in the adjustment of the Contract Sum; and/or

8.4.3 after consultation with the Contractor (who shall immediately consult with any relevant Nominated Sub-Contractor) issue such instructions requiring a Variation as are reasonably necessary as a consequence of such an instruction under *clause 8.4.1* or such confirmation under *clause 8.4.2* and to the extent that such instructions are so necessary and notwithstanding *clauses* 13.4, 25 and 26 no addition to the Contract Sum shall be made and no extension of time shall be given; and/or

8.4.4 having had due regard to the Code of Practice appended to these Conditions, issue such instructions under *clause* 8.3 to open up for inspection or to test as are reasonable in all the circumstances to establish to the reasonable satisfaction of the Architect the likelihood or extent, as appropriate to the circumstances, of any further similar non-compliance. To the extent that such instructions are so reasonable, whatever the results of the opening up for inspection or test, and notwithstanding *clauses* 8.3 and 26 no addition to the Contract Sum shall be made. *Clause* 25.4.5(2) shall apply unless as stated therein the inspection or test showed that the work, materials or goods were not in accordance with this Contract.

---

[1] *City of Westminster v Jarvis* [1970] 1 WLR 637, HL: Viscount Dilhorne suggested that the predecessor of these clauses in JCT63 in clause 6 applied before practical completion (of the defects liability provision) to both contractors and nominated sub-contractors.
[2] *Holland Hannen & Cubitts (Northern) Ltd v Welsh Health Technical Services Organisation* (1981) 18 BLR 120: A notice under this clause which does not require removal of anything is invalid. A similar point was made in *Fairclough Building v Rhuddlan* BC (1985) 30 BLR 26.

---

13 Variations and provisional sums

13.1 The term 'Variation' as used in the Conditions means;

13.1.1 the alteration or modification of the design, quality or quantity of the Works as shown upon the Contract Drawings and described by or referred to in the Contract Bills; including
    (1) the addition, omission or substitution of any work,
    (2) the alteration of the kind or standard of any of the materials or goods to be used in the Works,
    (3) the removal from the site of any work executed or materials or goods brought thereon by the Contractor for the purposes of the Works other than work materials or goods which are not in accordance with this Contract:

13.1.2 the imposition by the Employer of any obligations or restrictions in regard to the matters set out in *clauses 13.1.2*(1) to *13.1.2*(4) or the addition to or alteration or omission of any such obligations or restrictions so imposed by the Employer in the Contract Bills in regard to:
    (1) access to the site or use of any specific parts of the site,
    (2) limitations of working space,
    (3) limitations of working hours,
    (4) the execution or completion of the work in any specific order;
but excludes

13.1.3 nomination of a Sub-Contractor to supply and fix materials or goods or to execute work of which the measured quantities have been set out and priced by the Contractor in the Contract Bills for supply and fixing or execution by the Contractor.

13.2 The Architect/Supervising Officer may subject to the Contractor's rights of reasonable objection set out in *clause 4.1.1*, issue instructions requiring a

Variation and he may sanction in writing any variation made by the Contractor otherwise than pursuant to an instruction of the Architect/Supervising Officer. No Variation required by the Architect/Supervising Officer or subsequently sanctioned by him shall vitiate this Contract.

13.3 The Architect/Supervising Officer shall issue instructions in regard to:

13.3.1 the expenditure of provisional sums included in the Contract Bills; and

13.3.2 the expenditure of provisional sums included in a Sub-Contract.

13.4.1 (1) Subject to *clause 13.4.1*(2) all variations required by the Architect/ Supervising Officer or subsequently sanctioned by him in writing and all work executed by the Contractor in accordance with instructions by the Architect/Supervising Officer as to the expenditure of provisional sums which are included in the Contract Bills shall be valued by the Quantity Surveyor and such Valuation (in the Conditions called 'the Valuation') shall, unless otherwise agreed by the Employer and the Contractor, be made in accordance with the provisions of *clause* 13.5.

(2) The valuation of Variations to the Sub-Contract Works executed by a Nominated Sub-Contractor in accordance with instructions of the Architect/Supervising Officer and of all instructions issued under *clause 13.3.2* shall (unless otherwise agreed by the Contractor and the Nominated Sub-Contractor concerned with the approval of the Architect/Supervising Officer) be made in accordance with the relevant provisions of Sub-Contract NSC/4 or NSC/4a as applicable.

13.4.2 Where under the instruction of the Architect/Supervising Officer as to the expenditure of a provisional sum a prime cost sum arises and the Contractor under *clause* 35.2 tenders for the work covered by that prime cost sum and that tender is accepted by or on behalf of the Employer, that work shall be valued in accordance with the accepted tender of the Contractor and shall not be included in the Valuation of the instruction of the Architect/Supervising Officer in regard to the expenditure of the provisional sum.

13.5.1 To the extent that the Valuation relates to the execution of additional or substituted work which can properly be valued by measurement such work shall be measured and shall be valued in accordance with the following rules:

(1) where the work is of similar character to, is executed under similar conditions as, and does not significantly change the quantity of, work set out in the Contract Bills the rates and prices for the work so set out shall determine the Valuation;

(2) where the work is of similar character to work set out in the Contract Bills but is not executed under similar conditions thereto and/or significantly changes the quantity thereof, the rates and prices for the work so set out shall be the basis for determining the Valuation and the Valuation shall include a fair allowance for such difference in conditions and/or quantity;

(3) where the work is not of similar character to work set out in the Contract Bills the work shall be valued at fair rates and prices.

13.5.2 To the extent that the Valuation relates to the omission of work set out in the Contract Bills the rates and prices for such work therein set out shall determine the valuation of the work omitted.

13.5.3 In any valuation of work under *clauses 13.5.1* and *13.5.2*:

(1) measurement shall be in accordance with the same principles as those governing the preparation of the Contract Bills referred to in *clause* 2.2.2(1);

(2) allowance shall be made for any percentage or lump sum adjustments in the Contract Bills, and

(3) allowance, where appropriate, shall be made for any addition to or reduction of preliminary items of the type referred to in the Standard Method of Measurement, 6th edn, Section B (Preliminaries).

13.5.4 To the extent that the Valuation relates to the execution of additional or substituted work which cannot properly be valued by measurement the Valuation shall comprise:

(1) the prime cost of such work (calculated in accordance with the 'Definition of Prime Cost of Daywork carried out under a Building Contract' issued by the Royal Institution of Chartered Surveyors and the National Federation of Building Trades Employers which was current at the Date of Tender) together with percentage additions to each section of the prime cost at the rates set out by the Contractor in the Contract Bills; or

(2) where the work is within the province of any specialist trade and the said Institution and the appropriate body representing the employers in that trade have agreed and issued a definition of prime cost of daywork, the prime cost of such work calculated in accordance with that definition which was current at the Date of Tender together with percentage additions on the prime cost at the rates set out by the Contractor in the Contract Bills. Provided that in any case vouchers specifying the time daily spent upon the work, the workmen's names, the plant and the materials employed shall be delivered for verification to the Architect/ Supervising Officer or his authorised representative not later than the end of the week following that in which the work has been executed.

13.5.5 If compliance with the instruction requiring a Variation or the instruction as to the expenditure of a provisional sum substantially changes the conditions under which any other work is executed, then such other work shall be treated as if it had been the subject of an instruction of the Architect/Supervising Officer requiring a Variation under *clause* 13.2 which shall be valued in accordance with the provisions of *clause* 13.

13.5.6 To the extent that the Valuation does not relate to the execution of additional or substituted work or the omission of work or to the extent that the valuation of any work or liabilities directly associated with a Variation cannot reasonably be effected in the Valuation by the application of *clauses 13.5.1* to *13.5.5* a fair valuation thereof shall be made.

Provided that no allowance shall be made under *clause* 13.5 for any effect upon the regular progress of the Works or for any other direct loss and/or expense for which the Contractor would be reimbursed by payment under any other provision in the Conditions.

13.6 Where it is necessary to measure work for the purpose of the Valuation the Quantity Surveyor shall give to the Contractor an opportunity of being present at the time of such measurement and of taking such notes and measurements as the Contractor may require.

13.7 Effect shall be given to a Valuation under *clause* 13.5 by addition to or deduction from the Contract Sum.

16 Materials and goods unfixed or off-site

16.1 Unfixed materials and goods delivered to, placed on or adjacent to the Works and intended therefore, shall not be removed except for use upon the Works unless the Architect/Supervising Officer has consented in writing to such removal (which consent shall not be unreasonably withheld). Where the value of any such materials or goods has in accordance with *clause* 30.2 been included in any Interim Certificate under which the amount properly due to the Contractor has been paid by the Employer, such materials and goods shall become the property of the Employer, but, subject to *clause* 22B or 22C (if applicable), the Contractor shall remain responsible for loss or damage to the same.[1]

---

[1] *Dawber Williamson Roofing v Humberside County Council* (1979) 14 BLR 70: the provision in the contract that materials on site become the property of the employer when paid for is subject to the *nemo dat quod non habet* rule (see Glossary) even if the goods are supplied by a sub-contractor who is deemed to have notice of the main contract terms. But note that this case was argued on the wording of clause 1(1) of the Green Form; the wording of *clause* 2.2 of NSC/4 is more aggressive.

---

17 Practical completion and defects liability

17.1 When in the opinion of the Architect/Supervising Officer Practical Completion of the Works is achieved, he shall forthwith issue a certificate to that effect and Practical Completion of the Works shall be deemed for all the purposes of this Contract to have taken place on the day named in such certificate.[1]

17.2 Any defect, shrinkages or other faults which shall appear within the Defects Liability Period and which are due to materials or workmanship not in accordance with this Contract or to frost occurring before Practical Completion of the Works, shall be specified by the Architect/Supervising Officer in a schedule of defects which he shall deliver to the Contractor as an instruction of the Architect/Supervising Officer not later than 14 days after the expiration of the said Defects Liability Period, and within a reasonable time after receipt of such schedule the defects, shrinkages. and other faults therein specified shall be made good by the Contractor at no cost to the Employer unless the Architect with the consent of the Employer shall otherwise instruct; and if the Architect does so otherwise instruct then an appropriate deduction in respect of any such defects, shrinkages or other faults not made good shall be made from the Contract Sum.[2]

17.3 Notwithstanding *clause* 17.2 the Architect/Supervising Officer may whenever he considers it necessary to do so, issue instructions requiring any defect, shrinkage or other fault which shall appear within the Defects Liability Period and which is due to materials or workmanship not in accordance with this Contract or to frost occurring before Practical Completion of the Works, to be made good, and the Contractor shall within a reasonable time after receipt of such instructions comply with the same at no cost to the Employer unless the Architect with the consent of the Employer shall otherwise instruct; and if the Architect does so otherwise instruct then an appropriate deduction in respect of any such defects, shrinkages or other faults not made good shall be made from the Contract Sum. Provided that no such instructions shall be issued after delivery of a schedule of defects or after 14 days from the expiration of the Defects Liability Period.

17.4 When in the opinion of the Architect/Supervising Officer any defects, shrinkages or other faults which he may have required to be made good under *clauses* 17.2 and 17.3 shall have been made good he shall issue a certificate to that effect, and completion of making good defects shall be deemed for all the purposes of this Contract to have taken place on the day named in such certificate (the 'Certificate of Completion Making Good Defects').

17.5 In no case shall the Contractor be required to make good at his own cost any damage by frost which may appear after Practical Completion unless the Architect/Supervising Officer shall certify that such damage is due to injury which took place before Practical Completion.

---

[1] *City of Westminster v Jarvis* [1970] 1 WLR 637: Viscount Dilhorne said that Practical Completion means completion of all the construction work that has to be done, although there may be latent defects. *H W Nevill (Sunblest) Ltd v William Press & Son Ltd* (1982) 20 BLR 78: HH Judge Newey OR found that the architect has discretion to certify practical completion notwithstanding that there may be very minor *de minimis* work that has not been carried out.

[2] *H W Nevill (Sunblest) Ltd v William Press & Son Ltd* (1982) 20 BLR 78: These provisions for the rectification of defects by the contractor do not deprive the employer of his ordinary rights to claim damages for breach of contract.

---

18 Partial possession by employer

18.1 If at any time or times before the date of issue by the Architect of the certificate of Practical Completion the Employer wishes to take possession of any part or parts of the Works and the consent of the Contractor (which consent shall not be unreasonably withheld) has been obtained, then notwithstanding anything expressed or implied elsewhere in this Contract, the Employer may take possession thereof. The Architect shall thereupon issue to the Contractor on behalf of the Employer a written statement identifying the part or parts of the Works taken into possession and giving the date when the Employer took possession (in *clauses* 18, 20.3, *22.3.1* and 22C. 1 referred to as 'the relevant part' and 'the relevant date' respectively).

18.1.1 For the purposes of *clauses* 17.2, 17.3, 17.5 and *30.4.1*(2) Practical Completion of the relevant part shall be deemed to have occurred and the Defects Liability Period in respect of the relevant part shall be deemed to have commenced on the relevant date.

18.1.2 When in the opinion of the Architect any defects, shrinkages or other faults in the relevant part which he may have required to be made good under *clause* 17.2 or *clause* 17.3 shall have been made good he shall issue a certificate to that effect.

18.1.3 As from the relevant date the obligation of the Contractor under *clause* 22A or of the Employer under *clause* 22B.1 or *clause* 22C.2 whichever is applicable to insure shall terminate in respect of the relevant part but not further or otherwise; and where *clause* 22C applies the obligation of the Employer to insure under *clause* 22C. 1 shall from the relevant date include the relevant part.

18.1.4 In lieu of any sum to be paid or allowed by the Contractor under *clause* 24 in respect of any period during which the Works may remain incomplete occurring after the relevant date there shall be paid or allowed such sum as bears the same ratio to the sum which would be paid or allowed apart from the provisions of *clause* 18 as the Contract Sum less the amount contained therein in respect of the relevant part bears to the Contract Sum.

19 Assignment and sub-contracts

19.1.1 Neither the Employer nor the Contractor shall, without the written consent of the other, assign this Contract.[1]

19.1.2 Where *clause 19.1.2* is stated in the Appendix to apply then, in the event of transfer by the Employer of his freehold or leasehold interest in, or of a grant by the Employer of a leasehold interest in, the whole of the premises comprising the Works, the Employer may at any time after Practical Completion of the Works assign to any such transferee or lessee the right to bring proceedings in the name of the Employer (whether by arbitration or litigation) to enforce any of the terms of this contract made for the benefit of the Employer hereunder. The assignee shall be estopped from disputing any enforceable agreements reached between the Employer and the Contractor which arise out of and relate to this Contract (whether or not they are or appear to be a derogation from the right assigned) and are made prior to the date of any assignment.

[1] See *Helstan Securities Ltd v Hertfordshire County Council* [1978] 3 All ER 262.

20 Injury to persons and property and employer's indemnity

20.2 The Contractor shall, subject to clause 20.3 and, where applicable, *clause 22C.1*, be liable for, and shall indemnify the Employer against, any expense, liability, loss, claim or proceedings in respect of any injury or damage whatsoever to any property real or personal in so far as such injury or damage arises out of or in the course of, or by reason of the carrying out of the Works, and to the extent that the same is due to any negligence, breach of statutory duty, omission or default of the Contractor, his servants or agents or of any person employed or engaged upon or in connection with the Works or any part thereof, his servants or agents or of any other person who may properly be on the site upon or in connection with the Works or any part thereof, his servants or agents, other than the Employer or any person employed, engaged or authorised by him or by any local authority or statutory undertaker executing work solely in pursuance of its statutory rights or obligations.[1]

[1] *Scottish Special Housing Association v Wimpey Construction (UK Ltd)* (1986) 34 BLR 1, HL: The effect of the opening words of this clause are that if the employer is undertaking the insurance of *clause 22* perils (ie fire, explosion, flood etc) then the contractor is not liable for those perils even if caused by his own negligence. This House of Lords decision was in Scottish law, but follows the earlier English decisions in *James Archdale and Co Ltd v Comservices Ltd* [1954] 1 WLR 459 and *Coleman Street Properties Ltd v Denco Miller Ltd* (1982) 31 BLR 32. *City of Manchester v Fram Gerard* (1974) 6 BLR 74: The predecessor of this indemnity clause in JCT63 was to be strictly construed, and 'the Contractor, his servants or agents, or of any sub-contractor' did not include sub-sub-contractors.

23 Date of possession, completion and postponement

23.1.1 On the date of Possession, possession of the site shall be given to the Contractor who shall thereupon begin the Works, regularly and diligently proceed with the same and shall complete the same on or before the Completion Date.

23.1.2 Where *clause 23.1.2* is stated in the Appendix to apply the Employer may defer the giving of possession for a period not exceeding six weeks or such lesser period stated in the Appendix calculated from the Date of Possession.

23.2 The Architect/Supervising Officer may issue instructions in regard to the postponement of any work to be executed under the provisions of this contract.[1]

23.3.1 For the purposes of the Works insurances the Contractor shall retain possession of the site and the Works up to and including the date of issue of the certificate of Practical Completion, and subject to *clause 18*, the Employer shall not be entitled to take possession of any part or parts of the Works until that date.

23.3.2 Notwithstanding the provisions of *clause 23.3.1* the Employer may, with the consent in writing of the Contractor, use or occupy the site or the Works or part thereof whether for the purposes of storage of his goods or otherwise before the date of issue of the certificate of Practical Completion by the Architect. Before the Contractor shall give his consent to such use or occupation the Contractor or the Employer shall notify the insurers under *clause 22A* or *clause 22B* or *clause 22C.2* to 22C.4 whichever may be applicable and obtain confirmation that such use or occupation will not prejudice the insurance. Subject to such confirmation the consent of the Contractor shall not be unreasonably withheld.

23.3.3 Where *clause 22A.2* or *clause 22A.3* applies and the insurers in giving the confirmation referred to in *clause 23.3.2* have made it a condition of such confirmation that an additional premium is required the Contractor shall notify the Employer of the amount of the additional premium. If the Employer continues to require use or occupation under *clause 23.3.2* the additional premium required shall be added to the Contract Sum and the Contractor shall provide the Employer, if so requested, with the additional premium receipt therefor.

---

[1] *M Harrison & Co (Leeds) Ltd v Leeds City Council* (1980) 14 BLR 118: Postponement instructions include instructions which do not expressly give instructions to postpone, but which necessarily involve postponement because of the terms of a sub-contractor quotation that the contractor is instructed to accept.

---

24 Damages for non-completion[1]

24.1 If the Contractor fails to complete the Works by the Completion Date then the Architect/Supervising Officer shall issue a certificate to that effect.

24.2.1 Subject to the issue of a certificate under *clause* 24.1 the Contractor shall, as the Employer may require in writing not later than the date of the Final Certificate, pay or allow to the Employer the whole or such part as may be specified in writing by the Employer of a sum calculated at the rate stated in the Appendix as liquidated and ascertained damages for the period between the Completion Date and the date of Practical Completion and the Employer may deduct the same from any monies due or to become due to the Contractor under this Contract (including any balance stated as due to the Contractor in the Final Certificate) or the Employer may recover the same from the Contractor as a debt.[2]

24.2.2 If, under *clause 25.3.3*, the Architect/Supervising Officer fixes a later Completion Date the Employer shall pay or repay to the Contractor any amounts recovered allowed or paid under *clause 24.2.1* for the period up to such later Completion Date.

---

[1] See the discussion of *Peak Construction (Liverpool) Ltd v McKinney Foundations Ltd* (1970) 1 BLR 111; the omission of JCT63 to deal with delay in giving possession or access has now been resolved, at any rate in part, by *clause 25.4.12*. *Department of Environment for Northern Ireland v Farrans (Construction) Ltd* (1981) 19 BLR 1: It was held by the High Court in Northern Ireland that an Employer is entitled to deduct liquidated damages after the issue of a non-completion certificate, but he does so at the risk that a subsequent certificate might be issued which would supersede the original certificate and render him liable to the contractor for breach of contract in respect of the original deduction. *Peak*

Construction (Liverpool) v McKinney Foundations (1970) 1 BLR 114: In the Court of Appeal Lord Justice Salmon said that 'The liquidated damages and extension of time clauses in printed forms of contract must be construed strictly *contra proferentem*'. But see the contrary view expressed in *Keating* page 346.
[2] *Temloc Ltd v Erril Properties Ltd* (1987) CILL 376: This clause provided for liquidated damages to be payable at the rate set out in the appendix. If the rate in the appendix is inserted as 'nil' then the employer may neither recover any liquidated damages nor damages at large. *BFI Group of Companies Ltd v DCP Integration Systems Ltd* (1987) CILL 348: It was decided on the wording of the Minor Works agreement that damages at the rate set out in the appendix are payable notwithstanding that in the event the employer has suffered no loss whatsoever as a result of the delay.

25 Extension of time

25.1 In *Clause* 25 any reference to delay notice or extension of time includes further delay, further notice or further extension of time.

25.2.1 (1) If and whenever it becomes reasonably apparent that the progress of the Works is being or is likely to be delayed the Contractor shall forthwith give written notice to the Architect/Supervising Officer of the material circumstances including the cause or causes of the delay and identify in such notice any event which in his opinion is a Relevant Event.[1]

(2) Where the material circumstances of which written notice has been given under *clause 25.2.1*(1) include reference to a Nominated Sub-Contractor, the Contractor shall forthwith send a copy of such written notice to the Nominated Sub-Contractor concerned.

25.2.2 In respect of each and every Relevant Event identified in the notice given in accordance with *clause 25.2.1*(1) the Contractor shall, if practicable in such notice, or otherwise in writing as soon as possible after such notice:

(1) give particulars of the expected effects thereof; and

(2) estimate the extent, if any, of the expected delay in the completion of the Works beyond the Completion Date resulting therefrom whether or not concurrently with delay resulting from any other Relevant Event and shall give such particulars and estimates to any Nominated Sub-Contractor to whom a copy of any written notice has been given under *clause 25.2.1*(2).

(3) The Contractor shall give such further written notice to the Architect/Supervising Officer who may reasonably require for keeping up-to-date the particulars and estimate referred to in *clauses 25.2.1*(1) and *25.2.2*(2) including any material change in such particulars or estimate.

25.3.1 If in the opinion of the Architect/Supervising Officer, upon receipt of any notice, particulars and estimate under *clauses 25.2.1*(1) and *25.2.2*,

(1) any of the events which are stated by the Contractor to be the cause of the delay is a Relevant Event and

(2) the completion of the Works is likely to be delayed thereby beyond the Completion Date the Architect/Supervising Officer shall in writing to the Contractor give an extension of time by fixing such later date as the Completion Date as he then estimates to be fair and reasonable. The Architect/Supervising Officer shall, in fixing such new Completion Date, state:

(3) which of the Relevant Events he has taken into account and

(4) the extent, if any, to which he has had regard to any instruction under clause 13.2 requiring as a Variation the omission of any work issued since the fixing of the previous Completion Date,

and shall, if reasonably practical having regard to the sufficiency of the aforesaid notice, particulars and estimates, fix such new Completion Date not later than 12 weeks from receipt of the notice and of reasonably sufficient particulars and estimate, or, where the period between receipt thereof and the Completion Date is less than 12 weeks, not later than the Completion Date.

If, in the opinion of the Architect, upon receipt of any such notice, particulars and estimate it is not fair and reasonable to fix a later date as a new Completion Date, the Architect shall if reasonably practicable (having regard to the sufficiency of the aforesaid notice, particulars and estimate) so notify the Contractor in writing not later than 12 weeks from receipt of the notice particulars and estimate, or, where the period between receipt thereof and the Completion Date is less than 12 weeks, not later than the Completion Date.

25.3.2 After the first exercise by the Architect/Supervising Officer of his duty under *clause 25.3.1* the Architect/Supervising Officer may fix a Completion Date earlier than that previously fixed under *clause* 25 if in his opinion the fixing of such earlier Completion Date is fair and reasonable having regard to the omission of any work or obligation instructed or sanctioned by the Architect under *clause* 13 after the last occasion on which the Architect/Supervising Officer made an extension of time.

25.3.3 After the Completion Date, if this occurs before the date of Practical Completion, the Architect may, and not later than the expiry of 12 weeks after the date of Practical Completion, shall in writing to the Contractor either[2]:

(1) fix a Completion Date later than that previously fixed if in his opinion the fixing of such later Completion Date is fair and reasonable having regard to any of the Relevant Events, whether upon reviewing a previous decision or otherwise and whether or not the Relevant Event has been specifically notified by the Contractor under *clause 25.2.1*(1); or

(2) fix a Completion Date earlier than that previously fixed under *clause* 25 if in his opinion the fixing of such earlier Completion Date is fair and reasonable having regard to the omission of any work or obligation instructed or sanctioned by the Architect under *clause* 13 after the last occasion on which the Architect/Supervising Officer made an extension of time; or

(3) confirm to the Contractor the Completion Date previously fixed.

25.3.4 Provided always

(1) the Contractor shall use constantly his best endeavours to prevent delay in the progress of the Works, howsoever caused, and to prevent the completion of the Works being delayed or further delayed beyond the Completion Date;

(2) the Contractor shall do all that may be required to the satisfaction of the Architect/Supervising Officer to proceed with the Works.

25.3.5 The Architect/Supervising Officer shall notify in writing to every Nominated Sub-Contractor each decision of the Architect/Supervising Officer under *clause 25.3* fixing a Completion Date.

25.3.6 No decision of the Architect/Supervising Officer under *clause* 25.3 shall fix a Completion Date earlier than the Date for Completion stated in the Appendix.

25.4 The following are the Relevant Events referred to in *clause* 25;

25.4.1 force majeure;

25.4.2 exceptionally adverse weather conditions;

25.4.3 loss or damage occasioned by any one or more of the Specified Perils;

25.4.4 civil commotion, local combination of workmen, strike or lock-out affecting any of the trades employed upon the Works or any of the trades engaged in the preparation, manufacture or transportation of any of the goods or materials required for the Works[3];

25.4.5 compliance with the Architect/Supervising Officer's instructions

(1) under *clauses* 2.3, 13.2, 13.3, 23.2, 34, 35 or 36, or

(2) in regard to the opening up for inspection of any work covered up or the testing of any of the work, materials or goods in accordance with *clause* 8.3 (including making good in consequence of such opening up or testing) unless the inspection or test showed that the work, materials or goods were not in accordance with this Contract;

25.4.6 the Contractor not having received in due time necessary instructions, drawings, details or levels from the Architect/Supervising Officer for which he specifically applied in writing provided that such application was made on a date which having regard to the Completion Date was neither unreasonably distant from nor unreasonably close to the date on which it was necessary for him to receive the same[4];

25.4.7 delay on the part of Nominated Sub-Contractors or Nominated Suppliers which the Contractor has taken all practicable steps to avoid or reduce[5];

25.4.8 (1) the execution of work not forming part of this Contract by the Employer himself or by persons employed or otherwise engaged by the Employer as referred to in *clause* 29 or the failure to execute such work[6];

(2) the supply by the Employer of materials and goods which the Employer has agreed to provide for the Works or the failure so to supply;

25.4.9 the exercise after the Date of Tender by the United Kingdom Government of any statutory power which directly affects the execution of the Works by restricting the availability or use of labour which is essential to the proper carrying out of the Works or preventing the Contractor from or delaying the Contractor in, securing such goods or materials or such fuel or energy as are essential to the proper carrying out of the Works;

25.4.10 (1) the Contractor's inability for reasons beyond his control and which he could not reasonably have foreseen at the Date of Tender to secure such labour as is essential to the proper carrying out of the Works; or

(2) the Contractor's inability for reasons beyond his control and which he could not reasonably have foreseen at the Date of Tender to secure such goods or materials as are essential to the proper carrying out of the Works;

25.4.11 the carrying out by a local authority or statutory undertaker of work in pursuance of its statutory obligations in relation to the Works, or the failure to carry out such work:

25.4.12 failure of the Employer to give in due time ingress to or egress from the site of the Works or any part thereof through or over any land, buildings, way or passage adjoining or connected with the site and in the possession and control of the Employer, in accordance with the Contract Bills and/or the Contract Drawings, after receipt by the Architect/Supervising Officer of such notice, if any, as the Contractor is required to give, or failure of the Employer to give such ingress or egress as otherwise agreed between the Architect/Supervising Officer and the Contractor.

25.4.13 Where *clause 23.1.2* is stated in the Appendix to apply, the deferment by the Employer of giving possession of the site under *clause 23.1.2*.

[1] *London Borough of Merton v Stanley Hugh Leach Ltd* (1985) 32 BLR 51: Although this case was decided on JCT63, it seems clear that the contractor is in breach of contract if he fails to give written notice of delay as required by this provision, but the giving of the notice is not a condition precedent to the contractor's right to an extension. Under JCT63 failure to give notice may be taken into account by the architect in his extension; *Merton v Leach*. Under JCT80 there is specific provision in *clause 25.3.1* for review of the extensions granted by the architect after practical completion whether or not the contractor gave notice.

[2] *Temloc Ltd v Errol Properties Ltd* (1987) CILL 376: This clause provides that the architect should review his extensions of time not later than 12 weeks after practical completion. The employer's right to liquidated damages is not however conditional upon the architect complying with this stipulation.

[3] *Boskalis Westminster Construction Ltd v Liverpool City Council* (1983) 24 BLR 83: Delay caused by the industrial action of those undertaking work outside the contract does not fall under this sub-clause, but *clause 25.4.8(1)*.

[4] *Percy Bilton Ltd v Greater London Council* (1982) 20 BLR 1: Delay in receiving instructions includes delay in re-nomination, but does not include delay arising out of the need to re-nominate (usually, as in this case, because of the financial failure of a nominated sub-contractor). The words 'in due time' mean in 'a reasonable time' and not 'in time to avoid delay'. *London Borough of Merton v Stanley Hugh Leach Ltd* (1985) 32 BLR 51: The requirement for written application for instructions may be satisfied by a document in programme form delivered at the commencement of the work setting out the dates by when the contractor requires the information.

[5] *Percy Bilton Ltd v Greater London Council* (1982) 20 BLR 1: 'Delay' on the part of nominated sub-contractors does not include complete withdrawal. *City of Westminster v Jarvis* [1970] 1 WLR 637, HL: Delay on the part of nominated sub-contractors means delay in the completion of their work and does not include delay caused after such completion by the discovery of latent defects in their work.

[6] *Henry Boot Construction Ltd v Central Lancashire New Town Development Corporation* (1980) 15 BLR 8: Statutory undertakers working under contractual arrangement with the employer fall within this sub-clause, and not *clause 25.4.11*.

26 Loss and expense caused by matters materially affecting regular progress of the Works

26.1 If the Contractor makes written application to the Architect/Supervising Officer stating that he has incurred or is likely to incur direct loss and/or expense in the execution of this Contract for which he would not be reimbursed by a payment under any other provision in this Contract due to the deferment of giving possession of the site under *clause 23.1.2* where *clause 23.1.2* is stated in the Appendix to be applicable or because the regular progress of the Works or of any part thereof has been or is likely to be materially affected by any one or more of the matters referred to in *clause* 26.2; and if and as soon as the Architect/Supervising Officer is of the opinion that the direct loss and/or expense has been incurred or is likely to be incurred due to any such deferment of giving possession or that the regular progress of the Works or of any part thereof has been or is likely to be so materially affected as set out in the application of the Contractor then the Architect/Supervising Officer from time to time thereafter shall ascertain, or shall instruct the Quantity Surveyor to ascertain, the amount of such loss and/or expense which has been or is being incurred by the Contractor; provided always that[1]:

26.1.1 the Contractor's application shall be made as soon as it has become, or should reasonably have become, apparent to him that the regular process of the Works or of any part thereof has been or was likely to be affected as aforesaid, and

26.1.2 the Contractor shall in support of his application submit to the Architect/Supervising Officer upon request such information as should reasonably enable the Architect/Supervising Officer to form an opinion as aforesaid, and

26.1.3 the Contractor shall submit to the Architect/Supervising Officer or to the Quantity Surveyor upon request such details of such loss and/or expense as are reasonably necessary for such ascertainment as aforesaid.

26.2 The following are the matters referred to in clause 26.1[2]:

26.2.1 The Contractor not having received in due time necessary instructions drawings, details or levels from the Architect/Supervising Officer for which he specifically applied in writing provided that such application was made on a date which having regard to the Completion Date was neither unreasonably distant from nor unreasonably close to the date on which it was necessary for him to receive the same[3];

26.2.2 the opening up for inspection of any work covered up or the testing of any of the work, materials or goods in accordance with *clause* 8.3 (including making good in consequence of such opening up or testing) unless the inspection or test showed that the work, materials or goods were not in accordance with this Contract;

26.2.3 any discrepancy in or divergence between the Contract Drawings and/or the Contract Bills and/or the Numbered Documents;

26.2.4 the execution of work not forming part of this Contract by the Employer himself or by persons employed or otherwise engaged by the Employer as referred to in *clause* 29 or the failure to execute such work.[4]

26.2.5 Architect's/Supervising Officer's instructions under *clause* 23.2 issued in regard to the postponement of any work to be executed under the provisions of this Contract;

26.2.6 failure of the Employer to give in due time ingress to or egress from the site or the Works, or any part thereof through or over any land, buildings, way or passage adjoining or connected with the site and in the possession and control of the Employer, in accordance with the Contract Bills and/or the Contract Drawings, after receipt by the Architect/Supervising Officer of such notice, if any, as the Contractor is required to give, or failure of the Employer to give such ingress or egress or otherwise agreed between the Architect/Supervising Officer and the Contractor;

26.2.7 Architect's/Supervising Officer's instructions issued under *clause* 13.2 requiring a Variation or under *clause* 13.3 in regard to the expenditure of provisional sums (other than work to which clause 13.4.2 refers).

26.3 If and to the extent that it is necessary for ascertainment under *clause* 26.1 of loss and/or expense the Architect/Supervising Officer shall state in writing to the Contractor what extension of time, if any, has been made under *clause* 25 in respect of the Relevant Event or Events referred to in *clause* 25.4.5(1) (so far as that clause refers to *clauses* 2.3, 13.2, 13.3 and 23.2) and in *clauses 25.4.5(2), 25.4.6, 25.4.8* and *25.4.12.*

26.4.1 The Contractor upon receipt of a written application properly made by a Nominated Sub-Contractor under *clause* 13.1 of Sub-Contract NSC/4 or NSC/4a as applicable shall pass to the Architect/Supervising Officer a copy of that written application. If and as soon as the Architect/Supervising Officer is of the opinion that the loss and/or expense to which the said *clause* 13.1 refers has been incurred or is likely to be incurred due to any deferment of the giving of possession where *clause 23.1.2* is stated in the Appendix to apply, or that the regular progress of the Sub-Contract Works or any part thereof has been or is likely to be materially affected as referred to in *clause* 13.1 of Sub-Contract NSC/4 or NSC/4a and as set out in the application of the Nominated Sub-

Contractor then the Architect/Supervising Officer shall himself ascertain, or shall instruct the Quantity Surveyor to ascertain, the amount of such loss and/or expense.

26.4.2 If and to the extent that it is necessary for the ascertainment of such loss and/or expense the Architect/Supervising Officer shall state in writing to the Contractor with a copy to the Nominated Sub-Contractor concerned what was the length of the revision of the period or periods for completion of the Sub-Contract Works or of any part thereof to which he gave consent in respect of the Relevant Event or Events set out in *clause 11.2.3(5)(a)* (so far as that clause refers to *clauses* 2.3, 13.2, 13.3 and 23.2 of the Main Contract Conditions), *11.2.3(5)(b)*, *11.2.3(6)*, *11.2.3(8)* and *11.2.3(12)* of Sub-Contract NSC/4 or NSC/4a as applicable.

26.5 Any amount from time to time ascertained under *clause* 26 shall be added to the Contract Sum.

26.6 The provisions of *clause* 26 are without prejudice to any other rights and remedies which the Contractor may possess.[5]

---

[1] *London Borough of Merton v Stanley Hugh Leach Ltd* (1985) 32 BLR 51: The making of a timeous written application by the contractor is a condition precedent to the contractor's entitlement to loss and/or expense, and the lack of a notice is not a matter which may be cured by review of the arbitrator under the arbitration clause. But see notes on *clause* 26.6 below. *Rees & Kirbv Ltd* v *Swansea City Council* (1985) 30 BLR 1: On the facts, the employer may be estopped from enforcing his right to timeous application; in this case the estoppel arose out of negotiations between the parties. *Wraight Ltd v P H & T (Holdings)* (1968) 13 BLR 26: The expression 'direct loss and/or damage' which appeared in the determination provisions at *clause* 26 of JCT63 means the same thing as damages at common law. and thus includes loss of profit. *F G Minter v Welsh HTSO* (1980) 13 BLR 1: 'Direct loss and/or expense' is sufficiently wide to include financing charges although only, under the 1963 edition, for the period prior to each specific application by the contractor. Note that JCT80 now permits the contractor to apply for loss that he is likely to incur. *Rees & Kirby Ltd v Swansea City Council* (1985) 30 BLR 1: Under JCT63 the application must, if it is to be read as relating to financing charges, make some reference to the fact that the contractor has suffered loss and expense by reason of being kept out of his money. The Court of Appeal raised the question, which it did not answer, whether the same position would apply under JCT80. *Rees & Kirby Ltd v Swansea City Council* (1985) 30 BLR 1: There is no cut-off point for financing charges at practical completion. *Rees & Kirby Ltd v Swansea City Council* (1985) 30 BLR 1: There is no reason whv financing charges may not be calculated on a compounded basis.
[2] *London Borough of Merton v Stanley Hugh Leach Ltd* (1985) 32 BLR 51: This clause sets out the various matters which may give rise to an ascertainment of loss and/or expense. The contractor's entitlement is not dependent upon him being able to specify what loss flows from which of the listed matters. The position under JCT thus accords with the position under ICE as decided in *Crosbv & Sons Ltd v Portland Urban District Council* (1967) 5 BLR 121.
[3] See notes on *clause 25.4.6* above.
[4] See notes on *clause 25.4.8(1)* above.
[5] *London Borough of Merton v Stanley Hugh Leach Ltd* (1985) 32 BLR 51: If the contractor wishes to do so he can bring a claim for damages against the employer for breach of contract instead of or as well as making a claim for loss and/or expense. Such a claim for damages is not dependent upon timeous written application for loss and/or expense.

---

27 Determination by employer

27.1 Without prejudice to any other rights or remedies which the Employer may possess, if the Contractor shall make default in any one or more of the following respects, that is to say[1]:

27.1.1 if without reasonable cause he wholly suspends the carrying out of the Works before completion thereof; or

27.1.2 if he fails to proceed regularly and diligently with the Works; or

27.1.3 if he refuses or neglects to comply with a written notice from the Architect/Supervising Officer requiring him to remove defective work or improper materials or goods and by such refusal or neglect the Works are materially affected; or

27.1.4 if he fails to comply with the provisions of either *clause* 19 or 19A.

then the Architect/Supervising Officer may give to him a notice by registered post or recorded delivery specifying the default. If the Contractor either shall continue such default for 14 days after receipt of such notice or shall at any time thereafter repeat such default (whether previously repeated or not), then the Employer may within 10 days after such continuance or repetition by notice by registered post or recorded delivery forthwith determine the employment of the Contractor under this Contract; provided that such notice shall not be given unreasonably or vexatiously.

27.2 In the event of the Contractor becoming bankrupt or making a composition or arrangement with his creditors or having a proposal in respect of his company for a voluntary arrangement for a composition of debts or scheme or arrangement approved in accordance with the Insolvency Act 1986, or having an application made under the Insolvency Act 1986 in respect of his company to the court for the appointment of an administrator or, having a winding up order made or (except for the purposes of amalgamation or reconstruction) a resolution for voluntary winding up passed or having a provisional liquidator, receiver or manager of his business or undertaking duly appointed, or having an administrative receiver, as defined in the Insolvency Act 1986, appointed or having possession taken, by or on behalf of the holders of any debentures secured by a floating charge, of any property comprised in or subject to the floating charge, the employment of the Contractor under this Contract shall be forthwith automatically determined but the said employment may be reinstated and continued if the Employer and the Contractor, his trustee in bankruptcy, liquidator, provisional liquidator, receiver or manager as the case may be shall so agree.

---

[1] *Hounslow London Borough v Twickenham Garden Developments* (1970) 7 BLR 81: Principles of natural justice do not apply to the architect's default notice in the determination procedure. Further, the architect's notice need not give 'further and better particulars' of the default. but merely 'direct the contractor's mind to what is said to be amiss'. The employer's notice is not given 'unreasonably or vexatiously' for the employer having extraneous motives for wishing to determine provided he has one good and reasonable ground. *John Jarvis v Rockdale Housing Association* (1987) 36 BLR 48: Notice is not given 'unreasonably and vexatiously' unless 'a reasonable contractor, circumstanced in all respects as was the contractor at the time he gave the notice, would have thought it was unreasonable and vexatious to give such notice'. *J M Hill & Sons v London Borough of Camden* (1980) 18 BLR 31: It is not 'unreasonable and vexatious' for a party to give notice unless it would be 'totally unfair and almost smacking of sharp practice'. *Central Provident Fund Board v Ho Bock Kee* (1981) 17 BLR 21 and *Eriksson v Whalley* [1971] NSWLR 397 suggest that the formal requirements as to the service of notice are essential to its validity. *Goodwin v Fawcett* (1965) 175 EG 27 and *J M Hill & Sons v London Borough of Camden* 18 BLR 31 suggest that they are not.

28 Determination by contractor

28.1 Without prejudice to any other rights and remedies which the Contractor may possess, if

28.1.1 the Employer does not pay the amount properly due to the Contractor on any certificate (otherwise than as a result of the operation of the VAT Agreement) within 14 days from the issue of that certificate and continues such default for seven davs after receipt by registered post or recorded delivery of a notice from the Contractor stating that notice of determination under *clause* 28 will be served if payment is not made within seven days from receipt thereof; or

28.1.2 the Employer interferes with or obstructs the issue of any certificate due under this Contract; or

28.1.3 the carrying out of the whole or substantially the whole of the uncompleted Works (other than the execution of work required under *clause* 17) is suspended for a continuous period of the length named in the Appendix by reason of[1]:

(1) Architect's/Supervising Officer's instruction issued under *clause* 2.3, 13.2 or 23.2 unless caused by reason of some negligence or default of the Contractor his servants or agents or of any person employed or engaged upon or in connection with the Works or any part thereof, his servants or agents other than a Nominated Sub-Contractor or the Employer or any person employed, engaged or authorised by the Employer or by any local authority or statutory undertaker executing work solely in pursuance of its statutory obligations; or

(2) the Contractor not having received in due time necessary instructions, drawings, details or levels from the Architect/Supervising Officer for which he specifically applied in writing provided that such application was made on a date which having regard to the Completion Date was neither unreasonably distant from nor unreasonably close to the date on which it was necessary for him to receive the same; or

(3) delay in the execution of work not forming part of this Contract by the Employer himself or by the persons employed or otherwise engaged by the Employer as referred to in *clause* 29; or

(4) the opening up for inspection of any work covered up or the testing of any of the work, materials or goods in accordance with *clause* 8.3 (including making good in consequence of such opening up or testing), unless the inspection or test showed that the work, materials or goods were not in accordance with this Contract[2];

(5) failure of the Employer to give in due time ingress to or egress from the site of the Works or any part thereof through or over any land, buildings, way or passage adjoining or connected with the site and in the possession and control of the Employer, in accordance with the Contract Bills or the Contract Drawings, after receipt by the Architect of such notice, if any, as the Contractor is required to give, or failure of the Employer to give such ingress or egress as otherwise agreed between the Architect and the Contractor. Then the Contractor may thereupon by notice by registered post or recorded delivery to the Employer or Architect/Supervising Officer forthwith determine the employment of the Contractor under this Contract; provided that such notice shall not be given unreasonably or vexatiously.

28A.1 Without prejudice to any other rights or remedies which the Employer or the Contractor may possess, if the carrying out of the whole or substantially the whole of the uncompleted Works (other than the execution of work required under *clause* 17) is suspended for a continuous period of the length named in the Appendix by reason of:

28A.1.1 force majeure; or

28A.1.2 loss or damage to the Works occasioned by any one or more of the Specified Perils; or

28A.1.3 civil commotion

then the Employer or the Contractor may thereupon by notice, by registered post or recorded delivery to the Contractor or to the Employer forthwith determine the employment of the Contractor under this Contract; provided that such notice shall not be given unreasonably or vexatiously.

28A.2 The Contractor shall not be entitled to give notice under *clause* 28A.1 where the loss or damage to the Works occasioned by the Specified Perils was caused by some negligence or default of the Contractor, his servants or agents or of any person employed or engaged upon or in connection with the Works or any part thereof, his servants or agents other than the Employer or any person employed, engaged or authorised by the Employer or by any local authority or statutory undertaker executing work solely in pursuance of its statutory obligations.

28A.3 Upon such determination under *clause* 28A.1 the provisions of *clause* 28.2 shall apply with the exception of *clause 28.2.2*(6).

---

[1] See notes on *clause* 27.1 for decisions on whether a notice is given 'unreasonably or vexatiously'.

[2] *John Jarvis v Rockdale Housing Association* (1987) 36 BLR 48: The expression 'the Contractor' in this provision does not include nominated sub-contractors.

28.2.2 Lintest Builders v Roberts (1980) 13 BLR 39. CA: The reasonable cost of any necessary remedial works is to be taken into account in calculating the sum due to the contractor following a determination.

30 Certificates and Payments

30.1.1 (1) The Architect/Supervising Officer shall from time to time as provided in *clause* 30 issue Interim Certificates stating the amount due to the Contractor from the Employer and the Contractor shall be entitled to payment therefor within 14 days from the date of issue of each Interim Certificate.

(2) Notwithstanding the fiduciary interest of the Employer in the Retention as stated in *clause 30.5.1* the Employer is entitled to exercise any right under this Contract of deduction from monies due or to become due to the Contractor against any amount so due under an Interim Certificate whether or not any Retention is included in that Interim Certificate by the operation of *clause* 30.4. Such deduction is subject to the restriction set out in clause *35.13.5*(4)(b).

(3) Where the Employer exercises any right under this Contract of deduction from monies due or to become due to the Contractor he shall inform the Contractor in writing of the reason for that deduction.

30.1.2 Interim valuations shall be made by the Quantity Surveyor whenever the Architect/Supervising Officer considers them to be necessary for the purpose of ascertaining the amount to be stated as due in an Interim Certificate.

30.1.3 Interim Certificates shall be issued at the Period of Interim Certificates specified in the Appendix up to and including the end of the period during which the Certificate of Practical Completion is issued. Thereafter Interim Certificates shall be issued as and when further amounts are ascertained as payable to the Contractor from the Employer and after the expiration of the Defects Liability Period named in the Appendix or upon the issue of the Certificate of Completion of Making Good Defects (whichever is the later) provided always that the Architect/Supervising Officer shall not be required to issue an Interim Certificate within one Calendar month of having issued a previous Interim Certificate.

30.2 The amount stated as due in an Interim Certificate subject to any agreement between the parties as to stage payments, shall be the gross valuation as referred to in *clause* 30.2 less any amount which may be deducted and retained by the Employer as provided in *clause* 30.4 (in the Conditions called 'the Retention') and the total amount stated as due in Interim Certificates previously issued under the Conditions.

The gross valuation shall be the total of the amounts referred to in *clauses 30.2.1* and *30.2.2* less the total of the amounts referred to in *clause 30.2.3* and applied up to and including a date not more than seven days before the date of the Interim Certificate:

There shall be included the following which are subject to Retention:

30.2.1 (1) the total value of the work properly executed by the Contractor including any work so executed to which *clause* 13.5 refers, but excluding any restoration, replacement or repair of loss or damage and removal and disposal of debris which in *clauses 22B.3.5* and *22C.4.4*(2) are treated as if they were a Variation together with, where applicable, any adjustment of that value under *clause* 40¹;

(2) the total value of the materials and goods delivered to or adjacent to the Works for incorporation therein by the Contractor but not so incorporated, provided that the value of such materials and goods shall only be included as and from such times as they are reasonably, properly and not prematurely so delivered and are adequately protected against weather and other casualties;

(3) the total value of any materials or goods other than those to which *clause 30.2.1*(2) refers where the Architect/Supervising Officer in the exercise of his discretion under *clause* 30.3 has decided that such total value shall be included in the amount stated as due in an Interim Certificate;

(4) the amounts referred to in *clause 21.4.1* of the Sub-Contract NSC/4 or NSC/4a as applicable in respect of each Nominated Sub-Contractor;

(5) the profit of the Contractor upon the total of the amounts referred to in *clauses 30.2.1*(4) and *30.2.2*(5) less the total of the amount referred to in *clause 30.2.3*(3) at the rates included in the Contract Bills, or in the cases where the nomination arises from an instruction as to the expenditure of a provisional sum, at rates related thereto, or if none, at reasonable rates.

30.2.2 There shall be included the following which are not subject to Retention;

(1) any amounts to be included in Interim Certificates in accordance with *clause* 3 as a result of payments made or costs incurred by the Contractor under *clauses* 6.2, 7, 8.3, 9.2, and *21.2.3*;

(2) any amounts ascertained under *clause* 26.1 or 34.3 or in respect of any

restoration, replacement or repair of loss or damage and removal and disposal of debris which in *clauses 22B.3.5* and *22C.4.4*(2) are treated as if they were a Variation;
(3) any amount to which *clause* 35.17 refers;
(4) any amount payable to the Contractor under *clause* 38 or 39, whichever is applicable;
(5) the amounts referred to in *clause 21.4.2* of Sub-Contract NSC/4 or NSC/4a as applicable in respect of each Nominated Sub-Contractor.

30.2.3 There shall be deducted the following which are not subject to Retention;
(1) any amount deductible under *clause* 7 or *8.4.2* or 17.2 or 17.3 or any amount allowable by the Contractor to the Employer under *clause* 38 or 39, if applicable;
(2) any amount allowable by the Contractor to the Employer under *clause* 38 or 39, whichever is applicable;
(3) any amount referred to in *clause 21.4.3* of Sub-Contract NSC/4 or NSC/4a as applicable in respect of each Nominated Sub-Contractor

30.3 The amount stated as due in an Interim Certificate may in the discretion of the Architect/Supervising Officer include the value of any materials or goods before delivery thereof to or adjacent to the Works (in *clause 30.3* referred to as 'the materials') provided that:

30.3.1 the materials are intended for incorporation in the Works;

30.3.2 nothing remains to be done to the materials to complete the same up to the point of their incorporation in the Works;

30.3.3 the materials have been and are set apart at the premises where thev have been manufactured or assembled or are stored, and have been clearly and visibly marked, individually or in sets, either by letters or figures or by reference to a pre-determined code, so as to identify:
(1) the Employer, where they are stored on the premises of the Contractor, and in any other case the person to whose order they are held; and
(2) their destination as the Works;

30.3.4 where the materials were ordered from a supplier by the Contractor or by any Sub-Contractor, the contract for their supply is in writing and expressly provides that the property therein shall pass unconditionally to the Contractor or the Sub-Contractor (as the case may be) not later than the happening of the events set out in *clauses 30.3.2* and *30.3.3*;

30.3.5 where the materials were ordered from a supplier by any Sub-Contractor, the relevant Sub-Contract between the Contractor and the Sub-Contractor is in writing and expressly provides that on the property in the materials passing to the Sub-Contractor the same shall immediately thereon pass to the Contractor;

30.3.6 where the materials were manufactured or assembled by any Sub-Contractor, the Sub-Contract is in writing and expressly provides that the property in the materials shall pass unconditionally to the Contractor not later than the happening of the events set out in *clauses 30.3.2* and *30.3.3*;

30.3.7 the materials are in accordance with this Contract;

30.3.8 the Contractor provides the Architect/Supervising Officer with reasonable proof that the property in the materials is in him and that the appropriate conditions set out in *clauses 30.3.1* to *30.3.7* have been complied with;

30.3.9 the Contractor provides the Architect/Supervising Officer with reasonable proof that the materials are insured against loss or damage for their full value under a policy of insurance protecting the interests of the Employer and the Contractor in respect of the Specified Perils, during the period commencing with the transfer of property in the materials to the Contractor until they are delivered to, or adjacent to, the Works.

30.4.1 The Retention which the Employer may deduct and retain as referred to in *clause* 30.2 shall be such percentage of the total amount included under *clause 30.2.1* in any Interim Certificate as arises from the operation of the following rules:

   (1) the percentage (in the Conditions and Appendix called 'the Retention Percentage') deductible under *clause 30.4.1*(2) shall be 5 per cent (unless a lower rate shall have been agreed between the parties and specified in the Appendix as the Retention Percentage); and the percentage deductible under *clause 30. 4.1*(3) shall be one half of the Retention Percentage;
   (2) the Retention Percentage may be deducted from so much of the said total amount as relates to work which has not reached Practical Completion (as referred to in *clauses* 17.1, *18.1.1* or *35.1.6*) and amounts in respect of the value of materials and goods included under *clauses 30.2.1*(2), *30.2.1*(3) (so far as that relates to materials and goods as referred to in *clause 2.4.1*(2) of Sub-Contract NSC/4 or NSC/4a as applicable) and *30.2.1*(4);
   (3) half the Retention Percentage may be deducted from so much of the said total amount as relates to work which has reached Practical Completion (as referred to in *clauses* 17.1, *18.1.1* or 35.16) but in respect of which a Certificate of Completion of Making Good Defects under *clause* 17.4 or a certificate under *clause 18.1.2* or an Interim Certificate under *clause* 35.17, has not been issued.

30.4.2 The Retention deducted from the value of work executed by the Contractor or any Nominated Sub-Contractor and from the value of materials and goods intended for incorporation in the Works, but not so incorporated, and specified in the statements issued under *clause 30.5.2*(1), is hereinafter referred to as the 'Contractor's Retention' and the 'Nominated Sub-Contract retention' respectively.

30.5 The Retention shall be subject to the following rules[2]:

30.5.1 the Employer's interest in the Retention is fiduciary as trustee for the Contractor and for any Nominated Sub-Contractor (but without obligation to invest);

30.5.2 (1) at the date of each Interim Certificate the Architect/Supervising Officer shall prepare, or instruct the Quantity Surveyor to prepare, a statement specifying the Contractor's retention and the Nominated Sub-Contract retention for each Nominated Sub-Contractor deducted in arriving at the amount stated as due in such Interim Certificate;

   (2) such statement shall be issued by the Architect/Supervising Officer to the Employer, to the Contractor and to each Nominated Sub-Contractor whose work is referred to in the statement.

30.5.3 *[Number not used]*

30.5.4 Where the Employer exercises the right to deduct referred to in *clause 30.1.1*(2) against any Retention he shall inform the Contractor of the amount of that deduction from either the Contractor's retention or the Nominated Sub-Contract retention of any Nominated Sub-Contractor by reference to the latest statement issued under *clause 30.5.2*(1).

30.6.1 (1) Not later than 6 months after Practical Completion of the Works the Contractor shall provide the Architect/Supervising Officer, or if so instructed by the Architect/Supervising Officer, the Quantity Survevor with all documents necessary for the purposes of the adjustment of the Contract Sum including all documents relating to the accounts of Nominated Sub-Contractors and Nominated Suppliers.

(2) Not later than 3 months after receipt by the Architect or by the Quantity Surveyor of the documents referred to in *clause 30.6.1*(1)

    (*a*) the Architect, or, if the Architect has so instructed, the Quantity Surveyor shall ascertain (unless previously ascertained) any loss and/or expense under *clauses* 26.1, *26.4.1* and 34.3, and

    (*b*) the Quantity Surveyor shall prepare a statement of all adjustments to be made to the Contract Sum as referred to in *clause 30.6.2* other than any to which *clause 30.6.1*(2)(*a*) applies

and the Architect shall forthwith send a copy of any ascertainment to which *clause 30.6.1*(2)(*a*) refers and of the statement prepared in compliance with *clause 30.6.1(2)(b)* to the Contractor and the relevant extract therefrom to each Nominated Sub-Contractor.

30.6.2 The Contract Sum shall be adjusted as follows:

There shall be deducted:

(1) all prime cost sums, all amounts in respect of Sub-Contractors named as referred to in *clause* 35.1 the certified value of any work by a Nominated Sub-Contractor whose employment has been determined in accordance with *clause* 35.24, which was not in accordance with the relevant Sub-Contract but which has been paid or otherwise discharged by the Employer, and any Contractor's profit thereon included in the Contract Bills;

(2) any amount due to the Employer under *clause* 22A.2, *35.18.1*(2) or *35.24.6*;

(3) all provisional sums and the value of all work described as provisional included in the Contract Bills;

(4) any amount deducted or deductible under *clause* 7 or *8.4.2* or 17.2 or 17.3 the amount of the valuation under *clause 13.5.2* of items omitted in accordance with a Variation required by the Architect/Supervising Officer under *clause* 13.2, or subsequently sanctioned by him in writing, together with the amount included in the Contract Bills for any other work as referred to in *clause 13.5.5* which is to be valued under *clause* 13.5;

(5) any amount allowed or allowable to the Employer under *clause* 38, 39 or 40, whichever is applicable;

(6) any other amount which is required by this Contract to be deducted from the Contract Sum;

There shall be added:

(7) the total amounts included in the Interim Certificate issued under *clause* 30.7, being the Nominated Sub-Contract Sums or Tender Sums as finally adjusted or ascertained under all relevant provisions of Sub-Contract NSC/4 or NSC/4a as applicable;

(8) the tender sum (or such other sum as is appropriate in accordance with the terms of the tender as accepted by or on behalf of the Employer) for any work for which a tender made under *clause* 35.2 has been accepted;

(9) any amounts properly chargeable to the Employer in accordance with the nomination instruction of the Architect/Supervising Officer in

respect of materials or goods supplied by Nominated Suppliers; such amounts shall include the discount for cash of 5 per cent referred to in *clause* 36 but shall exclude any value added tax which is treated, or is capable of being treated, as input tax (as referred to in the Finance Act 1972) by the Contractor;

(10) the profit of the Contractor upon the amounts referred to in *clauses 30.6.2(7), 30.6.2(8)* and *30.6.2(9)* at the rates included in the Contract Bills or in the cases where the nomination arises from an instruction as to the expenditure of a provisional sum at rates related thereto or if none are reasonable rates;

(11) any amounts paid or payable by the Employer to the Contractor as a result of payments made or costs incurred by the Contractor under *clauses* 6.2, 7, 8.3, 9.2, 17.2, 17.3 or *21.2.3*;

(12) the amount of the Valuation under *clause* 13.5 of any Variation, including the valuation of other work included in the Contract Bills, as referred to in *clause 13.3.5*, other than the amount of the valuation of any omission under *clause 13.5.2*;

(13) the amount of the Valuation of work executed by, or the amount of any disbursements by, the Contractor in accordance with instructions of the Architect/Supervising Officer as to the expenditure of provisional sums included in the Contract Bills and of all work described as provisional included in the Contract Bills;

(14) any amount ascertained under *clause* 26.1 or 34.3;

(15) *[Number not used]*

(16) any amount paid or payable to the Contractor under *clause* 38, 39 or 40 whichever is applicable;

(17) any other amount which is required by this Contract to be added to the Contract Sum.

30.7 So soon as is practicable but not less than 28 days before the date of the Final Certificate referred to in *clause* 30.8 and notwithstanding that a period of one month may not have elapsed since the issue of the previous Interim Certificate the Architect/Supervising Officer shall issue an Interim Certificate which shall include the amounts of the sub-contract sums for all Nominated Sub-Contractors as finally adjusted or ascertained under all relevant provisions of Sub-Contract NSC/4 or NSC/4a as applicable and as reduced by any amounts to credited by Nominated Sub-Contractors under *clause* 2.2 of Agreement NSC/2 or NSC/2a as applicable.

30.8 The Architect shall issue the Final Certificate (and inform each Nominated Sub-Contractor of the date of its issue) not later than two months after whichever of the following occurs last:

(i) the end of the Defects Liability Period;

(ii) the date of issue of the Certificate of Completion of Making Good Defects under *clause* 17.4;

(iii) the date on which the Architect sent a copy to the Contractor of any ascertainment to which *clause 30.6.1(2)(a)* refers and of the statement prepared in compliance with *clause 30.6.1(2)(b)*.

The Final Certificate shall state:

30.8.1 the sum of the amounts already stated as due in Interim Certificates, and

30.8.2 the Contract Sum adjusted as necessary in accordance with *clause 30.6.2*

and the difference (if any) between the two sums shall (without prejudice to the rights of the Contractor in respect of any Interim Certificates which have not been paid by the Employer) be expressed in the said Certificate as a balance due to the Contractor from the Employer or to the Employer from the Contractor as the case may be, and subject to any deductions authorised by the Conditions, the said balance shall as from the 28th day after the date of the said Certificate be a debt payable as the case may be by the Employer to the Contractor or by the Contractor to the Employer.

30.9.1 Except as provided in *clauses 30.9.2* and *30.9.3* (and save in respect of fraud), the Final Certificate shall have effect in any proceedings arising out of or in connection with this Contract (whether by arbitration under article 5 or otherwise) as

    (1) conclusive evidence that where and to the extent that the quality of materials or the standard of workmanship are to be to the reasonable satisfaction of the Architect/Supervising Officer the same are to such satisfaction, and

    (2) conclusive evidence that any necessary effect has been given to all the terms of this Contract which require that an amount is to be added to or deducted from the Contract Sum or an adjustment is to be made of the Contract Sum save where there has been any accidental inclusion or exclusion of any work, materials, goods or figure in any computation or any arithmetical error in any computation in which event the Final Certificate shall have effect as conclusive evidence as to all other computations, and

    (3) conclusive evidence that all and only such extensions of time, if any, as are due under *clause* 25 have been given, and

    (4) conclusive evidence that the reimbursement of direct loss and/or expense, if any to the Contractor pursuant to *clause* 26.1 is in final settlement of all and any claims which the Contractor has or may have arising out of the occurrence of any of the matters referred to in *clause* 26.2 whether such claim be for breach of contract, duty of care, statutory duty or otherwise

30.9.2 If any arbitration or other proceedings have been commenced by either party before the Final Certificate has been issued the Final Certificate shall have effect as conclusive evidence as provided in *clause 30.9.1* after either:

    (1) such proceedings have been concluded, whereupon the Final Certificate shall be subject to the terms of any award or judgment in or settlement of such proceedings, or

    (2) a period of 12 months during which neither party has taken any further step in such proceedings, whereupon the Final Certificate shall be subject to any terms agreed in partial settlement,

whichever shall be the earlier.

30.9.3 If any arbitration or other proceedings have been commenced by either party within 28 days after the Final Certificate has been issued the Final Certificate shall have effect as conclusive evidence as provided in *clause 30.9.1* save only in respect of all matters to which those proceedings relate.[3]

30.10 Save as aforesaid no certificate of the Architect/Supervising Officer shall of itself be conclusive evidence that any works, materials or goods to which it relates are in accordance with this Contract.

---

[1] *Townsend v Stone Toms & Partners (No 2)* (1984) 27 BLR 26: The architect should only value the work that has been *properly* executed. It is not appropriate for him to take the view that the retention will cover minor defects of which he is aware; the purpose of the retention provisions is to protect the employer against latent defects.

[2] *Rayack Construction v Lampeter* (1979) 12 BLR 30: The employer was ordered to pay

the retention fund into a separate bank account. *Henry Boot Building Ltd v The Croydon Hotel and Leisure Co Ltd* (1987) 36 BLR 41: *Rayack* was not followed in a case where the employer had the benefit of a non-completion certificate entitling it to a sum in excess of the retention fund. *Re Arthur Sanders* (1981) 17 BLR 125: Where there are nominated sub-contractors, the due proportion of the contractor's beneficial interest in the retention fund is assigned by the contractor to the nominated sub-contractors.

[3] *Fairweather v Asden Securities* (1979) 12 BLR 40: Once the architect has issued the final certificate he is *functus officio* and thereby precluded from further certification. This case also decided that the final certificate under the then current version of the contract was conclusive of compliance by the contractor with his time obligation, but note the change in wording in later revisions of JCT63. Also see with regard to the conclusiveness of the final certificate under previous wordings *P & M Kaye Ltd v Hosier & Dickinson* [1972] 1 WLR 146 and *H W Nevill (Sunblest) Ltd v William Press & Son Ltd* (1982) 20 BLR 78.

---

35 Nominated sub-contractors

35.1 Where

35.1.1 in the Contract Bills; or

35.1.2 in any instruction of the Architect/Supervising Officer under *clause* 13.3 on the expenditure of a provisional sum included in the Contract Bills; or

35.1.3 in any instruction of the Architect/Supervising Officer under *clause* 13.2 requiring a Variation to the extent, but not further or otherwise,

(1) that it consists of work additional to that then shown upon the Contract Drawings and described by or referred to in the Contract Bills and

(2) that any supply and fixing of materials or goods or any execution of work by a Nominated Sub-Contractor in connection with such additional work is of a similar kind to any supply and fixing of materials or the execution of work for which the Contract Bills provided that the Architect/Supervising Officer would nominate a Sub-Contractor; or

35.1.4 by agreement (which agreement shall not be unreasonably withheld) between the Contractor and the Architect/Supervising Officer on behalf of the Employer.

The Architect/Supervising Officer has, whether by the use of a price cost sum or by naming a Sub-Contractor, reserved to himself the final selection and approval of the Sub-Contractor to the Contractor who shall supply and fix any materials or goods or execute work, the Sub-Contractor so named or to be selected and approved shall be nominated in accordance with the provisions of *clause* 35 and a Sub-Contractor so nominated shall be a Nominated Sub-Contractor for all the purposes of this Contract. The provisions of *clause* 35.1 shall apply notwithstanding the provisions of Section B.9.1 of the Standard Method of Measurement 6th Edition.

35.4.1 No person against whom the Contractor makes a reasonable objection shall be Nominated Sub-Contractor.[1]

35.4.2 Where the Tender NSC/1 and Agreement NSC/2 are used the Contractor shall make any such reasonable objection at the earliest practicable moment but in any case not later than the date when in accordance with *clause 35.10.1* he sends the Tender NSC/1 to the Architect/Supervising Officer.

35.4.3 Where the Tender NSC/1 and Agreement NSC/2 are not used so that the provisions of *clauses* 35.11 and 35.12 apply the Contractor shall make any such reasonable objection at the earliest practicable moment but in any case not later than seven days from receipt by him of the instruction of the Architect/Supervising Officer under *clause* 35.11 nominating the Sub-Contractor.

35.13.1 The Architect/Supervising Officer shall on the issue of each Interim

Certificate:

(1) direct the Contractor as to the amount of each interim or final payment to Nominated Sub-Contractors which is included in the amount stated as due in Interim Certificates and the amount of such interim or final payment shall be computed by the Architect/Supervising Officer in accordance with the relevant provisions of Sub-Contract NSC/4 or NSC/4a as applicable; and

(2) forthwith inform each Nominated Sub-Contractor of the amount of any interim or final payment directed in accordance with *clause 35.13.1*(1).

35.13.2 Each interim payment directed under *clause 35.13.1*(1) shall be duly discharged by the Contractor in accordance with Sub-Contract NSC/4 or NSC/4a as applicable.[2]

35.13.3 Before the issue of each Interim Certificate (other than the first Interim Certificate) and of the Final Certificate the Contractor shall provide the Architect/Supervising Officer with reasonable proof of the discharge referred to in *clause 35.13.2*.[3]

35.13.4 If the Contractor is unable to provide the reasonable proof referred to in *clause 35.13.2* because of some failure or omission of the Nominated Sub-Contractor to provide any document or other evidence to the Contractor which the Contractor may reasonably require and the Architect/Supervising Officer is reasonably satisfied that this is the sole reason why reasonable proof is not furnished by the Contractor, the provisions of *clause 35.13.5* shall not apply and the provisions of *clause 35.13.3* shall be regarded as having been satisfied.

35.13.5 (1) The Employer may, but where the Employer and the Nominated Sub-Contract have executed NSC/2 or NSC/2a, shall, operate *clauses 35.13.5*.3 and 4

(2) If the Contractor fails to provide reasonable proof under *clause 35.13.3*, the Architect/Supervising Officer shall issue a certificate to that effect stating the amount in respect of which the Contractor has failed to provide such proof, and the Architect/Supervising Officer shall issue a copy of the certificate to the Nominated Sub-Contractor concerned

(3) Provided that the Architect/Supervising Officer has issued the certificate under *clause 35.13.5*(2) and subject to *clause 35.13.5*(4) the amount of any future payment otherwise due to the Contractor under this Contract (after deducting any amounts due to the Employer from the Contractor under this Contract) shall be reduced by any amounts due to Nominated Sub-Contractors which the Contractor has failed to discharge (together with the amount of any value added tax which would have been due to the Nominated Sub-Contractor) and the Employer shall himself pay the same to the Nominated Sub-Contractor concerned. Provided that the Employer shall in no circumstances be obliged to pay amounts to Nominated Sub-Contractors in excess of amounts available for reduction as aforesaid.

(4) The operation of *clause 35.13.5*(3) shall be subject to the following:

(*a*) where the Contractor would otherwise be entitled to payment of an amount stated as due in an Interim Certificate under *clause 30*, the reduction and payment to the Nominated Sub-Contractor referred to in *clause 35.3.5*(3) shall be made at the same time as the Employer pays the Contractor any balance due under *clause 30* or, if there is no such balance, not later than the expiry of the period of 14 days within which the Contractor would otherwise be entitled to payment;

(b) where the sum due to the Contractor is the Retention of any part thereof, the reduction and payment to the Nominated Sub-Contractor referred to in *clause 35.13.5*(3) shall not exceed any part of the Contractor's retention (as defined in *clause 30.4.2*) which would otherwise be due for payment to the Contractor;

(c) where the Employer has to pay two or more Nominated Sub-Contractors but the amount due or to become due to the Contractor is insufficient to enable the Employer to pay the Nominated Sub-Contractors in full, the Employer shall apply the amount available pro rata to the amounts from time to time remaining undischarged by the Contractor or adopt such other method of apportionment as may appear· to· the Employer to be fair and reasonable having regard to all the relevant circumstances;

(d) *clause 35.13.5*(3) shall cease to have effect absolutely if at the date when the reduction and payment to the Nominated Sub-Contractor referred to in *clause 35.13.5*(3) would otherwise be made there is in existence either,

(i) a Petition which has been presented to the Court; or

(ii) a resolution properly passed for the winding up of the Contractor other than for the purpose of amalgamation or reconstruction,

whichever shall have first occurred.

35.13.6 Where, in accordance with *clause* 2.2 of Agreement NSC/2 or *clause* 1.2 of Agreement NSC/2a, the Employer, before the issue of an instruction nominating a Sub-Contractor, has paid to him an amount in respect of design work and/or materials or goods and/or fabrication which is/are included in the subject of the Sub-Contract Sum or Tender Sum;

(1) the Employer shall send to the Contractor the written statement of the Nominated Sub-Contractor of the amount to be credited to the Contractor, and

(2) the Employer may make deductions up to the amount of such credit from the amounts stated as due to the Contractor in any of the Interim Certificates which include amounts of interim or final payment to the Nominated Sub-Contractor; provided that the amount so deducted from that stated as due in any one Interim Certificate shall not exceed the amount of payment to the Nominated Sub-Contractor included therein as directed by the Architect.

35.14.1 The Contractor shall not grant to any Nominated Sub-Contractor any extension of the period or periods within which the Sub-Contract Works (or where the Sub-Contract Works are to be completed in parts any part thereof) are to be completed except in accordance with the relevant provisions of Sub-Contract NSC/4 or NSC/4a as applicable which requires the written consent of the Architect/Supervising Officer to any such grant.

35.14.2 The Architect/Supervising Officer shall operate the relevant provisions of Sub-Contract NSC/4 or NSC/4a as applicable upon receiving any notice particulars and estimate and a request from the Contractor and any Nominated Sub-Contractor for his written consent to an extension of the period or periods for the completion of the Sub-Contract Works or any part thereof as referred to in *clause 11.2.2* of Sub-Contract NSC/4 or NSC/4a as applicable.

35.15.1 If any Nominated Sub-Contractor fails to complete the Sub-Contract Works (or where the Sub-Contract Works are to be completed in parts any part thereof) within the period specified in the Sub-Contract or within any extended time granted by the Contractor with the written consent of the Architect/Supervising Officer and the Contractor so notifies the Architect/Supervising Officer with a copy to the Nominated Sub-Contractor, then, provided that the Architect/Supervising Officer is satisfied that *clause* 35.14 has been properly applied, the Architect/Supervising Officer shall so certify in writing to the Contractor. Immediately upon the issue of such a certificate the Architect/Supervising Officer shall send a duplicate thereof to the Nominated Sub-Contractor.

35.15.2 The certificate of the Architect/Supervising Officer under *clause 35.15.1* shall be issued not later than two months from the date of notification to the Architect/Supervising Officer that the Nominated Sub-Contractor has failed to complete the Sub-Contract Works or any part thereof.

35.25 The Contractor shall not determine any Nominated Sub-Contractor by virtue of any right to which he may be or may become entitled without an instruction from the Architect/Supervising Officer so to do.

---

[1] These clauses set out the procedure for nomination. In *Fairclough Building Ltd v Rhuddlan Borough Council* (1985) 30 BLR 26 the Court of Appeal considered *clause* 27(a) of JCT63, which is in substantially different form. It found that the provision applies to renominations as well as original nominations. These circumstances are dealt with expressly by JCT80 *clause* 35.24. It appears that the contractor may exercise his right of reasonable objection under *clause 35.4.1* if, on renomination, the proposed nominated sub-contractor will not undertake to complete within the main contract programme or, following *North West Metropolitan Regional Health Board v Bickerton & Sons Ltd* [1970] 1 WLR 607, if provision is not made for the incoming nominated sub-contractor to rectify the defects of the outgoing nominated sub-contractor.

[2] *Gilbert-Ash (Northern) Ltd v Modern Engineering (Bristol)* [1974] AC 689: This clause requires the contractor to discharge interim payments certified by the direction process as due to nominated sub-contractors. Lord Dilhorne said that its predecessor (JCT63 *clause* 27(b) 'is clearly intended to permit the contractor to deduct from the payment due to the sub-contractor under an interim certificate, a sum equivalent to the loss he had suffered in consequence of delay'. But note also the requirement under *clause* 23 of NSC/4 for prior notice of the intention to set off under *clause 23.2.3* and also, in delay cases, the need for the contractor to obtain a certificate under *clause 35.15.1* of the main contract.

[3] *Gilbert-Ash (Northern) Ltd v Modern Engineering (Bristol)* [1974] AC 689: This clause requires the contractor to provide reasonable proof that he has discharged payments due to nominated sub-contractors. Discharge may be 'by payment or by setting up a breach of warranty under the sub-contract in diminution or extinction of an instalment of the price then due'.

---

41 Settlement of disputes — arbitration

41.1 If a dispute or difference as referred to in Article 5 has arisen including:
  (i) any matter or thing left by this Contract to the discretion of the Architect; or
  (ii) the withholding by the Architect of any certificate to which the Contractor may claim to be entitled; or
  (iii) the adjustment of the Contract Sum under *clause* 30.6.2; or
  (iv) the rights and liabilities of the parties under *clauses* 27, 28, 32 or 33; or
  (v) unreasonable withholding of consent or agreement by the Employer or the Architect on his behalf or by the Contractor
then such dispute or difference shall be referred to the arbitration and final

decision of a person to be agreed between the parties to act as Arbitrator, or, failing agreement within 14 days after either party has given to the other a written request to concur in the appointment of an Arbitrator, a person to be appointed on the request of either party by the person named in the Appendix.

41.2.1 Provided that if the dispute or difference to be referred to arbitration under this Contract raises issues which are substantially the same as or connected with issues raised in a related dispute between:

(i) the Employer and Nominated Sub-Contractor under Agreement NSC/2 or NSC/2a as applicable, or

(ii) the Contractor and any Nominated Sub-Contractor under Sub-Contract NSC/4 or NSC/4a as applicable, or

(iii) the Contractor and/or the Employer and any Nominated Supplier whose contract of sale with the Contractor provides for the matters referred to in *clause 36.4.8(2)*,

and if the related dispute has already been referred for determination to an Arbitrator, the Employer and the Contractor hereby agree

(i) that the dispute or difference under this Contract shall be referred to the Arbitrator appointed to determine the related dispute;

(ii) that such Arbitrator shall have power to make such directions and all necessary awards in the same way as if the procedure of the High Court as to joining one or more defendants or joining co-defendants or third parties was available to the parties and to him; and

(iii) that the agreement and consent referred to in *clause* 41.6 on appeals or applications to the High Court on any question of law shall apply to any question of law arising out of the awards of such arbitrator in respect of all related disputes referred to him or arising in the course of the reference of all the related disputes referred to him;

41.2.2 save that the Employer or the Contractor may require the dispute or difference under this Contract to be referred to a different Arbitrator (to be appointed under this Contract) if either of them reasonably considers that the Arbitrator appointed to determine the related dispute is not appropriately qualified to determine the dispute or difference under this Contract.

41.2.3 Clauses 41.2.1 and *41.2.2* shall apply unless in the Appendix the words '*clauses 41.2.1* and *41.2.2* apply' have been deleted.

41.3 Such reference, except

41.3.1 on article 3 or article 4; or

41.3.2 on the question whether or not the issue of an instruction is empowered by the Conditions; or whether or not a certificate has been improperly withheld; or whether a certificate is not in accordance with the Conditions: or whether a determination under *clause 22C.4.3*(1) will be just and equitable; or

41.3.3 on any dispute or difference under *clause* 4.1 in regard to a reasonable objection by the Contractor, under *clause* 18.1 or *clause 23.3.2* in regard to withholding of consent by the Contractor and *clauses* 25, 32 and 33,

shall not be opened until after Practical Completion or alleged Practical Completion of the Works or termination or alleged termination of the Contractor's employment under this Contract or abandonment of the Works, unless with the written consent of the Employer or the Architect on his behalf and the Contractor.

41.4 Subject to the provisions of *clauses* 4.2, 30.9, *38.4.3*, *39.5.3* and 40.5 the Arbitrator shall, without prejudice to the generality of his powers, have power to direct such measurements and/or valuations as may in his opinion be desirable in order to determine the rights of the parties and to ascertain and award any sum which ought to have been the subject of or included in any certificate and to open up, review and revise any certificate, opinion, decision, requirement or notice and to determine all matters in dispute which shall be submitted to him in the same manner as if no such certificate, opinion, decision, requirement or notice had been given.

41.5 Subject to *clause* 41.6 the award of such Arbitrator shall be final and binding on the parties.

41.6 The parties hereby agree and consent pursuant to sections 1(3)(a) and 2(1)(b) of the Arbitration Act 1979, that either party

41.6.1 may appeal to the High Court on any question of law arising out of an award made in an arbitration under this Arbitration Agreement; and

41.6.2 may apply to the High Court to determine any question of law arising in the course of the reference; and the parties agree that the High Court should have jurisdiction to determine any such question of law.

41.7 Whatever the nationality, residence or domicile of the Employer, the Contractor, any sub-contractor or supplier or the Arbitrator, and wherever the Works or any part thereof are situated, the law of England shall be the proper law of this Contract and in particular (but not so as to derogate from the generality of the foregoing) the provisions of the Arbitration Acts 1950 (notwithstanding anything in s 34 thereof), to 1979 shall apply to any arbitration under this Contract wherever the same. or any part of it, shall be conducted.

The Sub-Contract — NSC/4

The following NSC14 provisions are reproduced with the kind permission of the Building Employers Confederation.

County & District Properties Ltd v C Jenner (1974) 3 BLR 38: Swanwick J found the predecessor of this contract, the 'Green Form' was not to be construed *contra proferentum* either party.

4 Execution of the Sub-Contract Works — instructions of Architect — directions of Contractor

4.1.1 The Sub-Contractor shall carry out and complete the Sub-Contract Works in compliance with the Sub-Contract Documents using materials and workmanship of the quality and standards therein specified and in conformity with all the reasonable directions and requirements of the Contractor (so far as they may apply) regulating for the time being the due carrying out of the Main Contract Works provided that where and to the extent that approval of the quality of materials or of the standards of workmanship is a matter for the opinion of the Architect, such quality and standards shall be to the reasonable satisfaction of the Architect.

4.1.2 The Sub-Contractor shall continually keep upon the Sub-Contract Works while such Sub-Contracts Works are being executed a competent person-in-charge and any instruction of the Architect given to him by the Contractor, or any direction given to him by the Contractor, shall be deemed to have been issued to the Sub-Contractor.

4.2 The Contractor shall forthwith issue to the Sub-Contractor any written instruction of the Architect issued under the Main Contract affecting the Sub-Contract Works (including the ordering of any Variation therein); and may issue any reasonable direction in writing to the Sub-Contractor in regard to the Sub-Contract Works.

4.3 The Sub-Contractor shall forthwith comply with any instruction or direction referred to in *clause* 4.2 save that where such instruction is one requiring a Variation within the definition of 'Variation' *clause 1.3, para* 2, the Sub-Contractor need not comply to the extent that he makes reasonable objection to such compliance. Upon receipt by the Contractor of any written objection by the Sub-Contractor, the Contractor shall thereupon submit that objection to the Architect.

4.4 If the Architect or Contractor purports to give any instruction or direction referred to in *clause* 4.2 otherwise than in writing to the Sub-Contractor or his person-in-charge then such instruction or direction shall be of no immediate effect but shall be confirmed in writing by the Sub-Contractor to the Contractor within seven days and if not dissented from in writing by the Contractor within seven days from the receipt of the Sub-Contractor's confirmation shall take effect as from the expiration of the latter said seven days. Provided always:

4.4.1 that if the Contractor within seven days of such instruction or direction otherwise than in writing having been given shall himself confirm the same in writing, then the Sub-Contractor shall not be obliged to confirm as aforesaid and the said instruction or direction shall take effect as from the date of the Contractor's confirmation, and

4.4.2 if neither the Contractor nor the Sub-Contractor shall confirm such an instruction or direction in the manner and at the time aforesaid but the Sub-Contractor shall nevertheless comply with the same, then the Contractor may confirm the same in writing (and must if the Architect has confirmed in writing in similar circumstances under the Main Contract) at any time prior to the final payment of the Sub-Contractor in accordance with the Sub-Contract NSC/4 and the said instruction or direction shall thereupon be deemed to have taken effect on the date on which it was issued.

4.5 If within seven days after receipt of a written notice from the Contractor requiring compliance with a direction of the Contractor the Sub-Contractor does not begin to comply therewith, then the Contractor may if so permitted by the Architect, employ and pay other persons to comply with such direction and all costs incurred in connection with such employment may be deducted from any monies due or to become due to the Sub-Contractor under the Sub-Contract or shall be recoverable from the Sub-Contractor as a debt.

4.6 Upon receipt of what purports to be an instruction of the Architect issued in writing by the Contractor to the Sub-Contractor, the Sub-Contractor may require the Contractor to request the Architect to specify in writing the provision of the Main Contract which empowers the issue of the said instruction. The Contractor shall forthwith comply with any such requirements and deliver to the Sub-Contractor a copy of the Architect's answer to the Contractor's request. If the Sub-Contractor shall thereafter comply with the said instruction then the issue of the same shall be deemed for all the purposes of the Sub-Contract to have been empowered by the provision of the Main Contract specified by the Architect in answer to the Contractor's request. Provided always that if before compliance the Sub-Contractor shall have made a written requirement to the Contractor to request the Employer to concur in the appointment of an Arbitrator under the Main Contract Conditions in order that it may be decided whether the provision specified by the Architect empowers the issue of the said instruction then, subject to the Sub-Contractor giving the Contractor such indemnity and security as the Contractor may reasonably require, the Contractor shall allow the Sub-Contractor to use the Contractor's name and if necessary will join with the Sub-Contractor in arbitration proceedings at the instigation of the Sub-Contractor to decide the matter as aforesaid.

5 Sub-contractor's liability under incorporated provisions of the main contract

5.1 The Sub-Contractor shall:

5.1.1 observe, perform and comply with all the provisions of the Main Contract as described by or referred to in the Tender, Schedule 1 on the part of the Contractor to be observed, performed and complied with so far as they relate and apply to the Sub-Contract Works (or any portion of the same). Without prejudice to the generality of the foregoing, the Sub-Contractor shall observe, perform and comply with the following provisions of the Main Contract Conditions; *clauses* 6, 7, 9, 16, 32, 33 and 34; and

5.1.2 indemnify and save harmless the Contractor against and from:

(1) any breach, non-observance or non-performance by the Sub-Contractor or his servants or agents of any of the provisions of the Main Contract referred to in *clause 5.1.1*; and

(2) any act of omission of the Sub-Contractor or his servants or agents which involves the Contractor in any liability to the Employer under the provisions of the Main Contract referred to in *clause 5.1.1*.

5.2 Nothing contained in the Sub-Contract Documents shall be construed so as to impose any liability on the Sub-Contractor in respect of any act or omission or default on the part of the Employer, the Contractor, his other sub-contractors or their respective servants or agents nor (except by way of and in the terms of the Agreement NSC/2) create any privity of contract between the Sub-Contractor and the Employer or any other sub-contractor.

11 Sub-contractor's obligation — carrying out and completion of sub-contract Works — extension of sub-contract time

11.1 The Sub-Contractor shall carry out and complete the Sub-Contract Works in accordance with the agreed programme details in the Tender, Schedule 2, item 1C, and reasonably in accordance with the progress of the Main Contract Works but subject to receipt of the notice to commence work on site as detailed in the Tender, Schedule 2, item 1C, and to the operation of *clause* 11.2.

11.2.1 (1) If and whenever it becomes reasonably apparent that the commencement, progress or completion of the Sub-Contract Works or any part thereof is being or is likely to be delayed, the Sub-Contractor shall forthwith give written notice to the Contractor of the material circumstances including the cause or causes of the delay and identify in such notice any matter which in his opinion comes within *clause 11.2.2(1)*. The Contractor shall forthwith inform the Architect of any written notice by the Sub-Contractor and submit to the Architect any written representations made to him by the Sub-Contractor as to such cause as aforesaid.

(2) In respect of each and every matter which comes within *clause 11.2.2(1)*, and identified in the notice given in accordance with *clause 11.2.1(1)*, the Sub-Contractor shall, if practicable, in such notice or otherwise in writing as soon as possible after such notice:

(*a*) give particulars of the expected effects thereof; and

(*b*) estimate the extent, if any, of the expected delay in the completion of the Sub-Contract Works or any part thereof beyond the expiry of the period or periods stated in the Tender, Schedule 2, Item 1C or beyond the expiry of any extended period or periods previously fixed under *clause* 11 which results therefrom whether or not concurrently with delay resulting from any other matter which comes within *clause 11.2.2(1)*, and

(c) the Sub-Contractor shall give such further written notices to the Contractor as may be reasonably necessary or as the Contractor may reasonably require for keeping up to date the particulars and estimate referred to in *clause 11.2.2(2)(a)* and *11.2.2* including any material change in such particulars or estimate.

(3) The Contractor shall submit to the Architect the particulars and estimate referred to in *clause 11.2.1(2)(c)* to the extent that such particulars and estimate have not been included in the notice given in accordance with *clause 11.2.1(1)* and shall, if so requested by the Sub-Contractor, join with the Sub-Contractor in requesting the consent of the Architect under *clause* 35.14 of the Main Contract Conditions.

11.2.2 If on receipt of any notice, particulars and estimate under *clause 11.2.1* and of a request by the Contractor and the Sub-Contractor for his consent under *clause* 35.14 of the Main Contract Conditions the Architect is of the opinion that:

(1) any of the matters which are stated by the Sub-Contractor to be the cause of the delay is an act, omission or default of the Contractor, his servants or agents or his Sub-Contractors, their servants or agents (other than the Sub-Contractor, his servants or agents) or the occurrence of a Relevant Event; and

(2) the completion of the Sub-Contract Works or any part thereof is likely to be delayed thereby beyond the period or periods stated in the Tender, Schedule 2, Item 1C, or any revised such period or periods;

then the Contractor shall, with the written consent of the Architect, give an extension of time by fixing such revised or further revised period or periods for the completion of the Sub-Contract Works or any part thereof as the Architect in his written consent then estimates to be fair and reasonable. The Contractor shall, in agreement with the Architect, when fixing such revised period or periods state:

(3) which of the matters, including any of the Relevant Events, referred to in *clause 11.2.2(1)* they have taken into account; and

(4) the extent, if any, to which the Architect, in giving his written consent, has had regard to any instruction requiring as a Variation the omission of anv work issued under *clause* 13.2 of the Main Contract Conditions since the previous fixing of any such revised period or periods for the completion of the Sub-Contract Works or any part thereof,

and shall, if reasonably practicable having regard to the sufficiency of the aforesaid notice, particulars and estimate, fix such revised period or periods not later than 12 weeks from the receipt by the Contractor of the notice and of reasonably sufficient particulars and estimates, or, where the time between receipt thereof and the expiry of the period or periods for the completion of the Sub-Contract Works or any part thereof is less than 12 weeks, not later than the expiry of the aforesaid period or periods.

11.2.3 After the first exercise by the Contractor of the duty under *clause 11.2.2*, the Contractor, with the written consent of the Architect, may fix a period or periods for completion of the Sub-Contract Works or any part thereof shorter than that previously fixed under *clause 11.2.2* if, in the opinion of the Architect, the fixing of such shorter period or periods is fair and reasonable having regard to any instructions issued under *clause* 13.2 of the Main Contract Conditions requiring as a Variation the omission of any work where such issue is after the last occasion on which the Contractor with the consent of the Architect made a revision of the aforesaid period or periods.

11.2.4 Not later than the expiry of 12 weeks from the date of practical completion of the Sub-Contract Works certified under *clause* 35.16 of the Main Contract Conditions or from the date of Practical Completion of the Main Contract, whichever first occurs, the Contractor with the written consent of the Architect shall either:

(1) fix such period or periods for completion of the Sub-Contract Works or any part thereof longer than that previously fixed under *clause* 11.2 as the Architect in his written consent considers to be fair and reasonable having regard to any of the matters referred to in *clause 11.2.2*(1) whether upon reviewing a previous decision or otherwise and whether or not the matters referred to in *clause 11.2.2*(1) have been specifically notified by the Sub-Contractor under *clause 11.2.1*, or

(2) fix such a period or periods for completion of the Sub-Contract Works or any part thereof shorter than that previously fixed under *clause* 11.2 as the Architect in his written consent considers to be fair and reasonable having regard to any instruction issued under *clause* 13.2 of the Main Contract Conditions requiring as a Variation the omission of any work where such issue is after the last occasion on which the Contractor made a revision of the aforesaid period or periods; or

(3) confirm in writing to the Sub-Contractor the period or periods for the completion of the Sub-Contract Works previously fixed. Provided always the Sub-Contractor shall use constantly his best endeavours to prevent delay in the progress of the Sub-Contract Works, howsoever caused, and to prevent any such delay resulting in the completion of the Sub-Contract Works being delayed or further delayed beyond the period or periods for completion; and the Sub-Contractor shall do all that may reasonably be required to the satisfaction of the Architect and the Contractor to proceed with the Sub-Contract Works.

11.2.5 The following are the Relevant Events referred to in *clause 11.2.2*(1):

(1) force majeure;

(2) exceptionally adverse weather conditions;

(3) loss or damage occasioned by any one or more of the *Clause 22* Perils';

(4) civil commotion, local combination or workmen, strike or lock-out affecting any of the trades employed upon the Works or any of the trades engaged in the preparation, manufacture or transportation of any of the goods or materials required for the Works;

(5) compliance by the Contractor and/or Sub-Contractor with the Architect's instructions;

   (*a*) under *clauses* 2.3, 13.2, 13.3, 23.2, 34, 35 or 36 of the Main Contract Conditions, or

   (*b*) in regard to the opening up for inspection of any work covered up or the testing of any of the work, materials or goods in accordance with *clause* 8.3 of the Main Contract Conditions (including making good in consequence of such opening up or testing) unless the inspection or test showed that the work, materials or goods were not in accordance with the Main Contract or the Sub-Contract as the case may be;

(6) the Contractor, or the Sub-Contractor through the Contractor, not having received in due time necessary instructions, drawings, details or levels from the Architect for which the Contractor or the Sub-Contractor, through the Contractor, specifically applied in writing

provided that such application was made on a date which having regard to the Completion Date or the period or periods for the completion of the Sub-Contract Works was neither unreasonably distant from nor unreasonably close to the date on which it was necessary for the Contractor or the Sub-Contractor to receive the same;

(7) delay on the part of Nominated Sub-Contractors (other than the Sub-Contractor) or of Nominated Suppliers in respect of the Works which the Contractor has taken all practicable steps to avoid or reduce;

(8) (*a*) the execution of work not forming part of the Main Contract by the Employer himself or by persons employed or otherwise engaged by the Employer as referred to in *clause* 29 of the Main Contract Conditions or the failure to execute such work;

(*b*) the supply by the Employer of materials and goods which the Employer has agreed to provide for the Works or the failure so to supply;

(9) the exercise after the Date of Tender by the United Kingdom Government of any statutory power which directly affects the execution of the Works by restricting the availability or use of labour which is essential to the proper carrying out of the Works, or preventing the Contractor or Sub-Contractor from, or delaying the Contractor or Sub-Contractor in, securing such goods or materials or such fuel or energy as are essential to the proper carrying out of the Works;

(10) (*a*) the Contractor's or Sub-Contractor's inability for reasons beyond his control and which he could not reasonably have foreseen at the Date of Tender for the purposes of the Main Contract or the Sub-Contract as the case may be to secure such labour as is essential to the proper carrying out of the Works; or

(*b*) the Contractor's or Sub-Contractor's inability for reasons beyond his control and which he could not reasonably have foreseen at the Date of Tender for the purposes of the Main Contract or the Sub-Contract as the case may be to secure such goods or materials as are essential to the proper carrying out of the Works;

(11) the carrying out by a local authority or statutory undertaker of work in pursuance of its statutory obligations in relation to the Works, or the failure to carry out such work;

(12) failure of the Employer to give in due time ingress to or egress from the site of the Works or any part thereof through or over any land, buildings, way or passage adjoining or connected with the site and in the possession and control of the Employer, in accordance with the Contract Bills and/of the Contract Drawings, after receipt by the Architect of such notice, if any, as the Contractor is required to give, or failure of the Employer to give such ingress or egress as otherwise agreed between the Architect and the Contractor;

(13) the valid exercise by the Sub-Contractor of the right in *clause* 21.8 to suspend the further execution of the Sub-Contract Works.

11.3 If the Sub-Contractor shall be aggrieved by: a failure of the Architect to give the written consent referred to in *clause 11.2.2*; and/or a failure of the Architect to give the written consent referred to in *clause 11.2.2* within the period allowed in that clause; and/or the terms of any written consent referred to in *clause 11.2.2* then, subject to the Sub-Contractor giving the Contractor such indemnity and security as the Contractor may reasonably require, the Contractor will allow the Sub-Contractor to use the Contractor's name and if necessary will join with the Sub-Contractor in arbitration proceedings at the instigation of the Sub-Contractor to decide the matter as aforesaid.

12 Failure of sub-contractor to complete on time

12.1 If the Sub-Contractor fails to complete the Sub-Contract Works (or any part thereof) within the period or periods for completion or any revised period or periods as provided in *clause 11.2.2*, the Contractor shall so notify the Architect and give to the Sub-Contractor a copy of such notification.

12.2 The Sub-Contractor shall pay or allow to the Contractor a sum equivalent to any loss or damage suffered or incurred by the Contractor and caused by the failure of the Sub-Contractor as aforesaid. Provided that the Contractor shall not be entitled so to claim unless the Architect in accordance with *clause* 35.15 of the Main Contract Conditions shall have issued to the Contractor (with a copy to the Sub-Contractor) a certificate in writing certifying any failure notified under *clause* 12.1.

13 Matters affecting regular progress — direct loss and/or expense — contractor's and sub-contractor's rights

13.1.1 If the Sub-Contractor makes written application to the Contractor stating that he has incurred or is likely to incur direct loss and/or expense in the execution of the Sub-Contract for which he would not be reimbursed by a payment under any other provision in the Sub-Contract by reason of the regular progress of the Sub-Contract Works or of any part thereof having been or being likely to be materially affected by any one or more of the matters referred to in *clause 13.1.2* the Contractor shall require the Architect to operate *clause* 26.4 of the Main Contract Conditions so that the amount of that direct loss and/or expense, if any, may be ascertained.
Provided always that:
    (1) the Sub-Contractor's application shall be made as soon as it has become, or should reasonably have become, apparent to him that the regular progress of the Sub-Contract Works or of any part thereof has been or was likely to be affected as aforesaid, and
    (2) the Sub-Contractor shall submit to the Contractor such information in support of his application as the Contractor is requested by the Architect to obtain from the Sub-Contractor in order reasonably to enable the Architect to operate *clause* 26.4 of the Main Contract Conditions; and
    (3) the Sub-Contractor shall submit to the Contractor such details of such loss and/or expense as the Contractor is requested by the Architect or the Quantity Surveyor to obtain from the Sub-Contractor in order reasonably to enable the ascertainment of that loss and/or expense under *clause* 26.4 of the Main Contract Conditions.
13.1.2 The following are the matters referred to in *clause 13.1.1*:
    (1) the Contractor, or the Sub-Contractor through the Contractor, not having received in due time necessary instructions, drawings, details or levels from the Architect for which the Contractor, or the Sub-Contractor through the Contractor, specifically applied in writing provided that such application was made on a date which having regard to the Completion Date or the period or periods for completion of the Sub-Contract Works was neither unreasonably distant from nor unreasonably close to the date on which it was necessary for the Contractor or the Sub-Contractor to receive the same; or

(2) the opening up for inspection of any work covered up or the testing of any of the work, materials or goods in accordance with *clause* 8.3 of the Main Contract Conditions (including making good in consequence of such opening up or testing), unless the inspection or test showed that the work materials or goods were not in accordance with the Main Contract or the Sub-Contract as the case may be: or

(3) any discrepancy in or divergence between the Contract Drawings and/or the Contract Bills; or

(4) the execution of work not forming part of the Main Contract by the Employer himself or by persons employed or otherwise engaged by the Employer as referred to in *clause* 29 of the Main Contract Conditions; or

(5) Architect's instructions issued in regard to the postponement of any work to be executed under the provisions of the Main Contract or the Sub-Contract; or

(6) failure of the Employer to give in due time ingress to or egress from the site of the Works, or any part thereof through or over any land, buildings, way or passage adjoining or connected with the site and in the possession and control of the Employer, in accordance with the Contract Bills and/or the Contract Drawings, after receipt by the Architect of such notice, if any, as the Contractor is required to give or failure of the Employer to give such ingress or egress as otherwise agreed between the Architect and the Contractor; or

(7) Architect's instructions issued under *clause* 13.2 of the Main Contract Conditions requiring a Variation or under *clause* 13.3 of the Main Contract Conditions in regard to the expenditure of provisional sums (other than work to which *clause* 13.4.2 of the Main Contract Conditions refers).

13.1.3 Any amount from time to time ascertained as a result of the operation of *clause* 13.1.1 shall be added to the Sub-Contract Sum or included in the calculation of the Ascertained Final Sub-Contract Sum.

13.1.4 The Sub-Contractor shall comply with all directions of the Contractor which are reasonably necessary to enable the ascertainment which results from the operation of *clause 13.1.1* to be carried out.

13.2 If the regular progress of the Sub-Contract Works (including any part thereof which is sub-sub-contracted) is materially affected by any act, omission or default of the Contractor his servants or agents, or any sub-contractor, his servants or agents or sub-sub-contractor (other than the sub-contractor, his servants or agents or sub-sub-contractor) employed bv the contractor on the Works the Sub-Contractor shall within a reasonable time of such material effect becoming apparent give written notice thereof to the Contractor and the agreed amount of any direct loss and/or expense thereby caused to the Sub-Contractor shall be recoverable from the Contractor as a debt.

13.3 If the regular progress of the Works (including any part thereof which is sub-contracted) is materially affected by any act, omission or default of the Sub-Contractor, his servants or agents, or any sub-sub-contractor employed by the Sub-Contractor on the Sub-Contract Works, the Contractor shall within a reasonable time of such material effect becoming apparent give written notice thereof to the Sub-Contractor and the agreed amount of any direct loss and/or expense thereby caused to the Contractor (whether suffered or incurred by the Contractor or by Sub-Contractors employed by the Contractor on the Main Contract Works from whom claims under similar provisions in the relevant sub-contracts have been agreed by the Contractor, Sub-Contractor and the Sub-

Contractor) may be deducted from any monies due or to become due to the Sub-Contractor or may be recoverable from the Sub-Contractor as a debt.

13.4 The provisions of *clause* 13 are without prejudice to any other rights or remedies which the Contractor or Sub-Contractor may possess.

21 Payment of sub-contractor

21.1 Interim payments and final payment shall be made to the Sub-Contractor in accordance with the provisions of *clause* 21.

21.2.1 Notwithstanding the requirement that the Architect shall issue Interim Certificates under *clause* 30 of the Main Contract Conditions, the Contractor shall, if so requested by the Sub-Contractor, make application to the Architect as to the matters referred to in *clauses 30.2.1*(4), *30.2.2*(5), *30.2.3*(3) of the Main Contract Conditions.

21.2.2 The Contractor shall include in or annex to any application under *clause 21.2.1* any written representations of the Sub-Contractor which the Sub-Contractor wishes the Architect to consider including those referred to in *clause 37.3.2*

21.2.3 The Sub-Contractor shall observe any relevant conditions in *clause* 30.3 of the Main Contract Conditions before the Architect is empowered to include the value of any off-site materials or goods in Interim Certificates.

21.3.1 (1) Within 17 days of the date of issue of an Interim Certificate (including the Interim Certificate referred to in *clause* 35.17 or *clause* 30.7 of the Main Contract Conditions) the Contractor shall notify to the Sub-Contractor the amount included in the amount stated as due therein in respect of the Sub-Contract Works and shall duly discharge his obligations to pay the Sub-Contractor such amount less only a cash discount of 2.5 per cent if discharge is effected within the said 17 days. Immediately upon discharge by the Contractor as aforesaid the Sub-Contractor shall supply the Contractor with written proof of such discharge so as to enable the Contractor to provide the Architect with the 'reasonable proof' referred to in *clause 35.3.3* of the Main Contract Conditions.

(2) Where the Employer has exercised any right under the Main Contract to deduct from monies due to the Contractor and such deduction is in respect of some act or default of the Sub-Contractor, his servants or agents the amount of such deduction may be deducted by the Contractor from any monies due or to become due under the Sub-Contract or may be recoverable by the Contractor from the Sub-Contractor as debt.

21.3.2 (1) The Contractor shall only be under an obligation duly to discharge any amount certified in an Interim Certificate issued under *clause* 35.17 of the Main Contract Conditions provided the Sub-Contractor shall have entered into Agreement NSC/2 including *clause* 5 of that Agreement unamended in any way and such Agreement is in full force and effect;

(2) Where the Contractor is under an obligation duly to discharge any amount certified in an Interim Certificate issued under *clause* 35.17 of the Main Contract Conditions the Sub-Contractor upon such discharge hereby agrees to indemnify the Contractor in respect of any omission, fault or defect in the Sub-Contract Works caused by the Sub-Contractor, his servants or agents for which the Contractor may at any time become liable to the Employer but subject

always to the terms of *clause 35.19.1* of the Main Contract Conditions.

21.4 Subject to any agreement between the Sub-Contractor, the Contractor and the Architect as to stage payments, the amount of an interim payment to the Sub-Contractor which is included in the amount stated as due in an Interim Certificate and to which the provisions of *clause* 35.13 of the Main Contract Conditions apply shall be the gross valuation as referred to in *clause* 21.4 less an amount equal to any amount which may be deducted and retained by the Employer as provided in *clause* 30.2 of the Main Contract Conditions (referred to in the Main Contract Conditions as 'the Retention') in respect of the Sub-Contract Works; and the total amount in respect of the Sub-Contract Works included in the total amount stated as due in Interim Certificates previously issued under the Main Contract Conditions.

The gross valuation shall be the total of the amounts referred to in *clauses 21.4.1* and *21.4.2* less the total amount referred to in *clause 21.4.3* as applied up to and including a date not more than seven days before the date of the Interim Certificate:

21.4.1 (1) the total value of the Sub-Contract work properly executed by the Sub-Contractor, including any work so executed to which *clause* 16.1 refers together with, where applicable, any adjustment of that value under *clause* 37;

(2) the total value of the materials and goods delivered to or adjacent to the Works for incorporation therein by the Sub-Contractor but not so incorporated provided that the value of such materials and goods shall only be included as and from such times as they are reasonably, properly and not prematurely so delivered and are adequately protected against weather and other casualties;

(3) the total value of any materials or goods other than those to which *clause 21.4.1*(2) refers where the Architect in the exercise of his discretion under *clause* 30.3 of the Main Contract Conditions has decided that such total value shall be included in the amount stated as due in an Interim Certificate.

21.4.2 (1) Any amount to be included in Interim Certificates in accordance with *clause* 3 as a result of payments made or costs incurred by the Sub-Contractor under *clause* 6 or 7 of the Main Contract Conditions as referred to in *clauses 5.1.1* and under *clause* 14.4.

(2) any amount ascertained as a result of the application of *clause* 13.1;

(3) any amount payable to the Sub-Contractor under *clauses* 35 or 36, whichever is applicable;

(4) an amount equal to one thirty-ninth of the amounts referred to in *clauses 21.4.2*(1), *21.4.2*(2) and *21.4.2*(3).

21.4.3 any amount allowable by the Sub-Contractor to the Contractor under *clause* 35 or 36, whichever is applicable together with an amount equal to one thirty-ninth of that amount.

21.5 The Retention which the Employer may deduct and retain as referred to in *clause* 30.2 of the Main Contract Conditions and *clause* 21.4 is such percentage of the total amount included under *clauses 21.4.1*(1) to *21.4.1*(3) in any Interim Certificate as arises from the operation of the rules set out in *clause* 30.4 of the Main Contract Conditions.

21.6 The Retention is subject to the rules set out in *clause* 30.5 of the Main Contract Conditions.

21.7 If the Sub-Contractor shall feel aggrieved by any amount certified by the

Architect or by his failure to certify, then subject to the Sub-Contractor giving to the Contractor such indemnity and security as the Contractor shall reasonably require, the Contractor shall allow the Sub-Contractor to use the Contractor's name and if necessary will join with the Sub-Contractor in arbitration proceedings at the instigation of the Sub-Contractor in respect of the said matters complained of by the Sub-Contractor.[1]

21.8.1 If:

(1) subject to *clause* 23 the Contractor shall fail to discharge his obligations to make any payment to the Sub-Contractor as hereinbefore provided; and

(2) the Employer has either

    (i) for any reason not operated the provisions of *clause 35.13.5* of the Main Contract Conditions; or

    (ii) has operated those provisions but for any reason has not paid the Sub-Contractor direct the whole amount which the Contractor has failed to discharge, within 35 days from the date of issue of the Interim Certificate in respect of which the Contractor has so failed to make proper discharge of his obligations in regard to payment of the Sub-Contractor,

then provided the Sub-Contractor shall have given 14 days' notice in writing to the Contractor and the Employer of his intention to suspend further execution of the Sub-Contract Works, the Sub-Contractor may (but without prejudice to any other right or remedy) suspend the further execution of the Sub-Contract Works until such discharge or until such direct payment is made whichever first occurs.

21.8.2 Such period of suspension shall not be deemed a delay for which the Sub-Contractor is liable under the Sub-Contract. The Contractor shall be liable to the Sub-Contractor for any loss, damage or expense caused to the Sub-Contractor by any suspension of the Sub-Contract Works under the provisions of *clause 21.8.1*. The right of the Sub-Contractor under *clause 21.8.1* shall not be exercised unreasonably or vexatiously.

21.9.1 The Contractor's interest in the Sub-Contractor's retention (as identified in the statement issued under *clause 30.5.2* of the Main Contract Conditions and referred to in *clause* 21.6) is fiduciary as trustee for the Sub-Contractor (but without obligation to invest) and if the Contractor attempts or purports to mortgage or otherwise charge such interest or his interest in the whole of the amount retained as aforesaid (otherwise than by floating charge if the Contractor is a limited company) the Contractor shall thereupon immediately set aside in a separate bank account and become a trustee for the Sub-Contractor of a sum equivalent to the Sub-Contractor's retention as identified in the aforesaid statement; provided that upon payment of the same to the Sub-Contractor the amount due to the Sub-Contractor upon final payment under the Sub-Contract shall be reduced accordingly by the amount so paid.

21.9.2 If any of the Sub-Contractor's retention is withheld by the Contractor after the period within which such retention should be discharged by the Contractor, the Contractor shall immediately upon the expiry of the aforesaid period place any such unpaid retention money in a separate trust account so identified as to make clear that the Contractor is the trustee for the Sub-Contractor of all such undischarged retention.

21.10.1 (1) Where *clause* 15.1 applied, either before or within a reasonable time after practical completion of the Sub-Contract Works the Sub-Contractor shall send to the Contractor or, if so instructed by him, to the Architect or the Quantity Surveyor, all documents necessary for the purpose of the adjustment of the Sub-Contract Sum.

(2) Subject to compliance by the Sub-Contractor with the requirements of *clause 21.10.1*(1) a statement of the final valuation of all Variations under *clause* 16 will be prepared by the Quantity Surveyor either within the Period of Final Measurement and Valuation stated in the Appendix to the Main Contract Conditions (Tender, Schedule 1, Item 10) or at such other time as is necessary to enable the provisions of *clause* 35.17 of the Main Contract Conditions to be operated and the Architect will send a copy to the Contractor and the Sub-Contractor.

21.10.2 The Sub-Contract Sum shall be adjusted as follows.

There shall be deducted:

(1) all provisional sums and the value of all work described as provisional included in the Sub-Contract Documents

(2) the amount of the valuation under *clause 16.3.2* of items omitted in accordance with a Variation required by an instruction of the Architect or subsequently sanctioned by him in writing together with the amount of any other work included in the Sub-Contract Documents as referred to in *clause 16.3.5* which is to be valued under *clause* 16.3;

(3) any amount allowed to the Contractor under *clause* 35, 36 or 37, whichever is applicable, together with an amount equal to one thirty-ninth of that amount.

(4) any other amount which is required by the Sub-Contract Documents to be deducted from the Sub-Contract Sum.

There shall be added:

(5) any amount paid or payable by the Contractor to the Sub-Contractor as a result of payments made or costs incurred by the Sub-Contractor under *clause* 6 or 7 of the Main Contract Conditions as referred to in *clause 5.1.1* and under *clause* 14.1;

(6) the amount of the valuation under *clause* 16.3 of any Variation including the valuation of other work, as referred to in *clause 16.3.5*, under *clause* 16.3 other than the amount of the valuation of an omission under *clause 16.3.2*;

(7) the amount of the valuation executed by, or the amount of any disbursements made by, the Sub-Contractor in accordance with the instructions of the Architect as to the expenditure of provisional sums included in the Sub-Contract Documents and of all work described as provisional included in the Sub-Contract Documents;

(8) any amount ascertained as a result of the application of *clause* 13.1;

(9) any amount paid or payable to the Sub-Contractor under *clause* 35, 36 or 37, whichever is applicable;

(10) any other amount which is required by the Sub-Contract to be added to the Sub-Contract Sum;

(11) an amount equal to one thirty-ninth of the amounts referred to in *clauses 21.10.1*(5), *21.10.2*(8) and *21.10.2*(9).

21.10.3 Before the Architect certifies final payment for the Sub-Contract Works under *clause* 35.17 or 30.7 of the Main Contract Conditions the Sub-Contractor shall be supplied through the Contractor with a copy of the computation of the Sub-Contract Sum adjusted in accordance with *clause 21.10.2*.

21.11.1 Where *clause* 15.2 applied, either before or within a reasonable time after practical completion of the Sub-Contract Works the Sub-Contractor shall send to the Contractor or, if so instructed by him, to the Architect or the Quantity Surveyor, all documents necessary for the purposes of computing the Ascertained Final Sub-Contract Sum.

21.11.2 (1) any amount paid or payable by the Contractor to the Sub-Contractor as a result of payments made or costs incurred by the Sub-Contractor under *clause* 6 or 7 of the Main Contract Conditions as referred to in *clause 5.1.1* and under *clause* 14.1;

   (2) the amount of the Valuation under *clause* 17;

   (3) any amount ascertained as a result of the application of *clause* 13.1;

   (4) any amount paid or payable to or allowed or allowable by the Sub-Contractor under *clause* 35, 36 or 37 whichever is applicable;

   (5) any other amount which is required to be included or taken into account in computing the Ascertained Final Sub-Contract Sum;

   (6) an amount equal to one thirty-ninth of the amounts referred to in *clauses 21.11.2*(1), *21.11.2*(3) and *21.11.2*(4).

21.11.3 The Sub-Contractor shall be supplied with a copy of the computation of the Ascertained Final Sub-Contract Sum before the Architect certifies final payment for the Sub-Contract Works under *clause* 35.17 or 30.7 of the Main Contract Conditions.

---

[1] *Lorne Stewart plc v William Sindall plc* (1986) 35 BLR 109: The predecessors of this clause, which provides for arbitration proceedings in which the sub-contractor would borrow the name of the main contractor, were considered at length and the following findings were made:

---

1 (*a*) There is a term to be implied into the sub-contract that 'Upon the sub-contractor exercising his right to use the main contractor's name in an arbitration against the employer, the main contractor will render to the sub-contractor such assistance and co-operation as may be necessary in order to enable the sub-contractor properly to conduct the said arbitration'.

   (*b*) Both main contractor and sub-contractor are parties to the arbitration and the arbitrator may order discovery against both of them.

2 (*a*) The amount of assistance and co-operation required depends upon the merits of each situation.

   (*b*) The sub-contractor is entitled to discovery against the main contractor even of documents that would have been privileged in the main contract arbitration. As against the sub-contractor, the employer is entitled to discovery of documents from the sub-contractor even if they would be privileged in the sub-contract arbitration.

3 The court has jurisdiction to intervene at its discretion to enforce these principles.

4 All documents properly discoverable by the main contractor in the sub-contract arbitration may properly be used by the sub-contractor in the name borrowing arbitration and vice versa.

Re Arthur Sanders (1981) 17 BLR 125: This clause, which provides for the main contractor to hold retention for the sub-contractor, takes effect as an assignment by the main contractor of a due proportion of the retention moneys held under the main contract.

22 Benefits under main contract

The Contractor will so far as he lawfully can at the request and cost, if any, of the Sub-Contractor obtain for him any rights or benefits of the Main Contract so far as the same are applicable to the Sub-Contract Works but not further or otherwise.

23 Contractor's right to set-off

23.1 The Contractor shall be entitled to deduct from any money (including any Sub-Contractor's retention notwithstanding the fiduciary obligation of the Contractor under *clause 21.9.1*) otherwise due under the Sub-Contract any amount agreed by the Sub-Contractor as due to the Contractor, or finally awarded in arbitration or litigation in favour of the Contractor, and which arises out of or under the Sub-Contract.

23.2 The Contractor shall be entitled to set off against any money (including any Sub-Contractor's retention, notwithstanding the fiduciary obligation of the Contractor under *clause 21.9.1*) otherwise due under the Sub-Contract the amount of any claim for loss and/or expense which has actually been incurred by the Contractor by reason of any breach of, or failure to observe the provisions of, the Sub-Contract by the Sub-Contractor provided[1]:

23.2.1 that no set-off relating to any delay in completion shall be made unless, in accordance with *clause* 12, the certificate of the Architect referred to in *clause* 12.2 has been issued to the Contractor with a duplicate copy to the Sub-Contractor:

23.2.2 the amount of such set-off has been quantified in detail and with reasonable accuracy by the Contractor[2]:

23.2.3 the Contractor has given to the Sub-Contractor notice in writing specifying his intention to set off the amount quantified in accordance with *clause 23.2.2* and the grounds on which such set-off is claimed to be made. Such notice shall be given not less than 20 days before the money from which the amount or part thereof is to be set off becomes due and payable to the Sub-Contractor; provided that such written notice shall not be binding in so far as the Contractor may amend it in preparing his pleadings for any arbitration pursuant to the notice of arbitration referred to in *clause 24.1.1(1)*.

23.3 Any amount set off under the provisions of *clause* 23.2 is without prejudice to the rights of the Contractor or Sub-Contractor in any subsequent negotiations, arbitration proceedings or litigation to seek to vary the amount claimed and set-off by the Contractor under *clause* 23.2.

23.4 The rights of the parties to the Sub-Contract in respect of set-off are fully set out in Sub-Contract NSC/4 and no other rights whatsoever shall be implied as terms of the Sub-Contract relating to set-off.[3]

---

[1] *Chatbrown Ltd v Alfred McAlpine Construction (Southern) Ltd* (1986) 35 BLR 44: this clause provides for rights of set-off for the contractor for loss and/or expense which has 'actually been incurred' by the main contractor. Loss and/or expense that is merely anticipated does not count.

[2] *Pillar PG Limited v DJ Higgins Construction Ltd* (1986) 34 BLR 43: The requirement that the main contractor must have quantified his set-off in detail and with reasonable accuracy applies to all species of set-off and not merely set-off for delay.

[3] *Tubeworkers v Tilbury Construction Ltd* (1985) 30 BLR 67: If the main contractor is not entitled to set-off under the terms of *clause* 23 then neither is he entitled to a stay of execution.

24 Contractor's claims not agreed by the sub-contractor — appointment of adjudicator

24.1.1 If the Sub-Contractor, at the date of the written notice of the Contractor issued under *clause 23.2.3*, disagrees the amount (or any part therof) specified in that notice which the Contractor intends to set off, the Sub-Contractor may, within 14 days of receipt by him of such notice, send to the Contractor by registered post or recorded delivery a written statement setting out the reasons for such disagreement and particulars of any counterclaim against the Contractor arising out of the Sub-Contract to which the Sub-Contractor considers he is entitled, provided always that he shall have quantified such counterclaim in detail and with reasonable accuracy (which statement and counterclaim if any, shall not however be binding insofar as the Sub-Contractor may amend it in preparing his pleadings for any arbitration pursuant to the notice of arbitration referred to in *clause 24.1.1*(1) and shall at the same time:

    (1) give notice of arbitration to the Contractor; and

    (2) request action by the Adjudicator in accordance with the right given in *clause 24.1.2* (and immediately inform the Contractor of such request) and send to the Adjudicator by registered post or recorded delivery a copy of the aforesaid statement and the written notice of the Contractor to which that statement relates and the aforesaid counterclaim (if any).

24.1.2 Subject to the provisions of *clause* 24 and of *clauses* 21.3 and 23 the Sub-Contractor shall be entitled to request the Adjudicator named in the Appendix, part 6 to act as the Adjudicator to decide those matters referable to the Adjudicator under the provisions of *clause* 24. In the event of the above-named being unable or unwilling to act as the Adjudicator a person appointed by the above named shall be the Adjudicator in his place. Provided that no person shall act as the Adjudicator who has any interest in the Sub-Contract or the Main Contract of which the Sub-Contract is part or in other contracts or sub-contracts in which the Contractor or the Sub-Contractor is engaged unless the Contractor, Sub-Contractor and the Adjudicator so interested otherwise agree in writing within a reasonable time of the Adjudicator's interest becoming apparent.

24.2 Upon receipt of the aforesaid statement the Contractor may within 14 days from the date of such receipt send to the Adjudicator by registered post or recorded delivery a written statement with a copy of the Sub-Contractor setting out brief particulars of his defence to any counterclaim by the Sub-Contractor.

24.3.1 Within seven days of any written statement by the Contractor under *clause* 24.2 or on the expiry of the time limit to the Contractor referred to in *clause* 24.2 whichever is the earlier, the Adjudicator, without requiring any further statements than those submitted to him under *clause* 24.1 and where relevant *clause* 24.2 (save only such further written statements as may appear to the Adjudicator to be necessary to clarify or explain any ambiguity in the written statements of either the Contractor or Sub-Contractor in person, shall, subject to *clause 24.3.2*, in his absolute discretion and, without giving reasons, decide, in respect of the amount notified by the Contractor under *clause 23.2.3*, whether the whole or any apart of such amount shall be dealt with as follows:

24.3.1 (1) shall be retained by the Contractor, or;

    (2) shall, pending arbitration, be deposited by the Contractor for security with the Trustee-Stakeholder named in the Tender, Schedule 2, Item 6; or

    (3) shall be paid by the Contractor to the Sub-Contractor; or

    (4) any combination of the courses of action set out in *clauses 24.3.1*(1), *24.3.1*(2) and *24.3.1*(3).

The Adjudicator's decision shall be binding upon the Contractor and the Sub-Contractor until the matters upon which he has give his decision have been settled by agreement or determined by an Arbitrator or the court.

24.3.2 The Adjudicator shall reach such decision under *clause 24.3.1* as he considers to be fair, reasonable and necessary in all the circumstances of the dispute as set out in the statements referred to in *clauses* 24.1 to 24.3, and such decision shall deal with the whole amount set off by the Contractor under *clause* 23.2.

24.3.3 The Adjudicator shall immediately notify in writing the Contractor and the Sub-Contractor of his decision under *clause 24.3.1*.

24.4.1 Where any decision of the Adjudicator notified under *clause* 24.3.3 requires the Contractor to deposit an amount with the Trustee-Stakeholder, the Contractor shall thereupon pay such amount to the Trustee-Stakeholder to hold upon the terms hereinafter expressed provided that the Contractor shall not be obliged to pay a sum greater than the amount due from the Contractor under *clause* 21.3 in respect of which the Contractor has exercised the right of set-off referred to in *clause* 23.2.

24.4.2 Where any decision of the Adjudicator notified under *clause* 24.3.3 requires the Contractor to pay an amount to the Sub-Contractor, such amount shall be paid by the Contractor immediately upon receipt of the decision of the Adjudicator but subject to the same proviso as set out in *clause* 24.4.1.

24.5.1 The Trustee-Stakeholder shall hold any sum received under the provisions of *clauses* 24.3 and 24.4 in trust for the Contractor and Sub-Contractor until such time as:

(1) the Arbitrator appointed pursuant to the notice of arbitration given by the Sub-Contractor under *clause 24.1.1*(1); or

(2) the Contractor and Sub-Contractor in a joint letter signed by each of them or on their behalf,

shall otherwise direct and shall, in either of the above cases, forthwith dispose of the said sums as may be directed by the Arbitrator, or failing any direction by the Arbitrator, as the Contractor and Sub-Contractor shall jointly determine. The Trustee-Stakeholder shall deposit the sum received in a deposit account in the name of the Trustee-Stakeholder but shall add the interest to the sum deposited. The Trustee-Stakeholder shall be entitled to deduct his reasonable and proper charges from the sum deposited (including any interest added thereto). The Sub-Contractor shall notify the Trustee-Stakeholder of the name and address of the Adjudicator and Arbitrator referred to in *clause* 24.

24.5.2 Where the Trustee-Stakeholder is a deposit-taking Bank then sums so received by it under the provisions of *clauses* 24.3 and 24.4 may, notwithstanding the trust imposed, be held by the Trustee-Stakeholder as an ordinary bank deposit to the credit of an account of the Bank as a Trustee-Stakeholder re the Contractor and Sub-Contractor referred to herein; and in respect of such deposit the Trustee-Stakeholder shall pay such usual interest which shall accrue to and form part of the deposit subject to the right of the Trustee-Stakeholder to deduct its reasonable and proper charges and any tax in respect of such interest from the sum deposited.

24.6 The Arbitrator appointed pursuant to the notice of arbitration given under *clause 24.1.1*(1) may in his absolute discretion at any time before his final award on the application of either party vary or cancel the decision of the Adjudicator given under *clause* 24.3 if it appears just and reasonable to him so to do.

24.7 Any action taken by the Contractor under *clause* 23.2 and by the Sub-

Contractor in respect of any counterclaim under *clause 24.1.1* is without prejudice to similar action by the Contractor or Sub-Contractor as the case may be if and when further sums become due to the Sub-Contractor.

24.8 The fee of the Adjudicator shall be paid by the Sub-Contractor but the Arbitrator appointed pursuant to the notice of arbitration under *clause 24.1.1*(1) shall in his final award settle the responsibility of the Contractor or Sub-Contractor or both for payment of the fee or any part thereof and where relevant for the charges of the Trustee-Stakeholder or any part thereof.

29 Determination of the employment of the sub-contractor by the contractor

29.1 Without prejudice to any other rights or remedies which the Contractor may possess, if the Sub-Contractor shall make default in any one or more of the following respects that is to say:

29.1.1 if without reasonable cause he wholly suspends the carrying out of the Sub-Contract Works before completion thereof; or

29.1.2 if without reasonable cause he fails to proceed with the Sub-Contract Works in the manner provided in *clause* 11.1; or

29.1.3 if he refuses or persistently neglects after notice in writing from the Contractor to remove defective work or improper materials or goods and by such refusal or neglect the Works are materially affected, or wrongfully fails to rectify defects, shrinkages or other faults in the Sub-Contract Works, which rectification is in accordance with his obligations under the Sub-Contract;

29.1.4 if he fails to comply with the provisions of either *clause* 26 or *clause* 32; then the Contractor shall so inform the Architect and send to the Architect any written observation of the Sub-Contractor in regard to the default or defaults of which the Contractor is informing the Architect. If so instructed by the Architect under *clause 35.24.4*(1) of the Main Contract Conditions the Contractor shall issue a notice to the Sub-Contractor by registered post or recorded delivery specifying the default (and send a copy thereof by registered post or recorded delivery to the Architect). If the Sub-Contractor shall either continue such default for 14 days after receipt of such notice or shall at any time thereafter repeat such default (whether previously repeated or not), then the Contractor may (but subject where relevant to the further instruction of the Architect to which *clause 35.24.4*(1) of the Main Contract Conditions refers) within 10 days after such continuance or repetition by notice by registered post or recorded delivery forthwith determine the employment of the Sub-Contractor under the Sub-Contract; provided that such notice shall not be given unreasonably or vexatiously.

29.2 In the event of the Sub-Contractor becoming bankrupt or making a composition or arrangement with his creditors or having a winding up order made or (other than for the purposes of amalgamation or reconstruction) having a resolution for voluntary winding up passed, or having a provisional liquidator receiver or manager of his business or undertaking duly appointed, or having possession taken by or on behalf of the holders of any debentures secured by a floating charge, of any property comprised in or subject to the floating charge, the employment of the Sub-Contractor under the Sub-Contract shall forthwith automatically be determined. Such determination shall be without prejudice to any other rights or remedies of the Contractor.

29.3 In the event of the employment of the Sub-Contractor under the Sub-Contract being determined under *clause* 29.1 or 29.2 the following shall be the respective rights and duties of the Contractor and the Sub-Contractor;

29.3.1 when the Employer through the Architect nominates a person to carry out and complete the Sub-Contract Works and use all temporary buildings, plant, tools, equipment, goods and materials intended for, delivered to and placed on or adjacent to the Works, and may purchase all materials and goods necessary for the carrying out and completion of the Sub-Contract Works;

29.3.2 (1) except where the determination occurs by reason of the bankruptcy of the Sub-Contractor or of him having a winding up order made or (other than for the purposes of amalgamation or reconstruction) a resolution for voluntary winding up passed, the Sub-Contractor shall if so required by the Employer or by the Architect on behalf of the Employer and with the consent of the Contractor within 14 days of the date of determination, assign to the Contractor without payment the benefit of any agreement for the supply of materials or goods and/or for the execution of any work for the purposes of the Sub-Contract but on the terms that the supplier or sub-sub-contractor shall be entitled to make any reasonable objection to any further assignment thereof to the Contractor;

(2) unless the exception to the operation of *clause 39.3.2* applies the Contractor, if so directed by the Architect, shall pay any supplier or sub-sub-contractor for any materials or goods delivered or works executed for the purposes of the Sub-Contract (whether before or after the determination) insofar as the price thereof has not already been paid by the Sub-Contractor;

29.3.3 the Sub-Contractor shall as and when required by a direction of the Contractor or by an instruction of the Architect so to do (but not before) remove from the Works any temporary buildings, plant, tools, equipment, goods and materials belonging to or hired by him. If within a reasonable time after any such requirement has been made the Sub-Contractor has not complied therewith, then the Contractor may (but without being responsible for any loss or damage) remove and sell any such property of the Sub-Contractor holding the proceeds less all costs incurred to the credit of the Sub-Contractor.

29.4 The Sub-Contractor shall allow or pay to the Contractor in the manner hereinafter appearing the amount of any direct loss and/or damage caused to the Contractor by the determination. Until after completion of the Sub-Contract Works under *clause 29.3.1* the Contractor shall not be bound by any provision of the Sub-Contract to make any further payment to the Sub-Contractor. Upon such completion the Sub-Contractor may apply to the Contractor who shall pass such application to the Architect who shall ascertain or instruct the Quantity Surveyor to ascertain the amount of expenses properly incurred by the Employer and the amount of direct loss and/or damage caused to the Employer by the determination, and shall issue an Interim Certificate certifying the value of any work executed or goods and materials supplied by the Sub-Contractor to the extent that their value has not been included in previous Interim Certificates; in paying that Certificate the Employer may deduct the amount of the expenses and direct loss and/or damage of the Employer as aforesaid. The Contractor in discharging his obligation to pay the Sub-Contractor such amount may deduct therefrom a cash discount of 2.5 per cent and, without prejudice to any other rights of the Contractor, the amount of any direct loss and/or damage caused to the Contractor by the determination.

30 Determination of employment under the sub-contract by the sub-contractor

30.1 Without prejudice to any other rights or remedies which the Sub-Contractor may possess if the Contractor shall make default (for which default a remedy under any other provisions of the Sub-Contract would not adequately recompense the Sub-Contractor) in any of the following respects:

30.1.1 (1) if without reasonable cause he wholly suspends the Main Contract Works before completion;

(2) if without reasonable cause he fails to proceed with the Main Contract Works so that the reasonable progress of the Sub-Contract Works is seriously affected;

then the Sub-Contractor may issue to the Contractor a notice by registered post or recorded delivery (a copy of which must be sent at the same time to the Architect by registered post or recorded delivery) specifying the default. If the Contractor shall continue such default for 14 days after receipt of such notice or if the Contractor shall at any time thereafter repeat such default (whether previously repeated or not) the Sub-Contractor may thereupon by notice by registered post or recorded delivery determine the employment of the Sub-Contractor; provided that such notice shall not be given unreasonably or vexatiously.

30.2 Upon such determination, then without prejudice to the accrued rights or remedies of either party or to any liability of the classes mentioned in *clause* 6 which may accrue before the Sub-Contractor shall have removed his temporary buildings, plant, tools, equipment, goods or materials or by reason of his so removing the same, the respective rights and duties of the Sub-Contractor and Contractor shall be as follows:

30.2.1 the Sub-Contractor shall with all reasonable dispatch and in such manner and with such precautions as will prevent injury, death or damage of the classes in respect of which he is liable to indemnify the Contractor under *clause* 6 remove from the site all his temporary buildings, plant, tools equipment, goods or materials subject to the provisions of *clause 30.2.2*(4);

30.2.2 after taking into account amounts previously paid under the Sub-Contract the Sub-Contractor shall be paid by the Contractor;

(1) the total value of work completed at the date of determination, such value to be ascertained in accordance with *clause* 21;

(2) the total value of work begun and executed but not completed at the date of determination, such value to be ascertained either under *clause* 16 as if it were a Valuation of a Variation (where *clause* 15.1 applies) or under *clause* 17 (where clause 15.2 applies);

(3) any sum ascertained in respect of direct loss and/or expense under *clause* 13.1 (whether ascertained before or after the date of determination);

(4) the cost of materials or goods properly ordered for the Sub-Contract Works (but not incorporated therein) for which the Sub-Contractor shall have paid or is legally bound to accept delivery and on such payment by the Contractor any materials or goods so paid for shall become the property of the Contractor;

(5) the reasonable cost of removal under *clause 30.2.1*;

(6) any direct loss and/or expense caused to the Sub-Contractor by the determination.

31 Determination of the main contractor's employment under the main contract

31.1 If the employment of the Contractor is determined under *clause* 27 of the Main Contract Conditions, then the employment of the Sub-Contractor under the Sub-Contract shall thereupon also determine and the provisions of *clause* 30.2 shall thereafter apply.

31.2.1 If the employment of the Contractor is determined under *clause* 28 of the Main Contract Conditions then the employment of the Sub-Contractor under the Sub-Contract shall thereupon also determine. The entitlement of the Sub-Contractor to payment shall be the proportion fairly and reasonably attributable to the Sub-Contract Works of the amounts paid by the Employer under *clause* 28.2.2(1) to (5) of the Main Contract Conditions inclusive together with any amounts paid in respect of the Sub-Contractor under *clause* 28.2.2(6) of the Main Contract Conditions provided the Sub-Contractor shall have supplied to the Contractor all evidence reasonably necessary to establish the direct loss and/or damage caused to the Sub-Contractor by the determination as referred to in *clause* 28.2.2(6) of the Main Contract Conditions.

31.2.2 Nothing in *clause* 31.2 shall affect the entitlement of the Sub-Contractor to the proper operation of *clause* 21 in respect of the amount, included in the amount stated as due therein, in respect of the Sub-Contract Works in an Interim Certificate of the Architect whose date of issue was prior to the date of determination of the employment of the Contractor under *clause* 28 of the Main Contract Conditions.

Appendix C

The ORSA Protocol

[The ORSA Protocol was written by ORSA's Information Technology Sub-committee, a group of lawyers and IT specialists.]

OFFICIAL REFEREES SOLICITORS ASSOCIATION

The Official Referees Solicitors Association (ORSA) was formed in September, 1990 to promote the interests of solicitors and their clients conducting business in the Official Referees' Courts and related domestic and international arbitration. In 1991 ORSA formed an Information Technology Sub-Committee to promote the use of technology in litigation and arbitration.

The sub-committee identified the lack of a dialogue between solicitors firms at an early stage of litigation or arbitration as the greatest barrier to the efficient use of technology. Accordingly, the sub-committee has prepared this Protocol. It is of the opinion that such a protocol is best tested in practice and revised through experience. Accordingly, it invites criticism and suggestions which will be considered for incorporation in subsequent versions. These should be addressed to me at Masons, 30 Aylesbury Street, London EC1R 0ER. Although the Protocol uses expressions consistent with litigation in the Official Referees' Courts, it is equally applicable to arbitration.

ORSA and its members take no responsibility for loss or damage caused to any user of this Protocol.

John Bishop
Chairman, ORSA

THE ORSA PROTOCOL
(VERSION 1.0)

The purpose of The ORSA Protocol is to facilitate and encourage the exchange of information amongst users of the Official Referees' Courts through the use of information technology (IT).

Central to the Protocol is the Questionnaire, reproduced here, which establishes the framework around which an agreement may be reached on appropriate standards for the interchange of information. There are a number of opportunities to use IT for the exchange of information, and the Questionnaire and the notes here cover these areas and suggest standard data and media formats. The potential areas are laid out below.

PLEADINGS

These would normally be exchanged as word processing (WP) files. It is useful to have these in electronic form since they can then easily be searched for particular words or phrases.

SCOTT SCHEDULES

These are also normally exchanged as WP files, although some firms use spreadsheets and still others use database systems. Given suitable co-operation, comments can be added to the relevant sections and the schedules returned, thus avoiding tiresome re-keying of data.

LISTS OF DOCUMENTS

These are best kept and exchanged as databases rather than WP files, since this enables searching and sorting of the lists. ORSA recommends the use of standard document characteristics (see 'Database Formats' in the Technical Notes).

TRANSCRIPTS

Electronic versions of trial (or arbitration) transcripts are now readily available from court reporters. These can be extremely valuable if exchanged as WP files since they can then be searched quickly for words and phrases.

LITIGATION SUPPORT

A number of systems are used to support the litigation process, although in this case the focus is on document management systems. These may take the form of structured databases (similar to Lists of Documents), full text retrieval systems (which contain, in addition to the indexed information, the full text of the documents) and imaging systems (which contain, in addition to the index information or the full text, an image or electronic photograph of the document). There are fewer established standards in this area, and close co-operation between parties will be required to achieve a successful exchange of information.

OTHER DOCUMENTS

This covers items such as witness statements or experts' reports, which should, in general, be exchanged as WP files.

How To Use
The ORSA Protocol

The purpose of using the ORSA Protocol is for parties to exchange information about their IT capabilities and systems as easily as possible. Before reading the notes for completing the Questionnaire and the Technical Notes presented in this document, users of the ORSA Protocol may find it helpful to consider the organisational and management issues laid out below.

Responsibilities

In cases involving only two parties, each party will be responsible to the other for the observation of the guidelines of this Protocol. If further parties are joined to any litigation after the initial exchange, it should be the responsibility of the solicitor whose client has joined a further party to inform him of the use of The ORSA Protocol and of any agreements as to the use of IT previously reached.

When litigation support techniques are being used, parties should consider the use of an independent third party to co-ordinate IT activities.

Initiation

Use of The ORSA Protocol should take place as soon as possible after the start of proceedings, which will give maximum benefit to all parties. An initiating party's solicitors should suggest use of The ORSA Protocol and the exchange of Questionnaires. Although any party may decide to volunteer a completed Questionnaire to any other, it is envisaged that the necessary spirit of co-operation would be engendered by an agreement between all parties to exchange Questionnaires. This will enable all parties to identify the most efficient formats to be used for the various types of information. Brief guidance notes are provided to aid completion, but it is essential that the parties' IT managers, or equivalent, be involved. The ideal scenario is that, following the exchange of Questionnaires, a meeting is held between solicitors and IT managers or advisers from all parties, so that queries and difficulties can be resolved expeditiously and a dialogue commenced as to how IT might be used most effectively in the case in question.

A fuller explanation of the questions and the reasons for their inclusion is given in the Technical Notes.

Operational Issues

Each party should agree to:

■ make available a contact person or persons to resolve issues arising from the use of The ORSA Protocol;

■ keep clear logs of all information sent and received and make such logs available to other parties on reasonable request;

■ make back-ups of all data received to protect against data loss or corruption;

■ check outgoing media for computer virus infection, data loss or corruption;

■ be wholly responsible for the detection of computer viruses on incoming media; and

■ provide accurate and comprehensive documentation to receiving parties covering media format and contents (see 'Documentation' in the Technical Notes).

Costs

Parties should attempt wherever possible to avoid duplication of data conversion costs. This applies particularly to litigation support systems and the production of images, indexes and full text, as well as common court reporters and the costs of machine readable versions of transcripts. If one party agrees to input all data relevant to a particular case, and another party enjoys the use of such data, a charge must be agreed between the parties and the clients.

There is uncertainty over the question of the recoverability of expenses incurred in using IT in litigation. As the Taxation issues become clearer, this document will be revised.

Legal Issues

It is envisaged that the parties will have no greater or lesser responsibility than if The ORSA Protocol and IT were not being used. However, parties should clarify in each case issues relating to:

■ data error and/or omission and its consequences;

■ computer viruses and consequential loss of information, if any;

■ copyright in material held in electronic form; and

■ the Data Protection Act 1984.

Notes For Completion Of Questionnaire

*T*he following notes offer guidance to assist with the completion of the Questionnaire printed opposite. Fuller explanations of some of the more technical terms are given in the Technical Notes overleaf.

Standard data formats are recommended for the exchange of information. Where there are several possibilities, a recommendation is made to use a particular format which is based upon prevailing standards within the legal sector and the personal computer industry.

If conversion from or to recommended formats is required, this is the responsibility of the sender or recipient as appropriate. If parties are using a common format not mentioned here, that format should be used to save unnecessary conversion.

Q6

Pleadings should be exchanged in WP format, preferably WordPerfect.

Q8

Lists of Documents should be exchanged in database format in preference to WP format. If possible, dBASE format should be used and, failing this, CSV.

Q9

Transcripts should be transferred in WP format, preferably WordPerfect.

Q10

Litigation Support covers a variety of systems and formats and no specific recommendations are made. Further details are given in the Technical Notes overleaf, but communication between parties is essential to identify possibilities for the exchange of information.

Q11

Other documents (for example, experts reports, witness statements, requests for further and better particulars) should be exchanged in WP format, preferably WordPerfect.

Q12

The use of 3.5", 720kb diskettes is recommended. Where both parties have the capability to read and write 3.5" 1.44 mb diskettes, these may also be used. Given that 5.25" diskettes are less robust, these should only be used where essential.

Multiple disks should be used where there is a large quantity of information. Where a single file spans more than one disk, MS-DOS Backup should be used and the version of DOS and the source directory clearly indicated.

Q13

LIX is preferred as the point-to-point communications system.

Q14

If LIX is not available but both parties have modem facilities and data communication software, file transfer may be possible, as may connection into existing electronic mail systems.

ORSA Information Technology Questionnaire

The purpose of this Questionnaire is to help to establish the best common formats amongst the parties.

Brief guidance notes are given opposite to assist with the completion of this Questionnaire. For a fuller description of the underlying issues please refer to the Technical Notes.

1 Name of your firm

2 Name of your client

3 Description of matter

4 Partner in charge

5 IT contact in your firm

Indicate with ticks in the following table which formats you are able to accept or supply for the functional areas. In the case of 'Other WP' and 'Spreadsheet' indicate your preferred system.

FUNCTIONAL AREA	Word Perfect 5.1	Word Perfect 5.0	Word Perfect 4.2	ASCII	Other WP	Spread sheet	SYLK	DIF	CSV	dBASE III	dBASE IV	TIFF Files
6 Pleadings												
7 Scott Schedules												
8 Lists of Documents												
9 Transcripts												
10 Litigation Support												
11 Other Documents												

Indicate with ticks in the following boxes which media formats you are able to accept or supply.

12 Media Formats   MS-DOS ☐   Size of Disk   5.25 ☐   3.5 ☐

    Optical Disk ☐   Capacity of Disk   360kb ☐   1.2mb ☐

                                              720kb ☐   1.44mb ☐

13 Indicate your LIX Point Number (if applicable)

14 Indicate your modem type and data communications package (if applicable)

TECHNICAL
NOTES

*T*hese Technical Notes provide guidance
in establishing the most efficient methods
for the exchange of information between
parties using the Official Referees' Courts.

The Notes define as far as is currently
thought appropriate by a number of users
of the Official Referees' Courts the format
of the data to be exchanged and the media
to be used. The notes are technical in
nature and are intended for the Information Technology manager within a law
firm or equivalent person. The following
guiding principles have been applied
throughout:

■ IBM-compatible personal computer
(PC) formats have been used wherever
possible, since these facilities are most
likely to be available.

■ No particular software packages are
recommended, but reference is made to
prevalent packages where appropriate.

■ Extensive reference is made to data
formats which are themselves connected with particular programs.
However, many other programs are
able to use data in these formats, and,
for the avoidance of doubt, it is the
formats and not the programs to which
these references are made. A specific
example is 'dBASE III format', which is
data produced by the dBASE III pro-
gram.

■ The most common and readily available media formats have been recommended. However, this is an area
where the highest common format
should be used to avoid unnecessarily
large quantities of media.

MEDIA

Ideally, MS-DOS format diskettes should be used. 3.5"
diskettes may be of either 720kb or 1.44 mb capacity.
To avoid data errors when writing to 5.25" diskettes
from 1.2mb drives, these diskettes should be of 360kb
capacity. For single files spanning more than the
capacity of a single disk, the MS-DOS Backup utility
should be used. The documentation (see below), should
clearly specify the version of MS-DOS used and the
source directories in order to facilitate restoration via the
MS-DOS Restore utility. Note that files backed up
cannot normally be restored by a version of Restore
lower than that of Backup, and that versions of Backup
and Restore are locked into their particular version of
MS-DOS.

Tape may be used where both parties are satisfied that
this is practical and in any event a test should be conducted to ensure compatibility. Tape streamer formats
are proprietary and therefore rarely compatible and such
exchange is only likely to be practical when all parties
are using the same system. Optical disk may be used for
large volumes of data, again providing both parties are
satisfied with the compatibility. Most modern drives
will read and write all common formats without problems.

DATA COMMUNICATIONS

For point-to-point transfer, either LIX or another package (such as Crosstalk) may be used. Again, the parties
must be satisfied that reliable transfer is practical and
error-free. Value Added Networks (VANs) such as the
IBM service may be appropriate, or access by one party
to another's in-house EMAIL system. Standards in this
area are lacking, and each case needs to be examined
individually.

DOCUMENT FORMATS

Given the industry dominance of WordPerfect, emphasis
is placed on the use of these formats whenever possible,
since this will also result in the capability to transfer
documents with the courts. If any party is using
WordPerfect, this should be the preferred format and the
other parties are responsible for the conversion of their
data into this format. Conversion systems are well-
known for causing loss of formatting or layout information, and to avoid this documents should be as simple as
possible consistent with relaying the relevant information effectively. The use of advanced features such as
automatic paragraph numbering is, generally, to be
discouraged in documents to be exchanged; a plain copy
is preferable. The exception to this guideline is when all

parties are using another common WP package, under which circumstances there is no benefit in converting to WordPerfect format.

At worst, documents, or more accurately text, can be exchanged in ASCII format, although this will involve the loss of all formatting information. If conversion is needed, it is the responsibility of each party to provide adequate conversion facilities, and a test should be conducted to establish the accuracy of the process.

DATABASE FORMATS

Structured information, for example, lists of documents, should be exchanged in database format rather than WP format, which will enable easier manipulation of the data. An outline structure is defined below:

NAME	LABEL	SIZE (CHARACTERS)	
Prefix	PX	2	Dn or Pn
Document number	DN	8	
Sender	SN	30	
Recipient	RC	30	
Document type	DT	20	
Original/Copy	OC	1	'O' or 'C'
Date	DA	10	

The potential uses for such a list are varied, and it is unlikely that all parties will be using the same data management package. The *de facto* PC standards of Comma Separated Value (CSV) or dBASE (III or IV as appropriate) should therefore be used if direct exchange is not possible. Most packages are capable of importing and exporting this format. (Note: parties using bespoke systems should therefore take care to specify as a requirement the capability to import and export in these formats.)

Dates present particular problems in that there is no single standard for their representation, although most packages will read and write a variety of formats. The 10 characters allocated should support any of these formats, and a test should again be conducted between parties to ensure compatibility of dates. Lists of senders, recipients and document types should be agreed prior to data inputting in order to normalise these descriptions as far as possible so that all parties refer to particular bodies in the same way. Each party will be responsible for notifying the others as to additions or amendments to these lists.

FULL TEXT FORMATS

If the full text of documents is to be exchanged, this will generally not be possible via the CSV format since the text will inevitably contain commas and quotation marks which may invalidate the protocol. Additionally, there are many full text packages but no standard or even common format has appeared. Exchange of full text should therefore be in ASCII. There are several possible scenarios. For instance, a separate file for each document may be preferred, linked to the list of documents via a unique document number. The integration of these files with the relevant application would be the responsibility of the receiving party. In the absence of industry or *de facto* standards, all parties should work together to develop and test a viable system.

IMAGE FORMATS

If images are to be exchanged, the Tagged Image Format File (TIFF) should be used. There are several flavours of TIFF and parties should ensure a common standard is being used which is compatible with all target systems. Again, there are no obvious standards for linking images into either standard or full text databases, although a scenario similar to that for full text is easily envisaged, with a TIFF file for each document linked via the document number. Again, all parties should work together to develop and test a viable system.

DOCUMENTATION

Each and every exchange of information should be accompanied by comprehensive documentation. Such documentation should be in hard copy and conform to the guidelines below.

■ All diskettes, tapes and optical disks should be clearly labelled with sender, recipient, and format. If MS-DOS Backup has been used, this should be indicated together with the version of MS-DOS. The hard copy should also contain a complete directory listing.

■ Each document contained on the media should be described by reference to its file name in the directory listing. Indications of content, format (including version number if appropriate) and relevant date should be given.

■ Databases should be described by reference to the directory listing. Format (including version number if appropriate) should be indicated. The structure should adhere to these standards. If not, any departures should be clearly indicated. The agreed date format (in the current absence of a single standard) should be shown.

■ Full text and image files should be appropriately described dependent upon the format(s) used and the sending and target systems, and as agreed between the parties.

Appendix D

Limitation Acts questionnaire

Introduction

This questionnaire is designed as a guide through the ungainly legislative code that is contained in the Limitation Act 1980 and the Latent Damage Act 1986. There are a couple of points which may be usefully made about it.

First, it makes no reference to the 'doomed from the start' doctrine. The minimal possibility that the doctrine might apply in the real world does not justify consideration here of the vast amount of judicial and other commentary that the doctrine has attracted.

Secondly, the questionnaire does not seek to take into account any special circumstances that might give rise to the defendant being estopped from pleading a limitation defence. By their very nature estoppel points tend to be peculiar to their facts.

See Chapter 17 as to when an action is brought. In short, where a defendant is named in the original writ the action is brought against him at the time the writ is issued. If he is added in by amendment later the action is brought against him when the proceedings are served on him. Arbitration proceedings are brought when the notice to concur is served.

Questionnaire

(1) Has the defendant been sued as a third party? If yes, go to (2). If no, go to (3).

(2) Did more than two years elapse between the date of judgment or settlement in the main action and the date of joinder of the third party (Law Reform (Married Women and Joint Tortfeasors) Act 1935 and Civil Liability (Contribution) Act 1978)? If yes, go to (3). If no, go to (43).

(3) Is there a direct contractual relationship between the plaintiff and the defendant? If yes, go to (4). If no, go to (24).

(4) Is the defendant under a contractual obligation to indemnify the plaintiff in respect of the loss in question? If yes, go to (5). If no, go to 15).

(5) Has the plaintiff's liability yet been established? If yes, go to (6). If no, go to (43).

(6) Is the contract under seal? If yes, go to (7). If no, go to (11).

(7) Was the liability of the plaintiff that is the subject of the indemnity established within 12 years before the date of the bringing of the action? If yes, go to (43). If no, go to (8).

(8) Has any fact relevant to the plaintiff's right of action been deliberately concealed from him by the defendant (Limitation Act 1980, s 32? If yes, go to (9). If no, go to (24).

(9) Did the plaintiff discover the concealment at least 12 years before the date of the bringing of the action? If yes, go to (24). If no, go to (10).

(10) Could the plaintiff have discovered the concealment at least 12 years before the date of the bringing of the action if he had exercised reasonable diligence? If yes, go to (24). If no, go to (43).

(11) Was the liability of the plaintiff that is the subject of the indemnity established within six years before the date of the bringing of the action? If yes, go to (43). If no, go to (12).

(12) Has any fact relevant to the plaintiff's right of action been deliberately concealed from him by the defendant? If yes, go to (13). If no, go to (24).

(13) Did the plaintiff discover the concealment at least six years before the date of the bringing of the action? If yes, go to (24). If no, go to (14).

(14) Could the plaintiff have discovered the concealment at least six years before the date of the bringing of the action if he had exercised reasonable diligence? If yes, go to (24). If no, go to (43).

(15) Was the contract under seal? If yes, go to (16). If no, go to (20).

(16) Was the date by which the defendant completed his contractual duties to the plaintiff within 12 years before the date of the bringing of the action? If yes, go to (43). If no, go to (17).

(17) Has any fact relevant to the plaintiff's right of action been deliberately concealed from him by the defendant? If yes, go to (18). If no, go to (24).

(18) Did the plaintiff discover the concealment at least 12 years before the date of the bringing of the action? If yes, go to (24). If no, go to (19).

(19) Could the plaintiff have discovered the concealment at least 12 years before the date of the bringing of the action if he had exercised reasonable diligence? If yes, go to (24). If no, go to (43).

(20) Was the date by which the defendant completed his contractual duties to the plaintiff within six years before the date of the bringing of the action? If yes, go to (43). If no, go to (21).

(21) Has any fact relevant to the plaintiff's right of action been deliberately concealed from him by the defendant? If yes, go to (22). If no, go to (24).

(22) Did the plaintiff discover the concealment at least six years before the date of the bringing of the action? If yes, go to (24). If no, go to (23).

(23) Could the plaintiff have discovered the concealment at least six years before the date of the bringing of the action if he had exercised reasonable diligence? If yes, go to (24). If no, go to (43).

(24) Were proceedings commenced prior to 18 September 1986 (s 4 of the Latent Damage Act 1986)? If yes, go to (25). If no, go to (34).

(25) Is there such proximity between the plaintiff and the defendant as to give rise to liability such as in *Junior Books Ltd v Veitchi Co Ltd* [1981] AC 520 where there is no need to show danger to the health or safety of occupants? If yes, go to (26). If no, go to (30).

(26) Did the damage occur within six years before the date of the bringing of the action? If yes, go to (43). If no, go to (27).

(27) Has any fact relevant to the plaintiff's right of action been deliberately concealed from him by the defendant? If yes, go to (28). If no, go to (44).

(28) Did the plaintiff discover the concealment at least six years before the date of the bringing of the action? If yes, go to (44). If no, go to (29).

(29) Could the plaintiff have discovered the concealment at least six years before the date of the bringing of the action if he had exercised reasonable diligence? If yes, go to (44). If no, go to (43).

(30) Was it within six years before the date of the bringing of the action that the damage to the building became so severe as to cause danger to the health or

safety of the occupants? If yes, go to (43). If no, go to (31).

(31) Has any fact relevant to the plaintiff's right of action been deliberately concealed from him by the defendant? If yes, go to (32). If no, go to (44).

(32) Did the plaintiff discover the concealment at least six years before the date of the bringing of the action? If yes, go to (44). If no, go to (33).

(33) Could the plaintiff have discovered the concealment at least six years before the date of the bringing of the action if he had exercised reasonable diligence? If yes, go to (44). If no, go to (43).

(34) Applying the questions set out between 25 and 33, would the action have been statute barred if it had been brought on 18 September 1986 (s 4(1)(a) of the Latent Damage Act 1986)? If yes, go to (44). If no, go to (35).

(35) Has any fact relevant to the plaintiff's right of action been deliberately concealed from him by the defendant (s 32 (5) of the Limitation Act 1980, introduced by s 2(2) of the Latent Damage Act 1986)? If yes, go to (25). If no, go to (36).

(36) Did more than 15 years expire between the date (or, if more than one, the last of the dates) of the alleged breach of duty and the date of the bringing of the action (s 14B of the Limitation Act 1980 introduced by s 1 of the Latent Damage Act 1986)? If yes, go to (44). If no, go to (37).

(37) Did the plaintiff acquire his interest in the property from a party which had a claim of which it was unaware (s 3 of the Latent Damage Act 1986)? If yes, go to (38). If no, go to (39).

(38) Did the plaintiff acquire his interest in the property at least three years before the date of the bringing of the action (s 3 of the Latent Damage Act 1986)? If yes, go to (39). If no, go to (43).

(39) Did the plaintiff acquire the knowledge that he had a claim at least three years before the date of the bringing of the action (see s 14A(6)–(10) of the Limitation Act 1980 introduced by s 1 of the Latent Damage Act 1986 for the statutory provisions on knowledge)? If yes, go to (40). If no, go to (43).

(40) Is there such proximity between the plaintiff and the defendant as to give rise to liability such as in *Junior Books Ltd v Veitchi Co Ltd* [1981] AC 520 where there is no need to show danger to the health or safety of occupants? If yes, go to (41). If no, go to (42).

(41) Did the damage occur within six years before the date of the bringing of the action? If yes, go to (43). If no, go to (44).

(42) Was it within six years before the date of the bringing of the action that the damage to the building become so severe as to cause danger to the health or safety of the occupants? If yes, go to (43). If no, go to (44).

(43) The action is *prima facie* NOT statute barred but consider whether there are any exceptional circumstances or changes in the law since March 1988).

(44) The action is *prima facie* STATUTE BARRED but consider whether there are any exceptional circumstances or changes in the law since March 1988).

Index